The Western Security Community, 1948–1950

STUDIES IN MILITARY HISTORY

General Editor: Militärgeschichtliches Forschungsamt

Rudolf Steiger, *Armour Tactics in the Second World War: Panzer Army Campaigns of 1939–41 in German War Diaries*

Horst Boog (ed.), *The Conduct of the Air War in the Second World War: An International Comparison*

Klaus Reinhardt, *Moscow: The Turning Point?*

The Western Security Community, 1948–1950

Common Problems and Conflicting National Interests during the Foundation Phase of the North Atlantic Alliance

EDITED BY
Norbert Wiggershaus and Roland G. Foerster

ASSISTED BY
Birgit Schulz and Winfried Heinemann

BERG
Oxford/Providence

First published in 1993 by

Berg Publishers

Editorial offices:
221 Waterman Street, Providence, RI 02906, USA
150 Cowley Road, Oxford, OX4 1JJ, UK

English edition © Militärgeschichtliches Forschungsamt, 1992
Originally published as Die westliche Sicherheitsgemeinschaft
1948–1950, = Militärgeschichte seit 1945, ed. by Militärgeschichtliches Forschungsamt, vol. 8, Harold Boldt Verlag Boppard/Rh.
Translated from the German by permission of the publishers © Harald Boldt Verlag

© Militärgeschichtliches Forschungsamt 1993

All rights reserved.
No part of this publication may be reproduced
in any form or by any means without the written permission
of Berg Publishers.

Library of Congress Cataloging-in-Publication Data
The Western security community, 1948–1950
  p. cm.
  ISBN 0-85496-692-7
  1. North Atlantic Treaty Organization--History. 2. Europe--Military policy--History--20th century. 3. Europe--Defenses--History--20th century. 4. National security--Europe--History--20th century.
  UA646.3.W468 1993   92-25569
  355'.031'091821--dc20   CIP

British Library Cataloguing in Publication Data
A CIP catalogue record for this book is available from the British Library

ISBN: 0-85496-692-7

Printed and bound in the United States by Edwards Brothers, Ann Arbor, MI.

Contents

Preface to the German Edition ix

Preface to the English Edition xiii

Introduction 1

Part I Preconditions 7

1 The Formation of the Blocs: Structures of the East-West Conflict, 1948–1950
   Wilfried Loth 9

2 Efforts towards Cooperation and Integration in Europe, 1948–1950
   Klaus Schwabe 29

Part II Member States' Interests and Viewpoints 43

3 Western Union and European Military Integration 1948–1950 – An American Perspective
   Lawrence S. Kaplan 45

4 Canada and the Security of Western Europe (1948–1950)
   Paul Létourneau 69

5 A Little 'Fish' in a Big Political 'Pool' – Belgium's Cautious Contribution to the Rise of Military Integration in Western Europe
   Luc De Vos 87

6 Military Integration from the Perspective of The Netherlands
   Jan Schulten 109

Contents

7 France and the Defence of Western Europe: from the Brussels Pact (March 1948) to the Pleven Plan (October 1950)
Pierre Guillen — 125

8 The British Labour Government and the Atlantic Alliance, 1949–1951
Geoffrey Warner — 149

9 Italy 1947–1949: Military Integration and Neutralist Tendencies
Romain H. Rainero — 173

10 The Reluctant European: Norway's Attitude to Military Integration, 1948–1950
Olav Riste — 185

11 Abandonment vs. Entrapment: Denmark and Military Integration in Europe, 1948–1951
Nikolaj Petersen — 199

Part III Problems of Cooperation and Integration — 227

12 Foundation and History of the Treaty of Brussels, 1948–1950
Wolfgang Krieger — 229

13 Foundation and History of NATO, 1948–1950
Wichard Woyke — 251

14 The Military Situation and the Idea of Threat
Eberhard Pikart — 273

15 Europe and America, 1948–1950: An Unequal Relationship
Pierre Melandri — 289

16 Strategic Concepts for the Defence of Western Europe, 1948–1950
Christian Greiner — 313

Contents

17	Economic Aspects of the Creation of the North American-Western European Alliance System (1948–1950) *Manfred Knapp*	343
18	The Problem of West German Military Integration, 1948–1950 *Norbert Wiggershaus*	375

Part IV Conclusion 413

19	Notes Towards a Synthesis *Donald Cameron Watt*	415

Abbreviations 449

Contributors 453

Index 459

Preface to the German Edition

The collapse of the Anti-Hitler Coalition at the end of the Second World War, and the rise of two ideologically opposed nation-states which were now active on a global scale, put the Old World countries firmly into second place in terms of their significance in foreign affairs. In spite of this they were not able to get on with the task of economic and political reconstruction after the end of hostilities, at the same time trying to make sure that the vanquished and divided German Reich would never again be capable of starting a war. On the contrary, they very quickly became embroiled in the ideological confrontation between East and West. As the Iron Curtain came down in front of the countries of Eastern Europe, the Western European nations, threatened (in their opinion) by an aggressive Soviet policy of consolidation and expansion, were forced to unite in a security pact in order to safeguard their free democratic systems and their sovereign territories.

This collection of essays attempts to answer the historical question of what preconditions, requirements and restraints led to the establishment of this alliance, what courses were taken up later to be abandoned and, finally, what subjective and objective perceptions of a threat to their security the member states used as the basis for the final results of their common effort. With the benefit of hindsight it is difficult to imagine the problems which had to be solved even at the start of the integration process, since the Alliance, in whatever form, meant the surrender of individual states' sovereign rights, the overcoming of seemingly intractable resistance within certain countries, the drastic reduction of national interests which had accumulated over generations and which had seemed to be inalienable, and finally, the mobilisation of economic resources which had not been considered feasible in the past.

While the United States wished to rid themselves once and for

Preface to the German Edition

all of her European obligations after the end of the Second World War, a Western Security Alliance, for Canada, meant the end of her former isolation in foreign affairs and a new 'window on the world'. France and Great Britain needed to rise above their centuries-old rivalry, and also examine their relationship to the new superpower, the USA. The concept of security in the Scandinavian countries was totally different to that of Central Europe, and great problems stemmed from the obvious imbalance between the size of the Benelux countries' demands and their quantitative options. Lastly, an integral role was played by the question of the west German state's integration into a Western security system, which was designed not only to guarantee security *for* the west Germans as an essential part of the Western European Security Alliance, but also security *against* them. There were not only financial problems but also those of military integration, and this particular phrase became a constant bone of contention over definition and interpretation, while there was a general call for equality within the Alliance. Thus, in a quite natural way, the early history of the Western Security Alliance became the touchstone of the process of compromise between the member states regarding, on the one hand, the surrendering of sovereign rights and prerogatives and, on the other, the gaining of objective security. Here one must add that most countries attempted to safeguard the first part before agreeing to the second, mostly for reasons of domestic policy.

An academic method of historiography prevents myths arising. To seek knowledge concerning the beginnings of military integration in Europe, however, is at the same time to enquire about the reality of a united Europe. Despite all attempts on the part of the historian to be objective, the choice of themes has a great influence upon the reader's perception. It is, therefore, extremely important for an objective judgement of how the Western Security Alliance began that the authors of the essays in this book come from many of the member states. Thus they make sure that there is a variety of viewpoints and approaches, which, in toto, offer an adequately critical appraisal of the initial stages of Western European military integration and of the Alliance itself. In addition to this, it is most pleasing to see an essay which tests and therefore qualifies the accuracy and verity of military historiography in a learned fashion, using this book as an example.

Preface to the German Edition

As part of its task of researching and writing military history, the Military History Research Office (MGFA) has included the history of the Western Security Alliance in its programme. This book is designed to lay the foundation for this project, following the tried and trusted method used by modern historical research institutes, including the MGFA.

DR. GÜNTER ROTH
Brigadier General, Commanding Officer
Militärgeschichtliches Forschungsamt

Preface to the English Edition

For the MGFA to publish an English edition of this book at this particular time is significant for two reasons. The first and most obvious reason is that the Western security community in Europe played a decisive role in shaping one of the longest periods of peace in modern history; its permanent and stable nature comprised a decisive factor in the solution of the 'German Question'. Secondly, the academic assessment of the Atlantic Alliance's foundation phase has a certain bearing upon today's international developments. The recent dramatic upheavals in the Central and Eastern European countries have led to a reappraisal of the post-war international system, as well as opening up perspectives for the return of these nations to the European fold, for a pan-European system of peace and a totally new kind of security partnership between East and West.

Against this background it is more and more important to know exactly what motives and common interests determined the foundation and development of NATO forty years ago, and to see which of the conditions for its creation then perhaps continue to apply today.

With this thought in mind, may this book catch the attention both of those with an interest in history and of policy-makers and political advisors.

Dr. Günter Roth
Brigadier General, Commanding Officer
Militärgeschichtliches Forschungsamt

Introduction

This collection of essays is the result of an international conference entitled 'The Initial Phase of Military Integration in Europe 1948–1950', which was held by the Military History Research Office (MGFA) in December 1985. The aims of this conference were, first, to collate the results of previous research and take initial stock of present work on the subject; second, to put forward new formulas and lines of research; third, to discuss opinions and theses; and, last but not least, to offer a platform to those colleagues who have shown themselves to be experts in the field in question. Apart from this, the MGFA hoped that the conference would prepare the ground and provide the impetus for the planned project 'Formation and Problems of the Atlantic Treaty to 1956', which will be pursued on the basis of international cooperation.

This book, however, is not designed merely to be of use to historians, but also to others with a special interest in the subject, in schools and universities, in military circles and also among the general public. While the work of the multi-national group of historical researchers, led by the Strasbourg historian Raymond Poidevin, pointed out how closely linked the effects of European political and economic integration were during the period 1948–1950,[1] this book deals with aspects of the narrower but equally important security side of the Western Alliance.

The period covered by this book is limited to the years 1948 to 1950, the initial phase of the military alliance, up to the decision to create an integrated NATO armed force in Europe. The troubled years in terms of international politics immediately following the Second World War form the background to the portrayal. During this period decisions were made which determined the balance of power for decades to come. Wilfried Loth is of the opinion that the ideological blocs in the East-West conflict were

Introduction

first formed between 1948 and 1950. In addition to this, the autumn of 1950 can be seen in many ways as a clear turning point in global terms.

Since the emphasis is on the initial phase of the security alliance, a limited span of time, it was not possible to go into its origins and prehistory. The risks in not doing so, however, as Donald Cameron Watt has lucidly pointed out in his convincing conclusion, are lessened by the fact that the individual essays describe the problems faced at the end of the 1940s and the beginning of the 1950s in the full light of past events, as well as considering long-term effects.

Regarding source material, the situation is fairly favourable, but it cannot yet be described as fully satisfactory. Great Britain, Canada and the USA allow full access to official files, while in other countries historians are kept on an extremely short 'leash'. However, in exceptional cases, some governments do allow access to material which is still off-limits to the general public. Fortunately, the Western European Union (WEU) has recently opened its archives for the period up to 1950, and it is expected that subsequent years will become available in the near future. Less fortunately, in the case of NATO, a similar decision is still not forthcoming; only certain historians have priority of access. Since almost all contributors were able to examine new archive material in their respective countries, sometimes having privileged access for the first time, conclusions were reached which, while necessarily of a temporary nature, were based on the largest possible amount of source material, and which give a positive impetus for further research into the foundation period of the Alliance.

As one of the two opposing poles of the world political system, the Atlantic European Alliance is the subject of this book. Two main aspects are dealt with in detail; first, the interests of the individual member countries, and second, the level of cooperation and integration within the alliance as a whole and the difficulties involved in these processes.

In the first section of the book the description of the conditions leading to early attempts at cooperation in security policy is limited to two viewpoints: on the one hand, the East-West conflict as the dominant structural problem in international relations, and, on the other, Western cooperation in the areas of economics and politics. In this regard, considering that the Soviet Union and the Eastern 'Bloc' are adequately covered in their role as the counterweight to the Western Alliance, equally strong emphasis is placed upon the economically and politically integrated system of democracies on both sides of the Atlantic.

When dealing with the interests of nations, whether in the field of foreign policy and security or in terms of economics, one should not just consider the 'great powers' but as many of the medium-sized and small powers as possible, both in Western Europe and across the Atlantic, giving them the chance to put forward their own national viewpoint. It is necessary to grasp how varied and complex the interests of individual alliance members are to appreciate fully the magnitude of the task and the difficulties some countries had in deciding whether or not to join the Western camp. It is only from a synopsis of the varied interests and contributions of all member states that one can arrive at a fairly accurate picture of the alliance itself, as well as of each country's role and room to manoeuvre. In order to conduct research into integration, it is still essential to point out national perspectives. Thus it is all the more unfortunate that it was not possible to portray the interests of Portugal, Luxembourg and Iceland.

We had to accept that neither the United States, the leading Alliance power, nor Great Britain nor France as the other main powers, could be allotted the space their importance deserves. This was acceptable, however, in as much as the role played by the United States has been adequately described in the essays by Wilfried Loth and Klaus Schwabe. The other national analyses also give a fair portrayal of American involvement, particularly those by Pierre Melandri and Manfred Knapp, on the relations between Europe and America, and on economic cooperation within the alliance, respectively.

In the essays the variety and the complexity of the aims, considerations, inherent necessities and decision-making processes become clear. Apart from this, a multi-faceted picture of the Western Alliance arises, one more complicated than could be seen at first, considering the stages leading to its foundation. On the whole, despite the many apparent security interests which finally resulted in integration, and despite frequent admissions that their own resources were limited, the results support the theory, formulated six years ago by Alan S. Milward on Western integration, in which he states that the member states' national interests were the decisive factors, and that integration was

Introduction

intended 'not to hasten their disappearance from the stage of history but rather to guarantee that they would continue to dominate that stage'[2]. This statement is also confirmed in the subsequent section which deals with international questions and cooperation, with the emphasis on the level and problems of cooperation and integration.

While the first section deals with purely national viewpoints, this part is international in scope. This is in line with the prevailing trend of (and also with the demands placed upon) historians, foreign affairs experts and international relations researchers in West Germany: namely that they steer away from a narrow, national perspective and look at foreign affairs, economic and security policy in terms of Europe and the Alliance.[3]

Historians are especially interested in the details of integrated defence concepts, forms of organisation and the ways in which states cooperate, as well as in the importance and the activities of the systems of military and security policy thus created. In addition to this, they want to examine the attempts made to solve common problems, and, equally importantly, to look at the security alliance's structural problems and the effect the international organisation and its decisions has on member states' policies.

In such a wide field it was not possible, and, indeed, it was not intended, to cover all imaginable questions. However, this book includes a number of important aspects of the difficulties involved in the foundation of the Brussels Treaty and NATO, the perception of threat, Western European military strategy, relations between the USA and Europe, the level of economic cooperation and West German integration, all of which dominated the scene during the years 1948 to 1950. Thus we should look first of all at the unequal relationship between the USA and Europe and the leading role played by the United States as an essential element in any systematic historical description and analysis of the Alliance and East-West relations. Next should come an examination of the economic side of the alliance's development, although (or perhaps because) security interests were often superimposed on economic ones.

Knapp's essay makes it clear how important it will be in any history of NATO to deal with the close correlation between political, economic, military and defence expenditure factors, and with the tensions resulting from this correlation.

It seemed obvious that certain themes which had been given a

Introduction

separate lecture would not only be taken up by others but would often be discussed from a different viewpoint and be given another emphasis. This, of course, is a sign of the importance and complexity of some of the problems. This means in effect that it is almost impossible to separate one problem from another.

In the light of such statements and tasks, some of them being dealt with for the first time, it is fitting that this book is rounded off by an essay written by Donald Cameron Watt concerning basic historiographical questions involved in researching and compiling a history of NATO. Cameron Watt places four critical viewpoints at the centre of his essay, entitled 'Notes Towards a Synthesis'.

First, the question of whether there is a typical development in modern historiography. Second, problems of interpretation, concepts and terminology (referring to the terms 'Cold War', 'blocs' and 'deterrence'). Third, the danger involved in historiography using the principle 'History begins now' – past political generations and their ideas. Last, the confusion of terminology and perception – the conception of the alliance.

This analysis which, in addition to the above, yields a whole range of advances on the previous state of research, gives an impression of the many methodological problems posed by a historical view of the North Atlantic Alliance. Cameron Watt's conclusions particularly warn us not to try to obtain the analysis from the evidence by force, as this analysis is not yet fully clear in terms of typology and terminology. He also admonishes us to be especially exact and precise in our use of terms and concepts. It is also essential to look back in time from the starting-point of an historical description so as to take account of the events which formed those involved in it. Above all, however, historians, in concert both with alliance institutions and the member states, seek a practicable answer to the question of access to source material, so that research into the period following the end of the Second World War can be conducted in a continuous and satisfactory fashion.

NORBERT WIGGERSHAUS
ROLAND G. FOERSTER

Introduction

Notes

1. *Histoire des débuts de la construction européenne (mars 1948–mai 1950)/ Origins of the European Integration (March 1948–May 1950)*. Sous la direction de Raymond Poidevin (ed.), Bruxelles, Milano, Paris, Baden-Baden, 1986.
2. Alan S. Milward, 'Entscheidungsphasen der Westintegration', in: *Westdeutschland 1945–1955. Unterwerfung, Kontrolle, Integration*, Ludolf Herbst (ed.), Munich, 1986, pp. 233 f.
3. Hans-Peter Schwarz, 'Die europäische Integration als Aufgabe der Zeitgeschichtsforschung. Forschungsstand und Perspektiven', in *VfZG* vol. 31 (1983) 4, pp. 555–72.

Part I
Preconditions

1
The Formation of the Blocs: Structures of the East-West Conflict, 1948–1950

Wilfried Loth

In the conflict between East and West the period 1948 to 1950 saw the formation of the ideological blocs. The shape of the postwar world had already been drawn to a great extent. The USA, mostly supported by (and sometimes under pressure from) her British allies, had adopted a policy of containment. The Soviet Union had answered the Marshall Plan by binding her satellite states to her own equivalent, and also by exhibiting a sabre-rattling hostility towards the West. In other words, there were no longer any reasons to go to the negotiating table over their common problems and differences. Instead there was a common fear (held by the Americans since 1945–6, by the Soviets from the summer and autumn of 1947 and by the Europeans since the winter of 1947–8) that the other side would mount more or less violent attacks upon their security zone. What started out as simply a struggle for spheres of influence and security zones between East and West, increasingly came to be regarded as a 'cold war', a battle for survival between two diametrically opposed societies. The reorganisation of Europe, including the solution of the German problem, for which both East and West were responsible, was completed by means of division, integration into blocs and the strengthening of the two new bloc leaders.[1]

It was not yet clear, however, what this bloc formation would look like. The new international system on the horizon demanded concessions from all the participants: concessions which for years some countries had refused to make. The USA had to face up to their firm commitments on the continent of Europe. The Europeans had to accept the limits placed on their sovereignty and the Germans had to cope with the division of their country.

Neighbouring states were obliged to accept the Germans as partners, and the Soviets were confronted with a capitalist bloc on their Western border which was both powerful and, despite theories to the contrary, fairly united. There was also a lack of experience on all sides in dealing with the new situation. Thus it was no simple matter to complete the creation of these bloc structures. It was at first unclear how large they would be and how extensive the confrontation between them would be. It was not even certain that these ideological blocs would continue to exist in their present form.

1

The first phase of bloc formation was somewhat uneven in both East and West. Within the Soviet camp, since the foundation of the Cominform (Communist Information Office), satellite states were bound to the Soviet Union and oriented towards the Communist model in a forceful (if not always consistent) fashion. The last remaining organised political groups within the 'people's democracies' were soon totally demolished, the Social Democratic parties being forced to merge with the Communists after a thorough purge. All workers' organisations were placed under Communist control, while the Party leaderships themselves were gradually purged of those suspected of not being completely loyal to Stalin at all times. Everywhere, heavy industry was given top priority for reconstruction, after the Soviet model, centralised planning methods were introduced, and the collectivisation of agriculture was pushed forward – not, however, without strong resistance. Economic production was devoted to the Soviets' own reconstruction efforts, with the result that the economic dominance of the Soviet Union was secured along with the political upper hand in Eastern Europe.[2] In the Soviet Union itself, the proponents of a more pragmatic line lost their influence. Eugen Varga was obliged to recant his theses concerning the possibility of reforming the West, while Andrei Zhdanov, who had based his demands for a policy of peaceful coexistence on Varga's ideas, lost his position as Stalin's deputy to the more dogmatic Georgi Malenkov.[3]

The process of 'Sovietisation' could be seen in its most dramatic form in the case of Czechoslovakia, at that time still a democratic state. When the Communists, faced with the prospect of losing popular support, embarked upon an anti-parliamentary strategy, the non-Communist coalition partners reacted by attempting to isolate the Communist Party. The result was a power struggle throughout the winter of 1947–8, which was bitterly fought on both sides. This ended in a victory for the Communists, at the end of February 1948, because President Benes did not dare give way to the demands for new elections made by the anti-Communists. The occupation of Prague by paramilitary police units under Communist control, the mobilisation of the Communist faithful in a general strike and the Soviet leadership's broad hint that the Soviet Union had troops just across the Czech border, gave Benes the impression that it would be unwise to continue the showdown tactics. Thus the way was open for the creation of a Communist one-party state on the Soviet model.[4]

The news of the neutralisation of the non-Communist element in Czechoslovakia strengthened Western fears that the Soviets would expand their empire by violent means. It caused a majority in Western Europe, who were already frightened by Communist-inspired strikes in France and Italy, to demand a military alliance with the USA. This news also brought home the idea to the governments in Washington, London and Paris that Soviet policy was aimed at 'ruling the world', and that the Soviet Union, at least in theory, would not shy away from the use of armed aggression in pursuit of this aim.[5] Apart from this, however, the formation of the Western bloc progressed in fits and starts. The British, and other smaller European states in their train, blocked the American suggestion aimed at economic integration under the aegis of the Marshall Plan. American politicians did not like the idea of a military commitment in Europe, partly because they did not see the immediate threat of a Soviet attack, and partly because they were not certain of convincing Congress of the need for such a commitment. The French were constantly against the Anglo-American-inspired creation of a West German state, partly due to their anxiety about a final split between East and West and also out of fear that such a move would provoke the Soviets, or even lead to a revival of the Soviet-German alliance.[6]

In spite of all this, there was a real breakthrough at the beginning of June 1948 regarding both US military commitment in Europe and the establishment of a west German state. There were mutual agreements on both issues. French Foreign Minister Bidault succeeded in convincing the American negotiators that there was to be no support from the French National Assembly for the West German state without a guarantee of American support sufficient to allay fears of a Soviet attack, as well as offering protection against any German threat to French security. In view of this package deal the State Department, which had hitherto rejected a military alliance on the grounds that it would endanger the economic recovery programme, came round to the idea of supporting a formal commitment. Also, as the French insisted upon parliamentary backing for American promises of support, the Senate passed the Vandenberg Resolution, thus clearing the way for a multilateral military alliance. Only then was the French government prepared to put the London proposals for the creation of a west German state to the National Assembly. Agreement was reached by a narrow majority.[7]

It was still not yet clear, however, how great the US commitment in Europe would be and how near to reality the Western bloc would be as a result. In Washington the idea was to have less of a concrete military organisation and more of a formal guarantee, so as to give moral support to the European Recovery Programme. There was no particular hurry to conclude a treaty, nor was there a willingness to make any great financial contribution to European rearmament. An automatic commitment to future allies did not figure in US plans.[8]

The Europeans, however, pressed for just such an automatic response, for quick assistance and a larger American presence in Europe. When they saw that this demand did not find favour with the Americans, they even began once more to doubt the wisdom of entering into a pact which might provoke the Soviet Union, but which at the same time offered no real protection against an act of aggression.[9] Thus it seemed improbable that the arrangement of early June 1948 would stand the test of time.

2

This, then, was the situation when the Soviets blocked the access routes to the western sectors of Berlin. They did this in a desperate attempt to halt the creation of a West German state and the establishment of a Western military alliance which went with it. Before this there had been a mixture of carefully aimed provocation and conciliatory gestures, obviously designed to persuade the Western Powers to return to the negotiating table and seek a mutual solution to the German problem. Seeing that these tactics had not had the desired effect, Stalin used the most drastic weapon at his disposal (one which some American officials had always foreseen as a possible reaction to the creation of a state in the western sectors of Germany). The chances of such massive pressure achieving a negotiated solution did not seem very great. There was the danger of a hardening of the Western viewpoint. But the Soviet leadership had no choice. The establishment of American-style capitalism in western Germany, the prospect of speedy rearmament and the creation of an American-European military alliance: all these factors seemed so dangerous that the Soviets gladly ran the risk of a dramatic loss of prestige. If they did not succeed in forcing the Western Powers back to the table by means of the blockade, there was still the possibility of driving the Western Allies out of Berlin, and therefore of removing a large obstacle in the way of creating a state in their own sector. This fact also justified the risks.[10]

Indeed, for a few weeks it seemed that Stalin's blockade had paid off. Despite warnings by the experts, the Western governments were not prepared for the crisis, and although the US air force had set up an improvised airlift to West Berlin, it was unclear if and for how long two million people could be fed by air. In addition to this, there was the widespread fear that the Soviets might block the air corridors as well. In fact this fear was unjustified because Stalin was not prepared to risk starting a war which the Soviets were bound to lose over the West German state, even if the latter went against Soviet interests. But the myth that the Soviets were strong caused the majority of Western politicians to forget how daring and how close to the limits of what was possible the Soviet ploy really was.[11] Thus the Western Powers seemed to be in an untenable position, seen in the long term. Soviet demands for the suspension of the London recommendations and of the Four-Power Conference on Germany found more and more support in the West – especially from France, who did not like the London compromise one bit, and, not least, from the Germans themselves, whose *Länder* Prime Ministers were at first clearly against the steps they were bound to take to found a state on west German territory.[12]

In any case, George Kennan, Head of Policy Planning Staff at the US State Department, in view of the obvious dilemma, pressed for an agreement between the Soviets and the West on the withdrawal of occupation forces from Germany followed by the restoration of an independent German state. The USA could then, he explained in a memorandum of 12 August, pull her troops out of Berlin without losing prestige, and the population of the Western sectors would not fall under Soviet control because the Soviet Union would also leave the city. This solution seemed to be more acceptable to him, in spite of the danger of considerable problems for the European Recovery Programme and the chance that the reunited Germans might turn away from the West. It certainly seemed more acceptable than being saddled with the Berlin problem on a long-term basis, with a West German state which could not survive economically without having both links to the East and a European federation, and with a West German people who would devote all their energies towards reunification. There would also be no foreseeable end to the division of Europe. Should the Soviet leadership not accept this solution, then there was still time to put the London proposals into effect, without now having the stigma (in the eyes of both the Germans and the Europeans) of being the cause of division. Kennan was now trying to fight against the very thing he had seen as being the result of the policy of containment, in 1945, and which he had indeed demanded. Such was the effect the Soviet threat in Berlin had upon him.[13]

Kennan's plan for a neutral Germany was seen at the State Department to be a serious alternative to retaining Western positions in Berlin, at least for a while. Both Secretary of State Marshall and the US Ambassador in Moscow, Smith, were convinced that time was on the side of the Soviets and that Berlin could not be retained in the long term. Thus they feared, in spite of President Truman's heartening words of encouragement, that a suspension of the west German state's creation process would be unavoidable.[14] Without knowing about the discussion going on in America, the British military governor in Germany, Sir Brian Robertson, argued along the same lines. His worry was that, judging by the Soviet action after the decision was made to found a west German state, the creation of two German states would inevitably lead to war with the Soviet Union. Therefore he wanted to make the one-nation solution more attractive for the Soviet leadership by offering them a share in the running of the Ruhr industrial zone, something hitherto rejected by the Western allies.[15]

Structures of the East-West Conflict

There were many reasons why the formation of the Western bloc did not falter. First there was a majority in the US administration who feared that an allied withdrawal from Germany would lead to a loss of confidence in the USA among the Europeans, and would also open the way for a gradual Finlandisation of Germany. Second, General Clay, convinced of the weakness of the Soviet position and the need for a 'Western solution', pushed the creation process along, so as to have a *fait accompli* behind which the Western government would be obliged to stand.[16] Third, the blockade created such a consensus of anti-Communist feeling in western Germany, Western Europe and the USA that a withdrawal was almost unthinkable in home-policy terms. Truman was afraid that the voters would see any decision in favour of neutralisation as a sign of weakness which would cost him re-election. Fourth, the French government did not take up the Soviet demand for a new Four-Power Conference, despite their dissatisfaction with the results of the London talks on the German question. In the meantime, the USA had made enough promises of support to keep French fears below the critical level concerning the risks involved in creating a west German state. They were also coming to see the division of Germany and the permanent presence of American troops on German soil as the lesser of two evils.[17]

Last, after the preparations for the new state had seen out the first critical weeks, the Berlin airlift proved to be a success, especially at the end of August 1948. It became clear to the experts that it was possible to supply the people of West Berlin by air even during the winter. On 26 August Marshall laid down the maintenance of the Allied Powers' responsibility for Berlin and the upkeep of the Western positions in western Germany as an essential part of any solution to the Berlin problem. Thus the worst phase of the Berlin crisis was over.[18]

What remained was a 'medium crisis' which made the Soviet threat seem real enough to the West to encourage the consolidation of the status quo under the banner of anti-Communism, without endangering Western positions and without the agreement over suitable reactions to provocation breaking down. The West had come through the trial of strength, and now the blockade proved to be the crucial psychological factor in the formation of the Western bloc. Western leaders lost all interest in a speedy end to the crisis. Both in the matter of the Euro-American military alliance and in the question of the West German state, it was now the fear of Soviet aggression which outweighed most other reservations and opposition. The formation of the Western bloc progressed all the more rapidly after the momentary insecurity caused by the blockade had passed. On September 1 the Parliamentary Council met in Bonn, and nine days later the Western negotiators agreed on the thesis that 'friendly coexistence' with the Soviet Union was 'impossible' in the long run, and that consequently there had to be a joint Western defence alliance.[19]

While the details of the pact and the new West German state were being thrashed out in the West, Soviet leaders still for a time hoped they could force the Western Powers to give up West Berlin and therefore halt the progress of the Western bloc. When the allied air force got through the winter unscathed, the Soviets began to recognise that the blockade was causing a hardening of the Western bloc, so they looked for a way out of the crisis without too much loss of face. The Western Powers, understandably enough, did not feel like making concessions. Not until the negotiations concerning the creation of the Federal Republic and the Atlantic Alliance were completed did they agree to a new meeting of the Allied Council of Foreign Ministers.[20] By lifting the blockade in May 1949, the Soviet leaders *de facto* accepted the foundation of the West German state. The only course now open to them was to create a state in the Soviet-occupied zone (SBZ) and thus, as they had started to do in 1947–8, draw the SBZ more and more into the fold of satellite 'people's democracies'.[21] Thus the formation of ideological blocs was institutionalised in Europe between the spring and autumn of 1949.

3

The widening of the split between East and West, however, did not mean that the division of Germany would be permanent, nor was it clear to what extent bloc formation would be a military phenomenon as well as a political one. Even after the Berlin blockade there was a limited understanding of the new alliance on the part of the USA. First, there was no question of an automatic promise of support for the Europeans. Second, financial help for the European efforts at rearmament was more or less meant to be a symbolic gesture. Third, the idea of a definite commitment of troops or matériel for the alliance was also not yet on the agenda.[22]

At that time it was politically unthinkable to bring the Federal Republic into the alliance, although it was inevitable both from a strategic and a military point of view. The psychological barriers against German rearmament and the return to economic health of the old enemy, together with a worsening of relations between East and West, formed such an effective obstacle to the use of West Germany's potential for containment that politicians did not even dare to discuss the issue internationally.[23] The West Germans themselves, or at least the majority, did not yet want any part of a military contribution to the Western Alliance either. Faced by Soviet aggression on the one side and American willingness to lead the way on the other, the West Germans accepted their new state. But this did not mean they necessarily saw their future within the Western Alliance.[24]

During the second half of 1949, however, three events made sure that this shaky alliance did not remain that way. First, news of the first Soviet atomic bomb explosion gave rise to doubts about America's current security concept. From 1945 up to that time, the administration, despite warnings by the experts, had relied on the American monopoly in atomics continuing, and had therefore decided that a low level of conventional arms was sufficient. Thus they had wanted to leave the conventional defence of Western Europe to the European allies themselves. But now the forces which, in the spring of 1948, had achieved a first small increase in terms of armaments, were growing stronger.

The trend towards an armed containment policy was strengthened by the victory of Mao Tse-Tung's troops in China. This victory, completed by the total withdrawal of the last of Chiang Kai-shek's forces from the mainland in December 1949, was forecast by Washington as early as the end of 1947. But the victory (which had surprised Mao himself by its speed) was viewed by the US leaders as a success for the Soviet Union. Neither Chinese internal factors nor the rivalry between the Soviets and the Chinese were considered. This compounded the American feeling of being threatened by the Soviets and also gave rise to a militant anti-Communist movement within the general public, which demanded a show of strength by their governments in dealing with Soviet Communism.[25]

Last, the disappointing progress of the Marshall Plan pushed US politicians towards a greater commitment in Europe. It became clear, in the autumn of 1949, that the shortage of dollars in the European states was growing rather than decreasing. Thus the restoration of European economic independence, planned for 1952, was seemingly going to take much longer, meaning that new US aid for Europe was essential.[26] In addition to this, it was obvious, since the British vetoed the recommendations made during the first session of the Consultative Committee of the Council of Europe, that Great Britain would have no part in an integrated Europe with supranational organisations. Thus it was doubtful whether there would be a European body capable of keeping an eye on the Germans, and so it seemed necessary to strengthen the Atlantic framework in order to integrate the Europeans.[27]

Seen together, these fears, realisations and pressures led the Truman administration to rethink its concept of global politics, which went far beyond the original Containment Doctrine. In memorandum NSC 68, commissioned by Secretary of State Acheson and prepared in February–March 1950 by leading experts from the State Department, the Pentagon and the Atomic Energy Authority, the aim of Soviet policy at that time was desribed as 'the domination of the Eurasian landmass'. The force behind this policy was described as the 'complete subversion or forcible destruction of the machinery of government and structure of society in the countries of the non-Soviet world'. The practical aspects of Soviet policy were only seen very selectively, different variants within international Communism were mostly ignored and a war in the near future was no longer viewed as impossible. The experts demanded, therefore:

> 'the development of an adequate political and economic framework ... a substantial increase in expenditures for military purposes [State Department planners were thinking of 35,000 to 50,000 million dollars per annum instead of the 14,400 million allocated for 1950] ... a substantial increase in the military aid program ... some increase in economic assistance programs and recognition of the need to continue these programs until their purposes have been accomplished [thus beyond the foreseen end of Marshall Aid Program in 1952] ... the development of internal security and civil defense ... [and last, but not least] increased taxes.[28]

Since the autumn of 1949 Secretary of State Acheson had been applying this enlarged containment concept to more and more foreign policy decisions. The new Chinese government was not recognised, nor was it allowed to join the UNO. Chinese President Zhou Enlai's overtures for a Sino-American settlement, his idea of a counterbalance to the Soviet threat, were rejected.[29] In order to halt the Soviet advance in Asia and bring French troops back to Europe as fast as possible, the US government started to give financial aid to the French intervention in Indochina (initially with $10 million which was granted on 1 May 1950). At the end of January 1950 Truman approved the controversial hydrogen bomb. With the promulgation of NSC 68, at the end of April, the resistance of the more conservative Secretary of Defence, Louis Johnson, against an increase in military spending was broken. After this Acheson concentrated his efforts on persuading Congress and the allies to accept a rise in defence spending, the strengthening of the alliance and the inclusion of the Federal Republic in the Western pact.[30]

There were, however, great difficulties once again in implementing this plan. The Europeans were certainly interested in increasing the US role in the European defensive network, but they were not able to increase their own defence expenditure. They feared that such an increase would threaten economic reconstruction, still at an early stage, and would have an effect on living standards that the population would find intolerable. Voices were heard, especially on the right wing of the Republican Party in Congress, condemning the Truman administration's attitude to the cold war as too 'soft'. Those same Republicans, however, were calling for a reduction in taxation and the Federal budget, and were thus vehemently against costly increases in armaments. At the conference of the Atlantic Council in May 1950 in London, while the Western foreign ministers agreed in principle with Acheson's demands for a stronger and more coordinated Western Alliance, they contented themselves with stating that the question must be 'examined', and agreed unanimously that it was 'too soon' to consider rearming Germany. After his return from London Acheson wanted to present his programme for strengthening the alliance to Congress. But the latter did not allow him to speak to both Houses, and those few Congressmen who finally did listen to his report were not very impressed. Even the current military-aid project for Europe, a 'symbolic' $1.2 billion, seemed threatened.[31]

4

It was the Korean War which supplied the final impetus for the defence-spending increase, the creation of an integrated defence organisation and the inclusion of the Federal Republic in the Western military alliance. This effect had been foreseen ever since the experiences of the Berlin blockade. For this reason, also, Stalin had hesitated before giving way to the pleas of his North Korean ally, Kim Il-sung, to be allowed to attack the south of the peninsula. Stalin's change of mind can only be explained by the fact that South Korea's president, Syngman Rhee, was also making warlike noises, and that the Chinese would gain prestige if the Soviets stood by and watched. Apart from this Stalin thought a speedy victory was possible without the danger of a protracted engagement and without the risk of the USA becoming involved. In view of the instability of Rhee's corrupt regime this was a good guess, also bearing in mind the American government's reluctance to support Rhee. Stalin, however, could not totally rule out US intervention, so he made no great show of diplomatic support for the North Koreans and carefully avoided sending Soviet troops into the theatre.[32] But Stalin's plan failed – there was no popular uprising in the South as he had hoped. Rhee's forces managed to escape encirclement by the North Koreans, and the South Korean dictator succeeded in persuading the US government, with the help of the American Commander-in-Chief in Japan, General MacArthur, to give him massive military assistance. At first Washington did not want to become involved in a war in the Far East, but many officials felt it no longer wise for the USA to appear weak in the eyes of the anti-Communist movement. Here was a chance for Washington to overcome resistance to the NSC 68 programme by means of a new, small-scale crisis. Thus MacArthur was given command of a force of US troops, which he continued to increase in size by demanding more and more manpower. What started out as a commando enterprise in a civil war very quickly became a global crisis.[33]

This only slightly changed the Western leaders' judgement of the world political situation, but public opinion concerning the idea of threat and security underwent a sea change, and this fact was instrumental in the Western bloc's continuing integration process. The advance of North Korea's forces was seen partly as the start of a worldwide military offensive by the Soviets and their allies, and partly as the beginning of a warlike expansion over the borders drawn in 1945, where more and more of the Western world would fall victim to takeover according to the 'domino principle'. The Korean War was sometimes seen as an attempt by the Soviets to fight a war by proxy. This ploy, one felt, would be used again in other regions when the right opportunity arose. In any case, the theory of Soviet aggression became much more popular, and there was a growing fear of a military attack against Western Europe. Many people began to draw a parallel between the Federal Republic, as the western part of a country whose other portion, under Communist control, was in the process of setting up an army of its own, and the situation of South Korea.[34] The dramatic events of the war and the conscious exaggeration of the Soviet threat in official government statements[35] served to increase the shock caused by the Communist attack on Korea.

Thus the US Congress reacted 'quite excellently', as Acheson's biographer later put it, to Truman's dramatic appeal of 19 July 1950, in which he demanded greatly increased military efforts so as to avoid a new world war. For fiscal 1951 the allocation of funds for the defence budget was nearly doubled (from $13.1 billion to $22.1 billion). For fiscal 1952, the sum was doubled again to $44 billion. It must be said, however, that only part of these funds were used for the Korean campaign. Most was allocated to the general strengthening of the US military arsenal. The plans to build up this force, envisaged within four years, were realised in two.[36] At the same time the barriers fell against a larger US presence in Europe and against her taking part in an integrated defence organisation for the European part of NATO. At the beginning of September the Truman administration was able to make offers to its European allies, on the condition that the Europeans agreed to the arming of the Federal Republic. They were not counting on meeting any great resistance, either from Congress or the American public. The Congressmen merely made sure that only four more divisions were to join the two already in Europe, instead of the six and a half wanted by the Pentagon.[37]

At the same time, in Europe there was a willingness to pay the price of an integrated army demanded by the USA. Among the smaller Western European nations, and even in France, the fear of Soviet attack led to the conviction that it was essential to have a West German force for the defence of the West, however difficult the political consequences might be. Otherwise, Western Europe, because of the strategic value of the west German front, the weakness of the European armies in terms of arms, and the resistance against falling living standards in favour of arms expenditure made defence using conventional weapons impossible. Churchill's House of Commons speech of 16 March, in which he demanded the activation of German units within a European army, found more disapproval than support among the Europeans themselves. On 11 August, however, at the meeting of the Advisory Committee of the Council of Europe, his plan for a European force, open to a West German contingent, and indeed built around it, appealed to a large majority.[38] The French merely stipulated, as a condition of their accepting the formation of German units, that either the European Union should become a supranational organisation, or else that the USA should take part in a fully integrated army.[39]

Since the American and French conditions matched one another, it was decided, at the beginning of September 1950, that there would be both an integrated NATO force, with US troops included, and a West German contribution to that force. It was just a question of precisely when a German force would be activated, what status it would have and the extent of US involvement in a common decision-making apparatus. However, because there was a great difference of opinion between the Americans and the French on this issue, it was December before the decisions of late summer 1950 became official. Even then, the final form of the West German contribution to the alliance was not yet clear.[40] The basic essentials of the arrangement, which was an addition to the original decision taken in the early summer of 1948 in answer to the threat from the East, were no longer a subject for debate.

To the Soviets, Western efforts to counter a threat which did not exist as such were bound to appear threatening in themselves. At the end of 1950, in a meeting with the Italian Communist leaders Togliatti, Longo and Secchia, Stalin described the world situation as 'serious', 'tense' and 'full of danger'. Their colleague, Giorgio Amendola, reports that the participants were agreed 'that the Cold War was at a turning-point both internally and externally ... the hypothesis of an outright war no longer seemed to be a figment of the imagination'.[41] In this vein Stalin also increased the rate of Soviet arms production, making sure the Eastern Bloc forces were firmly under the control of Moscow and accelerating the growth of heavy industry. At the same time the purges of 'unreliable' Communist leaders were at their height.[42] Thus, while the Western Bloc was forming, the Soviet Bloc was reaching its greatest degree of compactness.

5

The formation of the blocs in the period 1948 to 1950 realised (to a great extent) both the visions of the Truman Doctrine and the theories propounded by Zhdanov. It is true that the political relationships were much more complicated in both East and West than the bipolar view of the world, shared by both doctrines, would have it. One need only look at Stalin's break with Tito and the latter's successful independent stand to realise this.[43] But both blocs existed, each lived in fear that the other might get the upper hand, and therefore both camps sought to weaken each other by pointing up national contrasts and contradictions, and by dragging more regions of the world on to their own side. It had become tremendously difficult to get out of this bloc mentality, not only because economic interests and forms of society had aligned themselves to the polarisation in East and West, but above all because any unilateral weakening of defences would indeed have meant the other side taking advantage as a result. More feasible was a partial balancing-out of the two blocs in the form of a mutual recognition of spheres of influence and an agreement on reciprocal or joint interests. After all, both sides were afraid of an armed conflict, for good reason, and were also in any case not prepared to take risks (or incur great financial cost) to try to change the *status quo* to their advantage. These solutions, however, were neglected for a long time because, at least on the Western side, the ability to make a rational analysis of the conflict had been lost, and the Soviets' aggressive tone and the brutal methods they used in securing their power did not exactly help the West to remain rational.

Notes

1. Cf. on the decisions to divide Europe during the period 1945–7, Wilfried Loth, *The Division of the World 1941–1955*, London, 1988,

chaps. 5–7. It is clear that this rough outline of the process of bloc formation relies heavily on the above study, particularly upon Chapters 9 and 11. Where necessary, however, the results of new research have been brought in and certain relations have been more closely specified.
2. Cf. the survey by Jörg K. Hoensch, *Sowjetische Osteuropapolitik 1945–1975*, Kronberg, 1977, pp. 44–72. On the change of ideology and its function due to the break of 1947 see Heinrich Heiter, *Vom friedlichen Weg zum Sozialismus zur Diktatur des Proletariats.: Wandlungen der sowjetischen Konzeption der Volksdemokratie 1945–1949*, Frankfurt, 1977.
3. On this point see Werner G. Hahn, *Postwar Soviet Politics. The Fall of Zhdanov and the Defeat of Moderation, 1946–53*, Ithaca/London, 1982, pp. 20–5, 67–113.
4. Cf. François Fejtö, *Le Coup de Prague 1948*, Paris, 1976, and Karel Kaplan, *Der kurze Marsch: Kommunistische Machtübernahme in der Tschechoslowakei 1945–1948*, Munich/Vienna, 1981. For an interpretation of this, see Loth (see Note 1), pp. 165–7, and Peter Heumos, 'Der Februarumsturz 1948 in der Tschechoslowakei', in *Zeitgeschichte Osteuropas als Methoden– und Forschungsproblem: Gesichtspunkte zu einer strukturgeschichtlichen Interpretation*, Bernard Bonwetsch (ed.), Berlin, 1985 (= *Osteuropaforschung*, vol. 13). pp. 121–35.
5. Cf. the report of the National Security Council of the USA from 30.3.1948 (NSC 7) in *Foreign Relations of the United States. Diplomatic Papers, 1945–1950*, Washington, 1967–1980, FRUS, 1948, vol. I, pp. 546–50. For other accounts see Daniel Yergin, *Shattered Peace: The Origins of the Cold War and the National Security State*, Boston, 1977, ch. 13. For Europe see Loth (see Note 1), pp. 189–92, and Loth, *Sozialismus und Internationalismus: Die französischen Sozialisten und die Nachkriegsordnung Europas 1940–1950*, Stuttgart, 1977 (= *Studien zur Zeitgeschichte*, vol. 9), pp. 177–87.
6. On this point see Wilfried Loth, 'Die deutsche Frage in französischer Perspective', in *Westdeutschland 1945–1955. Unterwerfung, Kontrolle, Integration*, Ludolf Herbst (ed.), Munich/Vienna, 1985, pp. 37–49.
7. Ibid., p. 46f. Cf. also Timothy P. Ireland, *Creating the Entangling Alliance: The Origins of the North Atlantic Treaty Organisation*, Westport/London, 1981 (*European Studies*, No. 6), pp. 57, 63, 69, 85–100.
8. Cf. the recommendation made by the National Security Council of 28.6.1948, FRUS, 1948, III, p. 140f., and the statements by Under-Secretary of State Lovett during the first session of the Washington 'Exploratory Talks', ibid., pp. 149–151.
9. Ireland (see Note 7), pp. 101–4, Escott Reid, *Time of Fear and Hope. The Making of the North Atlantic Treaty, 1947–1949*, Toronto, 1977, pp. 114–18.

10. Cf. on the Soviet worries the testimony of Maurice Thorez (in a report of the autumn of 1947, which the US Embassy in Paris heard about: FRUS, 1947, III, p. 813f.) and that of Nikita Krushchev ('afraid of a new round of destruction'), in *Krushchev Remembers: The Last Testament*, Strobe Talbott (ed.), Boston, 1974, p. 191. On the aims of Stalin's statements during the conversation with Western ambassadors on 2.8.1948 (he had no intention of forcing Western troops out of Berlin, and that 'the only real issue' was the formation of a west German government) FRUS, 1948, III, pp. 999–1006. The fact that the Soviet leadership did not break off the negotiations when the Western Powers refused to put the London recommendation on ice, and instead made demands that amounted to forcing the Western Powers out of Berlin, cannot be taken as proof that 'the Soviet Union did not object to what was happening in the West ... as long as they were rewarded with the sole undisturbed possession of Berlin', (at least according to the recent book by Hermann Graml, *Die Alliierten und die Division Deutschlands. Konflikte und Entscheidungen 1941–1948*, Frankfurt, 1985, p. 208). The more plausible explanation for the Soviet tactic seems to be that she wanted to make it clear to the Western Powers how shaky their position was, and that she did not want to break off negotiations. In addition to this, Graml's theory misses the fact that the Soviet government was only ready to negotiate on the blockade if the discussion not only involved Berlin but also the decision to create a west German state (note of 14.7.1948, FRUS, 1948, II, p. 964; Molotov's statement of 31.7.1948, ibid., p. 997), and that the question of the new state came up time and again during the negotiations after the coded conversation with Stalin (according to Molotov on 6.8.1948, ibid., pp. 1018–21).
11. General Clay, who did not believe in this fiction, thus constantly urged the Allies to be allowed to break the blockade on the autobahns with the aid of tanks. Cf. Jean Edward Smith (ed.), *The Papers of General Lucius D. Clay: Germany 1945–1949*, Bloomington, 1974, p. 696f., 734–7; FRUS, 1948, II, p. 918, 957f.; John H. Backer, *Die deutschen Jahre des Generals Clay, Der Weg zur Bundesrepublik 1945–1949*, Munich 1983, pp. 277–9. How careful the Soviets were in their actions is shown by Hannes Adomeit in detail in *Die Sowjetmacht in internationalen Krisen und Konflikten. Verhaltensmuster, Handlungsprinzipien, Bestimmungsfaktoren*, Baden-Baden, 1983, pp. 97–143, 211–25.
12. Cf. on the fears held by the Americans, Bohlen to Marshall from 4.8.1948, State Department Papers, contained in Yergin (see Note 5), p. 385f., and Kennan's memorandum of 12.8.1948, FRUS, 1948, II, pp. 1288–96.
13. The text of memorandum PPS 37 can be found in FRUS, 1948, II, pp. 1288–96, the revised version as PPS 37/1 of 15.11.1948 (the so-called 'Plan A'), ibid., pp. 1320–38. Cf. also George F. Kennan, *Memoirs*

1925–1950, Boston/Toronto, 1967, with a somewhat confusing interpretation of his own motives.
14. Other testimonies, Cf. Bohlen to Marshall, 4.8.1948, in Yergin (see Note 5), p. 385f., and Smith to Clay, FRUS, 1948, II, p. 1006f., 1032. On the subject as a whole see also Avi Shlaim, *The United States and the Berlin Blockade, 1948–1949. A Study in Crisis Decision-Making*, Berkeley/London, 1983.
15. On this point see Rolf Steininger, 'Wie die Division Deutschlands verhindert werden sollte – Der Robertson-Plan aus dem Jahre 1948', in *MGM* 33 (1983), pp. 49–89.
16. Cf. Backer (see Note 11), pp. 299–302. In this respect Clay was instrumental in the founding of the Federal Republic.
17. At the end of April the Socialist ministers had formally urged the Prime Minister to arrange a new Four-Power Conference. Now, however, there was no longer a majority of the French Cabinet in favour of such a measure. Cf. Loth (see Note 6), p. 47.
18. FRUS, 1948, II, pp. 1083–85. Kennan put his plan forward again in November 1948 (see Note 13), but did not receive any support this time. Cf. also Axel Frohn, *Neutralisierung als Alternative zur Westintegration. Die Deutschlandpolitik der Vereinigten Staaten von Amerika 1945–1949*, Frankfurt, 1985.
19. The full text of the memorandum of 9.9.1948 (addressed to the member governments) can be found in FRUS, 1948, III, pp. 237–48; ibid., pp. 148–236 on the Washington negotiations and pp. 249–351 as well as FRUS, 1949, IV, pp. 1–281 on the later stages of negotiation in the autumn and winter of 1948–9.
20. Cf. the American documentation concerning the negotiations over the lifting of the blockade since January 1949 in FRUS, 1949, III, pp. 594–840, as well as on the Paris council meeting, ibid., pp. 856–1065.
21. Cf. Dietrich Staritz, *Sozialismus in einem halben Land: Zur Problematik und Politik der KPD/SED in der Phase der antifaschistisch-demokratischen Umwälzung in der DDR*, Berlin (GDR), 1976, pp. 155–74.
22. Cf. Lawrence S. Kaplan, *A Community of Interests: NATO and the Military Assistance Program, 1948–1951*, Washington, 1980, pp. 42–78; Kaplan, *The United States and NATO: The Formative Years*, Lexington, 1984, pp. 121–31; Ireland (see Note 7), pp. 119–37, 153–7, 161–3; Christian Greiner, 'Die alliierten militärstrategischen Planungen zur Verteidigung Westeuropas 1947–50', in *Anfänge westdeutscher Sicherheitspolitik 1945–1956*, vol.1: *Von der Kapitulation bis zum Pleven-Plan*, by Roland G. Foerster, Christian Greiner, Georg Meyer, Hans-Jürgen Rautenberg and Norbert Wiggershaus, Munich/Vienna, 1982, pp. 119–323.
23. Kaplan, *United States* (see Note 22), pp. 135–8; Norbert Wiggershaus, 'Die Entscheidung für einen westdeutschen Verteidigungsbeitrag 1950', in *Anfänge* (see Note 22), pp. 325–402, here pp. 325–38.

24. Cf. Wilfried Loth, 'Deutsche Europa-Konzeptionen in der Eskalation des Ost-West-Konflikts 1945–1949', in *Geschichte in Wissenschaft und Unterricht* 35 (1984), pp. 453–70, here pp. 464–6; Loth, 'Der Koreakrieg und die Staatswerdung der Bundesrepublik', in *Kalter Krieg und Deutsche Frage. Deutschland im Widerstreit der Mächte 1945–1952*. Josef Foschepoth (ed.), Göttingen/Zürich, 1985, pp. 335–61, here pp. 338–41.
25. On the rise of McCarthyism and its importance see Robert Griffith, *The Politics of Fear, Joseph R. McCarthy and the Senate*, Lexington, 1976, and Richard M. Fried, *Men against McCarthy*, New York, 1976.
26. Cf. Joyce and Gabriel Kolko, *The Limits of Power, The World and United States Policy 1945–1954*, New York, 1972, p. 457, 464, 470f., as well as the whole of ibid., pp. 453–76. Kolko's attempt to pin the blame for the worsening dollar crisis on the deflationary policy of the European Cooperation Agency is, however, less convincing.
27. Cf. Ireland (see Note 7), pp. 165–8.
28. The full text of memorandum NSC 68 can be found in FRUS, 1950, I, pp. 234–92; on how it was produced see Paul Y. Hammond, NSC 68: 'Prologue to Disarmament', in Warner R. Schilling, Paul Y. Hammond, Glenn H. Snyder, *Strategy, Politics and Defense Budgets*, New York, 1962, pp. 267–378; for data concerning the defence budget itself (not contained in the memorandum), see Yergin (see Note 5), p. 402. Cf. also John L. Gaddis, *Strategies of Containment. A Critical Appraisal of Postwar American National Security Policy*, New York/Oxford, 1982, pp. 83–109.
29. Cf. Michael H. Hunt, 'Mao Tse-tung and the Issue of Accommodation with the United States, 1948–1950', in *Uncertain Years: Chinese-American Relations, 1947–1950*, Dorothy Borg and Waldo Heinrichs (eds.), New York, 1980, pp. 181–233; and Nancy B. Tucker, *Patterns in the Dust: Chinese-American Relations and the Recognition Controversy, 1949–1950*, New York, 1983.
30. Kolko, (see Note 26), pp. 504–9; Yergin (see Note 5), pp. 400–7.
31. London conference: FRUS, 1950, III, pp. 94–125 and 828–1107, a summary of the discussions by Acheson on 14.5.1950, ibid., pp. 1061–7; Congress: Dean Acheson, *Present at the Creation: My Years in the State Department*, New York, 1970, p. 400f.
32. Cf. the deliberations in Loth (see Note 1), p. 235f., and Bernd Bonwetsch and Peter M. Kuhfus, 'Die Sowjetunion, China und der Koreakrieg', in *VfZG* 33 (1985), pp. 28–87, here pp. 46–52; on the prehistory of the Korean War see also Robert R. Simmons, *The Strained Alliance: Peking, Pyongyang, Moscow and the Politics of the Korean Civil War*, New York, 1975.
33. Cf. Kolko (see Note 26), p. 578f.; Glenn D. Paige, *The Korean Decision: June 24–30, 1950*, New York/London, 1968; also the American documents in FRUS, 1950, VII, pp. 125–270.

34. Cf. Loth, 'Koreakrieg' (see Note 24), pp. 341–3.
35. One need only compare the dramatic public statements made by the governments (e.g. Gunther Mai, *Westliche Sicherheitspolitik im Kalten Krieg: Der Korea-Krieg und die deutsche Wiederbewaffnung 1950*, Boppard, 1977 (= *Militärgeschichte seit 1945*, vol. 4), p. 29, 43f., 70, 74f.) with the relative calmness of internal views of the situation: Wiggershaus (see Note 23), pp. 340–5; Wiggershaus, 'Bedrohungsvorstellungen Bundeskanzler Adenauers nach dem Ausbruch des Koreakrieges', in *MGM* 25, 1979, pp. 79–122, here p. 106f.
36. Gaddis Smith, *Dean Acheson*, New York, 1972, p. 196f.; Kolko (see Note 26), p. 651f.; Hammond (see Note 28), p. 351f.; Yergin (see Note 5), p. 408.
37. Greiner (see Note 22), pp. 295–300.
38. Gerhard Wettig, *Entmilitarisierung und Wiederbewaffnung in Deutschland 1943–1955: Internationale Auseinandersetzungen um die Rolle der Deutschen in Europa*, Munich, 1967 (= *Schriften des Forschungsinstituts der Deutschen Gesellschaft für Auswärtige Politik e.V.*, vol. 25), p. 318f.; Loth, *Sozialismus* (see Note 5), p. 281f.
39. Cf. on this point explanations given indirectly by Foreign Minister Bidault to his American colleagues as early as the end of April 1950: Bruce to Acheson of 22.4.1950 and 25.4.1950, FRUS, 1950, III, pp. 60–5.
40. Cf. on the negotiations of autumn 1950 Lawrence W. Martin, 'The American Decision to Rearm Germany', in *American Civil-Military Decisions: A Book of Case Studies*, by Harold Stein (ed.), Birmingham (Alab.), 1963, pp. 643–65, here p. 656f.; Loth, *Sozialismus* (see Note 5), p. 282f., 286–9f., 384f.; Wiggershaus (see Note 23), pp. 355–3, 374–87, 392–9.
41. Cf. the testimonies of Secchia and Amendola during a public discussion in the spring of 1970 on Stalin's attempt to push Togliatti into the job of a secretary-general of the Cominform, documented in *Osteuropa* 20, 1970, pp. 703–18; for the context to this see Helmut König, 'Der Konflikt zwischen Stalin und Togliatti um die Jahreswende 1950/51', ibid., pp. 699–706.
42. After the trials of Kostoff in Bulgaria and Rajk in Hungary in 1949–50, the execution of former members of Zhdanov's staff in the autumn of 1950 (the Leningrad Affair) and the trial of Slansky in Czechoslovakia in 1951–2; Cf. Hoensch (see Note 2), p. 59f.; and Hahn (see Note 3), pp. 122–9.
43. On this point Lilly Marcou, *Le Cominform*, Paris, 1977, pp. 98–237.

2
Efforts towards Cooperation and Integration in Europe, 1948–1950

Klaus Schwabe

The plan for a European Defence Community (EDC) was the most ambitious attempt yet to create a form of supranational cooperation in Western Europe. Were the people on this side of the Iron Curtain prepared for this? Were they at all ready to work side by side with their former enemies, the Germans? In order to answer these questions, we must first look at the efforts made in the past to create a united Europe. Then it will be possible to appreciate the various organisations conceived on a European scale, which, from the Treaty of Brussels to the Schuman Plan, can be seen as experiments leading up to the EDC. On this basis we shall then examine the extent to which the process of creating the EDC had been made easier by these earlier attempts at cooperation, and how the EDC project in turn had an influence on the efforts to unite the Europeans, above all on the Schuman Plan negotiations, up to the end of 1950. In other words the question is whether the foundations for European cooperation laid down before the spring of 1950 were strong enough to serve as the base for the EDC, and also whether these foundations were themselves strengthened or weakened by the EDC project.

To find the roots of the efforts towards a united Europe after 1945 we must, as Walter Lipgens has proved,[1] look back to the 1920s; but for the immediate prehistory it will suffice to go back to the Second World War, when resistance movements both within and outside Germany examined the possibility of a federated Europe, among other solutions.[2] After the defeat of Nazi Germany, in the shadow of the calamity brought on Europe by overblown nationalism, and in the face of the resulting loss of power in the Old World, this discussion was continued. The growth of the USSR as a world power gave a new impetus to the subject. The 'cold war' and European unity became inextricably linked, and Churchill's famous Zürich speech of 19 September 1946, in which he called for the creation of 'a kind of United States of Europe', was inspired in no small measure by the failure of the Four Powers to come to an agreement on Germany at the Paris Conference in spring 1946. The dire economic state of Europe, which, according to Churchill, could only be exploited by Russia, was also a factor.[3] In the aftermath of the Communist takeover in Czechoslovakia in February 1948, the cause of a united Europe was taken up by both the parliaments and the public at large, reaching new heights of popularity.[4]

It should not, however, be forgotten how great a role the USA played in the movement for a united Europe. As early as the Second World War, in America, the concept of a European federation (on the lines of the American colonies after the War of Independence) had won support in high places.[5] Not until the spring of 1947, however, when the Marshall Plan was at the preparatory stage, did the aim of a united Europe, in whatever form, become official US policy and therefore, at the same time, a subject of debate for European governments. For in his well-known speech at Harvard University, on 5 June 1947, US Secretary of State Marshall had placed only one condition upon the economic aid he was offering: that the Europeans draw up a common list of requirements, and that they should form an organisation to coordinate the Marshall Aid Program.[6] This demand was deliberately kept somewhat vague, since the US Administration knew that a tightly organised structure would scare off many countries (certainly the Communist states, and possibly also some neutral countries) from taking part in the American recovery plan for Europe. The Americans, however, preferred a loose group containing the largest possible number of participating nations to a tighter organisation for the aid programme. It is clear that the 'inner circle' of planners went further in their hopes, banking on long-term trends that would ultimately lead to the long-term goal, a (Western) European political federation. Nevertheless, the US government did not want to be seen to be publicly supporting such future dreams. Over and above what was necessary, an organisation to coordinate aid, as Marshall had planned, the Americans felt it should be left to the Europeans themselves to find the best kind of union. For the

Americans this was primarily a question of European countries cooperating in order to rationalise economic aid, since the Americans saw the national economies as too isolated from one another and too small to make an effective use of US aid possible. The planners themselves had no doubt that a supranational organisation would be the best guarantee that such rationalisation would take place, although they took care not to make any definite public statements to that effect.[7]

The rationalisation of the economy of Europe was, for the Americans, merely the means to a greater end, which Marshall had described in his speech: namely the improvement of the sorry economic plight in which most European states found themselves, and thus the removal of the 'breeding ground' upon which Communism was threatening to grow. From the American point of view there was also a psychological side to this task. The Europeans must be given the hope that there were indeed ways out of their plight, and that the individual economies could be pulled from the chaos which sought to engulf them. One alternative to chaos was closer European economic cooperation, and thus the European ideal was a constructive vision of the future: at a time when more and more Europeans had serious doubts about what the future held. From the beginning Germany was included in all these economic, political and psychological considerations.[8]

If the US government was assuming the role of spokesman for the European ideal, then it was only reflecting the prevailing opinion among the public at large, which became more enthusiastic about Europe the more the chances of coming to an agreement with the Soviets over Europe faded. Since the start of 1948 this enthusiasm had produced one resolution after another from Congress, calling for the creation of a 'United States of Europe'.[9]

However easy it was, in the atmosphere of 1947–8, to support the idea of European union, it was a different matter to take the first real steps along the road the Europeans, both victors and vanquished, had to follow, at least according to the Americans. No false hopes were raised in Washington on this point. The events leading up to the founding of the Organisation for European Economic Cooperation (OEEC) served to confirm such an attitude. This body was the *first* attempt to organise Western European economic cooperation within the confines of the Marshall Plan, after the USSR and her satellites had excluded themselves from the group of recipient states.[10]

The OEEC was not only meant to organise the allocation of US aid in Europe, but would also, the American government hoped, become a 'continuing organisation', by means of which long-term Western European cooperation would be guaranteed. 'Long-term' meant after the end of Marshall Plan aid. If US wishes had been realised, the OEEC would have gained a supranational character, with a Secretary General not subject to national but only to the organisation's recommendations. This idea did not find favour with the British, however, and the OEEC became merely a steering group which did not impinge upon the sovereign rights of individual countries. Thus it was incapable of deciding how to distribute American aid.[11] Not until 1950 did it create something of real value – the agreement on the European Payments Union. But even this agreement was watered down, to please the British, to the extent that it precluded the opportunity of entering into a process of further economic integration in Western Europe.[12] The attempt to link the OEEC with other endeavours towards European unity were stifled (again due to British resistance) at a much earlier stage when the Belgian proposal to create a link between the OEEC and the Treaty of Brussels was rejected.[13]

Thus we arrive at the *second* effort to organise Europe – the Brussels Treaty. As this was in the main a military defence pact, it does not in itself qualify for coverage in this essay. However, the circumstances under which it came into being gave rise to hopes that it would have a wider function; and thus we should consider it, albeit briefly. Strangely enough, considering what I said before, it was the British Foreign Minister, Bevin, who supplied the initiative for this alliance of Western European states. Struck by the failure of the London Four-Power Conference on the German question (in November and December 1947), the resulting widening of the split between East and West and also a general Western crisis of confidence, Bevin proposed, in a note to the US government in January 1948, as well as in a speech to the House of Commons, the formation of a 'Western Union' as a counterpart to the Eastern Bloc which had already assumed concrete form. He spoke of a consolidation of the moral and spiritual strength of Western civilisation, closer consultation among the states of Western Europe (above all in economic matters) and of Britain's rapprochement to the continent of Europe backed by the USA and the Dominions. Italy and, later, even Germany would be included in this union.[14]

Efforts towards Cooperation in Europe

A short time later, Bevin went to America to explore the possibility of a military alliance between Western Europe and the USA. As in the Marshall Plan, the US administration made a united Europe the condition for taking up negotiations on an alliance, as Britain wanted. It is possible that Bevin, knowing the American position, put forward his sketchy idea of an extensive 'Western Union', while in reality only seeking a bilateral military alliance with the USA. The fact that the negotiations in Europe and the exploratory talks in Washington very quickly got round to military themes was also surely due to increasing tension in Europe following the Communist takeover in Prague. An Anglo-American alliance suited neither the Benelux countries, who sought membership of a Western European defence arrangement, nor the basic attitude held by the Americans, who wanted to speed the process of European union on the widest possible basis.[15] The Treaty of Brussels of 17 March 1948 contained merely a shadow of these wishes and of the hopes raised by Bevin's speech. Articles 1 to 3 recommended some sort of economic, social and cultural cooperation between the member states, while Article 7 created a consultative committee, which could advise on the possible the dangers to peace, including a revival of Germany's 'policy of aggression', but which could also propose common measures to maintain economic stability.[16] It was surely not this European disguise, but rather the worsening cold war, especially the Berlin blockade, which caused the USA to back up the Brussels Pact by concluding the NATO Treaty with the Western European states after protracted negotiations.[17]

The Consultative Committee envisaged in the Brussels Treaty, however, was not completely meaningless. For the first time it supplied the platform for negotiations concerning a political organisation of Western Europe – the Council of Europe, the *third* attempt to create European unity.

This time, officially at least, the initiative came from France. On 29 July 1948, French Foreign Minister Bidault suggested to the Brussels Consultative Committee the creation of a provisional European Parliament and a customs union between the five Brussels Treaty states.[18] This idea doubtless stemmed from a revaluation of French policy on Germany, which led to the conclusion, in Paris, that the recently initiated west German state could no longer be bound to the West using the dictatorial rule of occupation, but rather by integrating it into a European

Community.[19] But first of all this European Community had to be created. Such a proposal, once again, met with the whole-hearted approval of the Americans, although they refused to specify exactly what kind of political organisation they wanted.[20] This became the subject of protracted negotiations, above all between France and Great Britain. The French concept of an independent consultative parliament contrasts starkly with the British idea of an 'institutionalised intergovernmental conference'.[21] The final compromise envisaged a European Parliament with a mere advisory function, which needed a two-thirds majority to pass recommendations, and a Council of Ministers which could only act if it reached unanimous agreement. Here, since the founding of the Council of Europe on 5 May 1949, all initiatives aimed at creating a supranational European authority failed, mostly due to Britain's veto. Even if it had come about, the power of such an authority would have been very limited, as all military matters were specifically excluded from the Council of Europe's area of responsibility in deference to its neutral members.[22]

This was not the kind of Western European integration envisaged by the US government and the 'Europeans' within the French government; to be exact, not even a step in the right direction. Thus both the US and French foreign policies became caught on the horns of a difficult dilemma, a dangerous 'cul-de-sac', as Jean Monnet put it when looking back on the second half of the year 1949.[23] It was not the policy of containing the USSR which had run into a crisis (indeed, the NATO Alliance already existed), but rather the policy of containing Germany, or to be more exact West Germany, who had just formed herself into a new state of fifty million inhabitants and a disturbingly fast-growing economy.

It was clear that sooner or later this new Germany would rid herself of the shackles placed on her by the Occupying Powers, such as the International Authority for the Ruhr. Paris was afraid that the Anglo-Saxons, and the Americans in particular, were only too willing to support such efforts by the new Federal Republic to make herself independent, even to the point of rearmament. France would then become dangerously isolated were she to cling to the restrictions placed on the Federal Republic by the victors. And what if the USSR then decided to play her trump card, i.e., the offer of reunification for Germany? The ghost of a new Rapallo stalked the offices on the Quai d'Orsay, and not only there but also on the Potomac. From the point of view of both

France and the USA, European unity had to be achieved quickly in a way which would harness the new Federal Republic to the West once and for all. But how? The ideal solution for Paris and Washington would have been if Western Europe, including Great Britain, had been integrated within a supranational organisation. The US government even hoped for a Europe led by the British. But due to London's insurmountable aversion to such institutions, as was shown during debates in the Council of Europe, this ideal was out of reach. European unity *à l'anglaise* – in other words a loose, very informal federation of states – seemed to both Paris and Washington to be too weak to keep the Federal Republic in the West for good.[24]

Should the integration process go forward without Britain? In the summer and autumn of 1949 there had been long-winded debates on this very point within the US government as well as between Washington and London. Unlike its Western European ambassadors, in October 1949, the State Department was prepared to give its support to this partial union of Europe without Britain.[25] The Washington administration made this decision knowing that a rapprochement between Germany and France was the condition *sine qua non* for any kind of European integration; France had to take the lead in this process and if Britain did not want part of this, then so be it.[26] It took a few more months before the French government came to the same conclusion. Many factors guided Paris to this decision. First, the failure of French exploratory talks in London on the creation of an Anglo-French economic union (spring 1949)[27]; second, the unilateral devaluation of the pound by Britain in September 1949, which was understandably seen as a provocation by France;[28] third, unsuccessful attempts by France to widen the powers of the International Authority for the Ruhr[29] as well as the worsening conflict between Paris and Bonn over the future of the Saar in the spring of 1950.[30]

Against this background, France's foreign policy made a definite U-turn towards partial, sectoral but at the same time supranational integration of the European economy, which was to lead to the inception of the Schuman Plan and through this the Pleven Plan.

One essential element of the Schuman Plan, the *fourth* attempt to create a European organisation, was a High Commission as the top administrative body of the member countries' iron and coal industries when they were integrated. The decisions made by this commission should, according to Monnet's suggestion, be legal and binding on the member states. This 'breach' which had thereby been 'struck in the walls of national sovereignty'[31] was accepted without reservation by the West German government (which at that time had nothing to lose in this regard) and just as unreservedly welcomed by the US government. The British government, however, roundly rejected the principle of a supranational body.

Preliminary talks on the creation of a Western European Coal and Steel Community began without British participation and progressed rapidly in the summer of 1950. The participating governments, especially the French, were conscious of the fact that the Schuman Plan was only the first step on the road leading to a political federation of Europe. The European Coal and Steel Community was meant to provide the impetus for European unity in place of the Council of Europe, which had proved itself incapable of carrying out this task.[32]

At the end of June 1950 the outbreak of the Korean War cast its shadow on this encouraging new European initiative, and in Europe it led to anxious calls for some kind of German participation in Western Europe's defence. At the same time, both the Western Powers and the Federal Republic were agreed that a revival of an independent, national German armed force was out of the question. It thus seemed obvious that the problem of West Germany's defence contribution should be seen in a European perspective. Churchill voiced these thoughts in his speech to the Council of Europe on 11 August 1950, where he demanded the 'immediate creation of a European army under a single command'. He went further by proposing the appointment of a European Defence Minister, and his suggestion was accepted by a large majority of the Council.[33] It is clear that this decision was more noise than substance, since there was no doubt that the Council of Europe was in no position to organise what was in any case a vaguely formulated project.[34] But from that point on, the question of arming West Germany was closely linked to the difficulties in uniting Europe, at least from the perspective of public opinion in the West itself. The real negotiations aimed at reaching the first stage of union in the shape of the European Coal and Steel Community were, to say the least, complicated.

First, there was the suspicion on the part of the West that the Federal Republic would make use of the increase in her international status (which was expected to result from the efforts made by the West to secure a German contribution to defence) in order to press home her own interests more strongly within the Schuman Plan, and (if it came to the worst) perhaps even to accept the collapse of the whole project.[35] Therefore the USA wanted to avoid any link between plans for a German defence contribution and the Schuman Plan negotiations, as the French seemed to favour.[36] France, on the other hand, made the success of the Schuman Plan talks a prerequisite of any serious attempt to arm the Federal Republic.[37] Such a strategy ran the risk of bringing the Schuman Plan into disrepute in West Germany, since what started out as a far-sighted European initiative was now looked upon as an ultimatum from the victorious French. Adenauer was suitably displeased at the French behaviour. His reaction, which he did not allow the public to see, can be explained to a large extent in terms of the situation his government was facing at home, which made him afraid that the opposition would capitalise on his difficulties.[38]

In addition to this, it was an unhappy coincidence that this worsening of Franco-German relations should come at a time when the Schuman Plan talks were dealing with the knotty problem of how the body called Allied Controls was to be replaced by the European Coal and Steel Community, especially in the Ruhr. Such a lifting of the discriminatory controls by the former occupying powers was now seen within the German delegation as an essential prerequisite to the West German government's signing of the agreement on a European Coal and Steel Community.[39] This demand had been put forward at the start of negotiations and had only been delayed for technical reasons, so the German action should perhaps not be seen merely as a power-play, as the Americans and the French seemed to think. Also, there is no doubt that Adenauer at no time seriously thought of risking the failure of the Schuman Plan negotiations. In spite of this, Adenauer was forced to bear in mind the attitude of the Bundestag, which had to ratify the agreement. His pressure to have the last remnants of occupation removed in the Federal Republic of Germany had also received a boost from the debate on rearming the country.

Negotiations on the Schuman Plan, which continued into the spring of 1951, could not remain unaffected by this change in the political climate.[40] The Pleven Plan for a West German contribution to defence, which France put forward at the end of October

1950, was also bound to cast a bad light on the efforts to create a united Europe for a variety of reasons. The Pleven Plan, according to its French initiators, was meant to be a kind of Schuman Plan on the security front.[41] This idea was based on the misconception that it was possible to treat the defence of a country (always the real sign of national sovereignty) as a mere 'sector' of her entire policy, as was feasible with coal and steel production. Apart from this, the Americans considered the French project's practicality more than doubtful from a military point of view. The Pleven Plan, intended to be a European initiative, was suspected by the military planners of being a mere delaying tactic.[42] This sort of idea could only harm the image of a united Europe in the USA. While the US government had always been in favour of integration up to that point, it at once expressed doubts about the practicality of the supranational features of the Pleven Plan.[43]

But European union was damaged most by the fact that the long-term aim, a political Western European federation, was taken out of the context of the Schuman Plan by the Pleven Plan, and was linked with the controversial and, militarily speaking, questionable project of a European Defence Community. In fact this was obvious because this EDC was hard to imagine without a political parent organisation. The success or failure of the efforts to create a political union of Western Europe, however, were bound up with the progress of the creation of the project for military integration.[44] In any case, this was the view of leading Western European politicians, while the USA, with the Spofford compromise of December 1950 reached on the subject of a German defence contribution, left themselves room to manoeuvre should the EDC project come to nothing. This compromise envisaged separately running negotiations on rearming West Germany and on the formation of a military and political community of Western European states.[45] In the end (i.e. in 1954) the separation of the strictly military side of any European integration from its political-institutional aspects may have facilitated the rearming of West Germany outside the context of a European Defence Community. Until then, however, the uncertain fate of the EDC took some of the drive out of the endeavours to create a political union in Western Europe. It must be left to the imagination to decide whether a step-by-step process in this direction, as had been begun with the Schuman Plan, would have been successful.

Efforts towards Cooperation in Europe

Seen from the end of 1950–1, in any case, there was no solid political foundation for a European Defence Community. The consolidation which was expected from the continuation of the process begun by the Schuman Plan however, had been damaged by the hastily improvised Pleven Plan project.[46]

Notes

1. Walter Lipgens, *Die Anfänge der europäischen Einigungspolitik 1945–1950, part 1: 1945–1947*, Stuttgart, 1977, p. 43f.
2. Cf. for example Herman Graml, 'Die außenpolitischen Vorstellungen des deutschen Widerstandes', in *Widerstand im Dritten Reich: Probleme, Ereignisse, Gestalten*, Hermann Graml (ed.), Frankfurt, 1984, pp. 92–139, here p. 115f., 134, 137f.
3. Lipgens (see Note 1), p. 313f.
4. Walter Lipgens, 'Die Bedeutung des EVG-Projektes für die politische europäische Einigungsbewegung', in: *Die Europäische Verteidigungsgemeinschaft. Stand und Probleme der Forschung*, Hans-Erich Volkmann and Walter Schwengler (eds) for the Militärgeschichtliches Forschungsamt with contributions by Alfredo Breccia, Anselm Doering-Manteuffel, Alexander Fischer, Pierre Guillen, Peter Jones, Albert E. Kersten, Walter Lipgens, Klaus A. Maier, Wilhelm Meier-Dörnberg, Paul Noack, Raymond Poidevin, Jean-Pierre Rioux, Hans-Erich Volkmann, Donald Cameron Watt and Werner Weidenfeld, Boppard, 1985 (= *Militärgeschichte seit* 1945, vol. 7), pp. 9–30, here p. 13f.
5. For instance former Secretary of State John F. Dulles: Ronald Pruessen, *John Foster Dulles: The Road to Power*, New York, 1982, p. 190f.; Pierre Melandri, *Les Etats-Unis face à l'unification de l'Europe*, Paris, 1980, p. 15f. Lipgens slightly overplayed the USA's aversion to a regional European union during the period 1941 to 1946 (Lipgens (see Note 1), p. 61f.).
6. Michael J. Hogan, 'The Search for a "Creative Peace": The United States, European Unity, and the Origins of the Marshall Plan', in *Diplomatic History* 6, 1982, pp. 267–85; also Klaus Schwabe, 'Der Marshall Plan und Europa', in: *Histoire des débuts de la construction européenne (mars 1948–mai 1950)/ Origins of the European Integration (March 1948–May 1950), Actes du Colloque de Strasbourg 28–30 novembre*. Sous la direction de Raymond Poidevin (ed.), Bruxelles, Milano, Paris, Baden-Baden, 1986, pp. 47–69.

7. Schwabe (see Note 6), p. 52f.; Armin Rappaport, 'The United States and European Integration: The First Phase', in *Diplomatic History* 5, 1981, pp. 121–49, here p. 124, 128f.
8. John Gimbel, *The Origins of the Marshall Plan*, Stanford, Cal., 1976, p. 199f., 231f.; Melandri (see Note 5), p. 97f.
9. Rappaport (see Note 7), p. 122f.
10. Melandri (see Note 5), p. 103f.
11. Alan S. Milward, *The Reconstruction of Western Europe 1945–1951*, London, 1984, p. 169f., 206.
12. Ibid., p. 326; see also Imanuel Wexler, *The Marshall Plan Revisited: The European Recovery Program in Economic Perspective*, London, 1983, p. 155f.
13. Milward (see Note 11), p. 177.
14. *Foreign Relations of the United States, Diplomatic Papers, 1945–1950*, Washington DC, 1967–1980; FRUS, 1948, III, Washington, 1974, p. 3f.(Inverchapel to Marshall, 13.1.1948).
15. Ibid., p. 358f., Marshall to Embassy Belgium, 10.1.1948; ibid., p. 7f., Kennan to Marshall, 20.1.1948; ibid., p. 13, Memorandum of Conversation by Lovett, 27.1.1948.
16. Europa-Archiv (EA) 3, 1948, p. 1263f., and 4, 1949, 1st half-year, pp. 1755–67, 1810–17.
17. Timothy Ireland, *Creating the Entangling Alliance: The Origins of the North Atlantic Treaty Organisation*, London, 1981 (= European Studies, no. 6), p. 80f., 102f.
18. EA 4, 1949, 1st half-year, pp. 1817, 2011–24.
19. On this point Raymond Poidevin, 'Der Factor Europa in der Deutschlandpolitik Robert Schumans' (Sommer 1948–Frühjahr 1949), in *VfZG* 33, 1985, vol. 3, pp. 406–19, here p. 408f.; Pierre Gerbet, *La Construction de l'Europe*, Paris, 1983, p. 92.
20. FRUS, 1948, III, p. 222f., Marshall to Caffery, 27.8.1948.
21. Lipgens (see Note 4), p. 15.
22. Walter Lipgens, 'EVG und Politische Föderation: Protokolle der Konferenz der an den Verhandlungen über die europäische Verteidigungsgemeinschaft beteiligten Länder am 11. Dezember 1951', in *VfZG* 32, 1984, vol. 4, pp. 637–88, here p. 645f.; Gerbet (see Note 19), p. 96.
23. Jean Monnet, *Erinnerungen eines Europäers*, with a foreword by Helmut Schmidt, Munich, Vienna, 1978, p. 367f.
24. Ibid., p. 371f.; Gerbet (see Note 19), p. 103; Milward (see Note 11), p. 391f.; Schwabe (see Note 6), p. 62f.
25. Schwabe (see Note 6), p. 66f.
26. FRUS, 1949, IV, p. 469f., Acheson to Perkins, 19.10.1949; FRUS, 1949, III, p. 622f., Acheson to Schuman, 30.10.1949.
27. Monnet (see Note 23), p. 356f.

28. FRUS, 1949, IV, p. 841f., Holmes to Acting Secretary of State, 23.9.1949.
29. Milward (see Note 11), p. 388f.
30. Hans-Peter Schwarz, *Die Ära Adenauer. Gründerjahre der Republik 1949–1957*, Stuttgart, 1981 (= *Geschichte der Bundesrepublik Deutschland*, vol. 2), p. 88f.
31. Monnet, (see Note 23), p. 378.
32. The first French plan for this project shows us that the European Coal and Steel Community was already thought of as merely the first stage on the road to a gradual European union by its French supporters, quoted in Monnet (see Note 23), p. 376f. On the attitude of Great Britain and the USA cf. William Diebold, *The Schuman Plan: A Study in Economic Cooperation 1950–1959*, New York, 1959, p. 48f.; Melandri (see Note 5), p. 271f.; FRUS, 1950, III, p. 714f., Acheson, circular directive, 2.6.1950; also the author's work, 'Die Vereinigten Staaten und der Schuman-Plan', in Schwabe (ed.), *Die Anfänge des Schuman-Plans*, Baden-Baden, 1988.
33. Gerhard Wettig, *Entmilitarisierung und Wiederbewaffnung in Deutschland 1943–1955: Internationale Auseinandersetzungen um die Rolle der Deutschen in Europa*, Munich, 1967 (= *Schriften des Forschungsinstituts der Deutschen Gesellschaft für Auswärtige Politik e.v.*, vol. 25), p. 319f.
34. As Lipgens (see Note 4), p. 21, rightly states, Churchill totally overlooked the political basis for his suggested European army. He was happy that the Germans did not make the formation of a national army the precondition for their joining a European army later: FRUS, 1950, III, p. 207, Churchill to Truman, 13.8.1950.
35. FRUS, 1950, III, p. 752f., Webb to McCloy, 29.11.1950; McCloy was told to work against a hardening of the German position. Cf. also Diebold (see Note 32), p. 69f.
36. National Archives and Record Service: Modern Military Branch (NA, MMB), Washington DC, Record Group (RG) 59, 396.8, box 14, Department of State, Daily Summary, 4.8.1950; Monnet (see Note 23), p. 431.
37. FRUS, 1950, III, p. 378, Bohlen to Acheson, 15.10.1950.
38. *Die Kabinettsprotokolle der Bundesregierung*, Hans Booms, (ed.) for the Bundesarchiv, vol. 2, 1950. Revised by Ulrich Enders and Konrad Reiser, Boppard, 1984, p. 777, Note 51 (27.10.1950); Herbert Blankenhorn, Verständnis und *Verständigung: Blätter eines politischen Tagebuches*, Frankfurt/M., Berlin, Vienna, 1980, p. 115.
39. *Die Kabinettsprotokolle* (see Note 38), vol. 2, p. 880f., Notes 7, 116, Cabinet Meeting, 12.12.1950.
40. US High Commissioner McCloy supported Adenauer's position that West German integration into a Western European community had

to be linked to the lifting of the remaining occupation restrictions (McCloy to Truman, 10.9.1950). Harry S Truman Library, President's Secretary's File, 178, McCloy's answer to the two known memoranda by Adenauer of 29.8.1950.
41. Monnet (see Note 23), p. 432f. The Council of Europe had also supported the idea of sectoral integration, and Schuman made a point of this in connection with the Pleven Plan: Lipgens (see Note 22), p. 647.
42. FRUS, 1950, III, p. 411f., Acheson to Bruce, 27.10.1950; Acheson, Memorandum of Conversation with Secretary Marshall, 27.10.1950, Truman Library, Papers of Dean Acheson, box 65; Norbert Wiggershaus, 'Die Entscheidung für einen westdeutschen Verteidigungsbeitrag 1950', in *Anfänge westdeutscher Sicherheitspolitik*, vol. 1: *Von der Kapitulation bis zum Pleven-Plan*, by Roland G. Foerster, Christian Greiner, Georg Meyer, Hans-Jürgen Rautenberg and Norbert Wiggershaus, Munich, Vienna, 1982, p. 393f.
43. FRUS, 1950, III, p. 385, Acheson to Bruce, 17.10.1950.
44. Lipgens (see Note 4), p. 27f.
45. FRUS, 1950, III, p. 517f., Marshall, memorandum, 5.12.1950; Wettig (see Note 33), p. 387f.; Edward Fursdon, *The European Defence Community: A History*, London, 1980, p. 97f.
46. Lipgens (see Note 22), p. 644f., 650f.; Lipgens (see Note 4), p. 24f.

PART II
Member States' Interests and Viewpoints

3
Western Union and European Military Integration 1948–1950 – An American Perspective

Lawrence S. Kaplan

There has always been an air of unreality about the Brussels Pact military organisation. A critic might say that at most the organisation has had a shadow life, living on illusion, with the shadows changing sufficiently over a generation to permit different illusions.

In the mid-1980s the WEU – Western European Union, as it had been known since 1954 – was resurrected as an instrument of European political and military cooperation, either within the NATO structure or outside it as a potential element of an integrated Europe. There was a flurry of optimism following meetings in Rome in 1984 and Bonn in 1985 that generated such symposia as the round table on 'Relaunching the Western European Union', sponsored by the European Institute of Public Administration at Maastricht in May 1985. If nothing else should come of this new European attention to the WEU, the Maastricht round table at least produced intelligent and provocative analyses of the order of Reimund Speidelmann's 'WEU and EC – Competition or Cooperation for Western Europe's Security'.

Given its history, the prognosis of European military integration under the auspices of Western European Union is not good. Twice before the idea of integration has surfaced in the last forty years, and each time the Western Union seemed to be either a useful *ad hoc* device to solve a particular NATO problem, such as the admission of West Germany in 1954, or the involvement of the United States in a European alliance in 1948.

Historians in the future may wonder if the organisation ever took itself seriously. As recently as 1979 NATO officials in

Brussels and Casteau were not at all sure where the records of the original Brussels Pact were located. When the late Walter Lipgens began to search for documents on the political and military integration of Western Europe for a massive publication project sponsored by the European Community, he was first told that the files may have been stored in Paris or in Brussels. It required extensive enquiry before he learned that they were housed in the London headquarters of the WEU. Even when the WEU itself undertook to declassify and make available to scholars the records of the Permanent Commission and the Consultative Council in 1981, and subsequently the minutes of the Military Committee, Chiefs of Staff Committee, and Commander-in-Chief Committee in 1984, they seemed to evoke little interest among scholars.

Despite reasons for neglect, Western Europe's groping towards a new defence structure through the experience of the Western Union from 1948 to 1950 deserves more attention than it has received. NATO occasionally but only elliptically has acknowledged its debt to the work of the Brussels Pact units. Their names – Military Committee, Secretary-General, Military Supply Board, Finance and Economic Committee – were directly appropriated by the successor organisation. Montgomery's supreme command at Fontainebleau was a model for SHAPE. It is not too much to claim that the Western Union provided the basic infrastructure of NATO. Indeed, it is fitting that the very idea of infrastructure – installations crossing national lines needed to service multinational armed forces – was itself a symbol of integration, begun under Western Union auspices.

The American role in European military integration activities may be equally worth examining, despite its absence from official membership. There was a symbolic relationship from the beginning, centring on the vital military assistance that a revived and reshaped European defence would require and on the presence of such military leaders as Lyman L. Lemnitzer, A. Franklin Kibler and Clarence R. Huebner on a regular basis at meetings of the Military and Chiefs-of-Staff Committees.

The United States has played its part in denigrating the role of the Brussels Pact in the life of the Atlantic Alliance for some obvious reasons – and also for reasons that are less obvious. It would have been understandable if American leaders had dismissed the organisation as a ruse in 1948 to lure the United States into an entangling engagement. That the origins of the Brussels treaty lay in the plans laid by Ernest Bevin and Georges Bidault, the foreign ministers of the United Kingdom and France, respectively, to contrive an American-European alliance is indisputable. The British and French, not to mention the Benelux powers, had no expectations that their combined strength in 1948, or fifty years later, would be sufficient to cope with Soviet power. Only the United States commitment could make the difference.[1]

This recognition explains the major purpose of the Brussels Pact. It was designed to demonstrate to Americans that Europeans were performing on the political and military level what they had promised to do on the economic: namely, to help themselves through as much dedication as possible, and to collaborate with allies to break down barriers in the way of integration. By showing good faith they would then be worthy of the kind of support the Marshall Plan was in the process of giving. The outcome would involve assistance in strengthening their defences just as the Marshall Plan would revive the national economies. But more was at stake than military aid; it was the abandonment of America's 150-year-old isolationist tradition that was sought by the Europeans.

The effort ultimately succeeded as NATO's existence demonstrates. If Americans a generation ago were not resentful over the inspiration behind the Brussels Pact, it was because they were unaware of the Anglo-French deliberations of 1947 over the best means of bringing the United States into an alliance. Actually, European cunning was largely unnecessary. As early as New Year's Eve 1947 a leading State Department official, John D. Hickerson, observed to his colleague, Theodore C. Achilles, after some libations of fishhouse punch at the Metropolitan Club in Washington, that 'I don't care whether entangling alliances have been considered worse than original sin since George Washington's time. We've got to negotiate a military alliance with Western Europe in peace time and we've got to do it quickly.'[2]

While NATO was ultimately acceptable, including its blow to tradition, the Western Union could never overcome suspicion among Americans over the nebulous functions the Western Union had and over the accomplishments those functions achieved. The State Department perceived the Western Union countries to be aggressive prospective partners who wanted to cement a connection with the United States whereby they would become the negotiating agents for all the other powers in the alliance. It was also apparent that they wished for special privileges without accepting commensurate responsibility. The Defence Department was worried over Europe's incurring responsibilities for Europe's defence far beyond the resources available to it. The JCS was particularly concerned by demands that would be made on the armed services's limited supply of stocks. Western Union's indecent push for immediate military aid immediately after the signing of the North Atlantic Treaty seemed to justify their fears, particularly when American aid would obviously fill national needs, not the integrated plans of a united Europe.

Given the charade of integration, the Western Union was written off as a temporary expedient facilitating the security conversations of 1948 that led to the signing of the North Atlantic Treaty. Thereafter, its activities and its structure was subsumed under NATO. There was an element of pathos in Ernest Bevin's attempts to rally his colleagues on the Consultative Council in the summer of 1950. He reminded them of the potential of the Western Union to become the spokesman for the European component of NATO, even after the Korean War had broken out; if only the Five could translate their efforts into facts, and prevent the Americans from receiving the impression 'that the Brussels Treaty Powers were not doing their utmost'.[3]

It was much too late for such concerns. The United States long before had given up any idea that the Western Union could fulfil its promises. The record was a dismal one, particularly from the military perspective. From the time they gathered in London the Western Union seemed to be unable to do more than throw up committees with impressive names and equally impressive missions, but with no ability or even will to live up to their description or to carry out their objectives.

The immediate interest of the Allies was in securing American assistance to fill the gaps in equipment and in provisions. What they could not accomplish were the actual steps to be taken to implement their missions. National Security Council document 9/3 had made specific the requirement that Europe present a coordinated defence system with all means available to its members, then determine military needs and supply the United States with an inventory of deficiencies and a policy statement.[4]

A policy statement was deliverable. In fact it was available as early as August. Western Union noted that the primary objective was to 'hold enemy as far east as possible with the resources available at any given time'. Additionally, as air and sea defences were established, Africa would be defended and the Middle East would be used as an offensive base.[5]

But when the time came for the Western Union to meet the American deadline for specific information on which US aid could be based, they failed the test, and failed badly. There was no breakdown of material, troop, and financial deficiencies that would permit the kind of detailed screening that had been promised by November, to permit a rational military assistance programme to be put into effect.[6] The JCS accepted an 'interim solution' that called for the Western Union Chiefs of Staff to inform them by the end of November about the steps taken to plan Western European defence with means now available as well as the extent of outside assistance needed. Western Union chiefs would also provide a progress report on the standardisation of equipment, the coordination of production and the pooling of resources.[7]

Even this deadline for a scaled-down version of NSC 9/3 requirements was not met. The best they could manage was no more than a summary of forces available for mobilisation in 1949 if the necessary equipment could be acquired. If movement had begun to pool inventories and production resources in order to draft a balanced programme, it was sluggish when it was visible at all. The national lists of deficiencies were incomplete and haphazardly screened.[8] There was little that the United States could do about the response, or lack of response, of the Western Union allies, beyond accepting the results as a basis for a new military aid programme. There was no alternative despite the unhappiness of American military and political authorities. Western Union was too important to American plans in 1949 for its shortcomings to get in the way of progress. No matter how irritating its behaviour or deceptive its claims, the Brussels Pact was at the heart of the programme. Without its presence US politico-military policy toward Europe would follow the fireman's role in Greece – *ad hoc* action wherever trouble burst out – rather than the self-help and cooperation of the Marshall Plan approach.

The only time that the Western Union powers seemed to function as an integrated unit was when they could speak out against a specific US demand such as pressures on The Netherlands over

Indonesia in the spring of 1949, or demands for bases as reciprocity for military aid in the autumn of 1949. And the only specific details over needs that emerged from the Western Union powers dwelled on the special interests of the individual armed forces. France, for example, did not conceal its concerns for its own needs as a priority overriding such planning for integration the Defence Committee was making. Averell Harriman, US representative in Europe for the ECA, recommended, in July 1948 – fittingly on the 14th – sending a limited number of P-49s or P-51s to equip a selected unit of the French air force for the psychological effect a token response would have on French morale. Two months later President Truman approved the transfer of sufficient equipment and spare parts to bring three French occupation divisions in Germany up to combat status.[9]

Even when the issues seemed to be broader and to concern the Western Union as an entity, the focus was on American aid to the individual nation rather than to an integrated force. For example, the French representative on Western Union's Chiefs of Staff Committee, General Charles Lechères, recommended in October 1948 that all strategic planning be made in conjunction with Americans. 'It was only in that way,' he claimed, 'that the Western Union would be able to make a really economic distribution of effort. If the Americans undertook to plan the defence of North Africa, then additional French resources could be devoted to the battle in Western Europe'. Air Marshal Arthur William Lord Tedder, for the United Kingdom, agreed fully with Lechères's argument, but in the light of American sensibilities on the subject 'it would be undesirable to make a direct reference to the necessity for American assistance in any general statement on the subject'.[10]

If Western Union managed to keep any credibility at all in 1949, it was only as a result of the administration propping it up before a reluctant Congress as an example of European activity on behalf of self-help and integration. General Omar Bradley reported that the 'Western European countries which are the principal ones involved and to which a majority of this equipment goes, already have an organization set up which has been functioning for about a year and we do think they all have arrived at a point in their plans and their organization, where as far as they are concerned, the conditions you are talking about have been met'. Secretary of Defence Louis Johnson went even further on a limb when he labelled the Western Union as a 'working reality and not a mere paper organization. It has been studied by the Joint Chiefs of Staff, who consider it to be basically sound and in consonance with their strategic thinking.'[11]

None of these brave words accorded with anyone's reality, and no one knew this better than the JCS itself. Bradley did not need a special trip to Europe in early August to confirm the disarray he encountered there. Western Union at best was an embarrassment, at worst a scandal. This sentiment was clearly and regularly expressed to Americans by the most prominent of its military figures, Field Marshal Bernard Law Montgomery, the chairman of the Commanders-in-Chiefs Committee. Despite recognition of Monty as a contentious personality who ruffled sensibilities wherever he went, his judgements were respected in Washington. Nevertheless his conflict with French leaders, particularly Marshal Jean de Lattre de Tassigny, over command of forces, was widely known and cited as a further example of the problems of the Western Union as were demands for appropriate appreciation in the form of headquarters facilities at Fontainebleau. As late as 1950, in a serious review of the short-term defence plan approved by the Defence Committee, he seemed to give as much weight to the lack of a general headquarters building as he did to the inadequacy of forces available.[12] Yet the forcefulness of his personality, the distinction of his career, and the general good sense in his criticisms outweighed caveats about his judgement in American eyes. In the summer of 1950 he told the secretary-general of the Western Union that 'Our present organization will never produce military strength in Europe; after nearly two years work we are no better off than we started as regards the provision of effective forces'. The total effect was that of an 'opera bouffe'.[13]

While this language may have accorded with American prejudices, it was all the more damaging when the figure using it was a man whose qualities were cited by Secretary of State Marshall as precisely those needed for a supreme commander in Europe in August 1948. When he told US High Commissioner John J. McCloy and Ambassador to the UK Lewis Douglas in April 1950 that the 'defence of Europe was a façade', it was considered worthy of the special attention of Dean Acheson.[14]

So Western Union's defence network was left to wither as NATO took over the committee structure it had established a year earlier. Before the Korean War Western Union had shrunk to a Western European Regional Planning Group, where unlike its Military Committee and Chiefs of Staff Committee, the United States would not even be represented on a regular basis. Almost plaintively, Field Marshal Harold Alexander of the Defence Committee said 'He was sure that the US would continue to participate actively in the work done by the Brussels Treaty Defense Organisation'.[15] He was mistaken. The United States resisted, in order, as the JCS phrased it, 'to stimulate them more readily to greater measures of self-help and mutual aid'. If Americans had fully joined the group, it would have been equally logical for them to have joined the Northern European Regional Group and all the others as well. The only concession was 'participation as appropriate'.[16]

After Korea the WU virtually disintegrated. In the minutes of the Military Committee of 26 July 1950 there was recognition that 'its activities would be conducted in the wider framework of the principal staff officers committee of NATO'. By the end of the year the Consultative Council observed that 'the continued existence of the Western Union defence organisation is no longer necessary'. At the same time it resolved that 'the reorganization of the military machinery shall not affect the right of the Western Union Defense Ministers and Chiefs of Staff to meet as they please to consider matters of mutual concern to the Brussels Treaty Powers'.[17]

This attempt to keep alive Europe's separate efforts at integrated defence may have been simply a normal reflex action of any bureaucracy to justify its continued existence. Before the Korean War, General Paul Stehlin had outlined for the Military Committee at least three reasons for keeping distinctions between NATO and the Western Union. First was the obvious difference between Article IV of the Brussels Treaty which required automatic intervention by all the allies in the event of an attack against one of them, as opposed to Article 5 of the North Atlantic Treaty which only demanded such action as each party deemed necessary. Second, he pointed to the contributions the administrative machinery of Western European Defence Organisation (WUDO) had already made to the advancement of the pooling of resources, joint armament programmes and the standardisation of weapons. Third, he emphasised the vital European concern in strategic planning in a defence plan that would at least include the Rhine and the Alps.[18] This was a concern that was less pressing for the United States or for Britain, as the emergency war plan HALFMOON suggested. Any plan that is predicated on the evacuation of troops to strongholds across the Pyrenees or at the Channel would inevitably excite more hostile attention from continental Europeans than from Americans, Canadians or British.[19]

Of these three justifications for the survival of WUDO the first was specious. However elliptical the language of the Atlantic treaty may have been, its signals were as clear as the Brussels treaty, and far more persuasive in determining Europe's fate, and this was widely recognised on both sides of the Atlantic. NATO in 1949 held no other meaning more significant than America's entanglement in the fate of Europe.

However, French Defence Minister, Paul Ramadier, probably expressed some feelings common to most Europeans with memories of two World Wars when he said that historically 'between periods of crisis the United States was tempted to take a less active interest in Europe'. While he recognised and was grateful for the knowledge that Europe enjoyed 'at present the powerful and wholehearted backing of the United States', this aid had limits. 'Europe still must be built as an entity', with a sense of independence of the United States. This is language that was to be heard regularly over the next generation, but it ignores the reality of an American involvement through NATO that made that organisation and not the Western Union or any other strictly European group the source of Europe's security.[20]

The second reason for the maintenance of the WU has a tendentious ring to it. A case may easily be made that the Brussels powers had completed their service in making available to NATO the many committees and boards, and had little more to offer. Duplication of efforts might only serve to provide job security for WUDO officials. Stehlin's third justification was more persuasive than the other two. The pre-NATO planning of the WUDO committees deserved more attention than simply as building blocks for the NATO structure. Strategic planning under the WUDO not only exerted influence on the early years of NATO but continued to be felt throughout its history.

André Kaspi, a French historian with primary interests in Franco-American relations in the First World War had been one of the few scholars to look seriously at the actual workings of the military integration in the late 1940s. He observed that the integration of military forces, no matter how halting under NATO, 'stemmed from existing practices of the countries that signed the North Atlantic Treaty'.[21] It was obvious that Eisenhower's appointment as Supreme Allied Commander in 1951 made the integrated command of the Second World War, with SHAEF as a model for SHAPE. But the work of the Western Union functioning in peacetime may be a more appropriate precedent. From the beginnings of military planning in the summer of 1948 the Military Committee aimed at a Supreme Command, preferably with an American at its head. For a time the JCS, at the initiative of the British Chiefs of Staff, had even considered General Lucius Clay, US military governor in Germany, for this role, but occupation duties among other obstacles stood in the way.[22] There was considerable feeling among the JCS that such an arrangement would relieve Europeans of efforts toward integration that they otherwise would make, or would tempt to use Americans as 'reserve forces'. Only on the outbreak of a war would American troops be brought under an integrated command.[23]

As a result of this decision Europeans were left with the difficult matter of assigning authority, an issue that was personalised by the differences between Montgomery and Jean de Lattre de Tassigny over pride of place. Yet the differences were far more than personal; they reflected French concerns about placing power in the hands of a figure whose national interest could be in conflict with France's.[24] But for all the attention that has been given to the two rivals on the Commander-in-Chief Committee, it should be underscored that they ultimately agreed on strategy as well as distribution of commands. While Montgomery remained chairman of the committee, two out of the four allied commanders were French, and in wartime a Frenchman would command ground forces. As Kaspi had pointed out, 'The headquarters at Fontainebleau enabled the staff to become better acquainted and to learn how to cooperate in matters of daily routine.' This was no small achievement, and one that smoothed Eisenhower's command in NATO.[25]

Still a larger achievement was the European presence in the evolution of HALFMOON into the Medium Term Defence Plan of NATO. The emergency plan of evacuating Europe, which had been accepted by the American, British and Canadian planners in April 1948, was unacceptable to Europeans. Their demands for defence 'as far east as possible', a cornerstone of Western Union thinking, was realised in a plan that would accept the defence of the Rhine as a point of departure. This short-term WUDO plan was itself unsatisfactory to the Dutch, who would have to accept a line at the Rhine-Ijssel that would leave part of their country exposed.[26] It is not surprising that a year later the Middle Term Defence Plan (MTDP), nominally the product of NATO planners, represented the wishes of the European community far more than they did the American.

European expectations seemed impossible to meet, although the United States avoided communicating its judgement to the continental Western Union allies. Only the British Chiefs of Staff were aware of the American plans at a time when the Western Union announced their intentions to build up an 'impenetrable' defence at the Rhine-Ijssel line. Even after NATO was established, the JCS persisted through OFFTACKLE to keep to a plan of defending no more than southern Spain, Great Britain and the Mediterranean, while they tried to deflect their allies from a medium-term plan that would defend Europe at the Rhine. They were unhappy with both the scope of defence and with the lack of clear steps toward implementation. From an American perspective the NATO's MTDP was little more than a consolidation of the work of the regional planning groups. It omitted, among other things, plans for the defence of North America.[27]

What is noteworthy about this issue is not American suspicion and secrecy, except in their relations with Canada and Great Britain; rather it is the relative ease with which continental Europe broke down American resistance to its programme despite the hollowness of the Western Union's professions of self-help and integration and the inability, in the light of a restricted military budget, of the United States to fulfil its contribution to the MTDP. Yet its adoption by NATO represented the weight that a united Europe – at least on this issue – could bring to bear against the US.

It was in the context of the MTDP that the first infrastructure programme should be seen. If Europe was to be defended, the first slice of thirty airfields and thirty-four signal communications projects had to be built, and since lines would cross territories of member nations and since the organisation as a whole would be the beneficiary, this route to integration was a natural step to take. That the first slice was in reality a promissory note rather than an actual formula for sharing costs is hardly surprising. But the groundwork was laid for the North Atlantic Council to take over a project for European integration that was begun before SHAPE was established or for that matter before NATO as an organisation had come into being.[28] The JCS and Standing Group agreed a month after the Korean War broke out that progress in developing NATO's infrastructure was 'an integral part of the North Atlantic defense plan, taking into account the absolute priority granted it in the Western Union Defense Plan'.[29]

Less appreciated but also worthy of notice were attempts at military exercises of the kind that NATO would subsequently celebrate as unique to its functions. The manoeuvres and exercises in which the armies or navies of two or more allies would play war games were rightly identified as examples of allied cooperation in which normally hostile Greeks and Turks, for example, might work together in the eastern Mediterranean. The exhibitions of coordination sent messages to friends as well as to enemies. But it would be inaccurate to call these military exercises unprecedented. At a time when the idea of a NATO supreme commander was still in embryo, the summer of 1950, the Secretary General of the WUDO could report to the Consultative Council a variety of manoeuvres conducted by one or more of the allies, involving coastal convoys and minesweeping, under such names as 'Exercise Unity', 'Exercise Triade' and 'Exercise Cupola'.[30] Although they were not of the scale that would be found in the larger Atlantic association, they too provided precedents for NATO to follow when SHAPE was created in 1951.

All these activities were known to American planners, if only because the two major bodies of WUDO, the Military Committee and the Chiefs of Staff Committee, had American officers as regular observers. The observers dismissed the workings of the Western Union as trivial when not deceitful and manipulative. Reports from the American delegation to Brussels Pact committees seemed to confirm the charges that the allies were doing little or nothing to meet commitments for integration.

Yet an examination of the correspondence of the American representatives on Western Union committees and of the minutes of meetings of the Military Committee, the Chiefs of Staff Committee, and the Commanders-in-Chief Committee tell a different story. The work of the Brussels Pact was taken seriously, and American interest in advancing it was equally apparent. Generals Lemnitzer and Kibler of the Military Committee and Huebner on the Chiefs of Staff Committee were more than passive observers of the scene and more than mere conduits of information from London or Brussels to Washington. They were actors on the scene influencing their European colleagues on every major issue, and in turn influencing their superiors in the Pentagon.

This role of actor rather than witness was thrust upon them from the very beginning. The dispatch of General Lyman L. Lemnitzer by the JCS to London to head a joint group of seven officers assigned to the WU Military Committee on a 'non-membership basis' was a harbinger of things to come. The JCS had given him detailed instructions on what he may and may not do in talking with Europeans about a coordinated military supply plan. He was further informed of limits to the extent American troops in Europe would support Western Union's strategic concept of fighting as far east in Germany as possible. And most particularly he was cautioned against agreeing to military arrangements of any sort that might 'unduly influence' US global strategy.[31]

To dramatise the low profile he and his team were to adopt, Lemnitzer was to enter London in civilian clothes to conceal his identity from the press. Within a day, however, the London *Daily Express* noted his arrival under a headline reading 'America May Arm 35 Divisions'. Despite his own memories of anonymity the potential importance of his role was recognised, or at least hoped for, as the paper claimed that 'US General Lyman Lemnitzer, in London to advise the Military Committee on Western Union, had suggested that they set up a permanent staff and pool all military secrets and weapons. The United States will partly arm 35 European divisions of cadres before more first rated divisions are set up.'[32] From the moment of arrival he was a central figure at the Horse Guards headquarters in London.

If there was any doubt about the centrality of Lemnitzer's presence it should have been removed by his action in opening the first formal meeting of the Military Committee on 22 July 1948. The Committee then agreed that the United States and Canadian officers were free to express any views they wished without having the responsibility for the conclusions and recommendations of the MC and without signing reports to the

Defence Committee.[33] Lemnitzer responded to this treatment with equal enthusiasm. He had no hesitation about pushing the Committee to move ahead rapidly with the establishment of a Military Supply Board that would extend to logistical services and facilities and to their distribution among the allies. He took a particular interest in the Army Standardisation and Inventory Sub-committee and urged emphasis on practical aspects of implementing production resulting from standardisation rather than the theoretical fine points of standardisation on which the sub-committee dwelled. He applauded what seemed to be immediate action on cooperation among the Five when the committee recommended that Belgian and Dutch air forces be re-equipped with Meteors and the French re-equipped with Vampires. He accepted as a concomitant of these recommendations that the United States support their implementation with specific actions of its own. He concluded this despatch with the observation that the 'US may be approached by Western Union to assist in pilot training to a relatively limited degree (150 pilots over a two-year period) but no indication yet of other requests'.[34]

Also in his brief service as US representative to the Western Union Military Committee, which lasted less than a month, he observed with a proprietary interest the establishment of a Western Union Defence Organisation, from a Defence Committee managing political decisions through a Chiefs of Staff Committee to a Commander-in-Chief Committee.[35] Before he returned to Washington he made clear the importance that the United States should attach to the work of the emerging WUDO. He urged the JCS to adopt the elaborate security procedure known as METRIC established by the Western Union powers. His reasoning included the paralleling of this procedure with British and US practice, but it had other virtues as well for the United States. 'If US is to participate in activities of Western Union Military Committee as envisaged in JCS 1868/11 it will be necessary for US representative in London to have complete access to all committee information and documents'.[36] In making this recommendation he both attested to the potential importance of Western Union but also to the potential of American influence in all their councils.

There is no evidence that these communiqués from a respected but still relatively junior major general won over the sceptical JCS and other senior officials in the Pentagon at this time. They remained suspicious of European intentions. As suggested earlier, they worried particularly about two implications of massive aid to and involvement in the defence of Western Europe. The first was concern that NSC 9, calling for support of the Brussels Pact and the exploration of a larger mutual defence agreement, would commit the United States to military obligations beyond its capacity to handle, certainly under the tight military budgets imposed by the Truman Administration. Second was the danger of Europeans competing through the military aid programme for the same resources that the JCS needed so badly for American armed forces. Reluctantly, JCS dropped objections to NSC 9/2 when NSC 14, referring specifically to military aid, prohibited any assistance that would 'jeopardize the fulfillment of minimum materiel requirements of the United States armed forces'. Moreover, all aid would have to be consistent with 'strategic concepts provided by the Joint Chiefs of Staff'.[37]

Pressure from Secretary of Defence James V. Forrestal and the NSC more than conversion to faith in the defence efforts of Europeans accounted for JCS cooperation with the Western Union. It remained reluctant. Years later, Lemnitzer recalled General J. Lawton Collins, Army Deputy Chief of Staff, only half jokingly greeting him with the comment, 'Lem, I understand you're up there doling out all the equipment that you're going to take away from the Army and give to European allies'.[38]

Before Lemnitzer left London he had to contend with the possibility, as expressed in a communication from Lt. General Albert C. Wedemeyer, army deputy chief of staff, and Executive for the JCS, of withdrawing US representation in Western Union military talks.[39] The American delegate was emphatic in his rejection of the idea. The American presence, he felt, had done much to speed up the activities of the Committee and its removal could do serious damage to the developing Western Union structure. 'In addition', his cable continued, 'and without attempting to forecast what US attitude or alignment towards Brussels Powers may eventually take, I believe it would be unwise to abandon or neglect taking full advantage of the opportunity to observe and influence military planning'. His successor, he felt, must be a major general since heads of all the delegations were of that rank. This would assure the United States of participation in informal high-level discussions. Any downgrading in rank would be seen by Europeans as a sign of 'waning US interest in the Western

Union with consequent harmful effect on activities of the Military Committee.'[40]

Lemnitzer obviously won his case. When Major General A. Franklin Kibler replaced Lemnitzer in mid-August 1948 he was able to continue and deepen the connections his predecessor had made. Other Americans joined him. As noted earlier Lt. General Clarence R. Huebner, an experienced Second World War combat commander and General Clay's deputy in Germany, became the US representative on the Commanders-in-Chief Committee in April 1949, and Joseph H. Taggart of the Munitions Board was named representative on the WU's Military Supply Board.

In his authoritative history of the Office of the Secretary of Defence, Steven Rearden claimed that 'by the end of 1948, despite the Joint Chiefs' cautions, the United States had moved extremely close to a *de facto* alliance with the members of the Western Union'.[41] The logic of the American military presence in Europe side by side with the Brussels allies prevailed over formal American objections to linking American troops to defence planning. As long as an attack from the east would have to come through German territory, an American role was unavoidable, despite denials. In examining the variety of possibilities about attack from the east, the 'satellite' zone of Germany was constantly in mind. When the French Defence Minister suggested that an attack 'could also be made by German elements from the eastern zone going to the help of other subversive groups in western Germany at a time of crisis', the United States had a clear answer, and one that settled much of the question about American troops' involvement with Western defence: 'The American military governor in Germany would then join his forces with WUDO's.' Even before the Defence Committee had considered this subject General Kibler, speaking on the possibility of Soviet aggression through East Germany, asserted that 'any revolutionary movement in Germany would be considered by the American military authorities in the same light as an open aggression'.[42]

This centripetal movement had all come about at the very time both State and Defence officials were deprecating the activities of the European allies. When they were not disparaging them, they were venting their exasperation with the transparent attempts of the Brussels Pact powers to conceal the inadequacy of their efforts. Yet the record of correspondence between London and Washington and of the minutes of the Western Union committees reflect more collaboration, even conspiracy, between American and European members, than conflict and distrust.

This situation was particularly evident in the role that General Kibler played on the Military Committee. He was present in all its deliberations, and was party to its failings and failures as well as to its slim list of accomplishments. Indeed, he often seemed to serve as a coach to his European colleagues, pointing out what might or might not win over the hearts of suspicious Congressmen. On the basic question of US military assistance to the Western Union, one of the two vital *raison d'être* of the treaty, Kibler was fully aware of the inadequacy of the first estimate of equipment to be sought from the United States. But while also saying that it would be desirable to have indicated ultimate requirements based on a long-term plan, there was no time for this solution. So, inadequate as the proposals of the Military Committee were, based on the next few years' needs, he found nonetheless that it 'would afford the basis of a reasonable approach to the US Government'. As for its possible effect on Congress, the key to success, he offered, would be a perception that the Western Union was 'making the best possible use of the means at present available'. Hence, he predicted that the European powers had a 'fair chance' to make a convincing case to Congress.[43]

None of this encouraging advice to the European allies appeared in Kibler's cables to the JCS. Nor for that matter were his doubts about Western Union's approach to US aid reflected in his telegrams. Little of the substance of the committee meeting came through in his notation that the Chiefs of Staff 'plan will be recommended to Defense Ministers as a basis for an interim approach to United States (it is hoped by December 1948) for supplementary aid for equipping forces 5 powers intend to raise in the next year or so'.[44]

Even when he appeared criticial of WUDO practices, such as his reporting to the Chiefs of Staff Committee about the JCS being disturbed over the 'piece meal' approach to supply problems, he retreated in the face of a strong rebuttal. General Lechères complained that Kibler must understand the complexities and difficulties involved in tasks never attempted before. The American representative then made clear that he did not 'imply that the work accomplished was on the wrong lines'. He just wanted to alert his colleagues that Congress would be unhappy with a report that did not represent completed action by the Military Supply Board.[45]

This spirit of complaisance did not characterise the totality of Kibler's stances in WUDO circles. A few months later when the supply plan still turned out to be inaccurate as well as incomplete, he recommended the establishment of a permanent inter service logistics organisation as a prerequisite for US military aid.[46] When the supply board came up with new recommendations he condemned the results in no uncertain terms. The trouble, he claimed, was that the Military Committee approached the problem from the wrong direction. He urged the allies to present lists much greater than funds requested, along with clear priorities. Then, armed with lists, the Supply Board 'could match up total producted capacity within presently budgeted limitations and come up with a firm production program'.[47] Whatever discomfort the allies may have experienced over his didactic message, no rebuttal was recorded at these meetings.

Kibler articulated strong critical commentary on specific items as well. At a meeting of the Chiefs of Staff Committee on 26 August 1948 Belgium's Etienne Baele recommended an immediate decision in favour of the British .303 rifle which Montgomery had identified as the best field gun available. When Kibler demurred on the grounds that the US had no intention of abandoning the .300 rifle, the Chiefs of Staff, at the suggestion of Chairman Tedder, agreed to accept the American judgement that the decision was premature and that action be deferred. Standardisation in this instance would follow American specifications. Despite the obvious tensions raised in this meeting, Kibler's report to the JCS on the subject contained only a barebones mention of his enquiry into the British advocacy of the .303 weapon.[48]

Similarly, when the secretary-general had suggested to the Military Committee that it approve production of a French jeep, according to the Military Committee's Army Advisory Committee, Kibler complained. In reviewing French requirements of 23,000 jeeps, he noted that 7,000 were already on hand or reparable, and another 9,000 were to be supplied under the United States Mutual Defence Assistance Programme. Hence the jeep should have low priority. Moreover, he observed that the 'adoption of the French prototype jeep as standard was a step backwards in the standardization programme in that it increased to at least three the number of standard models of the same item'.

In this case, after General Chevillon claimed that the French would still be 7,000 jeeps short, the Military Committee did approve production as appropriate to French needs, but made it clear that Kibler's objections would be taken into account.[49]

It is difficult to escape from a conclusion that Pentagon strictures against the behaviour of the Western Union, first in enticing the United States into its web, and then in forcing it to accept its meagre efforts at integration as genuine, were overblown at best. It is obvious that American involvement with the activities of WUDO was so intimate that deception had no meaning. Either the American representatives were guiding – or controlling – their European colleagues on one issue or another, or were preparing them to win their cases in Washington, whether or not they had substance. In either instance the United States shared responsibility for results with the Brussels Pact powers. The US representative on the Military Committee dropped all pretences of concern for an integrated defence system after the outbreak of the Korean War. Anticipating $4 billion in supplemental military aid – over four times the amount in the original fiscal 1951 bill – General Kibler urged his colleagues on the Military Committee to review their deficiencies in materiél with 'utmost dispatch', in order to 'take advantage of and maintain the present momentum'.[50]

In all these deliberations at least two caveats must be emphasised, rather than merely assumed or alluded to in passing. One is the importance of what went unsaid in 1948 between the United States and its European associates. France's suspicions of an Anglo-American conspiracy may have been exaggerated but the exclusion of France from the Pentagon conversations of March 1948, along with the other Continental members of the Western Union, coloured if not distorted the dialogue between Americans and Britons on the one hand and the Europeans on the other. While suspicions about the extent of the Communist penetration of French public life may account for much of the exclusion, France's expectations of the United States inevitably differed from Britain's in this period. Both Britain and the United States had a global vision of foreign military policy that made Europe only one of the arenas of conflict with the Communist world. Herein lay an explanation for the short-term plan of evacuating Europe in the event of attack that went beyond a limited military budget and inadequate military forces on the field.

Another caveat follows from the natural gap between what the US military representatives in Europe said at meetings and what they reported, or failed to report, in their dispatches to Washington. It is not that there was a conscious attempt to deceive the JCS. There may not even have been an awareness of a distinction between the impression they might leave with their European counterparts and what they might make on their American superiors. The differences were often in tone rather than in substance. Or they were omissions rather than commissions. Lengthy exchanges in committee meetings could not always have been accurately encapsulated in a telegram. Nuances were missing in some cases, important commentaries in others. What could be said in extended give-and-take recorded in committee minutes in London or Brussels was not always shared with the generals in the Pentagon. The words of the telegrams were for the most part those of detached observers.

In sum, if there was a conspiracy to deceive, American military were collaborators in part of it. They did so in much the same spirit that Hickerson and Achilles drank toasts to the end of isolationism. There was no choice. A dangerously weak Europe had to be shored up, and the method acceptable to Congress lay through the enhancement of integrated measures. These were inevitably inadequate; a credible defence of Western Europe through even the most successful pooling of efforts or merging of sovereignties was never within the bounds of reality. Change would come only with a major American commitment, and in this endeavour Europeans and American military officials worked hand in hand. Their achievement – preparing the way for NATO – is worthy of more positive evaluation than has yet been accorded them.

Notes

1. Lawrence S. Kaplan, 'An Unequal Triad: the United States, Western Union, and NATO', in Olav Riste (ed.), *Western Security: The Formative Years*, Oslo, 1985, pp. 107–8.
2. Oral history interview, Theodore C. Achilles, Harry S. Truman Library, Independence, Missouri.

3. Records of the 9th session of Consultative Council, The Hague, 1 August 1950, DG1/1/2, Western European Union (WEU) Archives, London.
4. *Foreign Relations of the United States (FRUS)*, 1949, III, p. 291. Memorandum by the JCS to Secretary of Defence, 24 November 1948, 'Developments with Respect to Western Union'.
5. FP(48)27, 25 August 1948, Report by Chief of Staff to Military Committee, DG 1/15/30, WEU Archives, London; Ambassador of the United Kingdom to Secretary of State, 14 May 1948, III, p. 123, 126.
6. Memorandum, FC (48)23, Appendix B to Enclosure A to JCS 1868/58, 23 November 1948, CD 6-2-46, RG 330, NARS, Washington, DC.
7. Memorandum by the JCS to the S/D, 24 November 1948, NSC 9/6, 'Developments with respect to Western Union', FRUS, 1948, III, p. 291.
8. Report, JCS 1868/58, 11 February 1949, 'Military Aid Program', CD 6-2-46, RG 330, NARS.
9. US Special Representative in Europe to S/S, 14 July 1948, FRUS, 1948, 3, p. 183; Steven L. Rearden, *History of the Office of Secretary of Defence: The Formative Years, 1947–1950*, Washington, DC, 1984, p. 468.
10. FC(48), 2nd Meeting, Chiefs of Staff Committee, 6 October 1948, DG 1/6/36, WEU Archives, London.
11. *Military Assistance Program Hearings*, Committee on International Relations, Executive Session, 29 July 1949, US House of Representatives, Historical Series, vol. 1, p. 30; *Military Assistance Program Hearings*, Senate, Committees on Foreign Relations and Armed Services, 81 Cong. 1 sess., 9 August 1949, p. 49.
12. Sir Oliver Harvey to Kirkpatrick, 26 January 1949, FO 371, Public Record Office (PRO), London. The British Ambassador to France reported his embarrassment over Montgomery's complaints; FC (50), Minutes of First meeting of Chiefs of Staff Committee, 16 February 1950, DG 1/6/26, WEU Archives, London.
13. MD (50)12, 7 July 1950, DG 1/11/56, ibid.
14. Memorandum, S/S for President, 23 August 1948, 'Western Union Organisation of Defence Forces', CD6-2-46, RG 330, NARS; Douglas to Acheson, 11 April 1950, RG 59, NARS.
15. MD (49), 5th meeting, 23 November 1949, WU Defence Committee, Lancaster House London, DG1/5/34, WEU Archives, London.
16. JCS 1868/100, 19 August 1949, pp. 730–1, CCS 092, Western Europe (3–12–48), RG 218, NARS.
17. MC (50), 32nd meeting, Military Committee, 26 July 1950, DG 1/7/42, WEU Archives, London; Records, 10th session, Consultative Council, Brussels, 20 December 1950, DG1/1/2, ibid.

18. MC (49), 47th meeting, Military Committee, 26 October 1949, DG 1/7/40, ibid.
19. Kenneth W. Condit, *The History of the Joint Chiefs of Staff: The Joint Chiefs and National Policy*, Wilmington, Del., 1979, pp. 366–8.
20. MD. (49), 3rd meeting, minutes of Defence Committee, Luxembourg, 19 July 1949, DG 1/5/32, WEU Archives, London.
21. André Kaspi, 'Prelude to NATO: Two Examples of Integration of Military Forces', in L. S. Kaplan and R. W. Clawson, (eds), *NATO after Thirty Years*, Wilmington, Del., 1981, p. 185.
22. Rearden, *History of OSD*, p. 465.
23. Wedemeyer to CINCEUR, WAR X 90305, 6 October 1948, Leahy File, RG 218, NARS.
24. Kaspi, 'Prelude to NATO', p. 196; Memorandum of conversation between de Lattre and Public Affairs Officer of US Embassy in Paris, 11 February 1949, no. 165.840.00/2–1440, RG 59, NARS.
25. Kaspi, 'Prelude to NATO', p. 198.
26. Condit, *History of JCS*, II, p. 373; M.D. (49), 5th meeting of Defence Committee, 23 November 1949, Lancaster House, DG1/5/34/WEU Archives, London.
27. Rearden, *History of OSD*, p. 483; S/S Acheson to S/D Johnson, 24 March 1950, RG 330, CD6–2–46; Christian Greiner, 'The Defence of Western Europe and the Rearmament of West Germany, 1947–1950', in Olav Riste (ed)., *Western Security: The Formative Years*, Oslo, 1985, pp. 150–6.
28. Hastings, Lord Ismay, *NATO: the First Five Years, 1949–1954*, Paris, 1954, pp. 114–15; Robert S. Jordan, *The NATO International Staff/Secretariat 1952–1957. A Study in International Administration*, London, 1967, pp. 267–9.
29. JCS 2073/42, 29 July 1950, Appendix A to Enclosure B, CCS 092, Western Union (2–12048), RG 218, NARS.
30. WU 131/50, Draft Progress Report by secretary-general of Defence Organisation to Consultative Council, for meeting 1 August 1950, DG1/11/56, ibid.
31. Rearden, *History of OSD*, pp. 468–9.
32. Interview with Lemnitzer, 21 March 1974, pp. 3–4, Historian's Office of the Secretary of Defence (Historian's OSD) files, Pentagon, Washington, DC; 23 July 1948, London *Daily Express*, recorded in Delegation to the Western Union (DELWU) 3, Lemnitzer to Wedemeyer, Dept. of Army, 23 July 1948, CCS 092, RG 218, NARS.
33. DELWU 4, 23 July 1948, ibid.
34. DELWU 11, 1 August 1948, ibid.
35. DELWU 14, 6 August 1948, ibid.
36. DELWU 5, 26 July 1948, ibid.
37. Rearden, *History of OSD*, pp. 464–5.
38. Interview with Lemnitzer, 21 March 1974, pp. 10–12, OSD

Historian's files.
39. Wedemeyer to DELWU, WAR8661, 26 July 1948, CCS 092, Western Europe (3–12–18), RG 218, NARS.
40. DELWU 9, 31 July CCS 092, RG 218, NARS.
41. Rearden, *History of OSD*, p. 469.
42. MD (49), 1st meeting, Defence Committee, 17 January 1949. Brussels, DG 1/5/31, WEU Archives, London: MC (48), 5th meeting, Military Committee, 10 November 1948, ibid.
43. FC (48), 3rd meeting, Chiefs of Staff Committee, 26 October 1948, Whitehall, DG 1/6/36, ibid. General Huebner was not nominated to serve on this committee until 13 December 1948.
44. DELWU 86, 28 October 1948, Leahy File, Western Union, RG 218, NARS.
45. FC (48), 6th meeting, Chiefs of Staff Committee, 14 December 1948, DG 1/6/36, WEU Archives, London.
46. MC (49), 17th meeting, Military Committee, 21 April 1949, Whitehall, DG 1/6/38, ibid.
47. MC (49), 19th meeting, Military Committee, 4th May, Whitehall, DG 1/6/39, ibid.
48. FP (48) 33, 1st meeting, Chiefs of Staff Committee, 26 August 1948, London, DG 1/6/26, ibid.; DELWU 92, 30 October 1948, Leahy File, Western Union, RG 218, NARS.
49. MC (50), 1st meeting Military Committee, 4 January 1950, DG 1/7/41, WEU Archives, London.
50. MC (50), 32nd meeting, Military Committee, 26 July 1950, DG 1/7/42, ibid.

4
Canada and the Security of Western Europe (1948–1950)

Paul Létourneau

The failure to achieve nuclear disarmament, the expansionist policy of the USSR in Eastern Europe, the paralysis of the UN Security Council, the Berlin crisis, the failure of the commission on conventional disarmament, the civil war in Greece, Soviet influence in Iran and Turkey, the Prague coup and the weakness of Western European democracies: all these contributed to the foundation of a new military organisation comprising the most important Western nations. This set of international events, together with the fact that Canada, economically speaking, was more powerful than ever before, made it easier for her to commit to European security. The decision to participate in the new collective defence organisation, however, was not based solely on the Soviet threat. Several factors, among them the wish to play a greater role in international affairs, also influenced the Canadian government. First of all we shall make a brief survey of the most important Canadian initiatives concerning the security of Western Europe between 1948 and 1950, and, in the second section, deal with the main factors leading to Canada's entry into NATO.

Canadian Diplomatic Efforts

Between 1948 and 1950, against a background of high international tension, the West was mainly concerned with military security and the economic reconstruction of Western Europe as the prerequisites for political stability. Going against her traditional attitude, Canada played a large role in the creation of a regional security system, as did the United States, albeit somewhat more rapidly. After the end of the Second World War, in the course of restructuring international relations, Ottawa began to pursue an internationalist policy which led to Canada, a 'medium' power, acting as a major player in the definition and establishment of the new world order. During the postwar period, until 1957, Canada became a disciple of multilateralism, seeing compromise and consensus among the partners as a way of placing at least certain limits on the influence of the superpowers. She kept up this policy not only during the foundation of NATO, but also in her activities within the United Nations and in her efforts to consolidate the Commonwealth.

During this period, the Canadian government, for the first time, chose to link the country's destiny permanently, not just to France and the Benelux countries, but to Western Europe as a whole, thus superseding Canada's geographical ties to North America as well as her traditional historical ties to the British Empire. The threats facing Europe gave Canada's leaders the chance to judge Canada's international position from the widest possible angle. They took into account not only the large number of common interests but also the need to act in concert if the irreparable decline of Western civilisation was to be avoided. The Atlantic Alliance, with its main aim of protecting Europe, was for Canada a long-term political option, which brought to the fore her opinion that Canada's survival was closely linked to the security and progress of Western Europe.

Despite the qualms of Prime Minister Mackenzie King, the first Minister of External Affairs, Louis Saint-Laurent (who was appointed in September 1946 and who became Prime Minister himself in November 1947), as well as diplomats such as Lester B. Pearson, Hume Wrong and Escott Reid, gave a decisive impetus to Canadian diplomacy by breaking with the old isolationist views.[1] In the famous 'Gray Lecture',[2] which he held in Toronto on 13 January 1947, Louis Saint-Laurent turned away from the policy of 'no commitments' associated with Mackenzie King and thus founded the new Canadian doctrine. In particular, he said that Canada could accept the principle of assuming international responsibilities 'according to the concept of our role in international affairs' without damaging her internal unity. The experiences of war have shown us, said Saint-Laurent, that 'the security of this country depends upon the development of a stable international organization'.

On 13 August 1947, Escott Reid, during a public speech approved in advance by his superiors, suggested that 'the peoples of the Western world' should be given the option of creating their own international security organisation 'with teeth' without coming into conflict with the Charter of the United Nations.[3] The same idea was taken up by Saint-Laurent a month later in his speech to the General Assembly of the UN on 18 September. This was the clearest declaration of Western consideration of some kind of potential military alliance between the democratic nations. This speech can be seen as the public start of a process which was to lead to the Bevin declaration and the Vandenberg Resolution.[4]

Towards the end of 1947, the repeated, paralysing use of the Soviet veto in the United Nations, the failure of allied negotiations concerning a peace treaty with Germany, the USSR's condemnation of the Marshall Plan, the setting-up of Communist regimes in the Soviet sphere of influence, as well as the economic, political and moral weakness of the Western European democracies, all led to a coming together of the Western nations. In January 1948, the British Foreign Minister, Ernest Bevin, took the initiative and proposed the conclusion of a collective defence agreement with France and the Benelux countries, in order to prevent a Soviet attack and, above all, to reassure Western Europe.[5] These talks were speeded up by the Communist armed coup in Czechoslovakia, and thus the Treaty of Brussels was signed on 17 March.

This treaty provoked an immediate and enthusiastic response from both the United States and Canada. On 17 March, Prime Minister Mackenzie King called Parliament's attention to President Truman's declaration of the same day, and he described the treaty as a gesture which went far beyond a traditional military alliance since it represented 'a partial realization of the idea of collective security'. He went further by saying that: 'The peoples of all free countries may be assured that Canada will play her full part in every movement to give substance to the conception of an effective system of collective security by the development of regional pacts under the Charter of the United Nations.'[6]

The public declarations made by the President of the United States and the Canadian Prime Minister on 17 March were basic expressions of support for the secret British initiative of 11 March which envisaged the direct association of these two North American countries with European defence. On 29 April, before the Canadian House of Commons, Louis Saint-Laurent referred to Mackenzie King's declaration, reiterating Canada's interest in a new agreement on security which, he suggested, might eventually involve all free democratic nations. This second speech was also part of the trilateral negotiating process, as it not only supported the British initiative but was also an appeal to the recalcitrant elements within the US State Department [7] to reconsider their position.[8] Bevin responded quickly in a declaration to the British House of Commons on 4 May in which he supported the suggestions made by his Canadian colleague.[9]

Notwithstanding this fact, the Canadian Prime Minister rejected the suggestion that the tripartite secret talks take place in Canada, since 'he did not wish to give the impression that Canada had taken the initiative, as this might lead to unpleasant discussions in Québec and elsewhere in Canada, perhaps reminding people of the argument concerning conscription'.[10] This worry about catering to Canadian public opinion went hand in hand with what Saint-Laurent called his 'crusade' designed to convince his countrymen of the need for a security pact linking North America and Western Europe in peacetime. In the case of a war involving Great Britain and the United States, he said, Canada would also inevitably be dragged in. An alliance made defensive operations more effective.

During the long intergovernmental talks in Washington, which started off as trilateral but which then grew to a party of eight, and which finally led to the signing of the North Atlantic Treaty on 4 April 1949, Canadian diplomats insisted on the inclusion of a non-military cooperation clause. In this clause the contractual parties committed themselves to encourage economic cooperation and to eliminate sources of conflict between their economic policies. Although this Article 2 had little practical effect, it did indicate Canada's conviction that stability and economic might were indispensable means of removing the Communist menace from Western Europe.

Finally, although the Alliance's immediate priorities were the creation of a joint military command and the assembly of a force capable of standing up to the armed might of the USSR and her East European allies, the Canadian government did not think initially that the country was obliged to send troops to Europe. On the contrary, the idea was to make some kind of material contribution other than arms. Nonetheless, at the request of General Eisenhower, who had been appointed Supreme Allied Commander Europe (SACEUR) in 1950, and after the outbreak of the Korean War, the Canadian government, on 4 May 1951, announced its intention of forming a Brigade Group destined to serve in the NATO army. Until that time the Canadian army had merely had a symbolic significance and was basically a reserve organisation. Recruitment began on 7 May, mainly of reserve units.[11] It is somewhat strange that, in peacetime, it was the perception of immediate threat and pressure from her allies which forced Canada to set up operational land, sea and air forces, in order to turn them over to the alliance. This problem of adjustment underlines once more how great an influence political considerations had upon the initial decision to join NATO made by Canadian politicians.[12]

The Principal Reasons for Canada's Behaviour

In order to gain the widest possible Canadian perspective concerning European military integration between 1948 and 1950, we shall analyse seven main factors which played a part in Canada's decision.

The first and most important of these was Canada's efforts to have more control over her relations with the United States and to avoid having to engage in exclusive dialogue with a country which threatened, in the long term, to take away her independence. To paraphrase a former Canadian Defence Minister, at the signing of the North Atlantic Treaty, Canada thought that, with twelve people in one bed, there was less risk of one losing her virginity.[13]

The postwar period saw the world divided into two blocs. Since that time, due to her geographical position, Canada was not only the immediate neighbour and principal economic partner of the world's greatest power, but also neighbour to the other superpower. In the age of long-range bombers and atomic weapons, Russians and Americans faced one another across the Arctic: in other words, across Canada. From this point of view, Canada's situation in 1939 was, comparatively speaking, more comfortable. However, Canadian territory would play a certain role in any major operation directed against the North American continent as well as in any defensive operations. This was further emphasised by the development of atomic missiles and submarines, for which the Arctic Ocean was the perfect deployment area. In addition, Canada was incapable of defending herself and thus her national security depended to a large degree upon close military cooperation with the United States. This was further proof of the indivisibility of North American security.

In order to avoid a much too narrow and necessarily unequal relationship with the United States in matters of defence, Canada wanted to be a member of other collective defence organisations, which included other important nations whose values and national interests were similar to her own.[14]

To be more precise, by participating in NATO, Canada, if she played an important role in Western defence, could hope to maintain a definite influence in Washington. It seemed clear that an independent place in a collective security organisation of such importance for North America was one of the keys to Canada's continued national independence.[15] Under these conditions it was easy to see that politico-strategic and economic considerations, which played the greatest role compared to military matters, had provided the impetus for the creation of NATO.

Bilateral relations between Ottawa and Washington had had the greatest influence upon Canadian diplomacy. To this we must add six other important factors which, from 1945 onwards, explain the reasons for the Canadian attitude to military integration in Europe.

At the Canadian Department of External Affairs the thought was that security, economic progress and political stability in Western Europe were closely linked to Canada's own survival. There was a recognition of the common destiny of Canada and Western Europe, and also that the fall or decline of the latter would mark the end of their common civilisation.

The second preoccupation was that, from the beginning, NATO was not only planned as a military grouping but also as a way of developing a political and economic community. These last factors were even more important than the first.[16] Since government policy was to contribute to the creation of a cohesive group of states, and since the treaty was also meant to promote economic and political cooperation, the Canadian representatives in the Washington talks insisted that Article 2 be included.

Canada believed that the alliance could only survive through greater cooperation. Ottawa thought that it was the perception of a threat which had forced the Atlantic states to form the alliance, and that its lifespan might be dependent upon its contribution to their well-being and progress.[17] As Lester B. Pearson confirmed, on 20 January 1949, the Atlantic Union 'should include not only clauses against armed aggression but also in favour of peacetime cooperation in the economic, social and cultural fields'.[18]

This position was met with doubt and reticence. Canada was almost the only country who wanted to see the treaty extended as much as possible. The United States were much less enthusiastic and Congress was still suffering from the effects of the Marshall Plan. Europe had left out this aspect in the Treaty of Brussels, since it led to too many problems concerning members' sovereignty. No one could imagine how it was possible to achieve a certain level of economic integration without endangering the national independence of the smaller states.

For their part, the Canadian supporters of the treaty did not see the problem in the same light. They had no intention whatsoever of seeing their country renounce her sovereignty in favour of greater cooperation. They were also nationalists after a fashion, but they placed their emphasis not only upon independence but also upon the idea of being a respectable, committed member. In 1949 it was time for them to prove how committed they were.[19]

In spite of the other participants' many reservations, the Canadian delegation stood their ground successfully because, in the view of their government, there was the fear of negative public opinion reactions to a purely 'military' response to international problems in peacetime. They also guessed that economic conflicts would pose greater problems than the Soviet threat, and that, finally, they were convinced that Western Europe required political and economic reconstruction first of all. From this point of view military guarantees were a means of giving psychological comfort to the people of Europe, not an end in itself, nor was it a sufficient commitment to ensure the survival of the treaty beyond the crisis which brought it into being.

Even though we know that Article 2 had a restraining effect, at least at the beginning of the 1950s, Canada's commitment is nonetheless most important in that it throws light upon her position. The adoption of this article was greatly advantageous to domestic policy, since a more general guarantee was thus made to a group of countries including those with which Canada had had the strongest traditional links. This was an effort to make her participation in NATO more acceptable to the majority of the population of a country whose government had traditionally been isolationist.[20]

By orienting Canadian diplomacy in this way, Louis Saint-Laurent and Lester B. Pearson were not only seeking to gain support or give NATO greater power and stability. By committing Canada to the new alliance, by insisting on the role and status of all the partner states, even the smallest, in the Washington talks, they wanted to ensure that a middle power like Canada could make her voice heard in the concert of the Atlantic states. This third factor was the result of deep frustration immediately after the war. The victorious Great Powers took decisions without bothering to consult the allies with whose help the war had, after all, been won. As early as 29 August 1945, Canadian Prime Minister Mackenzie King declared that Canada would do all in her power to avoid being left out when it came to participating in the important decisions concerning the implementation of peace.[21] In a document sent to the House of Commons on 29 August 1947, the Canadian government pointed to Canada's substantial contribution to the allied victory, demanding 'an opportunity to participate in the negotiation of peace on the same basis of honourable cooperation as had characterized her contribution to the war'.[22] However, the Great Powers had no use for such advice, as they had not even reached agreement among themselves.

This Canadian frustration goes a long way towards explaining her conspicuous absence when the time came to maintain the allied airlift during the Berlin crisis. While the government was explaining to the people the necessity of creating a regional security alliance, it was reacting negatively, strangely enough, to the most serious crisis since 1945. This ambiguous position is clearly illustrated by a statement made by Prime Minister King in answer to British press reports which said he had been requested to send aircraft to help in the airlift:[23] 'I said that it was quite clear that, in the event of war between the three Great Powers and Russia, Canada would immediately become involved. The Cabinet agrees with me on this, and it thinks there will be no hesitation on its part in this matter. However, there is great hesitation (on the part of the Cabinet) on the question of how far we are prepared to go at this moment in time.'[24] Apart from the Prime Minister's old isolationist reflexes,[25] two other reasons can be given for this Canadian attitude. On the one hand, Canada wanted to remind the world of her political independence and, on the other she had already refused to assume continuing military responsibilities in Europe after she had been refused her own zone of occupation.[26] Thus, participation in the common defence effort was to go hand in hand with a political role for all the participating powers, even if they were not members of the 'Great Powers club'.[27]

The fourth factor which played a large role in the decision-making of Canadian diplomacy was the consciousness of the importance of maintaining peace in the world and of directly involving Canada in this process. The disappointments Canada experienced in the UN did not deflect her from this new approach to international problems. The fact that she was not a Great Power was no longer an excuse for her traditional non-involvement in such matters. For the first time in her history, the Canadian government signed a military alliance in peacetime. Participation in an alliance comprising the major Western countries seemed to her preferable to her former isolationism, a better way of guaranteeing her interests on a long-term basis. It must, however, be added that political leaders in Canada, just like public opinion, had been influenced in their decision by the Second World War.

Since it had become clear that Canada would inevitably be involved in any conflict which broke out in Europe, the hope was not only that she would be ready for this but also that a potential aggressor could be dissuaded from his action by a united Western front. The new factor was that Canada was now convinced of the virtues of deterrence for the maintenance of peace and was prepared to commit herself accordingly. The Minister of Defence, Brooke Claxton, stated that, if there had been an Atlantic pact in 1935, it 'would have prevented the outbreak of World War II in 1939'.[28] Opinions of this kind were quite common in Ottawa at this time.[29]

Canada's intention to assume her part of the joint responsibility and contribute to the upkeep of peace went hand in hand with the arrival of new personalities on to the Canadian diplomatic scene. During a period of twelve years, from 1945 to 1957, Canada's foreign policy had been largely guided by a small group of highly active professional diplomats, as well as by Louis Saint-Laurent, Minister of State and Prime Minister from 1948 to 1957. These men were to give foreign policy a new impetus and their concepts were to be the hallmark of this 'internationalist' period for Canada. This change in the top positions is the fifth important factor.

If Prime Minister Mackenzie King had been ahead of his government in wanting to accept responsibilities in 1939, during the postwar period he tended to put the brakes on his colleagues and diplomats on the road to internationalist commitment, even though he agreed with the process which led to Canada signing the NATO Treaty. In November 1948, after he had stood down in favour of Louis Saint-Laurent, professional diplomats had rather more freedom to manoeuvre. The war had not only led to a proliferation of Canadian embassies abroad, it had also convinced both political parties and public opinion that the acceptance of important international obligations was necessary in order to better guarantee Canada's security. The memories of the 1930s, when one country after another had fallen to Nazi aggression, were still fresh in the minds of top Canadian diplomats. Deterrence seemed much preferable to a return to the policy of 'appeasement'.[30]

The desire to get away for her traditional isolationism was made easier by relatively favourable economic conditions for Canada. For this reason, the wish to play a political role commensurate with her new economic power is the sixth factor.

The Second World War had led to a veritable industrial revolution in Canada. While Europe came out of the war exhausted, the United States and Canada were considerably stronger as a result. The contrast with the prewar situation was probably strongest in Ottawa, where, for what she knew was a temporary period, Canada was, for the first time, in a position to be able to make a substantial contribution to the reconstruction of those countries devastated by the war. This fact was very favourable from the point of view of foreign policy. Indeed, from 1943 onwards, Canada was in fourth place among the allies in terms of military production and in third and fourth place respectively among naval and aerial powers. On the commercial side, Canada was the second-biggest exporter in the world, mainly of raw materials (80 per cent of exports) vital for the continuing war effort, and of foodstuffs. The economic upswing due to the war effort continued to have an effect even after the war. This was reinforced by the fact that Canada was one of four countries possessing a major programme of arms research and development; not forgetting, of course, the minor though significant role she played in the development of the atomic bomb. Even though Canadian diplomats were able to take so many initiatives during this period and display such talent, it is easy to forget that they represented a country which, in 1945, was the fourth most powerful nation on earth, and that this fact was fully exploited by them.[31]

In certain sectors of international activity, particularly civil aviation and trade, Canada regarded herself not as a middle power but as a major one. However, taken as a whole, Canada's role was not commensurate with her relative economic weight, since she was an integral part of the Western sphere of influence led by the United States.[32] Even though Canadian diplomacy failed to extract the most from her economic situation, she did benefit from being able to play a greater role than before on the international stage.

The seventh factor is probably the most difficult to evaluate, but it had a profound influence on the environment in which Canadian diplomacy operated: the start of the cold war and the first tensions between the West and the Soviet regime. There was nothing comparable with MacCarthyism in Canada, although it was impossible to ignore it and to avoid all the repercussions, bearing in mind the proximity both in politico-cultural and geographical terms between these two North American neighbours.

Canada quite soon felt the effects of the changes in international relations on her own soil, beginning with the Guzenko affair. In September 1945, Igor Guzenko, an employee in the cipher department of the Soviet Embassy in Ottawa, had tried to get in contact with the Canadian government, saying he knew of the existence of a large espionage network operating in Canada. His story was rejected, however, and it was not until this persistent informer's life was in danger that the Canadian authorities decided to study the evidence material which had been given them. They were afraid of offending the Soviet Union and wanted to avoid any action which might be interpreted as a provocation. Mackenzie King, although he had mistrusted the USSR for a long time, did not believe Guzenko's revelations. In spite of this, he was forced to admit that the Soviet allies had been up to such tricks in Canada during the war. Following discreet consultations with London and Washington, suspects were arrested in February 1946, which led to the affair becoming publicly known. The whole country, and Ottawa in particular, suffered under the impact. The spirit of cooperation which had prevailed during the war had taken a serious blow. Until that time, Canadian public opinion had been sympathetic towards the USSR. However, a month after the revelations concerning the Guzenko affair, the Canadian Institute for Public Opinion held a poll in which the question was asked whether the samples believed that one superpower wanted to dominate the world; 50 per cent of the Canadians polled answered 'yes', saying that they suspected the USSR, while 3 per cent of the 'yes' answers specified the USA. By comparison, in answer to the same question, 25 per cent of Americans and 26 per cent of French men polled feared Soviet domination.[33] From this we can see how great the impact of the Guzenko affair was – and there were to be repercussions throughout the following years.

In direct contrast to public opinion, the Canadian government and diplomats were greatly concerned with limiting the damage. Mackenzie King even toyed with the idea of going to Moscow himself as a gesture of conciliation, and it was only the spirited opposition of his ambassador in Moscow, L. Dana Wilgress, which dissuaded him. Diplomatic relations were not severed, as Mackenzie King feared. The Soviet ambassador had left Canada before the revelations came to light and did not return. Ambassador Wilgress, for his part, did not leave Moscow until April 1947, but he was not replaced. For several years the Soviet Embassy in Ottawa and the Canadian Embassy in Moscow were run by chargés d'affaires. Only after the death of Stalin in 1953 were ambassadors exchanged.

Until 1947 at least, the Canadian government hoped that the wartime spirit of cooperation and good relations between the two superpowers might be maintained. At the creation of NATO, Saint-Laurent and Pearson worked hard to emphasise the defensive aims of the organisation in the hope of minimising the provocative aspect which NATO might entail for the Soviets.[34] The reason for this was not anti-Soviet feeling, as can be seen from diplomatic documents which seem not to have been affected by the Guzenko affair, but rather the preoccupation with lessening the risks of war. McCarthyism found some sympathy among the Canadian population, but it was too insignificant to dictate the course of Canadian diplomacy. Nonetheless, the Guzenko affair shocked Canadians and led to their becoming far more critical of the USSR. There can be no doubt that this event made the job of the Canadian government easier in its 'crusade' in favour of NATO two years later.

Conclusion

On 14 August 1946[35] Mackenzie King wrote in his personal diary: 'What folly it would be for any of our people to go poking their fingers into the European pie.' However, a few months later, Canadian diplomacy made itself the standard-bearer of the defence of Western Europe. During the postwar period, the guiding principles of Canadian diplomacy began to change, since the traditional isolationism had been replaced by the search for a role within the United Nations, and later, as the situation in Europe worsened, especially within the Atlantic Alliance. It was this opening-up of Canada to the world, rather than the struggle for power between the two blocs and the cold war, which motivated Canadian diplomats, together with their British colleagues, to become the first advocates of a regional security organisation in accordance with Article 52 of the United Nations Charter.

This analysis of the Canadian position in the face of the changes taking place in Europe, both in political and military terms, clearly shows that it rested upon mostly new factors. Indeed, apart from relations with the United States, it was mainly national factors which influenced the Canadian government's reaction to the change in the international situation: the recognition of a common destiny with Western Europe, the need to have structures in which the medium and smaller states could let their voice be heard, the fact that Canada was now convinced of the advantages of deterrence, a change in the upper echelons of Canadian diplomacy and politics, relatively favourable economic conditions and, finally, a certain mistrust of the Soviet Union. Apart from this, the above factors show quite clearly that Canadian reactions were influenced far more by matters of a political and economic nature than by military worries. There was no immediate fear of a massive Soviet military invasion. Without doubt, from the beginning, more than in other Allied nations, NATO was for Ottawa not only a reinforcement of the

Treaty of Brussels, but was also seen as a source of political, economic and psychological support for the free countries of Europe at a time of great political danger. It was also a welcome opportunity for Canada to play an international role which fitted in with her new political ambitions.[36]

Notes

1. Charles P. Stacey, *Canada and the Age of Conflict*, vol. 2: *1921–1948*, Toronto, 1981, pp. 374–426.
2. Ruddock A. MacKay (ed.), *Canadian Foreign Policy, 1945–1954: Selected Speeches and Documents*, Toronto, 1971, quotations pp. 388–99.
3. Escott Reid, *Time of Fear and Hope: The Making of the North Atlantic Treaty, 1947–1949*, Toronto, 1977, p. 30f.
4. John Holmes, *The Shaping of Peace*, vol. II, Toronto, 1982, p. 104; Jon B. McLin, *Canada's Changing Defence Policy: The Problems of a Middle Power in Alliance*, Baltimore, 1967, p. 13.
5. Alan Bullock, *Ernest Bevin: Foreign Secretary, 1945–1951*, London, Oxford, 1984, pp. 513–48.
6. Reid (see Note 3), p. 43.
7. Here the author is particularly referring to Charles Bohlen and George Kennan, who were against the conclusion of the treaty, preferring a kind of extension of the Monroe Doctrine to cover Western Europe. Cf. also Sir Nicholas Henderson, *The Birth of NATO*, Boulder, Col., 1982, p. 24f.; David P. Calleo, 'Early American views of NATO: then and now', in Lawrence Freedmann (ed.), *The Troubled Alliance: Atlantic Relations in the 1980s*, London, 1983, (*Joint Studies in Public Policy*, 8), pp. 7–27.
8. Reid (see Note 3), p. 59.
9. Henderson (see Note 7), p. 25f.
10. Stacey (see Note 1), p. 416f.
11. George F. Stanley, *Nos soldats*, Montreal, 1980, p. 528f. During this period, when the doctrine of massive counterattack was popular, conventional armed forces seemed superfluous. The Canadian armed forces sank in terms of numbers from 780,730 men at the end of the war to only 32,610 in 1947. Apart from this, the plan was to cut the reserve from 180,000 to 50,000 men.
12. Cf. also Holmes (see Note 4), pp. 229–36.
13. R. J. Sutherland, 'Canada's Long-Term Strategic Situation', in

International Journal, 1962, p. 207.
14. Cf. on this point: Nils Horvik (ed.), *Canada and NATO*, Kingston Centre for International Relations, 1982 (= *National Security Series*, No. 3), pp. 96–135.
15. Sutherland (see Note 13), p. 208.
16. On 25 October 1948, Defence Secretary Brooke Claxton, together with his colleagues, had pointed to this political, economic and military system in order that there be no doubt about the goal of Canada's entry into a security alliance. The text of this declaration can be found in *Études nationales et internationales*, série 'PPPO 6', Ottawa, Department of National Defence, 1982, p. 7.
17. Cf. on this point the statement made by Claxton in *Statements and Speeches*, Ottawa, Department of External Affairs, No. 48/56, 25.10.1948, p. 5; also *Etudes nationales et internationales* (see Note 16). However, this official opinion was not shared by several top officials in Ottawa; they saw problems in the practical execution of Article 2. Cf. also Holmes (see Note 4), p. 222f.
18. Quoted in Robert Spencer, *Canada in World Affairs: From UN to NATO 1946–1949*, Toronto, 1959, p. 273f.; cf. also Spencer, R., especially concerning the debate over Article 2, the 'Canadian article': 'Triangle into Treaty: Canada and the Origins of NATO', in *International Journal*, Spring 1959, p. 95; Reid (see Note 3), pp. 167–84; Holmes (see Note 4), pp. 112–17.
19. This 'loyal ally' nevertheless made use of the opportunity to stand up for her own opinion concerning the tactics to be chosen and the multilateral nature of the Alliance. Cf. Holmes (see Note 4), p. 221.
20. The public reaction was almost unanimously positive. Cf. the portrayal of the efforts to prepare the Canadian people for the signing of the treaty, which 'not only represents a military alliance': Spencer, *Canada in World Affairs* (see Note 18), pp. 268–82.
21. The text of the Commons debate is given in extract form in: MacKay (ed.) (see Note 2), p. 26; the whole text can be found in: *Journal des débats*, House of Commons, 27.9.1945.
22. Spencer, *Canada in World Affairs* (see Note 18), pp. 26–31; MacKay (ed.) (see Note 2), pp. 30–42.
23. Although the Prime Minister stated before Parliament that he had not been approached in a letter dated June 30 he did request that the Canadian High Commissioner in London inform the British government that 'a request for the supply of transport aircraft would place us in a difficult position'. Quoted from Stacey (see Note 1), vol. 2, p. 416.
24. In a statement of 30.6., ibid., p. 415f.
25. On 18.12.1947 he had declared that, in his opinion, 'Canada has made a great mistake in getting involved in problems in Asia and

Europe, which she knows nothing about, taking initiatives which run the risk of interfering in the affairs of the Great Powers without thinking about the possible consequences ... We know nothing about these questions and we should keep out of them.' Ibid., p. 415.

26. In spite of British objections, the last contingents of the Canadian occupation force left Europe during the summer of 1946. On 3 March Saint-Laurent explained the Canadian action as follows: 'We have withdrawn our forces from Germany because we have been left out. The Great Powers told us there were already three Zones of Occupation, and that France could form another if she wished, but that that was the end.' MacKay (ed.), (see Note 2), p. 177f. Cf. also Spencer, *Canada* (see Note 18), p. 266f.
27. As Pearson explained in his maiden speech as Canadian Defence Secretary, all multilateral decisions in the Atlantic Alliance should be made by all concerned, and that therefore Canada should not fall into the same trap as in 1939, when she saw herself getting involved in a war due to a policy in which she had had no part: *Statements and Speeches* (see Note 17), No. 48/48, 21.9.1948, p. 5.
28. *Statements and Speeches* (see Note 17), No. 48/56, 25.10.1948, p. 5.
29. Canadian Ambassador Wrong had also expressed this opinion in Washington, and had declared that such an alliance would have prevented not only the Second World War but also the First: *Foreign Relations of the United States, Diplomatic Papers, 1945–1950*, Washington, DC, 1967–1980 FRUS, 1948, III: 'Minutes of the Seventh Meeting of the Washington Exploratory Talks on Security, 10.9.1948, 4 P.M.', p. 249.
30. Cf. for example the article by Pearson, at that time Canadian Secretary of State: 'Canada's Stake in NATO', Foreign Affairs, October 1951, reprinted in MacKay (ed.) (see Note 2), pp. 208–11.
31. Sutherland (see Note 13), p. 203f.
32. The Canadian government, for example, actively supported the Marshall Plan; her financial contribution has been estimated at around Cdn$325,000,000 for the economic reconstruction of Europe. This considerable sum, however, was overshadowed by the much greater amount of aid rendered by the United States. The substantial aid Canada gave to Great Britain is also little known. The Anglo-Canadian financial agreement of 1946 allowed Britain loans of a total of Cdn$1,250,000,000 at an interest rate of 2 per cent, repayable over a period of fifty years from 1951 onwards. The interest-free loan of 1942 remained free of interest even after the end of the war until 1951. The remaining Cdn$425,000,000, under the auspices of the British Commonwealth Air Training Plan, was remitted from Great Britain. This generosity did not give Canada a greater sphere of influence, but was rather an expression of how little influence the Canadians had on Britain and the result of constant British pressure

on the Canadian negotiating partners. Cf. Stacey (see Note 1), pp. 399–402.
33. NB: in the same poll 25 per cent of the French samples feared an American domination: *Public Opinion Quarterly*, Princeton University, NJ, Spring 1946, p. 114.
34. Cf. on this point Saint-Laurent, *Statements and Speeches* (see Note 17), 49/9, March 1949. 'These efforts also made it clear why Canada had initially opposed the admission of Greece and Turkey to NATO in 1951. Ottawa ... had never been too enthusiastic about Washington's policy of encirclement.' John Holmes and Jean-René Laroche, 'Le Canada et la guerre froide', in Paul Painchaud (ed.), *Le Canada et le Québec sur la scène internationale*, Centre québecois des relations internationales, 1977, p. 282.
35. Cf. on this theme Holmes (see Note 4), pp. 24–8.
36. James Eayrs, *In Defence of Canada: Peacemaking and Deterrence*, Toronto, 1972, p. 169.

5
A Little 'Fish' in a Big Political 'Pool' – Belgium's Cautious Contribution to the Rise of Military Integration in Western Europe[1]

Luc De Vos

There have always been hiccups in relations between large and small states, regardless of whether or not they were on friendly terms. Sovereignty and equality of nations are important ideas in this field. Sovereignty means the right of unlimited self-determination. Since the Age of Enlightenment, German philosophers have associated sovereignty with the state, more so since the French Revolution. In spite of this, however, a small state always runs the risk of being annexed sooner or later. The absolute quality of sovereignty has been questioned since the end of the First World War and much more so since the end of the Second. But as long as the idea of absolute sovereignty existed, no individual state needed, in theory, to suffer unequal treatment in silence. Unanimous decisions were required in international negotiations. In many cases, however, large states took upon themselves the right to speak for a group of nations. Thus a functional inequality arose without changing the legal equality.[2]

Throughout her history Belgium has constantly tried to protect her sovereignty and to move on the same plane as the larger powers. But the Second World War and the feeling of powerlessness which came to the fore at this time forced a change in Belgium's traditional policy. The result was a series of regional military treaties which came into being not least because of the tension between East and West – the Brussels Pact and the North Atlantic Treaty Organisation.

In order to grasp the meaning of this change of opinion, we should briefly look at the last 150 years of Belgian history. Starting with the period of independence and neutrality from 1830 to 1940, we will then consider the influence of the Second World War and the resulting clear state of dependence upon other nations.

Belgium is the 'buffer zone' between the Romanic and Germanic worlds. There are, indeed, elements of both language groups – the Treaty of Vienna in 1815 combined what we today call Belgium, The Netherlands and Luxembourg to form the United Kingdom of The Netherlands, with the object of creating a bastion against France. But a national uprising led by liberal idealists in August 1830 resulted in Belgium making a unilateral declaration of independence on 4 October, which was recognised by the world powers on 4 December of the same year. Belgium was granted permanent, guaranteed and armed neutrality by the Treaty of London of 19 April 1839. The new state, with its limited sovereignty, became a cornerstone of the European balance of power. The Belgians themselves soon recognised that this neutrality best suited the needs of the country – she could serve as a meeting point for different cultures, on the one hand, and, on the other, maintain trade relations with all her neighbours on the basis of full equality. Throughout the nineteenth century, even in 1870, neutrality seemed to secure peace and maintain inner security. Neither of the language groups considered that the other community was being overly favoured.

The violation of this neutrality by Germany in 1914 was a heavy blow. The vast majority of politically aware Belgians had lost all faith in the system. During the negotiations on the peace treaty of 1919, Belgium asked to be relieved of her neutral obligations in order to gain complete sovereignty. Article 31 of the Treaty of Versailles dealt with Belgium's request. Belgium joined the League of Nations and hoped to assume the role of mediator between the larger neighbouring states. Alongside this increase in universal thinking, Belgium wanted to protect herself by means of regional agreements. Thus, in 1920, there were talks with France on military cooperation in the case of a new German attack. Flemish public opinion was against this treaty since there could be no corresponding treaty with Britain, although the Belgian government tried to conclude one. Many people, including the King and his generals, saw a threat to the country's sovereignty in the bilateral treaty with France. There was a fear that Belgium could be dragged into the conflicts of the 'big brothers'.

It was not until the Locarno Treaty of 1925 that Belgium was able to avoid a possible loss of sovereignty. This regional and collective security system as a whole, and above all the Rhineland Pact, made Belgium both a guarantor and a guaranteed state. The Belgian-German border was, as in the Treaty of Versailles, fixed and recognised. The Rhineland was to remain a demilitarised zone. However, the weakness shown by the League of Nations in punishing Italy for her aggression in Ethiopia, the Spanish Civil War and above all the rearmament of the Rhineland, but also pressure on the home front, brought Belgium back to a policy of independence a decade later.

This self-imposed neutrality, the policy of 'mains libres' (having a free hand) – a policy of not entering into any international obligations – was supported by the King, Catholic Prime Minister Paul van Zeeland and, above all, by Paul-Henri Spaak, the Socialist Foreign Minister. Great Britain and France offered their services as guarantors. In spite of this fact, there was one essential difference between the neutrality of 1839 and that of 1936. The former was imposed by the European powers for their own benefit, while the latter was self-imposed and so could be lifted again by the Belgians themselves at any time. Thus Spaak let it be known, on 19 December 1939, that he would regard an attack by the German Reich on The Netherlands as a violation of the strategic balance. In this case the Brussels government would call on the French and British for help.

For the second time in less than thirty years, on 10 May 1940, Belgian neutrality was ignored. Her calls to the two guarantors had little or no effect. After eighteen days the King capitulated as commander-in-chief of his forces. Meanwhile, the government was already in exile in France.

Hitler's unacceptable attitude forced Belgium to act. Thanks to the energy of Belgian politician Albert de Vleeshauwer, a rump government was formed in London consisting of four ministers, of which Spaak was Foreign Minister. This government was to carry on the fight.

Exile in London brought home two important facts, apart from the initial desperation and frustration: first that neutrality could never again be the basis of Belgian foreign policy, and second that, if there was to be a new international organisation, it should be more universally and practically constructed than the League of Nations.

Several ideas were taken up during 1941 in an effort to create a kind of European community after the war. Such future plans were above all produced by the governments in exile. They had enough time, and they lived close to one another, so that it was possible for friendships to arise, but also for tensions to continue. There were many reasons why no agreement was reached. The Belgian government was sceptical about the idea of universality from the start, as it was about a great European federation. More than The Netherlands and Luxembourg, the Belgians preferred a regional alliance in Western Europe. As early as 1941, Spaak had stated that the countries of Western Europe had never had disagreements over their borders, and that they had the same political, legal, social and moral aims. It was necessary, in his opinion, for these countries to form an alliance in order to guarantee security and prosperity.[3] Until 1942, however, Belgium was mainly interested in her own sovereignty, was afraid of being dependent upon a larger power and guarded her colonial possessions jealously. From 1943 on her thoughts tended more towards a Western Europe under the leadership of the British. Great Britain dismissed this plan, however. Churchill spoke scathingly of the Belgians as being too self-centred. Had Belgium not tried to wriggle out of her responsibilities during the Second World War, although she had been rescued by her British allies (among others) during the First? Had she forgotten the many British soldiers who fell at Ypres?[4] In any case the British Prime Minister had other things on his mind: he was worried about a possible Soviet reaction and wanted to avoid at all costs the Americans crawling back into their isolationist shell.

In the face of this British reluctance Belgium, The Netherlands and Luxembourg attempted to coordinate their own common efforts. Relative political calm and greater freedom of movement provided new chances for the various heads of government to meet. This regional cooperation took shape with the decisions of 21 October 1943, in favour of a stable parity between the Dutch florin and the Belgian and Luxembourg francs. With the signing of the Benelux Treaty in September 1944 the plan for a customs union came into being.

In fact it was Stalin who supplied the Western Alliance with a new lease of life. At the end of 1944, while looking for recognition of his planned Eastern European glacis, Stalin envisaged a similar system in the West.[5] But in October Belgium was the victim of a Soviet intimidation campaign, claiming that she was the instigator of a Western bloc.[6] All the Belgians wanted to do was to render active military assistance to Great Britain. A military agreement was signed by A. Eden and P.-H. Spaak on 9 November 1944. This agreement planned to constitute three Belgian divisions, the first within one year, the second in eighteen months and the third within two years. It can be considered as the start of future postwar military cooperation because there was no doubt that Germany would collapse before the two years necessary for the constitution of the last unit.

Five new infantry brigades would be formed in the immediate future and these, together with the brigade commanded by Colonel Piron, would comprise the new Belgian army. The five new brigades had to go to Ireland to be trained for a period of six months.

A second agreement planned the constitution of units whose mission was to safeguard the allied communication lines during the final phase of operations against Germany. These so-called Liberated Manpower Units boasted 75,000 men at the end of the war. On 6 December 1944, Spaak announced his foreign policy guidelines to Parliament. It was a policy which was preordained by Belgium's history, above all by the events of the Second World War. It was to consist of three levels: collective universal security at the highest level, at the middle level the Atlantic alliance, and finally, as the central element, at the lower level Western European integration.[7]

The new British Labour government under Attlee, with Bevin as Foreign Secretary, had very little interest in regional agreements. Its main interest lay in the United Nations. France, too, wanted little to do with an alliance with small states, preferring to hold on to her former status as a great power. Belgium had to be content with the concept of the UN, under strong pressure from the USA.[8] The Belgian people were more interested in the foundation of the UN in the euphoria of victory in 1945. Like Australia and New Zealand, Belgium was opposed to the veto system as agreed at Jalta. Not until Article 51, the principle of legitimate self-defence, and Article 52, regional security, were brought into the Charter of the UN, was there a sense of relief. Belgium had enthusiastically supported the efforts of US

Republican Senator Vandenberg and the Latin American countries. The same viewpoints came up again during the debate in the Belgian Parliament on the ratification of the Charter. The spokesman of the Foreign Affairs Committee, MPs from the Christian Peoples' party (CVP) and August De Schryver, Vice-President of the Belgian delegation at the UN negotiations, all pointed to the possibility, on 23 October 1945, that Articles 51, 52 and 53 could be combined. The Speaker defended the idea that the right of collective self-defence by means of a regional treaty or a mutual assitance pact need not be subject to approval by the Security Council.[9]

Foreign Minister Spaak again showed himself to be a supporter of a regional pact when, on 31 October 1945, he stated, during the same debate, 'I am convinced that there are problems which can only be solved within geographical limits.'[10] Unlike the Dutch, who were much more enthusiastic about the UN, there was little support for an Atlantic community in Belgium. During the debates only CVP politician, V. Cossée de Maulde, said anything in its favour. He said that 'Belgium is bound to support a federation, in a strong community of free nations, an Atlantic Community uniting the great maritime powers; a federation in which each member retains her full independence, occupying a place commensurate with the size of her population, her economic importance and her intellectual brilliance; a federation whose impressive military might matches her immense territory and her incomparable prosperity; a federation which commands the most important global communications, a decisive element in any armed conflict'.[11] Shortly afterwards CVP politician, Van Cauwelaert, reiterated this idea in several lectures and articles. Some other politicians held the same opinion, but public opinion and most politicians in 1945 and 1946 did not want to go beyond a security pact between the nations of Western Europe.[12]

Apart from the Communists, Senator Rollin of the Socialists was among the few who spoke out against a regional agreement. He feared the creation of blocs, which, as in previous wars, would sooner or later take up arms against each other. Also, the fact that the Communists were a factor in the Belgian governments from 11 February 1945 to 20 March 1947 put a brake on the development of the regionalist idea. Besides, the French and the British did not want to do anything which might have upset either the USA or the USSR.

Spaak was the chairman of the UN General Assembly, and Belgium received a non-standing seat on the Security Council, which was taken up by the Secretary General of the Foreign Ministry, F. Vanlangenhove.[13]

Western European policy was geared towards disarmament, faith in the United Nations and agreement and cooperation with the Soviet Union. The West, however, was very soon disappointed because, while the West had run down her armed forces to a great extent, the USSR (perhaps as a counterbalance to America's monopoly of atomic weapons) had a very large army at its disposal. The many Russian vetoes during the UN sessions, increasing mistrust and the fear, whether justified or not, that the other side might be a threat to their security, quickly led to a changed situation.

But the most important factors leading to Western European union were the attitude of the USSR in Eastern Europe and the fear of totalitarian Communist ideology. Spaak expressed this in the following words, 'Many Western statesmen have, in the course of the last twenty years, been called the "father of Europe" or the "father of the Atlantic Alliance". None of them are worthy of this title. Stalin, on the other hand, is – without his aggressive policies, without the threat he posed to the free world, the Atlantic Alliance would not have been created, and the movement for a united Europe, including Germany, would not have been so astonishingly successful.'[14]

Seeing the increasing power of the Soviet Union and her self-imposed isolation from the rest of the world, Churchill, at that time Leader of the Opposition, gave a fiery speech at Fulton in the USA, on 5 March 1946, in which he used the phrase 'Iron Curtain' for the first time in public. He called on the Anglo-Saxon peoples to unite against any ambitions the Soviet Union might have of increasing her power. This sensational, albeit unofficial speech, was the first sign of a turning away from the universal list idea. The failure of the Moscow Conference of April 1947, which was meant to lead to a peace treaty with Germany, marked the end of the superpower alliance.

It was also the catastrophic state of the economy in Western Europe which brought these countries together. Belgium had suffered much less as a result of the Second World War than The Netherlands and above all Luxembourg. If the damage were to be expressed in financial terms, Belgium had lost only two-thirds as much as The Netherlands and only half as much compared to Luxembourg.[15] For this reason, too, the planned Benelux customs union had to be put on ice for the time being. The low level of war damage, cash payment for the stationing of large numbers of US, Canadian and British troops in Belgium between September 1944 and January 1945, the successful anti-inflationary measures taken by Liberal Minister Gutt and the speedy recovery of the Belgian economy all provided the country with a positive balance of payments. Most European countries got into great difficulties during the very cold winter of 1946–7. Their last reserves were exhausted and their populations could not understand why things were still so bad in spite of the fact that the war was over. Belgium was one of the few countries which were not so sorely tested, and thus she could improve her position in the world to a great extent. But Belgium, too, welcomed the American aid plan for Europe, announced by Secretary of State Marshall in Harvard on 5 June 1947. For the former general, one of President Roosevelt's more left-leaning advisors, this was the last chance to avert the division of Europe.

But reality was different. The founding of the Committee for Economic Cooperation in Europe, in July 1947, was limited to Western Europe, and its successor, the Organisation for European Economic Cooperation (OEEC), founded on 16 April 1948, was aimed, as was the Truman or Containment Doctrine of 12 March 1947, at a regional alliance which seemed more advantageous than anarchy or a *de facto* surrender to the Eastern Bloc. It is curious, to say the least, to note that the Communists disappeared from the Belgian government on the same day. On 20 March 1947, the Socialists and the Catholics formed a new government with Spaak as Prime Minister and Foreign Minister. The BLEU (Belgian-Luxembourg Economic Union) received $740.9 million (4.8 per cent of the total of $15,378.1 million) from the American aid programme over four years. The Netherlands received 7.2 per cent.[16] Only the Communists in Belgium wanted no part of the OEEC; one Socialist MP and a Senator of the same party abstained.

In answer to the Marshall Plan, the Soviet Union founded the Cominform (Communist Information Bureau), which took up the tradition of the Comintern (Communist (Third) International), disbanded in 1943. This new, regionally structured organisation was to encourage talks in order to increase the spread of Communism in Europe.

In 1947 it became clear that the universalist idea was impossible to realise. There were several reasons for this: the Soviet vetoes, the Communist take-over in Eastern Europe and bilateral treaties between the USSR and these countries meant that there was already a kind of Eastern Bloc in existence.[17] The 'cold war' had begun, and Belgian public opinion feared a new war.[18] Belgium waited impatiently for signs of action from her bigger neighbours.

On 22 January 1948, British Foreign Minister Bevin made a momentous speech to the House of Commons, in which he condemned Soviet power politics and put forward the speedy creation of a 'Western Union'. Bevin had already expounded these ideas in November 1945 during a foreign policy debate in the House of Commons. He suggested that Britain should conclude bilateral treaties with France and the Benelux countries as a first step. Later such countries as Italy could be included. Bevin had discussed his plans beforehand with his French opposite number Bidault. However, one cannot help thinking that the British politician wanted to go much further than the Frenchman. Bevin, the trade-union man, had spoken openly, but he had also given up a little of his discretion. On 13 January 1948, Bevin had already informed the USA of his plan after consultations with the most important and loyal member of the Commonwealth, Canada.

Like many others, Spaak thought that Bevin's plan was an offer of a regional pact. But when he asked for a more exact breakdown, he found only a series of bilateral treaties, as in the Treaty of Dunkirk of 4 March 1947. As early as that year, Spaak had considered a similar anti-German pact with Britain and France, or even with the Soviet Union, but he was now disappointed that no one would recognise the Soviet threat. For this time he, as the representative of a country which was economically relatively well off, wanted more, in other words a regional, multilateral pact. The Benelux countries, although not yet very important in economic terms, became the backcloth for further talks. Apart from negotiations of an economic nature on the planned customs union, the Benelux countries sought a common political standpoint during a conference held in Luxembourg from 29–31 January 1948.

On 18 February 1948, the French plan was announced in Brussels, and a very similar British proposal was voiced on 19 February. Both states wanted a number of bilateral treaties modelled on the Treaty of Dunkirk, a total of six. The partners promised mutual aid in the case of a renewed attack by Germany. The British, and especially the French, were afraid that the Soviet Union would look upon a Western Alliance as a provocative act. There was still the worry that America might fall back into isolationism.

The joint Benelux note was sent on 19 February 1948, so that both the French and British notes remained unconsidered. The Benelux note underlined what the countries had been trying to impress upon the French and the British since 3 February: that it was not the divided and occupied Germany which was the source of danger but rather the expansionist Soviet Union. For this reason an alliance erga omnes was the best solution. Spaak also wanted to include economic cooperation in any regional pact, and in this he was supported by his Dutch counterpart. A pragmatic kind of politician, he knew that such a treaty needed a strong economic base so that the citizens could see it in their daily lives. Permanent organisations also had to be created in order to lend a recognisable form to the pact. There was one earlier example of military integration: the Rio Pact of 20 September 1947, which had been signed by all American countries except Ecuador and Nicaragua was, in terms of the right of self-defence (Article 51), fully compliant with the Charter of the United Nations. The attitude of the Benelux countries was remarkable, differing totally from the Belgian position at the beginning of 1947. Of course The Netherlands were now prepared to face Soviet anger, and Great Britain and France were on their side. At the same time Spaak had already been once bitten due to the failure of Belgium's independence policy between 1936 and 1940. Above all, however, he regarded this as a unique opportunity to achieve 'political and economic cooperation between the countries of Western Europe'.

The first talks, involving the Benelux countries, Britain and France, which began on 4 February 1948, led to great disquiet on the part of the two 'pseudo'-superpowers. This, however, was soon watered down in view of US enthusiasm for the Benelux plans. The Benelux had, indeed, pointed out what the Americans wanted to hear. Had the USA not already tried to encourage European cooperation by means of the Marshall Plan? The Communist coup in Prague on 27 February 1948 allowed the British and the French to change tack on the Benelux plans without too much loss of face. Bidault rightly said, on 3 March, that he could see an 'orientation nouvelle' ('new movement'), while Bevin said much the same thing in a memorandum to his Cabinet. Spaak also repeated almost verbatim what he had said on 6 December 1944, 'In my opinion it is totally impossible, at this time, to create a defence concept for Belgium using exclusively Belgian finance and manpower.'[19]

On 4 March 1948, the Brussels Conference began. It was held in the Palais des Académies, and security measures in and around the building were impressive. Bevin was particularly well-guarded, both when he arrived and when he left. There was a chance that Jewish groups connected with the uprising in Palestine might attempt an attack on his life. Chairing the negotiations was top diplomat and head of the Belgian delegation, Fernand Vanlangenhove. As Secretary General of the Foreign Ministry, he had made his mark on both the policy of independence and that of the exile government in London. From 1948 he was the first standing Belgian representative at the UN, and also a member of the Security Council from time to time. The Benelux countries had formed a single delegation and had conducted trilateral talks. Negotiations between them (also ironically termed 'Spaakistan') and the two 'pseudo'-superpowers were conducted at ambassadorial level, without interpreters and in French. The atmosphere was pleasant and even relaxed. Old friends met once again.

At the start of the first session the French and the British expressed their agreement with the Benelux proposals. The term 'Union de l'Europe Occidentale' (Western European Union) had to be dropped. However, the British and French delegations wanted Germany to be specifically described as a danger. The economic plans failed to materialise due to the stubbornness of the British. The Benelux countries demanded that the treaty, which was to run for fifty years, should only be applied in the case of an attack on the European territory of a member state, a clause which was included because of the Falklands. The assistance should be immediate, automatic and mutual.

On the day the treaty was signed by the five foreign ministers (17 March), the Belgian Christian Democratic Finance Minister, Gaston Eyskens, and the four ambassadors accredited in Brussels, there was a definite feeling of euphoria. As Spaak put it, this was a European day. Several of the ideas put forward by the 'three little brothers had been accepted. This is all to the credit of the "two big brothers"'.[20]

On the fringes of the conferences, the Belgian Socialist MP, Fayat, made a highly interesting suggestion. Would it not also be good to have a joint colonial policy? This was almost certainly an attempt to show solidarity with The Netherlands, who were having great difficulties with the Dutch East Indies (what is now called Indonesia) at that time. The suggestion points to a willingness to coordinate international policy.[21]

Belgium had signed the Brussels Treaty, but this still had to be ratified by Parliament. There Spaak brilliantly defended his convictions. The Communists thought it was pointless to conclude a defensive treaty without evidence of an immediate threat. Spaak then asked the House if there had been an immediate threat in 1914 or 1939. In spite of this, Belgium had been caught up in the proceedings each time. 'From now on the question is whether or not Belgium must take a variety of diplomatic and military measures to protect herself in the case of European or even world war in the future.'[22] Spaak said that the 150 million Europeans should unite for their own salvation, 'to save themselves in a military, political and economic sense. The five-nation pact, as it has been concluded, and as it has been interpreted by those who wanted it, is nothing other than the first stage in this magnificent edifice. One would have to be crazy not to want it.'[23]

Important politicians from the three largest Belgian parties, the Liberal Jean Rey, the Walloon Socialist, Max Buset, and the Flemish Christian Democrat, De Schryver, pointed out that the idea of neutrality was a thing of the past. The general situation as well as the geographical location made a change of policy vital. The Flemish Christian Democrat, Bruynincx, repeated an earlier theory when he said, 'There is only one possible solution – to integrate our armed forces into an international system of organisation and rearmament, a system in which each country must bear the same financial burden in relation to the size of its population.'[24] He went on, 'There should no longer be any silly illusions about a potential attacker coming from Western Europe. International politics has become much more realistic. The danger comes from the East, it is a fact, and all of Western Europe must defend itself against this danger by taking the necessary steps. The union of the total military and economic might of Western European nations, in which the Benelux countries are to play a great role, has a two-fold aim – firstly, to serve the cause of peace, and secondly, to defend the integrity of our territory if necessary.'

In the Senate, Christian Democrat, Count C. d'Aspremont Lynden, went further, 'The Soviets' desire for ideological expansion makes us fear the worst for Western civilisation. This civilisation will defend itself because it has to protect its freedom, which is under threat from those who seek to suppress it.'[25]

The Socialists pointed out even more strongly that the treaty was the last chance to avoid the formation of blocs. Senator H. Vos expressed this in the following statement: 'If we welcome this pact enthusiastically, it is because this is the last chance, and because we want to make a last attempt to prevent these large, dangerously sharp contrasts turning into real political blocs, which could very soon face each other with weapons drawn.'[26]

For the Socialists, who had once been so positive towards the Soviet Union, this was the least they could do. Christian Democrat, Theodore Lefèvre, summed up the feelings of the overwhelming majority of Parliament thus: 'Belgium's defence can no longer be considered alone, but rather as a part of the defence of the West. Our army will have to be a part of the armed forces capable of protecting Western Europe.'[27]

The Communists were unanimous in their opposition to the pact because they did not think the country's security was in danger; the pact did not encourage the economic upturn, but rather served only to defend capitalism and not peace. Besides this, it was aggressive and was directed against the Soviet Union. One hundred and thirty eight Senators voted for the Brussels Treaty on 24 March 1948, out of a total of 153. The fifteen Communists all voted against.[28] Out of 202 MPs, 171 took part in the vote, of which 150 voted for and twenty one Communists voted against the Brussels Treaty. Two Communists were missing.[29]

One might be forgiven for thinking that this new military alliance would have spurred Belgium on to greater efforts in this area. Nothing was further from the truth. As Defence Minister Col. DeFraiteur explained in his speech on the budget on 27 May 1948, 'The reorganisation of the armed forces will include National Service of one year's duration, the build-up of the air force and the creation of a base in the Congo. Arms and equipment leave much to be desired, and new supplies are difficult to come by. The financial pressure caused by this rearmament will be spread over a number of years.'[30] It was clear that the gap between the fourteen West European divisions and the estimated 200 Soviet divisions would not be closed in this way. However, military cooperation between the member states only started a few months later. In the case of the air forces this cooperation was already a reality. In September 1948 the 'Organisation de défense de l'Union Occidentale' came into being. British Field Marshal Montgomery became chairman of the Commanders in Chief Committee, much to the dismay of the Belgians. The land forces were under the command of French General de Lattre de Tassigny, the air forces were to be commanded by British Air Marshal Robb and the navies by French Vice-Admiral Joujard. Belgium received a few staff officer posts. A Belgian General, Albert Tromme, became de Lattre's deputy chief of staff in December 1948. The military organisation, with its HQ in Fontainebleau, was named 'Uniforce'.

The signing of the Brussels Treaty marked the victory of the regional defence concept over the universalist idea. The hope contained in the treaty, that other countries would join, was the basis for a larger alliance. Besides the Marshall Plan this meant another step on the road to European integration. The role played by the Benelux countries showed that the smaller states had not yet had their last word. They certainly did not join the Alliance in order to gain prestige, although, as it turned out, they could work to that end within the alliance itself.

On 17 March 1948, the very same day on which the Brussels Treaty was signed, US President Truman praised the initiative of the Western Europeans during a speech before Congress, 'This development deserves our full support. I am confident that the United States will, by appropriate means, extend to the free nations the support which the situation requires. I am sure that the determination of the free countries of Europe to help themselves will be matched by an equal determination on our part to help them to do so.'[31] On the following days secret discussions were held in Washington, in which Americans, Canadians and British negotiators laid the foundations for the later Atlantic Alliance.

The US President was able to convince the powerful chairman of the Senate Foreign Affairs Committee, the Republican Vandenberg, of the need for America to break with isolationism for good. Supported by the Democratic Senator for Texas, Connally, Vandenberg succeeded in having Resolution 239 passed by sixty four votes to four. Thus, from now on, the USA could conclude treaties for collective defence to strengthen her own security outside the American continent within the bounds of the Charter of the United Nations.

The final communiqué of the second session of the Brussels Treaty Council of Ministers, dated 20 July 1948, emphasised the fact that the five governments, in agreement with other countries, had the same goal: in other words to do their utmost to defend their integrity and way of life.

In the meantime the land links between the Western zones of occupation and West Berlin were cut, partially from 1 April and completely from the end of June 1948. The blockade of Berlin and the resulting airlift of supplies caused a change in public opinion. As early as 6 July 1948, Secretary of State George Marshall headed talks with the ambassadors of the Five in Brussels and Canada. On 9 September 1948, the joint note was ready. This time The Netherlands, under the leadership of Minister van Kleffens, more in favour of an Atlantic solution, had more of a hand in the formulation of the note than the Belgians, who were aiming at an independent Europe.[32]

Of course the negotiations did not remain fully secret, as Donald Maclean, a member of the British delegation, was already spying for the Russians. The Soviets were thus suitably displeased, but the smaller European states regained their confidence. In September 1948, during a session of the UN General Assembly in the Palais Chaillot in Paris, Vychinsky condemned the policies of the USA and the Brussels Five. On 28 September Spaak tore the accusations to pieces in his now-famous speech. The intuitive Belgian voiced the feelings of many in a powerful fashion as he explained his view of the reasons behind the Brussels Treaty: 'Fear of the USSR, fear of her government, fear of her policies.' Fear was also the direct result of Soviet imperialism.

> What is the reality of recent history? There is but one great power who has increased her territory, and that country is the USSR. During and because of the war, you have annexed the Baltic states. During and because of the war, you have taken a part of Finland. During and because of the war, you have taken a part of Poland. Thanks to your audacious and elastic policies you have become all-powerful in Warsaw, Prague, Belgrade, Bucharest and Sofia. Thanks to your policies you have occupied Vienna and Berlin, and there is no sign of your leaving them. Your policies now make you demand control of the Ruhr. Your empire stretches from the Black Sea to the Baltic and to the Mediterranean. You would like to be on the banks of the Rhine, and

you ask us why we are worried. The truth is that your policies are more audacious and more ambitious than those of the Tsars themselves. Last of all, you make us afraid because you have a Fifth Column in every country represented here which makes Hitler's Fifth Column look like a troop of boy scouts. There is nowhere in the world and no government, whether in Africa, Europe or Asia, which is in difficulties, and you are not there to make things worse. In each of our countries, at this moment in time, there is a group of people who are not only sympathisers and defenders of your foreign policy (which is, after all, not a crime), but who also never miss an opportunity to weaken the state in which they live, politically, morally and socially'.[33]

This speech was continually interrupted by applause, and there was overall approval from the members.

In Belgium itself public opinion was mobilised in another way. On 7 February 1949, the Archbishop of Brussels-Malines, Cardinal Van Roey, had a pastoral letter read out in every church. In a Catholic country where people still went to church regularly, this was highly important. In his letter the Archbishop defended the clergy in the countries occupied by the Communists.[34]

Meanwhile, the talks between the USA, Canada and the Brussels Five were still in progress. Finally there was agreement on a draft treaty. On 16 March 1949, Denmark, Iceland, Norway, Italy and Portugal were invited to join. Would an increase in the number of members mean a weakening of the Benelux position? On 19 March 1949, the US State Department published the text of the draft in a White Book. On 31 March came Moscow's furious reaction. In a note to the countries concerned, the Soviet Union explained her position. The USSR maintained that the future treaty was aggressive in intent and that the Statute of the UN, the Franco-Soviet and Anglo-Soviet agreements and the decisions of Potsdam and Jalta were all being violated. The Belgian government answered post haste and referred to Article 51 of the United Nations Charter. Spaak gave the Belgian view when he said, 'As is so often the case in Communist documents, the text was long-winded, confused and brusque.'[35] On 4 April the treaty was signed in Washington by the USA, Canada, Great Britain, France, Belgium, The Netherlands, Luxembourg, Denmark, Iceland, Norway, Italy and Portugal.

The North Atlantic Treaty is a defensive pact, in which the members agree to render assistance to each other in protecting their territory north of the Tropic of Cancer. The treaty did not go as far as the Treaty of Brussels. Under strong pressure from the Americans, Articles 4 and especially 5 contained no automatic military assistance clause, but rather provision for prior consultation. The partners decided for themselves what measures were required. Article 9 of the Atlantic Treaty was also already present in the Treaty of Brussels. This article set out a standing, integrated organisation. The Brussels Pact administration and buildings were very soon simply taken over.

The discussion in the Belgian Parliament on the ratification of the agreement was very similar to that concerning the Brussels Pact itself. The Communists pointed out the aggressive character of the treaty and said it did not necessarily agree with the statutes of the UN Charter. The North Atlantic Treaty was passed in the Belgian House of Representatives on 4 May 1949 by 139 votes; twenty two Communists voted against and one Socialist abstained. Forty MPs, including one Communist, were missing at the vote. In the Senate, the treaty was ratified by 127 votes to thirteen from the Communists. There were four Communists among those not present.[36]

On 12 May the Berlin Blockade also came to an end. On 2 June 1949, Belgium's membership of the North Atlantic Treaty Organisation (NATO) was made official by law. Many member states promised a great deal, but not many of these promises were kept before the Korean War. Belgium, for example, had agreed, under the auspices of the Brussels Treaty in Luxembourg on 15 July 1949, that she would ensure the mobilisation of four and a half infantry divisions and one armoured division (around 40,000 men).

Spaak, who had played such an important role in the creation of an integrated Europe, militarily speaking, was forced to resign from office in August 1949, both as Premier and as Foreign Minister, due to problems at home. On top of this, his party lost much ground in the elections. There was a strong influence on the voters due to the question of the constitutional role of the King, who had capitulated and gone into captivity during the war, and also from the international situation to a certain extent. The Communists lost 41 per cent of their 1947 votes, and thus the number of MPs fell from twenty three to twelve. Against the advice of the elder statesman (i.e. Spaak), the Belgian Socialist Party went into opposition and elected Eyskens, another signatory to the Brussels Treaty, as the new Prime Minister. He was one of Spaak's rivals; but an even more fervent supporter of the Atlantic idea, Catholic politician, Van Zeeland, became Spaak's successor as Foreign Minister.

Since the end of the Second World War the Belgian public had been bombarded with news on conferences, treaties, etc., and were obviously becoming less and less interested. At the end of 1949 only 4.1 per cent of Belgians polled said they knew the details of the North Atlantic Treaty.[37] Home affairs, particularly the controversy about the King, overshadowed even the news of the first Soviet atomic bomb test, which was given in a joint Anglo-Canadian-American communiqué.

The Belgian constitution was mostly put together in the nineteenth century, at a time when nationalism was at its height. Thus one might be tempted to ask how this constitution was to allow the integration of Belgium into a larger group of states. Article 9 of the North Atlantic Treaty, which formed the basis of the standing NATO organisation, took away a good part of Belgium's national prerogatives. This meant that responsibility for the Belgian army was partly in the hands of foreigners, and many other important decisions were taken away from the government and Parliament. Article 68 of the Belgian constitution states, 'The King is Commander-in-Chief of the land and sea forces, declares war, concludes peace treaties and forms alliances.' Due to historical circumstances, Kings Leopold I, in 1831, Leopold II, in 1870, Albert, in 1914–18 and Leopold III in 1940, were personally in command of the troops. But in peacetime, too, the monarch placed a very influential role in the country's defence policy. During the arguments over the King, a commission in 1949 emphasised the fact that the ministers had the final responsibility. However, the article remained intact, and the oath taken by the King at his coronation was just as Article 80 of the constitution stipulates: 'I swear that I shall abide by the Constitution and the laws of the Belgian people, safeguard the country's independence and preserve the integrity of her territory.'[38]

But the government also lost important decision-making powers due to NATO. Even if it makes use of its right of veto against a decision, there is often such psychological pressure from the other members that national governments often go further in their defence efforts than they might have done on their own. Parliament also faces a difficult task. The secret nature of many decisions, the complexity and the dogmatic sticking to principles encountered when taking part in NATO negotiations leaves little room to discuss matters.

In order to secure the main essentials of her sovereignty, Belgium has had to give up part of her rights in favour of the Benelux union and larger communities such as the Brussels Treaty and NATO. Within these international organisation she plays quite a large role, has found a position equal to most other countries, and has even been able to have an influence on international events. 'The representative of a small country can have a say in international politics, but she must show that she can exercise discretion, and she must at all costs avoid giving the impression that she wants to preach to the others, especially to the powerful countries. She could not lose her sense of proportion. It was only because no one doubted my loyalty towards the Atlantic Alliance and the European union that I was able to take some useful initiatives.'[39]

Even if being a member of an international organisation meant Belgian sovereignty was limited, it also gave her the chance to play a role in international affairs. This was, of course, most true in the Brussels Treaty organisation where there were only a few members. The three French-speaking states took the lead here. NATO, on the other hand, with its twelve original members and its Anglo-Saxon influence, gave the Belgians less opportunity to come to the fore. Belgium's special contribution to the Brussels Treaty and to NATO was her striving towards the goal of a regional defensive alliance.

Defence and the economy have always been two important elements of the state. The fact that some power was transferred to international organisations took much of this importance away from the Belgian state and led to an inner weakness, for many other political problems can also be solved very effectively at a regional level.

Notes

1. For this article I found the bulk of my information in Frans Govaerts, 'Belgium, Holland and Luxembourg', in *Small Powers in Alignment*, Omer DeRaeymaeker, Willy Andries, Luc Crollen et al. (eds), Louvain, 1974 (= *Studies in International Relations*, no. 2), pp. 182–278, as well as in other books by DeRaeymaeker. I would particularly like to thank Prof. Dr. Jean Stengers, the Nestor of Belgian historians, who gave me the text of his lecture, which he held in 1984 in Strasbourg, entitled 'Paul-Henri Spaak et le traité de Bruxelles de 1948', now published in *Histoire des débuts de la Construction européenne (mars 1948–mai 1950)/ Origins of the European Integration (March 1948–May 1950), Actes du Colloque de Strasbourg 28–30 novembre 1984*, sous la direction/Raymond Poidevin (ed.), Bruxelles, Milano, Paris, Baden-Baden, 1986, pp. 119–42. There are great problems in Belgium for those wishing to conduct research using postwar archives. Legally they are secret for 100 years, *de facto*; however, they can be seen after fifty, or in exceptional cases, thirty years.
2. Omer DeRaeymaeker, *Les petit pays et la collaboration internationale*, Brussels, 1950, p. 37.
3. Paul-Henri Spaak, *Combats inachevés: De l'independance à l'Alliance*, Paris, 1969, p. 148; Fernand Vanlangenhove, *La sécurité de la Belgique, Contribution à l'histoire de la période de 1940 à 1950*, Brussels, 1971, p. 74, 82f.
4. Stengers (see Note 1), p. 130.
5. Spaak (see Note 3), p. 159.
6. Vanlangenhove (see Note 3), p. 138.
7. Paul Smets, *La pensée européenne et atlantique de Paul-Henri Spaak (1942–1972), part 1*, Brussels, 1980, p. 52f.
8. Vanlangenhove (see Note 3), p. 164.
9. Omer DeRaeymaeker, 'Regionale accorden en wettige zelfverdediging', in *Politica, Tijdschrift voor Staatkunde en Sociologie*, VII–3, 1957, p. 196.
10. Original text in DeRaeymaeker (see Note 9), p. 196f.
11. Ibid., p. 198f.
12. Michel Dumoulin, 'Opinion publique et politique extérieure en Belgique de 1945 à 1962: Orientation des études et perspectives de la recherche en Belgique', in *Res publica: Revue de Science Politique*, XXVII–1, 1985, p. 13. The Institut Universitaire d'Information Sociale et Economique (INSOC) held opinion polls. The following questions could be found in vol. 2 for 1946: 'Avez-vous confiance en l'action de l'ONU pour le maintien de la paix?' (Do you trust UNO peace initiatives?). 36 per cent yes, 36.95 per cent no and 28.05 per cent do not know. 'Etes-vous partisan d'une entente des nations occidentales?'

(Are you in favour of a Western alliance?). 68.86 per cent yes, 8.01 per cent no and 23.13. per cent do not know.
13. Jean-Claude Ricquier, 'Souvenirs d'un Sécretaire général des Affaires étrangères: Fernand Vanlangenhove', in: *Revue Générale*, Nos. 6 and 7, 1981, pp. 3–26.
14. Spaak (see Note 3), p. 249f.
15. Govaerts (see Note 1), p. 195 (Jean van de Mensbrugghe, *l'Union Economique. Réalisations et Perspectives*, Bruxelles, 1949, p. 40).
16. Govaerts (see Note 1), p. 199 (US Overseas Loans and Grants, p. 117, 129).
17. Treaty with Czechoslovakia on 12.12.1943; with Yugoslavia on 11.4.1945; with Romania on 4.2.1948, and with Bulgaria on 18.3.1948.
18. Dumoulin (see Note 12), p. 16.
19. Original text in *Parlementaire Handelingen, Kamer 1947–1948*, Bruxelles, no. 36, 3.3.1948, p. 11.
20. Spaak (see Note 3), p. 258.
21. Dumoulin (see Note 12), p. 14f.
22. *Parlementaire Handelingen, Kamer* (see Note 19), no. 57, 27.4.1948, p. 13.
23. Ibid., p. 16.
24. Ibid., nos. 68 and 69, 26.5.1948, p. 34.
25. *Parlementaire Handelingen, Senaat 1947–1948*, Bruxelles, nos. 35 and 36, 23.3.1948, p. 721.
26. Ibid., p. 717.
27. *Parlementaire Handelingen, Kamer* (see Note 19), nos. 70 and 71, 27.5.1949, p. 21.
28. *Parlementaire Handelingen, Senaat* (see Note 25), nos. 37 and 38, 24.3.1947, p. 781.
29. *Parlementaire Handelingen, Kamer* (see Note 19), no. 58, 28.4.1948, p. 21f.
30. Original text in Antoine Snoeck, 'La cooperation militaire européene et les efforts d'intégration', in *Le Rôle des Belges et de la Belgique dans l'Edification Européenne. Studia Diplomatica*, part XXXIV, 1981, pp. 481–515, here p. 485.
31. Govaerts (see Note 1), p. 204 (US, Congressional Record, Part XCIV–3, p. 2997).
32. Henry Truman, *Memoirs: Years of Trial and Hope*, New York, 1956, p. 248.
33. Original text in Spaak (see Note 3), p. 216f.
34. Joseph van Roey, *Au service de l'Eglise: Ecrits et allocutions de doctrine et d'action pastorale*, part VII, Tournai, 1955, p. 127.
35. Spaak (see Note 3), p. 264.
36. *Parlementaire Handelingen*, Kamer (see Note 19), 4.5.1949, p. 13; *Parlementaire Handelingen, Senaat* (see Note 25), 12.5.1949, p. 1448.
37. Dumoulin (see Note 12), p. 16; INSOC, 1949, nos. 5 and 6, p. 22.
38. On the role of the monarchy in politics see Luc De Vos, 'België tegen

wil en dank beschermd door zijn dynastie?', in *'Wij, Koning der Belgen ...
' 150 jaar Grondwettelijke Monarchie*, Bruxelles, 1981, pp. 159–80; and
De Vos, *Het effectief van de Belgische krijgsmacht en de militiewetgeving
1830–1914*, Bruxelles 1985, p. 460.
39. Original text in Spaak (see Note 3), p. 343.

6
Military Integration from the Perspective of The Netherlands

Jan Schulten

In 1950, General Heinz Guderian, in his pamphlet 'Kann Westeuropa verteidigt werden?' (Göttingen, 1950, p. 39), wrote, concerning the Dutch defence contribution, 'Holland's army is, at the moment, merely a plan.' General Dwight D. Eisenhower, during a visit to The Netherlands in January 1951, was equally unimpressed by her defence measures.[1] I must add, however, that The Netherlands were by no means exceptional in this, for the Americans also criticised the other Western European countries. As former President Herbert Hoover said in February 1951, 'The continent is not going to do this job.'[2] The situation did, however, improve dramatically in the following years, at least as far as Holland was concerned. In 1952, 30,000 Dutch soldiers took part in the NATO HOLDFAST exercise, while the navy and the air force also participated in various NATO exercises. Military integration in Europe had begun.

Dutch postwar defence policy has already been dealt with by other historians.[3] These studies all based themselves on the fact that Holland had given up her policy of neutrality since the Second World War and had gone over to an alliance policy. Influences from both home and abroad were considered in this. However, little attention was given to the problems which arose concerning the development of defence policy within the Defence Ministry and the General Staff. In view of the fact that access to archive files is still limited, this is hardly surprising. This essay is an attempt to shed some light on the problems of military integration, despite closed files, in the hope that the result will be a better understanding of the situation.

Jan Schulten

2

On 10 May 1940, the Dutch policy of neutrality was finally destroyed by the German attack on Holland. The Netherlands joined the allies. After a short period of confusion and desperation, as the Queen and her government fled to Britain on 13 May 1940, the Dutch government resumed its work in London at the end of 1940. Immediately after the Japanese attack on Pearl Harbor, the Dutch declared war on Japan and thereby became one of the first allies of the United States. At the end of the war, as the United Nations came into being, Holland had to face a difficult decision. It was clear to all that a return to neutrality was out of the question. There was really only a choice between two options: either to join the UN and create a system of collective security or to seek an alliance with the US, Britain and other Western European nations.[4] Although the government chose the latter solution during the war, they opted for the United Nations after the war despite their negative experience with the League of Nations. The Dutch were not overly interested in foreign affairs, as they had troubles of their own. The goal of political and social reform was more important at the time. The central question was the war in Indonesia, which dominated the scene in Holland between 1945 and the end of 1949.

There was also the German problem. It was obvious to the Dutch government that Holland's survival depended on the economic health of Germany. The Ruhr area was especially important for the Dutch economy. One danger was German militarism. In a memorandum, published by the Dutch government in English and Dutch, this was made clear. 'It was with great satisfaction that the Netherlands government learned that the discussion of a draft of a long-term treaty, aiming at the demilitarization and disarmament of Germany, has been placed on the agenda of the ensuing Moscow conference, as well as the consideration of other measures for the economic and military control of Germany. Like other peace-loving countries, the Netherlands believe that such a treaty should be concluded to cover a long period. At present there were already sufficient indications proving that the fall of Hitlerism has not meant the end of Prussian nationalism.'[5]

During 1947 it became more and more obvious to the Dutch government that the real danger had moved further east. This resulted in a change in foreign and security policy, which meant that an alliance with the USA, Britain and other Western European countries became feasible. In spite of this a lot of mistrust had to be overcome. For example, there was disagreement with Britain and the US on the question of Indonesia. In addition to this was the fear of American and British economic expansion. The government, however, was convinced that only an alliance with the United States could guarantee Dutch sovereignty on a long-term basis. The Prague coup made sure that The Netherlands did not hesitate to join the Western European Union. The Brussels Treaty was not the final solution for Holland, however, but rather a way of persuading the United States to participate in questions of European security.

In The Netherlands most people mistrusted the Soviet Union. According to a survey in 1948, 71 per cent of the Dutch population expected a Third World War. The government did not, however, think a direct Soviet attack was likely.[6] Social discontent was the greatest danger, because this did not exclude the possibility of an attempt by the Communists to take over. This meant that a rise in living standards was top priority. Against public opinion, the Dutch government thought that it was vital to have a German defence contribution. Thus the Council of Ministers decided, on 18 January 1949, that Western Germany was to be included in the Western Union's defence plans. As a result of this, the idea arose to move the forward line of defence to the Elbe, which meant that a West German contribution would be essential owing to the sheer length of this line. The government was sure that this could be achieved in a short time.[7] It decided to limit itself to the defence of Dutch territory, at the same time working to get West Germany included in the Western European security system.

Holland's entry into NATO on 4 September 1949 was the logical consequence of her policy on security at that time. During the signing of the NATO Treaty in Washington, Minister Stikker said, 'The treaty we are about to sign marks the end of an illusion: the hope that the United Nations would, by itself, ensure international peace.'[8] 'The government was in favour of military integration, but did not have a clear idea of what that really meant. Moreover, cooperation between the Dutch Foreign Office and the Defence Ministry was, as always in Holland at that time, thin on the ground.[9] Although relations with the US had improved since the problem of Indonesia had been solved, the Dutch government still feared being abandoned by the Americans should the

Soviets attack. Thus Eisenhower's successor as SACEUR (Supreme Allied Commander Europe), General Matthew B. Ridgway, had to calm the Dutch in 1952. He described it thus in his memoirs:

> In Holland and Belgium, the two countries most exposed to Red aggression, there was a particularly well-nourished feeling that we had no serious intentions of staying to fight if attacked. In an effort to allay these fears, I talked to the Dutch Cabinet for forty-five minutes, in a plain-spoken, informal session at which neither side minced words. I told them that it was our unalterable decision to defend every foot of European soil that we could defend – subject only to one proviso – that we were not going to throw away any of our troops in a hopeless last-stand defense of a non-defensable position. Our resources in manpower were too meager for that.[10]

For the Dutch government this meant that the USA would only support Western Europe militarily if the Europeans made their own contribution to the defence of their continent.

During the Second World War Holland had gained little experience of military cooperation. Just after the end of the war the Allied forces left the country, and The Netherlands did not take part in the occupation of Germany. The war in Indonesia was the first priority of interest when the Dutch armed forces were being built up. British weapons and equipment were bought and, not least due to this, British organisational structures were adopted. Officers and NCOs were trained in Britain.

At the beginning of 1947 all that changed, and the Dutch were left to their own devices in terms of defence. The hope was that two divisions could be created for the defence of The Netherlands in 1952.[11] Between 1945 and 1959 Holland created an army which was very similar to that of 1940.[12] One could say the same about the Dutch concept of defence itself. The old defensive positions, such as Grebbe and the Maas Line, were reactivated and improved. The Germans were still regarded as the enemy. But the British and Americans were not necessarily looked on positively in military circles. This was also due in large measure to the US and British attitude on the Indonesian question. Especially between 1948 and 1949, the Dutch felt they had been left in the lurch by both Britain and the United States.

3

When we speak of military integration, we mostly limit ourselves to integration or cooperation between different countries' armed forces. I believe we must also consider the integration of the navy, air force and army in one country. The Dutch navy was mainly involved in Indonesia before the Second World War. As it became obvious that the colonial empire had come to an end, they tried to build up a new sphere of influence in the West Indies.[13] As an independent force, but in conjunction with the United States, the navy was to have its own objectives there. Further, the navy was to avoid playing merely a secondary role. Dutch security policy had been too concentrated on the continent of Europe. The ideal role for the navy was ruling the waves, or at least making a contribution to securing the shipping lanes.[14]

The army did not agree with such ideas and followed its own interests. The first priority was to ensure that sufficient manpower was available for the war in Indonesia. Then territorial forces were to be organised for the defence of The Netherlands. At the end of 1947 it became clear to the Chief of the General Staff, General Kruls, that Britain was too weak in both military and economic terms to support Holland in the future. Only the United States were in a position to offer Holland long-term military aid. The Commander-in-Chief of the army in Indonesia, General Spoor, was of the same opinion.[15]

American equipment and organisational structures were to be the norm for the Dutch army. American tactical command regulations were also to be adopted after they had been adapted to Dutch conditions. General Kruls often warned against letting the British and Americans lead them around by the nose.

The Dutch air force tried in an inconspicuous way to build up its own empire. It did not become an independent arm until 1948 and was still in the process of finding its feet. As a power factor it was not in the same league as the army or the navy. The air force command was therefore cautious. It had airbases built and sent pilots to the USA to be trained. The air force was furthest along the road to military integration.

In spite of all the Dutch royal navy's efforts, the army had the lion's share of Holland's defence. For this reason this essay will continue to look at the development of the Dutch army as a factor in military integration. As a whole, however, it must be said the reformation of three independent arms had a negative effect on later military integration.

4

The signing of the Treaty of Brussels meant that Holland was able to take the first steps along the road leading to integration. It was a small beginning. A few officers were sent to London and Paris, but there were no troops for the Western Union. This did not change when Holland joined NATO. Not until the 1950s did things start to happen. On 27 January 1950, the MDAP (Mutual Defence Assistance Programme) treaty was signed in Washington, and on 4 May 1950 the first US ship carrying military equipment arrived at Rotterdam.[16] Now the Dutch could begin reorganising the army. Holland's defence policy was, however, a two-headed affair. On the one hand, efforts were made to achieve military integration with common aims, and on the other there were national interests. This dilemma was at its most striking in the case of the defence of the Rhine line. We shall deal with this question later.

The Brussels Treaty was meant to produce definite plans for Western Europe's defence. But this aim could just as easily be achieved by means of the existing agreements between the USA, Britain and France. The central issue was the defence of the Rhine. If the Soviets attacked, the plan was to withdraw across the Rhine and defend there. To make a stand further east was not feasible due to the low level of manpower. This defence plan meant that most of Holland would be left to the enemy.[17] The Dutch army command was against this idea. They rightly feared becoming merely a passive member of the new alliance rather than an equal partner. One problem was that there were almost no troops available in Holland in 1948, because the majority of the armed forces were needed for the war in Indonesia. Also, there had not been so much contact with the former Western allies since the end of the Second World War. According to the Dutch General Staff, Belgium was in a far better position in this respect. Because Belgium had taken part in the occupation of Germany, they had better relations with the Americans, the British and the French. The General Staff reacted to this new situation brought on by the Brussels Treaty by increasing the pace of cooperation with Belgium, which had already begun. The aim was to create a common block by means of the Benelux agreement as quickly as possible in order to prevent France and Britain gaining too much influence in the new alliance.

Let us look back at the Rhine defence. In 1947 it was clear to the USA, France and Britain that there were too few troops in Europe to resist a Soviet attack. Three plans were devised: the Long Term Plan (LTP), the Medium Term Plan (MTP) and the Short Term Plan (STP). The STP envisaged a withdrawal behind the Pyrenees as soon as the attack came from the east, with Europe being reconquered from there. But this plan was quickly shelved. It was a different story with the MTP, in which the Rhine was to be the line of defence. This was, of course, very good for France. The French had still not forgotten how the British, in 1940, had retreated to their island and left them to their fate. The Rhine defence was to stop history repeating itself, at least according to the French.

For the Western Allies the MTP, however was merely a last resort. The real aim was the LTP, and this meant a defensive line as far east as possible, preferably at the Iron Curtain.[18] As Holland did not agree with the Rhine defence, they suggested to their new allies that the line of defence should be extended to the Ijsselmeer. The River Ijssel, which flows from Arnhem to the Ijsselmeer, should be the new line of defence.

Field Marshal Montgomery and General de Lattre de Tassigny, however, were not convinced of the effectiveness of the Ijssel line. The Dutch General Staff immediately developed ways of improving the line. Dams were to be built in the Rhine at Arnhem and in the Waal at Nijmegen, which would be closed in the case of an enemy attack. The level of the Ijssel would rise and flood large areas between the Reichswald forest and the Ijsselmeer. The defensive stand could then be made behind this huge water obstacle. The Dutch succeeded in getting their way, and the Rhine defence was modified. They could, of course, mention that Rotterdam had to be secured: an extremely important strategic point for the Western Allies. The Dutch General Staff had in this way achieved two aims – Holland was not to be abandoned in a crisis, and was not to be ignored when the whole system of defence was being created. However, Dutch military circles were convinced that defence should be pushed further east in the long term.

I have, in this chapter, spoken only in fairly sketchy terms about the Ijssel line, as it appeared only as a detail in the complete defensive plan. However, it is worth looking at the Dutch plans in greater detail. The idea of creating a defensive line with the help of water was, of course, nothing new for Holland. This kind of defence had been used in The Netherlands since the seventeenth century. The only new element was that the line was drawn somewhat further east. For the Dutch, though, it meant the defence of their country rather than a part of the defence of Western Europe. There is also something to say about the actual building of the line. After much testing and trials, building really began in 1952.[19] Everything was shrouded in secrecy. The project became more and more complicated and cost much effort and money. The plan was out-of-date in 1952, when building started, and it was being dismantled nine years later. The Ijssel line was a negative influence on the build-up of the Dutch armed forces. There was a certain similarity with the Maginot line – it cost a great deal in economic terms and began to become an end in itself. Apart from this it was a prime example of static defence, although many did not realise this at the time.

Plans to reconstitute the Dutch armed forces were afoot in Britain during the Second World War. One major element of this was that in future Holland should always operate within an alliance. However, what this alliance would look like was unclear. One certainty was that the army should be built up with the aim of protecting Holland against a new attack – but more effectively than in 1940, of course. Although all efforts were made to train men for the struggle in Indonesia after the war, there were preparations made to rebuild the new army. In his memorandum of 16 February 1946, General Kruls, the Chief of the General Staff, wrote that the Dutch armed forces' job would be different to that during the period of the policy of neutrality. Holland should join an alliance and provide troops for a common plan of operations. The General made a point of saying that any new battles should take place outside Holland.[20] It was a good guess that the United States and Britain would be the new allies.

During the next few years the General Staff's image of the enemy changed, and the Soviet Union took the place of Germany. This meant that the objective hardly needed to be changed, but just that the fighting would be further east. Manpower was required, though, and as yet they had none. This was not so bad, as the General Staff did not expect a Soviet attack at that moment. There was just a fear of internal unrest, for which the Communists would be responsible. The few territorial units which Holland had at her disposal were told to guard important targets such as post and telegraph offices, bridges and power stations.

In 1948 it became imperative that the army field forces be reconstituted. The new Commander-in-Chief of the Western Union's troops, Field Marshal Montgomery, informed the Dutch army command that the war in Indonesia should not prevent the country raising three divisions by 1950.[21] He received the reply that this would only be possible after a victory in Indonesia. Therefore it would be advantageous for the Western Union if the British supported the Dutch action in the East Indies.[22] The British were not over-enthusiastic about this suggestion. The Dutch Foreign Ministry was also annoyed that the General Staff had made such a statement. This was one of many areas of friction between the two parties. This brought the tensions between General Kruls and the government more and more to a head. On 8 March the build-up of the field forces finally began, and a working staff was formed with Maj.-Gen. Adrianus T.C. Opsomer as its head.[23]

But the way forward was slow. There was increasing pressure from the Western Union and later from NATO. US public opinion reacted with impatience to the slow progress of military build-up in Europe. Thus American reporter Hanson Baldwin wrote about the Dutch army in the *New York Times* in August 1949, 'Army built on three divisional basis, but all three divisions are now in the Netherland's East Indies, with units not larger than brigades at home. Little air power at home.'[24]

In September 1949 the army command knew that Indonesia had been finally lost. General Kruls regretted having sent arms shipments to Indonesia at such a late stage. These were needed in Europe,[25] as the assumption was to be able to activate three divisions by 1952. From 1 August to 4 August 1950 the TRIADE map exercise was carried out at Fontainebleau, in which the Rhine-Ijssel defence was rehearsed. The result was that, for the moment, only the MTP was feasible. The Dutch agreed to this, and the field force, later called the First Dutch Army Corps, was assigned to the defence of the Rees-Ijsselmeer line.

On 9 October 1950, General Kruls sent a stiff note to the Defence Minister. The General accused the government of not putting enough effort into rearmament, and put forward the idea that Holland should raise five divsions by 1954. A lot more money was necessary for this, and National Service should be extended. He spoke out strongly in favour of rearming Germany and of forward defence. Also, Dutch forces should be permanently stationed in Germany.[26] Due to the solution of the Indonesian problem the government had more room to manoeuvre than in the past. However, factors such as the Korean War, increased pressure from the USA and increased arms and equipment sent by them all contributed to a faster reconstruction of the Dutch armed forces. On 1 September 1950, the Dutch field force, or rather the First Dutch Army Corps, was complete in all but minor details.[27]

However, it was 17 November 1952 before the first operational order came for the Dutch army corps. It was based on the Northern Army Group's plan of operations, and also on the Emergency Defence Plan of Allied Land Forces Central Europe. The Dutch assignment was, in the case of a Soviet attack, to pull back in a delaying action from the Dortmund-Ems Canal line between Rheine and Haren to behind the Rees-Ijsselmeer line. The Dutch air force was to be placed under the command of the Second Allied Tactical Air Force (ATAF). Two ATAF was to gain air supremacy over the northern army group's area of operations and give it tactical air support. Indeed, integration was given a start by the operation order of 17 November 1952. The preparatory stage of military integration was over. Up to the end of 1952, as far as Holland was concerned, the talk was more of forced cooperation between Europe and America to meet the threat from the Soviets than of military integration.

The Chief of the General Staff, General H. J. Kruls, played a dominant role in Dutch security policy. He came into more and more conflict with the government,[28] for Kruls did not restrict himself to military matters, but wanted to have a say in politics and the economy. There were stormy arguments, in particular with Piet Lieftink, the Finance Minister. In February 1952 the General was obliged to give notice of discharge from his post. His successor, General Hasselman, did not achieve any great change either. Montgomery and de Lattre de Tassigny were strongly criticised in Holland. Both were considered by the Dutch General Staff to be completely unsuitable to be Commanders-in-Chief of integrated armed forces. The Dutch military attaché in Brussels reported that the Belgians and the French were of the same opinion.[29] This criticism did not come to an end until Eisenhower was appointed as the first SACEUR.

Dutch-Belgian cooperation in military matters is worth closer scrutiny. As early as during the Second World War the Dutch government sought contact with the Belgians with an eye to future military cooperation. On 13 July 1943, the Dutch Defence Minister wrote to his Belgian opposite number, H. Pierlot: 'I am happy to see that the officers of our two countries are cooperating on the basis of cordiality and mutual trust.' He ended the letter as follows: 'In this regard I am thinking of close cooperation between our countries, and I hope that we will be able to discuss the matter at a suitable time.'[30] Although the Belgian minister was happy about the good relations, he was hesitant, because he thought Parliament should give the word before closer cooperation could be entered into.[31] In mid-1944 the whole affair was taken up anew.

Following on from earlier talks, the then Colonel H. J. Kruls wrote on 2 June 1944, in London, to his Belgian colleague, Colonel P. J. Diepenrijkx, that it was vital to have close military cooperation after the war between Belgium and The Netherlands. In his opinion the two countries had the same security interests, and 1940 had made it obvious that cooperation was necessary. On 8 June the Belgians replied: Diepenrijkx was in agreement.[32] After that there was a pause, and the idea was not taken up again until 19 February 1946. This time it was the Belgians who started the ball rolling.[33] The Belgian Foreign Ministry asked the Dutch military attaché in Brussels whether The Netherlands was interested in comprehensive military cooperation with Belgium. Holland, however, was too embroiled in her own problems to have time for the Belgian proposal. It was not forgotten, though, for Holland came back to it the very next year. The Dutch military attaché in Brussels, Major-General Sas (none other than the Major Sas who had been warned of the German attack by Colonel Oster in Berlin in 1940) checked this time how prepared the Belgians were to cooperate.[34] The answer was positive, and the two defence ministers decided to create a Belgian-Dutch military committee. The aim was to exchange useful experience, to make common use of firing ranges, to train together in order to save costs and so on; it was thus a question of practical military matters.

The chairman of the Dutch delegation, Major-General Droste, received a special assignment; he was told personally, under great secrecy, that this military technical cooperation was to be merely the start. It was very important to build up good relations with Belgium, and efforts had to be made to further this cooperation.[35] On 10 May 1948, the treaty was signed, and the preamble reads as follows, 'Whereas, within the framework of the Charter of the United Nations and the international agreements aimed at keeping the peace and for the defence of the Netherlands and Belgium against attack, it is important for the two countries to take military steps to ensure both their own cooperation and their position with regard to Powers which might make them offers of cooperation.' It was laid down very clearly that, 'This cooperation shall at no time whatsoever impinge upon the sovereignty of either of the Governments or upon their territories.'[36] The Dutch press was told that this was just a treaty concerning military cooperation, and nothing was said about the wider political implications of the agreement. The Dutch Parliament was also kept in the dark.

The Dutch-Belgian military committee rapidly got up steam. There were more and more sub-committees which took on a variety of problems such as the allocation of radio frequencies. A common position among the Benelux countries was laid down in matters concerning the Western Union and NATO. In 1951 a joint coastguard was formed. This cooperation among the Benelux countries was, at least for the Dutch, a first and very important step along the road to military integration within NATO.

On 26 May 1952, General Matthew B. Ridgway arrived in Paris to take over the post of SACEUR from General Eisenhower. As he discussed the main problems of NATO with Eisenhower, Ridgway was amazed at how complicated it all was. He was particularly worried about the lack of a central command. Eisenhower explained that this was the greatest weakness of the alliance. The cause was the mutual distrust of the members during the early years. There had also been many difficulties caused by national pride. 'Ike' added that not only military know-how was needed to be Commander-in-Chief of NATO but also a great degree of political tact, as the situation in Europe was very complicated. As opposed to Eisenhower, who had to deal almost exclusively with political problems, Ridgway was able to concentrate on the real job of building up the NATO armed forces.

During the period from 1945 to 1949 the Dutch were almost completely occupied with their own problems. Cooperation with the Belgians was born out of mistrust of France and Britain rather than resulting from the idea of European unity. Not until after 1950 did Holland start to recruit troops for the defence of Western Europe. The ambitious aims, such as five divisions, were never reached. It is, however, interesting that the notion of defence from as far forward as possible was discussed very early on in Holland.

One of the most important reasons for this was that a future war would be fought in Germany and not on Dutch soil. Until 1950 there was a wish to cooperate with other countries in a military alliance, but that was still a long way from real integration. Only after 1952 did this become possible. Seen from a purely theoretical point of view, the Treaty of Brussels offered better prospects for military integration than the NATO Treaty, for equality in a normal prerequisite for integration. During the early build-up phase of the Western Union's armed forces, there was little to be seen of this integration. This changed when the Americans joined NATO. Because the other members were mostly dependent upon the USA, they found themselves forced to work together, and not until after 1952 can we speak of real military integration.[37]

Conclusion

In Holland, between 1948 and 1950, military integration was discussed, but the term was not defined in detail. Thus politicians and soldiers had their own idea of what the term meant. The politicians were almost exclusively concerned with the political and economic aspects of military integration. The preservation of national sovereignty was one of their main goals. They had no interest in the day-to-day workings of integration. In this way they did not realise what an influence integration has on politics.

For the soldiers, military integration means above all the answer to many practical questions, such as, 'Where do I get fuel and ammunition, where can I have my vehicles repaired, and how can I combine my artillery fire with that of my neighbours?' Little by little, often unseen, the Dutch General Staff created a structure which was almost completely outside the writ of the politicians. Dutch cooperation with the Belgians had a stimulating effect on later military integration within NATO.

Jan Schulten

It is noticeable how much influence prewar military thinking had on Holland between 1945 and 1952. There has already been much discussion about whether the Second World War was a turning point. In Holland the general opinion is that one can indeed talk of a turning point, at least in terms of foreign and security policy. My belief is that this idea is somewhat overemphasised. Traditional military thinking played too great a role in the country's security policy.

Notes

1. Stephen E. Ambrose, *Eisenhower. Soldier, General of the Army, President-Elect 1889–1952*, New York, 1983, p. 502.
2. *New York Times*, 28.2.1951.
3. Adrian F. Manning, 'Die Niederlande und Europa von 1945 bis zum Beginn der fünfziger Jahre', in *VfZG*, vol. 29, 1981, vol. 1 pp. 1–20. Albert E. Kersten, 'Niederländische Regierung, Bewaffnung Westdeutschlands und EVG', in *Die Europäische Verteidigungsgemeinschaft. Stand und Probleme der Forschung. Im Auftrag des Militärgeschichtlichen Forschungsamt hrsg. von Hans-Erich Volkmann und Walter Schwengler. Mit Beiträgen von Alfredo Breccia, Anselm Doering-Manteuffel, Alexander Fischer, Pierre Guillen, Peter Jones, Albert E. Kersten, Walter Lipgens, Klaus A. Maier, Wilhelm Meier-Dörnberg, Paul Noack, Raymond Poidevin, Jean-Pierre Rioux, Hans-Erich Volkmann, Donald Cameron Watt und Werner Weidenfeld*, Boppard am Rhein, 1985, (*Militärgeschichte seit 1945*, Bd 7), pp. 199–219; Joris C. Voorhoeve, *Peace, Profits and Principles: A Study of Dutch Foreign Policy*, The Hague, 1979.
4. See Samuel I. P. van Campen, *The Quest for Security: Some Aspects of Netherlands Foreign Policy 1945–1950*, Den Haag, 1958.
5. Handelingen Tweede Kamer, 1946–1947, Bijlage Nr. 383.
6. Hans Blom, 'Jaren van tucht es ascese', in *Bijdragen en Medelingen betreffende de Geschiedenis der Nederlande*, Aflevering 2, 1981, pp. 300–33.
7. Algemeen Rijksarchief, Den Haag, Notulen Ministerrat 1948.
8. J. H. Leurdijk (ed.), *The Foreign Policy of The Netherlands*, Alphen aan de Rijn, 1978.
9. Van Campen (see note 4), p. 109.
10. Matthew B. Ridgway, *Soldier: The Memoirs of Matthew B. Ridgway*, New York, 1956, p. 247f.

Military Integration: The Netherlands

11. Sectie Militaire Geschiedenis Landmachtstaf (=SMG), Den Haag, Collectie Schrek Nr. 187A, Note to the Chairman of the Council of Ministers, 9.6.1947.
12. See Jan Schulten, 'Die Aufstellung des Königlich-niederländischen Heeres nach 1945', in *Entmilitarisierung und Aufrüstung in Mitteleuropa 1945–1956*, mit Beiträgen von Alexander Fischer, Christian Greiner, Klaus A. Maier, Ulrich de Maizière, Wilhelm Meier-Dörnberg, Georg Meyer, Manfred Rauchensteiner, Jan Schulten, Hans-Erich Volkmann und Norbert Wiggershaus, Herford, Bonn, 1983 (*Vorträge zur Militärgeschichte*, vol. 4), pp. 209–23.
13. Centraal Archieven Depot (CAD), Den Haag, Defence Ministry, Notulen Vergadering Comité – Verenigde Chefs von Staven (CVS), 11.12.1948. Archief Hoofdkwartier Generale Staf (HKGS), 1940, doos. 1.
14. See Ger Teitler, *Enkele aspecten van het maritiem-strategisch denken in Nederland. 1945–1955*, Den Helder, 1980.
15. CAD (see Note 13), HGKS, 1948, doos. 11, Note to the Minister for War, no. G 4/3652/47.
16. See Ine Megens, *De Amerikaanse Hulpverlening aan Nederland*, Glimmen, 1980.
17. Christian Greiner, 'Die alliierten militärstrategischen Planungen zur Verteidigung Westeuropas 1947–1955', in *Anfänge westdeutscher Sicherheitspolitik 1945–1956*, vol. 1: *Von der Kapitulation bis zum Pleven-Plan*, von Roland G. Foerster, Christian Greiner, Georg Meyer, Hans-Jürgen Rautenberg, Norbert Wiggershaus, Munich, Vienna, 1982, pp. 119–232, here pp. 206–25.
18. James A. Blackwell Jr., 'In the Laps of the Gods: The Origins of NATO Forward Defense', in *Parameters, Journal of the US Army War College*, vol. 15, no. 4, 1985, pp. 64–95.
19. Jan H. M. A. Erven and Edward A. I. M. Vriends, Plannen C en D, 1948–1956, Breda, 1984 (unpublished MS).
20. CAD (see Note 13), HGKS 1945–1946, doos. 1, Voorstellen betreffend de Legervorming, nr. 69, 16.2.1946.
21. CAD (see Note 13), HGKS 1948, doos. 1, CVS-Vergaderingen, 13.11.1948.
22. Ibid., Letter from Military Attaché, no. 3978, 18.8.1948.
23. SMG (see Note 11), Collectie Schrek, No. 123. HKGS No. G2/17543/A5, 8.3.1949.
24. CAD (see Note 13), doos. 6, Letter from Mil. Attaché, 18.8.1949.
25. Ibid., Archief Kruls, Memorandum, October 1948.
26. Ibid., HKGS 1952, doos. 146, Note by Chief of General Staff, Nr. Kab. 50/1083, 22.11.1950.
27. SMG (see Note 11), Collectie Schrek, no. 124, Order of the Day.
28. Hendrik J. Kruls, *Generaal in Nederland*, Bussum, 1975.
29. CAD (see Note 13), HGKS 1948, doos. 26, Letter from Military

Attaché, no. 30788, 18.8.1948.
30. Ibid., Archief Kruls, Letter of 13.7.1943.
31. Ibid.
32. Ibid., Letter no. 1651P, 27.6.1944.
33. Ibid., HGKS 1946, doos. 1, Letter from Military Attaché, 22.2.1946.
34. Ibid., HGKS 1947, doos. 14, Letter by Maj.-Gen. Sas, No. 49, 1.10.1947.
35. Ibid., HGKS 1948, doos. 14, Note to Quartermaster-General, 10.1.1948.
36. Ibid., Arch., Belg.-Dutch Agreement of 10.5.1948, doos. 625.
37. Han N. Boon, *Afscheidsaudientie*, Den Haag, 1976, pp. 162–9.

7
France and the Defence of Western Europe: from the Brussels Pact (March 1948) to the Pleven Plan (October 1950)

Pierre Guillen

From 1947–8 onwards, leading French politicians argued with their Western partners in favour of a joint defence organisation for Western Europe. This change of attitude – up to that time they had placed their emphasis upon a policy of national independence – was due to the sudden recognition that France was unable to guarantee her own security. Difficulties in terms of currency, financial and economic problems, social unrest and political instability all made it impossible at that time to rebuild the armed forces. As early as the summer of 1947, General Humbert, Etat-Major de la Défense Nationale (EMDN, Chief of the General Staff), pointed to France's military weakness, which was such that she could not mobilise her forces and intervene in a conflict without the assistance of foreign powers.[1]

To give up a part of her national sovereignty, in the field of defence, was such a break with tradition that the speakers for the majority faction in government, during the debates on the Brussels Pact, worked hard to demonstrate that any limits placed on French sovereignty would also apply to the other signatories; that the costs and the service connected with the coordination of military efforts would be shared out equally; and that 'interdependence does not mean subjection'. The speakers went on to say that France had no alternative: 'Independence on her own would mean independence in weakness for France,' declared Teitgen on behalf of the National Defence Committee, while Ramadier, the Defence Minister, explained: 'We will accept neither the idea of going it alone nor the policy of being a satellite. We will choose solidarity, which will give us the power to make others respect our independence.'[2] The setting-up of joint bodies enabled the partners to share out the tasks, to standardise materials and industrial products; each country saw that this made life easier, and they benefited from the power of collective defence.

The Brussels Pact was the first step on the road to this joint defence organisation for Western Europe. It offered France a double guarantee: against Germany and against the USSR. To be sure, the first guarantee, considering that there was no longer the fear of her mounting an attack, was a political rather than a military one: to counter the weight of Germany, whose rebirth was seen as a danger in itself, to allay the fear that France might one day have to face alone the west German state which was being constituted, and which, with the help of the British and the Americans, would soon become powerful once more. The second guarantee, against the USSR, whose expansionist aims and aggressive intentions were more and more obvious to the majority of French political leaders, was less a question of assembling a European armed force capable of successfully repelling an attack by the Red Army – the Soviet forces were simply too large – than of persuading Stalin not to invade Western Europe by demonstrating their will to organise themselves to resist such an attack.

However, the French were quickly convinced that the Brussels Pact, whose 'birth was so difficult' and whose 'realisation was so accompanied by dissent',[3] was no real answer to the problem. On the one hand, due to the small amount the Five could put into it, the guarantees were an illusion. Britain did not really want to commit herself, the Benelux countries were military lightweights, and thus it was left to France to bear the brunt of the defence of Western Europe under the auspices of the Western European Union (WEU). The National Defence Committee, in defining the tasks of the French armed forces, decided that top priority was to 'ensure, with the help of the allies, the coverage of the Rhine frontier'.[4]

However, the military leaders found themselves incapable of fulfilling this aim as there were insufficient means at their disposal. In the National Defence Committee, General Révers, the Chief of the General Staff in the EMDN, the Defence Minister and the Secretary of State for the Armed Forces made bitter complaints: the matériel was worn out and out-of-date, they had insufficient manpower; in order to meet the minimum requirements of the WEU (five divisions), they would have to spend 360 billion francs. But the Finance Minister, with the support of the President of the Council of Ministers, rejected the idea of increasing the defence budget, saying there would be a monetary and economic catastrophe if he did. The President of the Republic confirmed this statement: '1949 will be a critical and decisive year. We are about to win the social battle, we must now win the economic battle and keep down inflation.' The Minister of the Interior declared that it was impossible to cut the cost of maintaining law and order, while the Minister for the French colonies was unable to reduce the expenditure for Indochina.[5] Not only were the funds for the defence of Europe not increased, but the planned orders for tanks and aircraft were put on ice for lack of dollars, while it was decided, in January 1949, to reduce the levels of manpower in the air force and the navy.[6]

On the other hand, the French criticised the dominating influence which the British planned to exert within the WEU. With the exception of the air force, the French military leaders refused to subordinate themselves to the British. There were constant power struggles between Montgomery and de Lattre de Tassigny. The French were also annoyed about Britain's efforts to speak on behalf of the Five in Washington, with France as the brilliant substitute.[7] Above all, as Paris saw it, the British were unwilling to commit themselves on the Continent. During the meeting of the Brussels Pact foreign ministers in July 1948, Bevin adopted a completely negative attitude, which was also regretted by the Americans who emphasised the unfavourable consequences this would have in Congress when it decided on allocating aid for Europe.[8] In July 1949, at the meeting of the five defence ministers, there was still complete uncertainty over Britain's contribution. The British responded to the French complaints by casting aspersions on the value and moral fibre of the French army.[9]

All this revealed a profound difference between the British and French strategic concepts. British strategy, guided by the experience of the Second World War, was based on the idea of 'Fortress Britain'; even in the air forces, where Anglo-French cooperation was a reality, the RAF's defence plans were solely concentrated on the defence of the British Isles. The French, on the other hand, refused to accept the scenario of another invasion followed by a new liberation; the WEU was to be strong enough to contain an attacker, but it was necessary that the British commit themselves from the start to moving their main point of effort to the Continent. But they refused to do so. The French thought that the WEU was about to come under British control, reducing France and the Benelux countries to mere helpers in the defence of the Commonwealth: 'the system as it is risks becoming a source of immediate advantage to the British' and it 'is of doubtful benefit to France'. Thus it had to be admitted that 'the key to our security lies not in London but rather in Washington'.[10]

As early as the end of 1947, the French government regarded US aid as indispensable: France was powerless against a Soviet attack on Europe, and a declaration of neutrality would be no insurance against the threat.[11] In February 1948 the Prague coup strengthened the fears of such an attack, and, even while negotiations for the Brussels Pact were going on, the French government, knowing how lacking in teeth this agreement was, sent three urgent appeals to the United States (on March 4, March 18 and April 13), saying that without US commitment the defence of Western Europe was impossible.[12]

Without American guarantees, any kind of military alliance between the European countries was incapable of ensuring their security, maintained the EMDN, which went on to emphasise the inequality of forces existing at the time; there was no doubt that the European states together would be able, in the long term, to raise a force capable of balancing out that of the USSR, but the Russians would not allow them to do so, 'unless the United States guaranteed their safety during the development of such a force'.[13]

This was the reason why, in a note sent to Washington dated 20 May 1948, the French government expressed their concern 'at the turn of international events, and (our) conviction that urgent measures must be taken which will allow us to stand up to the dangers facing the Western nations'. Because of her geographical situation, France was particularly exposed to these dangers, so it was in her best interests that the Western defence organisation be put together 'without weakness or delay', and she 'anxiously' awaited 'definite assistance measures' from the United States: measures which had been demanded by the signatories of the Brussels Pact.[14]

Under the assumption that official approval would be given to US assistance, which alone would lend 'any kind of credibility' to the efforts to solve the problem of Western European defence,[15] the French foreign minister, Robert Schuman, met General Marshall in October 1948, to discuss the participation of

American occupation troops in joint defence on German soil. Marshall assured Schuman that the United States were prepared to organise defence in Germany, in cooperation with the other WEU countries, and also to equip several tens of divisions, which were to be raised as soon as possible.[16]

Thus the Atlantic Alliance, which Paris regarded as an essential complement to the Brussels Pact, was to a great extent the result of French initiatives and pressure on the American government. In the press and radio statements which the French government issued in an effort to justify the conclusion of the Atlantic Pact in the public's eyes, there was a reminder of the events of 1914 and 1939. France had been invaded because America had failed to commit herself. Western Europe's situation was once again most dangerous: the East European states were rapidly becoming Soviet satellites, the Russians were building up a system of alliances and creating the Cominform 'with the task of preparing the way for the total victory of Communism in Europe'. It would be 'an unpardonable crime to leave our fatherland in such an unarmed solitude, open to any attacker ... Our people would not forgive either our blindness, our isolationism nor our passivity.'[17] By bringing the United States into the defence of Western Europe, the Atlantic Treaty realised 'the main aim of French diplomacy since 1918'.

This pact, which was made inevitable by the necessary solidarity in the face of the threat, and also by the powerlessness of the UN to prevent an attack, was based upon the democratic states' right to collective defence against what they saw as the danger posed by the 'military bloc in Eastern Europe'. In reply to those who objected that this would be abandoning the European ideal, the government said that the Atlantic Pact was, on the contrary, 'the prerequisite for a strong Europe, a guarantee for the future of the values of European civilisation'. To those who pointed critically towards the costs of Atlantic defence, they replied that Western Europe had to make an effort to rearm itself at all costs if it wanted to survive; thanks to American aid and the pooling of defensive means, the costs for the European economies would be lessened.

Once the Atlantic Treaty was finally signed, the French government was concerned that there were not merely declarations of intent and affirmations of principle, but rather that the defence of Western Europe was begun without delay. Apart from this, the

Council of the Republic, in a motion adopted on 27 July 1949, made the ratification of the treaty dependent upon effective military assistance and the setting-up of the planned bodies. This position was taken up by the government in a note addressed to the US Administration, whose reaction was most negative and who refused to accept the note. Since the positions had become bogged-down, the above note was finally replaced by a letter to the representatives of all signatory states in Paris, in which the government stated that individual and collective defence could not be effective until military assistance was rendered and until a definite organisation was set up as quickly as possible.[18]

Above all, through the Atlantic Alliance, the French government wanted the other states to recognise that the defence of the continent of Europe was the top priority ('NATO must give absolute priority to the defence of Western Europe by means of a joint strategy') and they wanted to get a formal commitment from the United States on this. The directives for the French delegation at NATO insisted upon the immediate need for a first stage of rearmament, where Western Europe must be the first to benefit, and also upon the need to have the United States included in the Western European Regional Planning Group, under the same conditions as the member countries of the WEU.[19] In the opinion of the French General Staff, the American aid had to be sufficient to allow them 'to move most of our joint defensive system beyond the Rhine'.[20]

In the opinion of the French military leaders, the essential point in the definition of a joint strategy was that the Americans committed themselves to participate 'with all means at their disposal' in the defence of Continental Europe.[21] The Americans had to be made aware that their own security would no longer be assured if Western Europe fell into the hands of the USSR. In order to liberate it again, enormous efforts would be needed, much greater than those now required. To rely solely upon the deterrent effect of the strategic air forces was not enough; the United States had to take in hand the 'direct security' of Western Europe by increasing her military presence on the Continent and by leading the way in a joint defence organisation. She alone had the material and financial wherewithal and she alone was in a position to impose effective structures and to overcome the reticence of the Europeans, who still clung dearly to the intangibility of their national sovereignty.[22] The government took this position and charged the Defence Minister to present it in Washington.[23]

Although the decisions taken by the Atlantic Council on 17 September 1949 and the American Military Assistance Act for Europe complied with French wishes, 'on paper' at least, it was again time to put these decisions into practice.[24] However, the United States still seemed to think that France 'could once more be a common battlefield'.[25] Meanwhile, during the next few months, the French leaders recognised 'a change in US military thinking towards giving priority to the defence of Continental Europe and a more active US participation in this defence'.[26] In accordance with the directives issued by the French Chiefs of Staff Committee, General Paul Ely, the French representative in the Standing Group, succeeded in having the importance of the defence of Western Europe recognised in the Medium-Term Plan adopted by the Standing Group on 13 March 1950 (the point of main effort was to be placed here from the outset and the maximum reinforcements were to be employed). Also included was the necessity 'of keeping the enemy as far to the east in Germany as possible', the participation of the entire allied air forces in any land battle which might occur, the commitment of the strategic air force as support on the battlefield, and an increase in the US initial commitment.[27] However, the latter still seemed to think she would intervene mainly with her air force and navy, while France and the other states would supply 'the Alliance's infantry'.[28]

To have the opportunity to be able to guide the definition of Atlantic Alliance global strategy towards priority for the defence of Western Europe was the main reason why France continued to demand the creation of a kind of triumvirate at the top echelon of NATO, the Steering Group (which later became the Standing Group). As early as the summer of 1948, the French government demanded a say in this top body, which drew up the strategy for the future alliance, and, during the negotiations, under pressure from the Defence Ministry, this demand became a sort of prerequisite, since, in the Ministry's opinion, this was the only way France could avoid 'the disadvantages for her security of the Anglo-American tête-à-tête, in which our basic needs are pushed to one side or even completely ignored'. Continental interests had to be represented, otherwise Western Europe would run the risk of being left open to invasion again.[29] In this way it was made clear to the American allies that Western Continental Europe was the nearest, the most vulnerable and the most tempting objective for the USSR; that France was the heart of this objective – a fact which made it fitting for France 'to employ the necessary strategic means for the protection of the Continent', all the more so because it would be her forces above all which would guarantee coverage – and it would be her bases, resources and communications which France would place at the alliance's disposal, in the country itself as well as in the Union Française. Not to mention the fact that her troops were defending Indochina, the 'front against Soviet expansion' in South-East Asia.[30]

Another advantage of such a triumvirate would be that the French would represent the Continent, and in this way she would be recognised for her role in setting up a European union; 'since the interests of the small European states coincide to such a great degree with those of France, she would be the natural choice as their representative'.[31] To those who noted that the 'smaller European powers' seemed to object to the role cast for them, the President of the Council, Queuille, replied: 'The smaller powers run the risk of disappearing in wartime, and so they will have to get used to a situation which will help strengthen their security.'[32] All the same, in order to comply with the wishes of the small countries, the Standing Group was portrayed from the start as a working party, aimed at orientation and coordination; however, even then the British and Americans had to concede that it would become 'the military high command' as soon as possible.

Among the French reasons, there was, of course, the jealousy of the privileged role played by Britain, and the wish to put an end to it: 'We must reject any kind of organisation which does not put us on an equal footing with Britain in the Washington talks,' it said in a letter from the Secrétariat Genéral to the Defence Ministry, and Ramadier, the minister, took the same position before his colleagues: France's presence in the Standing Group would prevent Britain from being 'in a position to exert an overriding influence upon the realisation of the Alliance'. But the aim was above all a strategic one: 'To emphasise the absolute necessity of the land defence of Continental Europe'.[33]

France got her way and, thanks to General Ely's activity within the Standing Group, Anglo-American conceptions developed along the lines favoured by France. Because of this the government thought it had been right to insist upon creating this body, an 'indispensable nerve-centre of the coalition',[34] and the government took care to see that the plans to reform the Atlantic Pact, which came up for discussion from time to time, did not weaken 'the decisive influence upon global strategy' of the Standing Group, 'which for us represents one of the essentials of the Atlantic Pact'.[35] Care was also taken to prevent any other countries being admitted to the 'club': to turn the triumvirate into a four-way (in August 1949 the Italian application was rejected), or even a body with eight, ten or twelve members would have meant losing any kind of capacity to make clear decisions and would have led to a rebirth of the Anglo-American tête-à-tête: 'the strategic decisions will be taken elsewhere'.[36]

Since the Atlantic Alliance seemed to comply with French government wishes, what was to be done with the Brussels Pact organisations? At the start, the top civil servants in the Defence Ministry thought that the two systems were in no way conflicting and had to be kept apart: while the Atlantic Alliance was of a temporary nature, the Brussels Pact was 'one of the seeds of a permanent European federation'. Apart from this, the Brussels Pact, whose commitments were more precise than the Atlantic Alliance, guaranteed France immediate assistance in a *casus belli*, while the Atlantic Alliance could be revised after ten years and might then no longer offer the same guarantees for French security.[37]

In the end it was agreed that the WEU bodies should not be done away with ('the experience of London, imperfect as it may be, is of great value') but rather adapted to the new situation: the Military Committee in London would be limited to a coordinating role in organising mobilisation, information, training and logistics; any strategic competence would disappear. The Military Supply Committee would continue to deal with the standardisation of matériel and the allocation of production contracts. The Western Union Chiefs of Staff Committee in Fontainebleau would become the working party for the Western European theatre. However, it would be 'completely illogical, at a time when a European union is in the offing, to do away with the organisations which make it possible to work together'.[38] The Comité de Défense Nationale (CDN) agreed to these conclusions, since it thought (in answer to a question raised by the President of the Council, Queuille, on the possibility of the Americans consenting to participate fully in the WEU and on the functionality of all the bodies created in London and Fontainebleau) that, on this basis, the Americans should actively participate in all discussions relating to operational planning, but also that they should merely have observer status in all other matters.[39]

Apart from this, the Foreign Ministry emphasised that France was concerned to keep her power and influence within the Brussels Pact institutions: 'In this way we can defend our concept of Europe and Western European defence and effectively play an increasing role on the Continent, both in political and military terms.' In addition to this, maintaining the London organisations was a means of combating Britain's tendency to 'abandon the Brussels Pact for the Atlantic Alliance and to wriggle out of her Continental commitments, to which she bound herself within the Pact'.[40] As a result of this, while the Finance Ministry, guided by the need to save funds, speculated upon the imminent breakup of the Brussels Pact organisations, which they considered to be mere doubles for the Atlantic Alliance bodies, the Foreign Ministry took its stand on the side of the Brussels Pact, making use of two further arguments. On the one hand an organisation set up to guard against a renaissance of the German peril should not be placed in jeopardy at a time when that country was recovering, and when US policy was making her risk committing herself to 'dangerous measures'; 'Faced by a Germany whose growing power might tempt her to be less than true to the ideal of cooperation in Europe', some valuable mechanisms of support could be found in the Group of Five to counter her. On the other hand, the WEU allowed France to get Benelux backing before going to the Americans and British to discuss European questions and, with the support of the Benelux countries, to make herself the mouthpiece for Western Europe in the Atlantic Alliance.[41]

Meanwhile, in the course of the last months, the WEU had been nothing but a source of disappointment for the French leaders. The difference in concepts between the French and British high commands were striking, and they jeopardised the cohesion of the Western camp. President Auriol demanded that the British be told that their policy was becoming more and more 'insular in character' and that it risked isolating the Continent. Despite soothing words from the British defence minister, the French government's opinion was that the British wanted to drop the WEU in favour of the Atlantic Alliance.[42] In March 1950 the Quai d'Orsay condemned the fact that the debates in the Brussels Pact committes were so ineffectual. Indeed, the Economic and Finance

Committee had been brought to a 'complete standstill'; by putting off any practical application of the commitments to mutual assistance, leaving unanswered, among other things, the basic question of how to divide up the costs of defence among the Five, the Brussels Pact had been effectively paralysed.[43] Hervé Alphand, the French representative on the North Atlantic Council Deputies, stated that the execution of WEU programmes had hardly started, while the integration of forces and strategic planning had not progressed one iota. The Economic and Finance Committee, after months of trying to find an equitable formula for the division of the costs of joint defence, had had to give up as no agreement had been reached.[44]

General Jean Cherrières, Etat-Major Permanent à la Présidence du Conseil, had even tougher things to say: the Brussels Pact was more of a collection of declarations of intent than a fair and balanced integration of each country's means against a common threat; the Armaments Committee, despite the efforts of the French representatives, had not succeeded in setting up a coordinated long-term arms-production programme, and had got nowhere in standardising matériel. The Economic and Finance Committee's results were even more disappointing. General Cherrières blamed British delaying tactics and the lack of realism among the technical committees, who were incapable of coming to a decision, and where hair-splitting and toothlessness prevailed; the whole thing was a source of difficulties and a waste of time. Considering that France expected more security from the Brussels Pact thanks to cooperation, in the face of a common adversary, not only in terms of resources but also in terms of the advantages to be gained from a united Western Europe, the balance was completely negative. Due to a lack of coordination in military, economic and financial policy, the Brussels Pact had ended up in an impasse.[45]

Under these circumstances, the French leaders no longer placed their trust in the WEU; the solution was to seek a reform of the Atlantic Pact, by way of an integrated defensive organisation for Western Europe within NATO. This was sketched out by Hervé Alphand as early as February 1950, and he returned to the matter in several notes in March and April. These were based on a conviction and a confirmation. The conviction was that the USSR would be capable of conducting a war in less than five years, and thus it was vital to strengthen Western Europe militarily and economically in order to deter the Russians. It was useless to negotiate with the Soviets. As neutrality was also pointless, the only way to secure peace was to enlarge and organise the West's armed forces, so as to nip the Russian plans in the bud and convince her that such plans had no chance of success. On the other hand, there was the confirmation that although Western Europe's potential was considerable, her efforts remained uncoordinated; European cooperation had not got off the ground, and there was no real coordination of defensive forces. In addition, in spite of the Marshall Plan, Western European economic and financial recovery was not sufficient to allow them to carry out an armaments programme on a large scale. What was needed was a grouping on an Atlantic level; this would also remove the difficulties caused by Britain, who wavered between the European and Atlantic camps. It would also remove the Franco-German antagonism by driving out 'the spectre of a Franco-German head-on collision in Europe'.

According to Alphand, this integrated organisation meant limitations placed upon national sovereignty in favour of Atlantic alliance. In military terms, it was necessary to begin to apply the rule of majority decisions in coordinating and organising the armed forces. There would be an executive organ at the top, which would put into practice the military policy of the West on behalf of the governments. The United States hesitated so as not to provoke a negative reaction from the Europeans; France should take the lead, if possible in concert with Britain. This was of great interest to France, as she could then continue her efforts at rearmament without fear of causing serious economic and social problems. The Chiefs of Staff thought it vital to increase military expenditure by 300 billion francs in the next budget, an idea which was rejected by both government and Assembly; how could they increase military spending at a time when the economic situation was detrimental, when income was diminishing and there was a balance-of-payments deficit? The monetary, financial and economic problems facing France made it necessary to create a Western defence budget in order to realise an effective defence system. The United States and Canada would help to bear the burden of expenditure which was too great for the Western Europeans. Apart from this, a reform of the Atlantic Alliance's institutions would allow the most modern US technology to be transferred to Europe. 'Faced by the numerical superiority of our enemies, our military security can only rest upon technical superiority, our scientific advances and the higher quality of our weaponry.'[46]

Alphand's views were shared by General Cherrières, who, on 18 March 1950, discussed them with Defence Minister Pleven; he sent him a long note on the same subject, approved by the Chiefs of Staff Committee, on 22 March, and the main points were repeated in a letter to the Quai d'Orsay of 27 March. General Cherrières emphasised that General Ely was of like mind in the Standing Group, having the initial defence-plan project, which had just passed through the Group, presented as an attempt to integrate the regional plans. From this standpoint, it was advisable for the French government to request that the Atlantic Council draw up a list of joint defence requirements, define the rules for the spreading of the costs among the members, and allocate the military tasks for each country, formulating the list of standardised matériel to be adopted and produced.[47] The Direction des Affaires politiques took up these recommendations and, in a letter to Foreign Minister Robert Schuman, emphasised their urgency. 'While it is true that France has an interest, in political and diplomatic terms, to keep the maximum possible freedom of action and to avoid the Atlantic Alliance turning into a kind of Cominform under the direction of the United States, it is nonetheless essential to involve the Americans in ever-closer cooperation and to freely accept the limitations on our sovereignty which will place us in a better position to safeguard our national independence.' An effective defence of Western Europe demanded the creation of a 'driving force' at the head of the alliance, which would be able to take decisions and which would be capable of exercising 'a supra-national authority based on the common interest'.[48]

All this was repeated once again, in July 1950, in the instructions given to the French delegation at the North Atlantic Council Deputies. They were to insist upon the setting-up of an integrated Atlantic armed force. In order to keep the enemy in check, it was necessary to have in Western Europe 'a land and air force of a size which cannot be raised by the sole efforts of the Continental countries. The United States and Great Britain must take part in the initial battle using the elements already in place', and contribute to the establishment of the necessary infrastructure.[49] The invasion of south Korea in June reinforced the French view: it showed that the defence had to be organised in a permanent way.

The American memorandum of 23 July 1950, in which the United States suggested that, in exchange for an increase in military aid to the Europeans, they should increase their own defence efforts, presented the French government with an opportunity to make their views known. Alphand discussed the matter with the US representative at the Council Deputies, Spofford, and requested, in the name of the government, the formulation of a precise strategic plan, the strengthening of the US and British military presence on the Continent, the setting-up of a joint fund to finance rearmament and infrastructure programmes, an initial American payment into this fund so as to permit the production of the first list of weapons, and, finally, American financial participation in the war in Indochina. Alphand pointed to the conclusion which Europe had to draw from the Korean War: the US Chiefs of Staff had to revise their strategic plans (Western Europe could not resist an invasion for more than three to four weeks, and the Americans would not intervene on a massive scale for a longer period), where France would be a mere bridgehead for the 'reconquest' of Europe, a prospect which gave rise to neutralist and defeatist thinking among the French public. Strategic plans were needed, based on a successful resistance to an attack from the initial battle on, something the Western Europeans were incapable of doing.[50]

The French memorandum of 5 August, in answer to the US note of 23 July, reiterated the demands presented by Alphand; it particularly pointed out that accelerated rearmament, imposed by the Korean War, had to be seen 'as a collective enterprise, not as a juxtaposition of national efforts', which implied the creation of central bodies for planning and direction, in order that decisons on financing, sharing of costs, production and manpower were taken on a collective basis and carried out jointly.[51] The French ambassador in Washington was charged with commenting upon the memorandum: France wanted the defence of Europe to be organised on a realistic basis; the assembly of a few new French divisions was not enough; on the contrary, there should be forty to fifty divisions stationed in Europe, conforming to a joint defence plan and a system of finance based on the concept of 'Atlantic nations' joint action', not on that of 'addition and juxtaposition of national efforts'. A second French note, sent to the US government on 17 August, went into greater detail concerning the reform of the NATO structures demanded by Paris. The various proposals were aimed at a collective organisation pursuing a common direction, in all aspects of defence policy; they implied the absorption of the WEU into the new system and the disappearance of the military structure of the Brussels Pact.[52]

The reform project which the Atlantic Alliance Defence Committee had to study on 28 October contained many of the French concepts: the creation of a Supreme Allied Command in Europe, divided into three theatres of operations, North, Centre and South, with three commands. The French government demanded the post of Deputy Supreme Commander for the French forces, and above all that of Commander of the Central European theatre, whereby they expressed reservations about subordinating the whole French forces in NATO to a supranational command, as they represented all the large elements; the government wanted to be able to use some of them in 'certain circumstances' – for example keeping internal order and defending the 'Union française'.[53]

In order to justify their request for the reform of NATO structures and increased US commitment, the French government pointed out the failure of the Brussels Pact organisation, whereby they placed the blame on the other partners, principally the British. However, one of the main reasons for the French insistence upon the complete integration of Western European defence within NATO was France's inability to fulfil the commitments she had made within the WEU.

In London, on 15 March 1949, the Five had agreed upon an additional arms production programme to the military budgets and the arms shipments from America under the Military Assistance Programme. France's portion was $160 million in two years. As well as this, at the Pact meeting in Luxembourg on 15 July 1949, France committed herself to assembling a modern army of twenty and a half divisions up to the end of 1951, which represented costs amounting to 2,347 billion francs. However, the United States, which was expected to finance a good deal of these programmes, decided, on 5 October, that her aid was to be solely material and not in financial terms. Thus the cost of rearmament fell entirely upon the European budgets. When, in November 1949, the CDN examined the problem, the Finance Minister, Petsche, exploded: he had never been kept informed of these commitments which, because of the financial situation, were completely unrealistic. 'We have gone beyond the limits of what we can afford. It is no use having an army if the country is in debt because of it.' The Defence Minister admitted that it was necessary to keep their efforts within the bounds of what France could afford, and thus to reduce the commitments made in Luxembourg. But the President of the Council, Bidault, thought it was impossible for France to renege on these commitments; they would have to be carried out. The CDN decided that France should therefore ask the USA for financial aid.[54]

The situation remained bogged down until the US government had replied. On the one hand, the Chiefs of Staff, through General Cherrières, demanded a substantial increase in France's spending, since they could not let everything rest on American aid. The United States were on France's side, but they could not fool her for too much longer: 'the Americans will not shut their eyes to our military weakness for ever'. In September 1949, Dean Acheson had declared to French Ambassador Bonnet that France should take the lead in Western Europe at once. If she proved to be incapable of doing this, the United States would choose another partner; there were already several voices in favour of Germany. It was vital to put into effect the commitments made in the WEU up to 1950.[55] On the other hand, Petsche did not agree that the build-up of a modern French army and France's commitments within the WEU and NATO would entail financial sacrifice; he repeated that the currency, the finances and the economy would not stand it.[56] The CDN, which met in March 1950 to solve the matter, came to the conclusion that the way out was to internationalise the costs of joint defence within the Atlantic Alliance; until this happened, the Chiefs of Staff Committee had to review and reduce the Luxembourg programme.[57] As a result of this decision, the Foreign Ministry and the Chiefs of Staff defined the position they were to adopt before the Consultative Council of the Brussels Pact as follows: to postpone the deadline for the 1949 military programmes from the end of 1951 to July 1954, and to request that the Atlantic Alliance organisations supply the essential resources, i.e., that the USA commit herself financially over and above the current military-aid programme.[58]

The problem was made worse for France by the increasing cost of the colonial war in Indochina. From the autumn of 1949 onwards, the French government had drawn the attention of the

United States to this point again and again. In February 1950, the CDN stated that France was in no position to continue her struggle in South-East Asia alone – she had to choose between her commitments in Indochina and the defence of Western Europe. The CDN decided to confront the US Administration with the matter. At the beginning of April, following two meetings between the Foreign and Defence Ministries, priority was given to European rearmament: the Luxembourg plan was to be continued, as long as it was integrated into NATO planning and carried out in stages with the help of the USA. France would pay 50 per cent of the costs, Britain 25 per cent, and the Benelux countries 25 per cent. The French portion would be financed by massive savings on expenditure for Indochina and the 'scraping together' of credits for the defence of Europe; in order to cover the deficit for the Indochina adventure, the United States would be asked for substantial financial assistance. The ministries would make it clear to Washington that rearmament could not be financed by national budgets alone without placing European economic and financial recovery in jeopardy. In accordance with these decisions, Schuman informed Acheson that France would be forced to review her military policy in Europe if US aid for Indochina was not forthcoming.[59]

However, the government was not yet out of the woods. There was a conflict between the Defence and Finance Ministers, on the subject of the financing of the infrastructure (airfields and telecommunications) for the WEU, which required the help of the President of the Council as referee. But the judgement passed by Bidault on 19 June was interpreted differently, and the argument started up once more in the CDN, with the result that President Auriol told Finance Minister Petsche to give ground.[60] Apart from this, the CDN had given the figure of 500 billion francs in 1951 as the additional costs of French participation in European rearmament, and they hoped that the Americans would supply most of this sum; if US aid did not reach this figure, European rearmament would have to be reduced, as the expenditure for Indochina had been cut to the bone. However, the Americans played the waiting game. The French government sent them a note describing the nature and importance of the assistance they had to render in order to allow France to pursue her struggle in Indochina (the financial aid was meant to pay for the assembly of Vietnamese troops so as to free French soldiers for Europe). At the same time the note explained to the Americans that, due to

French military expenditure in Indochina, they had to increase their contribution to the defence of Europe! In order to justify her requests (170 billion francs for French defence in Europe, 100 billion for Indochina), the French government pointed out that they were fighting in South-East Asia for the common interest, that the security of the Union française had to be assured, and that they had to face 'the danger of a substantial fifth column' at home. France's defence spending should not lead to internal instability 'which would facilitate the enemy's plans'.[61]

Despite French persistence ('The French government is faced by an urgent and tragic problem'), the Washington talks of September 1950, conducted by Defence Minister Pleven, did not come to a satisfactory conclusion: the USA cut her aid from the requested 270 billion francs to a credit of seventy billion francs, to be spent before 30 June 1951, and seventy billion more for the second half of 1951. Moreover, in the matter of Indochina, she decided that aid should be in the form of matériel, refusing to render any kind of financial assistance or politico-military commitment. However, following the disaster of Cao Bang in October 1950, and the mission by the Minister for the French Overseas Territories, Letourneau, to survey the situation in Indochina, the matter was judged to be so serious that the government decided to give 'absolute priority' to spending on Indochina: this had to be done whatever the repercussions might be for the assembly of European forces. This turn around in priorities (up to that time the government had given the top slot to the joint defence of Europe, believing that the Indochina campaign could be handled as well) led to protests from the Chiefs of Staff Committee: 'France cannot pull out of Europe, as any security system in Europe can only be built around the French army. But the fact that Indochina has been given top priority will jeopardise our programme in Europe.' In fact the CDN, on 21 October, decided that, due to the part failure of the Washington talks, which modified the financial base upon which the rearmament programme had been established, it was necessary to 'adjust' this programme in order to take this cut in credits into account.[62]

More than ever, the French leadership tended towards seeking the solution to the problem of financing rearmament in the integration of Western European defence within NATO and in the reform of the Atlantic system which they had been demanding for months.

This situation placed the French government in a position of weakness *vis-à-vis* the US administration on the question of German rearmament. Since France had proved incapable of raising the divisions she had promised, how could she oppose the assembly of German divisions, upon which the Americans had only decided after the French failure, which threatened European rearmament? To tell the truth, the idea of recreating German armed forces had been on the table for a long time; the Americans had been hinting at it since the autumn of 1948, and the matter was openly raised during the Paris tripartite conference of November 1949.[63] Although, since the spring of 1948, most of the French military leaders were convinced that German rearmament was not only inevitable but indispensable in order to increase Western Europe's defensive potential,[64] the government was categorically opposed to it and continually warned the US government that such an action would create a dangerous situation in the eyes of the USSR, who would not fail to react; and it would lend more weight to those who argued, in the United States and Britain, that British and American troops be pulled out of the Continent. Finally, it would weaken the organisation of Europe, strengthening opposition in France to a united Europe and Franco-German cooperation.[65]

Meanwhile, American persistence, the problems faced by the French government in fulfilling their military commitments in Europe, as well as the effects of the Korean War, led, in the course of 1950, to a softening of the French position. Although President Auriol remained firmly opposed to any kind of German rearmament, Pleven, Defence Minister and (from July) President of the Council, was no longer against the idea in principle: the recreation of German armed forces was, he said, premature at that time, and it could not occur until French rearmament, and that of Western Europe in general, within NATO, had reached a certain level. For the time being, it was necessary to limit German participation in her own defence to financial contributions towards the costs of joint defence, and also industrial contributions the production of matériel and building an infrastructure on NATO's behalf). This position was taken up by the government and represented in Washington during the exchange of notes between the French and US governments on Western rearmament in July–August 1950; the French emphasised, at the same time, that the limit had been reached, reiterating their reasons for opposing, at that time, the reconstitution of German armed forces.[66] At the end of August, the French government, conscious of their isolation and the growing US pressure, went one step further: they accepted a substantial increase in the west German police force.[67]

On the eve of the Atlantic Council meeting, in September, the French government made their position public, in that they said once again that the rebuilding of the German army was premature. Pleven, in his Strasbourg speech, reminded his audience of the form in which his government would allow a West German participation in Western European defence.[68] It was decided that Robert Schuman and Dean Acheson would have 'a very frank discussion': before integrating German elements into a Western army for the defence of Europe, this army and this Europe had first of all to be created; priority had to be given to rearming the member countries of the Atlantic Alliance, with the aid of the USA, and also to the reform of NATO itself into a Western defence organisation with a solid structure.[69]

The idea of an integrated European armed force, containing German contingents, had, however, never for one moment been envisaged by the French. They placed their trust in a new NATO, with a massive increase in US financial and military commitment, in order to find a way out of the impasse facing Western European rearmament. It was only as a result of the meetings in New York and Washington, in September 1950, where France, due to her isolation, was unable to resist the pressure of the other alliance members on the subject of German rearmament, that the French government decided to come out of her isolation and to agree to the plan for a European army.

Notes

1. Pierre Melandri and Maurice Vaïsse, 'France: From Powerlessness to the Search for Influence', in *Power in Europe? Great Britain, France, Italy and Germany in a Postwar World, 1945–1950,* Josef Becker and Franz Knipping (eds.), Berlin, New York, 1986, pp. 461–72.
2. *Journal Officiel de la République française* (= JO), Débats parlementaires, Assemblée nationale, Meeting of 27.12.1948, Debate on the credit for

the installation of the Western European Union command in Fontainebleau.
3. Maurice Vaïsse, 'L'échec d'une Europe franco-britannique ou comment le pacte de Bruxelles fut crée et délaissé', in *Histoire des débuts de la construction européenne (mars 1948–mai 1950)/ Origins of the European Integration (March 1948–May 1950)*, Actes du Colloque de Strasbourg 28–30 novembre, sous la direction de/ Raymond Poidevin (ed.), Bruxelles, Milano, Paris, Baden-Baden, 1986, pp. 369–89.
4. Service Historique de l'Armée de Terre, Vincennes, decision taken by the National Defence Committee (= CDN), 30.11.1948.
5. Ibid.
6. Ibid., meetings of 30.11.1948 and 20.1.1949. The government was unable even to take delivery of thirty aeroplanes, which Britain was to lend free of charge, because there was no money for spare parts. Archives ministère Relations extèrieures Paris, *Europe 1944–49*, 23, Foreign Ministry (Affaires étrangères = AE) to the British Embassy in Paris, 4.10.1948 (hereafter Europe 1944–49).
7. Vaïsse (see Note 3).
8. *Europe 1944–49* (see Note 6), 23, note from European Directorate, 27.10.1948.
9. CDN (see Note 4), Meeting of 2.8.1949. Auriol and Queuille reported in detail on Montgomery's statements.
10. Ibid., note from EMDN to AE, spring 1948.
11. Ibid., Council of Ministers dated 17.12.1947.
12. Melandri and Vaïsse (see Note 1).
13. CDN (see Note 4), Présidence du Conseil, EMDN, 'Mémoire sur les accords militaires en cours d'élaboration', April 1948.
14. *Europe 1944–49* (see Note 6), 23, notes to Washington and London, 20.5.1948.
15. Ibid., note dated 1.7.1948.
16. Ibid., record of conversation between Schuman and Marshall, 4.10.1948.
17. Ibid., 26, Auriol's speech to the Association of Daily Regional Newspapers, 10.3.; Commentary by the Head of the Information and Press Service at the Quai d'Orsay, 18.3.; Radio speech by R. Schuman, 18.3.; Report by the Information and Press Service, 19.3.: 'Factors which can be of use in the Press' representation of the Atlantic Alliance'; Note concerning the statements made by R. Schuman before representatives of the French and foreign press on 24.3.1948.
18. Archives ministère Relations extérieures, Paris, *Europe 1949–55* (hereafter Europe 1949–55), 17, note dated 23.8.1949.
19. Secrétariat général de la Défense nationale, Service Historique de l'Armée de Terre, Vincennes (hereafter SGDN), French draft directives concerning the military organisation of the Atlantic Alliance,

27.8.1949; France's position had been defined in a note from the Défense nationale dated 2.8.
20. Ibid., French thesis on the military organisation of the Atlantic Alliance, 27.8.1949.
21. Ibid., Definition of the French position regarding the organisation of the Atlantic Alliance, 27.8.1949.
22. Ibid., French draft directives.
23. Meeting of CDN (see Note 4), 29.8.1949.
24. SGDN (see Note 19), note of 28.9.1949.
25. Statement by J. Chauvel, Secretary-General of the Quai d'Orsay, at the meeting of the CDN (see Note 4), 29.9.1949.
26. CDN (see Note 4), Etat-Major Permanent à la Présidence du Conseil, note from General Cherrières, 30.11.1949.
27. Ibid., Report by General Ely to the Defence Minister, 16 March 1950, Note by the Defence Minister for the meeting of the CDN on 24.3.1950.
28. Ibid., Pleven's statement before the CDN, meeting of 17.5.1950.
29. Ibid., letter from Rear-Admiral Laurin, Deputy Chief of Staff of the EMDN, to the Defence Minister, 28.1.1949, 'Re the Brussels Pact and the orientation necessary for the Atlantic Alliance so that the insufficiencies and gaps in our defensive system can be closed', letter approved by the Chiefs of Staff Committee. See also *Europe 1944–49* (Note 6), 25, General Mast, Chief of the Institut des Hautes Etudes de la Défense nationale (= IHEDN), to Ramadier, 5.3.1949, 'Concluding study concerning the Atlantic Alliance'.
30. SGDN (see Note 19), French study on the military organisation of the Atlantic Alliance, 27.8.1949.
31. Ibid., French draft directive concerning the military organisation of the Atlantic Alliance, 27.8.1949.
32. Queuille's statement before the CDN (Note 4), meeting of 29.8.1949.
33. SGDN, (see Note 19), French draft directive, and meeting of CDN (see Note 4), 29.8.1949, 'France's position on NATO'.
34. Pleven's statement before the CDN (see Note 4), meeting of 24.3.1950.
35. Archives Secrétariat général du ministère des Affaires étrangères, Paris, Quai d'Orsay (hereafter SG), 4, Deputy Director Political Affairs, note to Minister, 10.4.1950.
36. Letter from SGDN (see Note 19), for the CDN (see Note 4), meeting of 16.12.1950.
37. Letter from Rear-Admiral Laurin, Deputy Chief of General Staff of the EMDN, to the Defence Minister, 28 January 1949, letter approved by the Chiefs of Staff Committee. Note by SGDN (see Note 19), 28.9.1949.
38. Ibid., note of 27.8.1949, and French draft directives.
39. CDN (see Note 4), meeting of 29.8.1949, 'France's attitude to NATO'.

40. Here and the following, ibid., note of 28.9.1949.
41. *Europe 1949–55* (see Note 18), chargé d'affaires in London at the European directorate, 2.9.1950.
42. SGDN (see Note 19), note of 27.8.1949; meeting of CDN (see Note 4), of 29.9.1949; Europe 1949–55 (see Note 18), 15, London 22.4.1950.
43. Chief of General Staff, SG (see Note 35), 4, Note by the Service de Cooperation Economique, 16.3.1950.
44. Ibid., Note by Alphand, 21.3.1950.
45. Ibid., note from General Cherrières to Pleven, 22.3.1950.
46. Ibid., notes by Alphand, 21.2., 10.3., 11.4.1950.
47. Ibid., letter from General Cherrières to Parodi, 27.3.1950, with the note for Pleven of 22.3. as an enclosure.
48. Ibid., note from the Political Department to the Minister, 10.4.1950.
49. General directives for the French representatives in the Atlantic Council, 23.7.1950.
50. SG (see Note 35), 4, US memorandum dated 23.7.1950 and minutes of conversation between Alphand and Spofford in London, 27.7.1950.
51. Ibid., Draft of 1.8. and French memorandum of 5.8.1950.
52. Ibid., AE to the embassy in Washington, 11.8.1950, French memorandum of 17.8.1950.
53. SGDN (see Note 19), note of 20.10.1950, 'Reorganisation of the Atlantic Alliance', meeting of CDN (see Note 4) of 16.12.1950.
54. Meeting of CDN (see Note 4), 28.11.1949. SG (see Note 35), 3, note from Alphand to the President, 21.3.1950, in which the main points of the problem are reiterated.
55. CDN (see Note 4), note by General Cherrières, 30.11.1949, 'Re the necessity of taking effective measures in 1950 to strengthen our national defence and the insufficient nature of the funds allocated to this purpose'.
56. SG (see Note 35), 4, note from the 'Service de coopération économique', 16.3.1950.
57. CDN (see Note 4), meeting of 24.3.1950, 'France's military commitment within the Brussels Pact'.
58. SG (see Note 35), 4, notes to Alphand, 1. and 5.4.1950.
59. CDN (see Note 4), meeting of 29.9.1949 and ditto of 17.2.1950, 'Assessment of the military situation in Indochina in the framework of the defence of the Union française and global strategy'. SG (see Note 35), 4, minutes of meeting of Quai d'Orsay, 7.4., notes from H. Alphand of 8. and 11.4., note to the Minister, 12.4., note to the President, 13.4.1950. SG, 8, minutes of meeting between Schuman and Acheson in London on 8.5.1950.
60. SG (see Note 35), 4, note by the European Directorate to Schuman, 5.6.1950, CDN (see Note 4), meeting of 22.6.1950.
61. CDN (see Note 4), Défense nationale (DN) to AE, 1.7.1950, Chairman of the Chiefs of Staff Committee to DN, 12.8.; CDN (see Note 4),

meeting of 18.8. and 2.10.1950. SG (see Note 35), 'General directives for the French representative in the Atlantic Council', 23.7.1950; meeting between Alphand and Spofford in London, 27.7.; draft reply to US government, 1.8.; French memorandum dated 5. and 17.8. Note to the President, 7.9.1950.
62. SGDN (see Note 19), note dated 20.10.1950, meeting of CDN (see Note 4), on 21.10., note by Chiefs of Staff Committee, 3.12.1950.
63. *Europe 1944–49* (see Note 6), Allemagne 21, telegram by Seydoux dated 15.10.1948, AE to Bonnet, 16.12.1948. SG (see Note 35), 2, note by European Directorate, 18.11.1949.
64. Pierre Guillen, Die französische Generalität, die Aufrüstung der Bundesrepublik und die EVG (1950–1954), in: *Die Europäische Verteidigungsgemeinschaft. Stand und Probleme der Forschung.* Hrsg. im Auftrag des Militärgeschichtlichen Forschungsamtes von Hans-Erich Volkmann und Walter Schwengler. Mit Beiträgen von Alfredo Breccia, Anselm Doering-Manteuffel, Alexander Fischer, Pierre Guillen, Peter Jones, Albert E. Kersten, Walter Lipgens, Klaus A. Maier, Wilhelm Meier-Dörnberg, Paul Noack, Raymond Poidevin, Jean-Pierre Rioux, Hans-Erich Volkmann, Donald Cameron Watt und Werner Weidenfeld, Boppard am Rhein, 1985 (*Militärgeschichte seit 1945*, Bd 7).
65. *Europe 1944–49* (see Note 6), Allemagne 21, AE to Bonnet, 16.12.1948. SG (see Note 35), 2, Note from the European Directorate, 18.11.1949.
66. CDN (see Note 4), meeting of 24.3. and 17.5.1950. SG (see Note 35), 2, Note from the European Directorate, 18.4.1950, telegram Subdept. Central Europe: in Washington and London dated 9.8.; telegram from Bonnet of 16.8.1950. SG, 4, Draft of an answer to the US government dated 1.8.1950, telegram from Washington of 19.8. (conversation between Harriman and Bonnet on German rearmament).
67. SG (see Note 35), 2, European Directorate to Bonn, 23.8.1950, Washington, 23.8. (conversation between Dean Acheson and Bonnet).
68. *Europe 1949–55* (see Note 18), Pleven's speech in Strasbourg on 2.9.1950 and Schuman's press conference on 6.9.
69. SG (see Note 35), 4, Note to Chairman (Schuman) dated 19.9.1950. SG, 2, Pol. Dept. to the embassies in the capitals of the Atlantic Alliance members, 9.10.1950.

8
The British Labour Government and the Atlantic Alliance, 1949–1951*

Geoffrey Warner

Introduction

Historians of British policy towards the Atlantic Alliance labour under considerable difficulties where source material is concerned. Although the British government normally applies a 'thirty-year-rule' for access to official papers, this most emphatically does not apply in respect of NATO. Documents emanating from NATO itself are under the control of the alliance and the consent of all member governments is apparently required before any can be released. This is bad enough, but the position has been made considerably worse by the fact that, presumably on grounds of economy, the British government has not felt able to 'weed out' NATO documents from its own files, with the result that the principal Foreign Office, Treasury and Ministry of Defence files dealing with the alliance have not yet been transferred to the Public Record Office and are therefore not available for research. One must perforce piece the story together from other sources, notably the records of the Prime Minister's and the Cabinet Office. Not only are these records incomplete in themselves; they are also being made available only gradually. It is for this reason that the present chapter deals only with the Labour government and concentrates upon broad issues rather than detailed analysis.

Geoffrey Warner

The Basis of the Labour Government's Policy towards NATO

Before examining the major problems of alliance policy during the period in question, it is important to look at some of the underlying assumptions of British policy-makers. In February 1949 the Foreign Secretary, Ernest Bevin, authorised the establishment of a Permanent Under-Secretary's Committee in the Foreign Office 'to consider long-term questions of foreign policy'.[1] This committee produced a steady stream of papers on all sorts of questions which are invaluable in elucidating the principles which guided the Foreign Office, and not infrequently the government as a whole, in formulating its policy.

Particularly interesting from our point of view are PUSC 22, originally drafted in May 1949 under the title 'A Third World Power of Western Consolidation?' but submitted to the Cabinet in October as the more concise 'European Policy'; PUSC (50) 9 of April 1950 on 'Western Organisation'; and PUSC 51, also of April 1950, on 'Anglo-American Relations: Present and Future'. Between them these papers provide a detailed and revealing statement of the Foreign Office's view of the Atlantic Alliance.

The main purpose of PUSC 22 was to throw cold water upon any suggestion that Western Europe, with or without the support of the Commonwealth, could form a 'Third Force', independent of both the United States and the Soviet Union in world affairs. 'The conclusion seems inescapable,' a key paragraph declared, 'that for the present at any rate the closest association with the United States is essential, not only for the purpose of standing up to Soviet aggression but also in the interests of Commonwealth solidarity and of European unity.'[2] This led, in PUSC (50) 9, to a heavy emphasis upon the importance of NATO:

> The advantages of building on the North Atlantic Treaty are considerable: (a) It is the most spectacular achievement of Western diplomacy since the war and is therefore attractive to public opinion; (b) It has behind it the compulsive force of unity for collective self-defence and is therefore unlikely to wither away in the chill winds of political disagreement; (c) Since it includes both the United States of America and Canada, as well as Western Europe it reflects in itself all the three main aspects of British foreign relations; (d) It is the most satisfactory vehicle for a further positive gesture by the United States Government ... ; (e) The present dependence of most nations of

Western Europe on United States military and economic assistance gives strength to the links binding the Atlantic community together; (f) Problems are most likely to be fully considered in a world-wide context by the North Atlantic Treaty Organisation than by any purely European body; and it is in the interest of the United Kingdom that they should be so considered; (g) It provides a grouping for the nations of Western Europe which is free from the disadvantages inherent in the non-governmental character of the Council of Europe; (h) It might provide an ante-chamber for Germany's entry, in a non-military capacity, into the Atlantic community, of which the Federal Republic might eventually become a member.[3]

PUSC 51 was generally optimistic concerning Anglo-American relations, arguing 'that there need be no fundamental conflict on interests between the USA and the United Kingdom in any part of the world, provided that the United Kingdom can achieve a position, closely related to the USA, and yet sufficiently independent of her, to be able to influence American policy in the directions desired'. In order to do this, however, Britain had to retain its strength. 'Americans do not hesitate to scrap ruthlessly something which is not working well,' the paper warned, 'whether it be an automobile or a policy, and to try a new model'. Possible 'new models' were a retreat into isolationism, an accommodation with the Soviet Union, or reliance upon West Germany or France as America's principal ally. All were considered inimical to British interests. 'The interests of the United Kingdom therefore demand,' PUSC 51 concluded, 'that her present policy of close Anglo-American co-operation in world affairs should continue. Such co-operation will involve a sustained political military and economic effort.'[4]

Consideration of relations with the United States, of course, reinforced British support for NATO. As Bevin told the Cabinet in a report on the fourth session of the North Atlantic Council in May 1950:

[t]he general attitude of the Americans throughout the Conference showed that they are determined to make a reality of the North Atlantic Treaty and that increasingly they regard it as the focus for the further development of the Western world. For us this means that our future relations with the United States will largely be determined by the success of our collaboration in the Atlantic Treaty. Since it is the kernel of their policy, it must also be the kernel of ours.[5]

This bundle of attitudes and assumptions led to an exaggerated 'Atlanticism' in British policy. One form it took was profound suspicion of anything which appeared to threaten the idea of an Atlantic community, particularly schemes like the Schuman Plan or the European Army, which looked towards a European federation. Since France was responsible for both these initatives, moreover, the French came to be regarded as the main threat to 'Atlantic' ideals. Reflecting on the tripartite talks which preceded the North Atlantic Council in May 1950, Bevin's second-in-command at the Foreign Office, the Minister of State Kenneth Younger, noted in his diary that '[w]e and the Americans want to start building up an Atlantic Community which includes and transcends Western Europe, while the French still hanker after a European solution in which the only American function is to produce military and other aid. This difference is important because it stems from two quite different conceptions.'[6]

Another form of British 'Atlanticism' was the assumption of a superior attitude towards the other European members of the alliance. British spokesmen at NATO meetings sometimes acted like prefects at a public school, chiding unruly junior pupils for failing to heed the wishes of the American headmaster. A classic example was the intervention of the Minister of Defence, A.V. Alexander, at the first meeting of the North Atlantic Defence Committee in Washington in October 1949. As he subsequently reported to his colleagues on the Cabinet's Defence Committee in the meeting on 5 October:

> it was noticeable that many of the comments which were made by the smaller Powers were concerned with prestige points and that there is a strong desire on the part of the smaller countries to secure recognition for their equality of status with ourselves, France and the United States ... I thought it would be of some advantage to remind the Committee that the purpose of our meeting was to forge an effective and efficient instrument for our common defence, and to warn against the danger in which the democracies tend to stand of being so concerned to ensure that all voices are heard at all times as to place us at a notable military disadvantage as compared with the authoritarian States. I think this did some good; ....[7]

Such behaviour was, of course, merely a reflection of the British government's determination to present itself as the most reliable ally of the United States. On a number of occasions, indeed, the British adopted policies at American behest about which they were not entirely happy and then became *plus royaliste que le roi* in urging them upon the rest of the alliance.

Anything that was seen as a threat to Britain's position as the indispensable right arm of the United States in NATO affairs was strenuously resisted. One illustration of this was the reaction to a seemingly innocent American suggestion in early 1951 that the headquarters of the alliance should be moved from London to Paris. The interdepartmental committee of officials which dealt with NATO matters, the Atlantic (Official) Committee, was fertile in objections to the transfer: '...the location of NATO in Paris would reinforce the concept of a European community against the concept, which we supported, of an Atlantic community ...'; Anglo/ United States cooperation, on which the whole success of the North Atlantic Treaty depended, would be achieved with much greater difficulty if NATO were located in Paris '... there was no doubt whatever that if NATO were located in Paris Communist penetration must be expected...'; '...this was some four months before the defection of Burgess and Maclean) ... 'the removal would lead to a lessening of United Kingdom influence in NATO affairs ...' Ministers were in complete agreement with officials. 'London was the natural location for NATO,' it was stated at a meeting of the Defence Committee. 'It was the link between the Continent of Europe on the one hand and the Continent of North America on the other, and it was the natural focal point for the association of the Commonwealth with NATO.' The general feeling of the meeting was 'that the American proposal should be strongly resisted....'[8]

It is not the intention of the present chapter to discuss whether or not the basic assumptions which underlay British policy towards the Atlantic Alliance between 1949 and 1951 were correct. For one thing, this would require an assessment of Soviet intentions which the author is not competent to undertake. What it will attempt to show, however, is that on the two major issues which confronted the alliance during this period – German rearmament and defence expenditure – these assumptions gave rise to policies which divided the government, split the Labour Party for several years, and imposed unacceptably heavy strains upon the British economy.

German Rearmament

Approval by the North Atlantic Defence Committee of the so-called 'Strategic Concept' for Atlantic defence in December 1949 and of the Medium Term Defence Plan in April 1950 inevitably stimulated discussions of the role of West Germany in allied strategy, even before the outbreak of the Korean War. The Foreign Office view, expressed in a PUSC paper of 19 April 1950 on 'The Future of Germany', was that 'Germany should remain disarmed.' The Prime Minister, Clement Attlee, did not believe that this was feasible. 'I think it unlikely that Germany will settle down without some armed forces,' he wrote to Bevin on 2 May. 'One must consider the tradition of the German state.'[9] The Chiefs of Staff went even further in their review of defence policy and global strategy later in the month. They argued that unless West Germany became an integral part of the West, both politically and militarily, she would become an integral part of the East. The military vacuum between the Rhine and the Elbe could not last and a strategy based upon the defence of the former would inevitably lead the West Germans to conclude that, since they were to be abandoned by the West in the event of a war, they had better reinsure with the East. The Chiefs of Staff recommended that the ultimate aim should be the formation of a German contingent within the forces of Western Europe, a conclusion with which Bevin was said to have agreed.[10]

It was also felt that the rest of Western Europe could not be defended without German help. 'A defence of Western Europe based mainly upon France and Britain would be very shaky,' wrote Kenneth Younger in July 1950, since French morale was even lower than it had been in 1940. What was needed was 'a large and immediate contribution from the United States or Germany or both'. The Americans seemed unlikely to send large ground forces to Europe, however, especially in view of their commitments in the Far East. This left Germany, and it was Younger's view that 'her rearmament seems essential if Western defence is to be real'. Not only 'might (it) then be possible to defend the Elbe instead of the Rhine, with great effect upon the morale of the Low Countries and France' but 'it would (also) make available efficient manpower on a significant scale'.[11]

At the same time, the question was one of acute political sensitivity. Even after the Korean war had left the Chiefs of Staff to throw all caution to the winds to advocate in August 1950 the formation over the next five years of a West German army of twenty divisions (plus ten in reserve), an air force of 2,100 planes, and some naval units to boot, the most Bevin felt able to put before the Defence Committee and the Cabinet was the suggestion that there should be established a 100,000-strong gendarmerie in West Germany, together with another 3,000 in West Berlin, to match the *Bereitschaften* in the Soviet zone. In the Cabinet, moreover, Bevin chose to link this proposal, in typical 'Atlanticist' fashion, with American policy, explaining to his colleagues that the United States now favoured the creation of an integrated defence force in Europe under unified command and that if this force – which might include a German contingent – were formed, the Americans would be prepared to increase the strength of their own forces in Europe. The more ambitious proposals of the Chiefs of Staff never reached the Cabinet. They were countered in the Defence Committee by reference to French susceptibilities, the opposition of the SPD within Germany itself, and the danger of provoking a Russian reaction. No one seems to have raised an equally fundamental objection – that German rearmament would split the government and the Labour Party wide open – but all were no doubt aware of its existence.[12]

When the British, French and American foreign ministers met in New York prior to the September meeting of the North Atlantic Council, however, it soon became clear that the formation of a West German gendarmerie was not enough to satisfy the Americans. They wanted the constitution of regular military units, although they did not specify the number or the period during which they should be formed. Following a serious of frantic telegrams, Bevin obtained the Cabinet's 'general agreement to an acceptance in principle of German participation in Western defence', although it is obvious, even from the typically circumspect Cabinet minutes, that there was a great deal of opposition to the idea.[13]

The issue was muddied still further, moreover, when the French, who had refused to accept even the principle of German rearmament, came forward in October 1950 with the Pleven Plan for a European Army as their solution to the dilemma in which they had been placed by the American demand for German participation in Western European defence. Although divided themselves, British ministers seemed quite unable to appreciate the difficulties experienced by the French. 'The French attitude left the whole western world in doubt and anxiety,' Attlee exclaimed at a meeting of the Defence Committee on 8 November 1950. 'Were the French in fact intending to fight, or had they already made up their minds to give in?'[14] Bevin had his own explanation for the French attitude. 'Present French policy is, I believe, at bottom antipathetic towards NATO and the Americans,' he stated in a paper for the Defence Committee on 24 November. 'The proposal for a European Army is only one of many aspects of this covert antipathy ... If we are even to break down this antipathy and to make the French good members of NATO, we cannot afford to allow the European federal concept to gain a foothold within NATO and thus weaken instead of strengthening the ties between the countries on the two sides of the Atlantic. We must nip it in the bud.' The Foreign Secretary's bizarre alternative to the European Army – an Atlantic Federal Force – was not surprisingly rejected by his colleagues, who had objected to the French proposal in part precisely because of its federal implications, but no one questioned his interpretation of French motives.[15]

Castigating the French did not, however, resolve the British government's own divisions. Kenneth Younger recorded in his diary on 4 February 1951:

> The whole subject is in an unholy muddle – largely, I think, through Ernie [Bevin]'s fault. He has wavered from one view to another on German rearmament, first trying to delay it, then joining the Americans in bullying the French for greater speed, then having cold feet about it and vainly thinking of going back. The whole thing has been quite inadequately explained to the Cabinet from time to time with the result that they are now shocked to find how far they have been committed. The Americans, on the other hand, who have been pushing ahead in their usual bullheaded manner have not really given any reason to think that we are still half-hearted and anxious for delay – which is clearly the actual position of the Cabinet at the moment. The French, having been subjected to great pressure not only by [the] US but by us too, now seem to have given up the fight and to be, if anything, more resigned than we are to a fairly rapid start to German rearmament. If therefore the Cabinet, worried by the undoubted reluctance of the Labour Party to accept the policy, now want to change the pace or alter the direction I foresee great difficulty and pretty well justified annoyance on the American side and even, perhaps, the French.[16]

A temporary respite was provided by the newly appointed NATO Supreme Commander, General Eisenhower. As Younger noted on 25 February 1951, the important debate in the House of Commons on the 12th 'went off fairly smoothly' as far as German rearmament was concerned. 'We owed that,' he explained, 'as much as anything to Eisenhower, who ended a tour of Europe by making a speech in which he appeared almost uninterested in German forces and put all his emphasis upon the prior build up of the other western countries.[17] As that coincides exactly with our view here, we were able to take the same line which allayed the fears of all sides – both those (mainly Labour) who hate all idea of a German army, and those (mainly Tory) who feared that we were going to try and wriggle out of our earlier commitment...?' Attlee told the House of Commons:

> We have accepted the need for a contribution from Germany, but the time, method and conditions will require a great deal of working out. There is, first of all, the provisions of arms. Obviously, the rearmament of the countries of the Atlantic Treaty must precede that of Germany. Second, I think the building up of forces in the democratic States should precede the creation of German forces. Third, the arrangement must be such that German units are integrated in the defence forces in a way which would preclude the emergence again of a German military menace. Fourth, there must be agreement with the Germans themselves.[18]

By July 1951, however, the situation had evolved in a number of important respects. First, the Americans, who if anything had been even more hostile to the European Army than the British when the idea had first been mooted, had now come out in favour of it. Second, the Four-Power talks in Paris in the spring of 1951, which had offered some slender hope of a trade-off between German rearmament and Soviet concessions in other fields, had broken down. Finally, the West Germans themselves seemed to be becoming more accustomed to, and indeed more enthusiastic about, the idea of their rearmament, provided that they were treated on a basis of complete equality with other contributors to the Western European defence force. The time had clearly come, as Herbert Morrison, who had taken over from the ailing Bevin as Foreign Secretary the previous March, told the Defence Committee on 26 July 1951, when the government had to take a further decision on the matter.

Lengthy debates in the Defence Committee, and in the Cabinet itself four days later, only revealed the continuing division within the government. The Secretary of State for War, John Strachey, told the Defence Committee that:

> [t]he military advice which had been given to him had always emphasized that German rearmament would be a provocation to the Soviet Union and that, as a result of it, the risks of war would grow greater. In fact, he had been told that because of his increased risk it would be necessary in 1952 to undertake a partial mobilization. He accepted that opinion, but he thought that it was essential that we should first create an effective shield of ourselves and our Allies, and that we should not take any open practical action with regard to the Germans which might provoke the Soviet Union into a preventive war during the next two years, when we should be far from ready.[19]

Another strong opponent of German rearmament was Hugh Dalton, whose post as Minister of Local Government and Planning belied his stature in both the government and the Labour Party. He told the Cabinet that, although it had accepted the principle of a German contribution to Western defence, 'he believed that several of his colleagues had shared his reluctance to see Germany rearmed'. He felt that the German attitude was quite different from that of the NATO partners. 'Whereas we were rearming in self-defence, the Germans were capable of rearming for purposes of aggression, and many of them would have a positive interest in provoking war with Russia to recover their lost homes ... The Germans were not a peace-loving or trustworthy people and he himself would not like to see a German army in being, even if it formed part of a European Army.' For these and other reasons:

> He was ... in favour of delaying as long as possible any actual rearming of Germany. We should not bring pressure on the French to speed up German rearmament and we should certainly not agree to the organisation of any German units outside the European Army, where at least there would be some chance of preventing the growth of a dominant German General Staff. Planning and preparations could go forward, but we should delay the provocative step of putting arms into the hands of the Germans.[20]

On the day after the Cabinet meeting, Dalton wrote to the Prime Minister to complain that the minutes did not include the statement in the latter's summing up, to which Dalton and others attached great importance, 'that you should wish this whole thing to be played very slow'. Apart from the interesting footnote that it provides to the accuracy of the Cabinet minutes, Dalton's minute gives a very rare glimpse of the precise division of opinion within the Cabinet, which the minutes never do. 'You will recall.' Dalton wrote, 'that a number of the Ministers who spoke, including the Chancellor of the Duchy [Lord Alexander], the Colonial Secretary [James Griffiths], the Secretary of State for Scotland [Hector McNeil], and the Secretary of State of War [John Strachey], were very definitely of the same opinion, on this point, as you and I. The Minister of Labour [Alfred Robens] also told me afterwards that, though he had not spoken, he shared our view.' Attlee did not deny the existence of this small but by no means unimportant bloc. He merely commented that he thought 'the second sentence of my summing up safeguards your point'. This read: 'He [the Foreign Secretary] would doubtless consult the Cabinet before agreeing to any proposal involving the early implementation of the principle of German rearmament.'[21]

Dalton's reference in Cabinet to the possibility of preventing the rise of a dominant German General Staff shows how this much-maligned French proposal was coming to be seen as a way out of the impasse for precisely the same reason which MM. Monnet and Pleven had originally proposed it: not to subvert the 'Atlantic Community', but to make the bitter pill of German rearmament more palatable. On 4 September 1951 the Cabinet endorsed the Prime Minister's proposal that the Foreign Secretary should express support for the European Army in his forthcoming meeting with the American and French foreign ministers. This lay behind the statement which Morrison, Acheson and Schuman issued in Washington on 14 September 1951 and which welcomed the plan for a European Army 'as a very important contribution to the effective defence of Europe, including Germany'.[22]

Defeat in the general election of 25 October 1951 deprived the Labour government of any further responsiblity for representing Britain in the negotiations over German rearmament. It was probably as well, for the Labour Party's conduct in opposition showed that it remained bitterly divided on the issue.

Defence Expenditure

Divisive through it was, the question of German rearmament did not precipitate any resignations from the Labour government. The second of the two major issues which confronted the Atlantic Alliance during this period, defence expenditure, brought about precisely that.

In the same way that acceptance of the Medium Term Defence Plan, with its proposals for a massive expansion of Western Europe's defences, made a discussion of German rearmament inevitable, so it also raised the question of increased defence expenditure. Indeed, at the meeting of the North Atlantic Defence Committee on 1 April 1950 which approved the plan, the Norwegian defence minister 'drew attention to the economic implications of the acceptance of the plan and reminded the Committee that substantially increased military budgets would endanger economic recovery, which was admitted to be fundamental to the military strength of the countries concerned'. His British counterpart, Emmanuel Shinwell, responded with one of those characteristically prefectoral interventions to which reference has already been made:

> Obviously a target was required, and that had been given to us by our Military Committee. But it was no good proceeding to a meeting with Finance and Foreign Ministers without a great deal more preparatory work than had so far been done. While we must avoid a position in which the separate bodies established by the North Atlantic Treaty Organization operated in water-tight compartments, it was no less important to avoid 'passing the buck'. It was our job as Defence Ministers to face the position realistically and to state the requirements, not be deterred or over-awed by the apparently astronomical requirements submitted by our military advisers.

The Committee went on to invite the Defence Financial and Economic Committee of NATO 'to recognize the additional finance which would be required to meet the requirements of the Medium Term Plan over and above anything envisaged in the current defence budgets and to get down to a study of how such additional expenditure could be borne'.[23]

This recommendation infuriated the Chancellor of the Exchequer, Sir Stafford Cripps, who told the Cabinet's Defence Committee on 10 May 1950 that 'he did not regard himself as committed to the provision of any extra finance for Atlantic Treaty Defence'. Caution was also displayed by Bevin at the meeting of the North Atlantic Council later in the month when he explained that he 'could not at present accept any modification of the general principle that economic recovery enjoyed priority over defence requirements'. Other ministers shared his view and the relevant resolution was accordingly worded in non-committal terms. The fact remained, however, as Kenneth Younger pointed out in July, that 'the present Western Defence budgets are clearly inadequate if we are to reach our targets for 1954 or 1957. The deficiencies are large and increasing, and it seems clear that only a major alteration of priorities as between "guns and butter" could fill the gap.'[24]

The post-Korea panic prompted the Americans to confront their European allies with a specific demand for action, just as they were to confront them in the case of German rearmament two months later. Informing NATO members of its own plans for an increased effort in the field of defence, the United States asked them to provide, by 5 August, the 'firmest possible statement ... of (the) nature and extent of (the) increased effort, in terms of increases in both forces and military production, they propose to undertake'.[25]

Cripps tabled the British government's proposed reply for discussion by the Cabinet on 1 August 1950. Existing plans involved expenditure totalling £2,590 million over the three years 1951/52–1953/54, and Cripps proposed to increase this to £3,400 million. Since it was felt that an annual outlay of £950 million was the most that could be afforded 'on general economic grounds', he intended to ask the United States for assistance in plugging the gap between three years' expenditure at this level and the full cost of the expanded programme, or £550 million.[26]

In view of what happened later, it is interesting to note that the main objection to Cripps' proposals came from the Minister of Health, Aneurin Bevan. 'Our foreign policy,' he told his Cabinet colleagues, 'had hitherto been based on the view that the best method of defence against Russian imperialism was to improve the social and economic conditions of the countries threatened by Communist encroachment. The United States Government seemed now to be abandoning this social and political defence in favour of a military defence. He believed that this policy was misjudged, and that we should be ill-advised to follow it.' Although

Britain might be able to support the additional defence burden without 'fatal damage to its economic and social structure', he doubted whether this was true of France and some other European allies, while even in Britain the social services might have to be cut. Other ministers, however, felt that 'the great danger was that these proposals might appear, to the United States Government and to public opinion on both sides of the Atlantic, to take insufficient account of the danger of the present international situation ... The fact was that our forces were insufficiently equipped to meet the dangers with which we now were faced. It was abundantly clear that we must spend substantially more on defence if we were to play our full part under the North Atlantic Treaty.' Mr Bevan's anxieties were overruled and the Chancellor's proposals accepted.[27]

In accepting them, everyone of course assumed that the United States would provide the £550 million required of it. After all, had not the Americans expressed a willingness 'to give (their allies) further assistance to help them to make their maximum contribution to the common defence'?[28] It soon became clear, however, that British and American views did not coincide in this matter. Summing up bilateral discussions between the two countries on 6 September 1950, a Treasury official reported that not only did the Americans regard the £3,400 million programme – in common with those of all the other NATO countries – as insufficient, but also that the £550 million for which the British had asked went 'far beyond' anything they had contemplated.[29]

In October 1950 – by which time the cost of the defence programme had risen to £3,600 million as the result of a particularly generous increase in pay for the armed services – Bevin and the new Chancellor of the Exchequer, Hugh Gaitskell, proposed that the negotiations for the greater portion of American aid should be transferred to a multilateral basis within the framework of the so-called 'Nitze Exercise'. This was a scheme in which all the NATO countries would work out an equitable procedure for sharing defence expenditure within the context of the alliance. Direct assistance on the lines of the European Recovery Programme, they argued, could lead Britain to forfeit its growing economic independence and lose the position it was just regaining as the principal partner of the United States in world affairs.

We shall be back again in the European queue, and our loss of power and influence will reflect itself in many ways. It will be more difficult to hold the Commonwealth together. Our position in Europe will be weakened. In the many negotiations and arrangements to be made in the months ahead we shall find that we are treated not as partners, though of unequal power, but as just another necessitous European nation. In general, the preservation of good relations between ourselves and the United States would become increasingly difficult.

At the same time, Bevin and Gaitskell warned that acceptance of the 'Nitze Exercise' involved 'financial and economic risks as well as advantages'. In particular, it was predicated upon acceptance of the Medium Term Defence Plan, which would require 'a military effort for the United Kingdom far in excess of our £3,600 million programme' (the estimate was £6,000 million) and it was thus 'essential for us to establish that any plan for multilateral distribution provides that the shares allotted to each country are not only equitable but also tolerable, and that this may involve a revision of total defence requirements as well as their distribution'.[30]

Given the mood in the United States, there was not much likelihood that this would happen. Indeed, during Attlee's visit to Washington in December 1950, he was put under considerable pressure to increase British defence expenditure still further. At a private meeting on 7 December, Averell Harriman, the President's senior adviser on aid to Europe, told him that:

> [w]hile in July an effort of £3,600 million including American help was perhaps a reasonable contribution by the United Kingdom, he felt sure that it would be considered inadequate in the present situation. This he thought might make the American people – already somewhat disillusioned about the prospects of NATO in view of the difficulties with the French over Germany – be inclined to withdraw. He wished therefore to put forward a strong plea for a substantially increased defence programme in the United Kingdom.[31]

There were those in London who agreed with Mr Harriman. Referring to Chinese intervention in Korea, the threat from the *Bereitschaften* in East Germany, and a possible Soviet or satellite attack upon Yugoslavia, the Minister of Defence told the Chiefs of Staff on 13 December 'that it was quite clear to him that we had got to increase the tempo of our defence preparations'. The

Chiefs of Staff were invited 'to prepare a statement setting out the present position and pointing out what they considered to be the threat in 1951. From this it could be deduced that all possible steps short of general mobilisation should be taken to increase our defence preparedness.' It seems that the Chiefs were reluctant to do this until they had the opportunity of discussing the situation with the Chief of the Imperial General Staff, Field Marshal Sir William Slim, who had accompanied the Prime Minister on his visit to Washington. Slim told his colleagues on 14 December, however, 'that he was in general agreement with the view that recent events had increased the danger that a world war might break out in 1951'. Furthermore, said Slim, '[t]he United States were convinced that war was inevitable, and that it was almost certain to take place within the next eighteen months....'[32]

Another threat of American pressure – although this time one which did not in fact materialise – precipitated a decision on the part of the British government. On the basis of an inaccurate report that the American Secretary of State, Mr Acheson, intended to ask the European members of NATO at the alliance's Council meeting then taking place in Brussels to double their pre-Korean rate of defence expenditure, the Prime Minister asked the Cabinet on 18 December to authorise the Foreign Secretary to say that the British government had decided to increase and accelerate its defence preparations still further and to invite the Chiefs of Staff to work out the details. 'In there talks in Washington,' Attlee explained, he 'had persuaded the Americans to accept Anglo-American partnership as the mainspring of Atlantic defence. Much of the advantage we had gained would be lost if we were not to be treated as merely one of the European countries which were being urged by America to make a larger contribution to the common defence effort. We should align ourselves with the Americans in urging the others to do more.' Although there was clearly some disquiet, the Cabinet accepted the Prime Minister's proposals.[33]

When the details were worked out in the New Year, they involved increasing the £3,600 million programme to one of £4,700 million. Commenting on the economic implications of the proposals, the Chancellor of the Exchequer did not disguise their seriousness. In a memorandum for his Cabinet colleagues he wrote:

The general character of the prospect which faces us may ... be summarised as follows. Total expenditure on defence, civil defence and stockpiling will be rising from £865 million in 1950/51 to nearly £1,900 million in 1953/54. Within this total expenditure, we have to increase production for defence by about £250 million in 1951/52, and by a further £250 million in 1952/53. At the same time, to pay our way abroad, we must raise total exports by some £100 million (at present prices) within two years, with little or no help from the industries contributing most to the recent expansion and in the face of a certain decline in exports of some classes of goods. Meanwhile, raw material shortages and the disturbance of output caused by transfer of resources from civilian to military work, are bound to limit the expansion of industrial output. It would not be safe to count on a rate of increase of manufacturing output of more than say 4 per cent a year ... which would add some £225 million a year (at present prices) to total output of manufactured goods. Consequently, for the first time since the war we must face a reduction in the standard of living (apart from food ...), in the rate at which industry is re-equipped with plant and machinery for civil production, and in the amount of building for civil needs.

At the same time, due to the worsening terms of trade, 'we shall have to struggle hard to achieve a balance of payments position which, at best, will be precarious and vulnerable and if not quickly improved on will lead to serious cumulative strains in our external financial relations'. A few paragraphs later, he warned that while colleagues would not expect him to deal with budgetary matters, 'there is no doubt that we shall be faced with some exceedingly painful decisions in this field.'[34]

Although the Cabinet minutes do not indicate that there was any serious opposition to the proposals when they were discussed at two meetings on 25 January 1951,[35] the budgetary time-bomb which Gaitskell had referred to exploded two months later. On 22 March the Cabinet discussed a proposal by the Chancellor to place a ceiling of £400 million on expenditure on the National Health Service. This would involve charging patients for false teeth and spectacles, which had hitherto been provided free of charge. The two points of view were summed up by Bevan, the architect of the National Health Service, although now Minister of Labour, and Shinwell, the Minister of Defence. The reason for the Health Service charges, said Bevan, 'was the cost of the increased defence programme; and if the Chancellor of the

Exchequer was not prepared to accept a tolerance of a few million in his budgeting, he should meet his difficulties by reducing defence expenditure. Shortage of raw materials would in any event make it impossible to spend wisely the amount now allocated for defence.' It was unthinkable,' replied Shinwell, 'that at the present juncture in international affairs the United Kingdom Government should endeavour to meet the serious financial difficulties with which the Chancellor of the Exchequer was faced by cutting a defence programme which the Government had pledged themselves in pursuance of their obligations to Allied Governments.'[36]

The battle raged for a month until Bevan, who was heavily outvoted, resigned from the government on 21 April 1951, together with Harold Wilson, the President of the Board of Trade, and one other junior minister. Although Bevan was in a tiny minority in the Cabinet, his line of argument, as Kenneth Younger recorded in his diary on 13 March, 'clearly had quite a strong demagogic appeal in the country, since it brings under one umbrella all pacifists, all anti-Americans, and all who believe in a neutral 3rd. force between [the] USA and [the] USSR or else don't believe that the Soviet Union is a genuine danger at all. Most of us have misgivings on some or all of these grounds.'[37] Bevan's stand certainly split the Labour Party and he himself did not make his peace with the leadership until 1956.

Bevan's fears that the rearmament programme would prove excessive were realised as the terms of trade continued to worsen during 1951. Alluding to Bevan's views, Gaitskell told fellow-OEEC finance ministers in July that:

> [t]here would have been little or no discontent if rearmament could have been carried out in a period of stable prices. What was really causing the trouble was the rapid rise in raw materials price and the consequent deterioration in the terms of trade. This development increased the burden of rearmament enormously. The United Kingdom was now paying on an average 42% more for its imports than the average price ... in 1950. Export prices on the other hand had only risen by 18%. In fact, the increased cost of imports in 1951 was roughly speaking as great as the total rearmament effort that year.[38]

The hope was that the NATO discussions on burden-sharing would produce satisfactory results, but the omens did not look too promising. The Prime Minister reported to the Cabinet at the end of August that there would be a clash with the United States at the NATO Council meeting in Ottawa the following month because the Americans seemed to be thinking not only of asking the European members of the alliance to meet the requirements of the Medium Term Defence Plan, but also to find most of the financial wherewithal themselves. This was unacceptable, especially as the imminent report of NATO's Financial and Economic Board, which had been looking at burden-sharing, was likely to show that Britain's defence programme might already represent 'more than its fair share', while that of the United States might not. The task of the British Foreign Secretary, therefore, was to convince the Americans that 'short of an imminent threat of war there are only two ways of closing the gap between existing programmes and the Medium-Term Defence Plan, namely a large increase in the American effort or a downward reassessment of the requirements of the Plan itself'.[39]

Morrison, Gaitskell and Shinwell informed their colleagues shortly before the general election that their objectives in the financial field at Ottawa 'were to a relative extent achieved'. Gaitskell had:

> made it clear that our overall balance of payments deficit, combined with the threat of a severe dollar crisis, was making our situation increasingly difficult. While production for defence was so far up to schedule, we might be forced ... to increase our export of goods produced by the metal-using industries, which could only be at the expense of rearmament orders. There was a danger, therefore, that the United Kingdom might not be able to complete the projected £4,700 million defence programme on time; and it was clearly quite out of the question, in present conditions, for us to contemplate anything in the nature of an increase over our present plans ... we could not accept our force allocation under the Medium-Term Defence Plan as a realistic target....

Since time at Ottawa was too short for a thorough examination of all the issues involved, a temporary committee of the NATO Council, known jocularly as 'the Wise Men', was set up to explore them and to report by early December.[40]

By that time, of course, the Labour government was out of office, a casualty to a large extent of the economic crisis exacerbated if not brought about by its own rearmament programme. It is interesting to note, moreover, that one of the first assessments of the situation by the new Conservative Chancellor of the Exchequer, Mr R.A. Butler, concluded that 'with the resources likely to be available to us over the next two years some diminution or re-balancing of the defence burden is inevitable'.[41] And so it proved to be.

Conclusion

'It is given to few men to see their dreams fulfilled,' Ernst Bevin is reported to have said after the Brussels meeting of the NATO Council in December 1950. 'Three times in the last year I know I have nearly died, but I kept myself alive because I wanted to see this North Atlantic Alliance properly launched. This had been done today.'[42] What he was referring to, of course, was the appointment of General Eisenhower as Supreme Commander of the alliance's integrated force and the placing of the American troops in Europe under his command. But Bevin's remarks might also be interpreted to include the whole system of collective security which NATO represented; and in so far as British policy had consistently sought to establish such a system since 1948, he was justified in his pride. Nevertheless, as this chapter has tried to show, the price paid was in some important respects a very heavy one, and the historian is legitimately entitled to wonder whether there might not have been other, less damaging ways of achieving the same objectives.

Notes

* First published in: Western Security. The Formative Years. European and Atlantic Defence 1547–1953. Ed. by Olov Risle. Oslo 1985, pp. 247–265.
1. Strang minute, 9 May 1949, *Foreign Office Records*, Public Record Office, London, FO 371/76384/W3113/G. Crown Copyright records in the Public Record Office are reproduced by permission of the Controller of Her Majesty's Stationery Office.
2. *Idem: Cabinet Office Records*, Public Record Office, London, CP (49)208, 18 October 1949, CAB 129/37/1. In August 1949, Strang,

who was Permanent Under-Secretary of State at the Foreign Office, wrote that '[t]he conclusion of the paper cannot be taken as representing finally approved government policy; but the paper was passed by the Foreign Secretary and has been seen by certain of his colleagues, including the Chancellor of the Exchequer, some of whom have expressed general agreement and none of whom have expressed dissent'. (Strang minute, 13 August 1949, FO 371/76384/G). It is also worth pointing out that, at a Cabinet meeting on 8 May 1950, '[t]here was general support for the Foreign Secretary's view that the strength of the Soviet Union and her satellites could not be matched by the Commonwealth and Western Europe without the full support of North America; and that, from the point of view of foreign policy and defence, reliance must be placed on the greater strength of the Atlantic community...' (CM(50)29th Conclusions, Minute 5, 8 May 1950, CAB 128/17).
3. PUSC(50)9, 21 April 1950, *Prime Minister's Office Records*, Public Record Office, London, PREM 8/1203.
4. PUSC 51, 28 April 1950, CAB 21/1761.
5. CP(50)118, 26 May 1950, CAB 129/40.
6. *Younger Diary*, 14 May 1950, Younger Papers. I am greatly indebted to Lady Younger for access to these papers, which I am preparing for publication.
7. DO(49)68, 2 November 1949, CAB 131/7.
8. AOC(51)4th Meeting, Minute 1, 29 January 1951, CAB 134/38; DO(51) 4th Meeting, Minute 3, 28 February 1951, CAB 131/10. The Conservative Foreign Secretary was still fighting this battle in December 1951. '...[y]ou know that I wish to maintain the headquarters of the organisation...' 'he wrote to the Prime Minister. 'I think we should fight hard for this ... London is the true Atlantic capital.' (Eden minute, 21 December 1951, PREM 11/160.) The battle, however, was lost at the Lisbon meeting of the North Atlantic Council in May 1952.
9. PUSC (49)62, 19 April 1950, PREM 8/1203; Attlee minute, 2 May 1950, ibid.
10. Shinwell minute, 13 June 1950, PREM 8/1203; DO(50)67, 30 August 1950, CAB 131/9. Both the text of the Chiefs of Staff's review of defence policy and global strategy and the Defence Committee's discussion of it remain classified. One is therefore forced to reply upon extracts and summaries in other documents.
11. Younger memo, 6 July 1950, Younger Papers.
12. DO(50)66, 29 August 1950: DO(50)67, 30 August 1950, CAB 131/9; DO 17th Meeting, Minute 3, 1 September 1950, CAB 131/8; CM(50)55th Conclusions, Minute 3, 4 September 1950, CAB 128/18.
13. Bevin telegrams, 13, 14 September 1950, PREM 8/1429/1; CM(50) 58th Conclusions, Minute 3, 14 September 1950; CM(50) 59th

Conclusions, Minute 1, 15 September 1950, CAB 128/18.
14. DO(50) 21st Meeting, Minute 4, 8 November 1950, CAB 131/8. Attlee's vehemence is particularly hard to understand in view of his own proposals the previous May that the idea of an integrated European Army as a means of facilitating German rearmament should be examined. See his minute of 2 May 1950 cited in Note 9 above.
15. DO(50)100, 24 November 1950, PREM 8/1429/1. (For some reason this document is missing from the Defence Committee files.) DO(50) 22nd Meeting, Minute 1, 27 November 1950, CAB 131/8.
16. Younger Diary, 4 February 1951, Younger Papers.
17. The speech was presumably Eisenhower's report to a joint session of Congress on 1 February 1951 when he said: 'I personally think that there has to be a political platform achieved, an understanding that will contemplate an eventual and an earned equality on the part of that nation [Germany] before we should start to talk about including units of Germans in any kind of army.' See *The Times*, 2 February 1951, p. 6.
18. Younger Diary, 25 February 1951, Younger Papers; Attlee speech, 12 February 1951, Denise Folliott (ed.), *Documents on International Affairs 1951*, London: Oxford University Press for the Royal Institute of International Affairs, 1954, pp. 105–6.
19. DO(51) 16th Meeting, Minute 1, 26 July 1951, CAB 131/10.
20. CM(51) 56th Conclusions, Minute 6, 30 July 1951, CAB 128/20.
21. Dalton minute, 31 July 1951; Attlee minute, 31 July 1951, PREM 8/1429/2; CM(51) 56th Conclusions, Minute 6, 30 July 1951, CAB 128/20.
22. CP(51)240, 30 August 1951, CAB 129/47; CM(51) 58th Conclusions, Minute 2, 4 September 1951, CAB 128/20; Tripartite Communiqué, 14 September 1951, *Documents on International Affairs 1951*, p. 136. The British, of course, had no intention of joining the European Army themselves.
23. DO(50) 31, 28 April 1950, CAB 131/9.
24. DO(50) 8th Meeting, Minute 7, 10 May 1950, CAB 131/8; CP(50) 118, 26 May 1950, CAB 129/40; Younger memo, 6 July 1950, Younger Papers.
25. Acheson circular telegram, 22 July 1950, US Department of State, *Foreign Relations of the United States 1950*, Volume III, *Western Europe*, Washington: US Government Printing Office, 1977, p. 138.
26. CP(50)81, 31 July 1950, CAB 129/41.
27. CM(50) 52nd Conclusions, Minute 4, 1 August 1950, CAB 128/18.
28. Acheson circular telegram, 22 July 1950, *Foreign Relations of the United States 1950*, vol. III, p. 138.
29. Strath minute, 6 September 1950, *Treasury Records*, Public Record Office, London, T 229/243.

30. CP(50)246, 30 October 1950, CAB 129/42. This was accepted on 16 November. See CM(50) 74th Conclusions, Minute 4, CAB 128/18.
31. Unsigned memo, 7 December 1950, PREM 8/1200.
32. COS(50) 205th Meeting, Confidential Annex, 13 December 1950; COS(50) 207th Meeting, Confidential Annex, Minute 7, 14 December 1950; COS(50) 206th Meeting, Confidential Annex, Minute 2, 14 December 1950, *Ministry of Defence Records*, Public Record Office, London, DEFE 4/38.
33. CM(50) 87th Conclusions, Minute 1, 18 December 1950, CAB 128/18.
34. CP(51)20, 19 January 1951, CAB 129/44.
35. CM(51) 7th Conclusions, Minute 4; 8th Conclusions, Minute 2, 25 January 1951, CAB 128/19.
36. CM(51) 22nd Conclusions, Minute 1, 22 March 1951, CAB 128/19.
37. Younger Diary, 13 May 1951, Younger Papers.
38. Unsigned Memo, 11 July 1951, FO 371/94136/M107.
39. CP(51)239, 30 August 1951, CAB 129/47. The report of the Financial and Economic Board was indeed something of a triumph for British diplomacy. As Sir Eric Roll, the British representative on the Board, put it, 'Notwithstanding concessions we had to make in order to get the report through in time, it remains in structure, in doctrine, and even largely in language, a "United Kingdom document".' MAC(51)129, 4 September 1951, CAB 134/491.
40. CP(51)266, 22 October 1951, CAB 129/47.
41. EA (E) (51) 1, 30 November 1951, CAB 129/47.
42. Lord Ismay, *NATO: The First Five Years 1949–1954*, (no publishing information), p. 37.

9
Italy, 1947–1949: Military Integration and Neutralist Tendencies

Romain H. Rainero

After the Second World War, the Italian army, generally speaking, had no role to play in the ranks of the victorious Allied forces: although the allied strategic commands had accepted Italian participation in the operations against Germany after 13 October 1943, they had not, however, offered this new 'ally' the status of an ally in the true sense of the word during the final assault on Germany. Neither had the allies drawn the logical consequences from this war effort, as can be seen from the second ceasefire agreement concluded with Italy in Malta on 24 September 1943 which mentions joint command and united effort in the war against a common enemy. The declaration of war against Germany made by the 'New Italy' and her contribution to the final phase of the war in Europe, with a balance of more than 70,000 dead soldiers alone,[1] together with the bloody guerilla war in Northern Italy, were merely accepted by the allies. They did not, however, recognise the part played by the democratic government of the South (il Regno del Sud), although this fact had been clearly proved in numerous documents, particularly in the Hyde Park Declaration, the basis for Italian participation in the conflict.

At no time did the allies succeed in keeping to one single position with regard to Italy: on the one hand, she was seen as an aggressor, a founder member of the Axis, and thus as a culpable and defeated power. On the other hand, there was the new Italy, a land with a democratic tradition, herself a victim of the violent Mussolini regime. Apart from this Fascist hiatus, she was fully justified in claiming a long period of suffering. The simple fact that many of the 'new' politicians were identical to those who had stood up to Mussolini (Sforza, Sturzo, De Gasperi, Pacciardi, Amendola, etc.) was proof of the exceptional nature of the Fascist period as against the 'real Italy'.

For the allied Italian policy, these two elements were brought into play in order to justify a policy which was neither coherent, fair nor generous. We must return to the mistakes and contradictions of this policy in order to establish points of reference within public opinion, which had withstood all the battering caused by this political development, but which was scarcely able to make out the basic direction of allied government policy, because a vain attempt was made to look for rationality and uniformity within it. While it is true that political reactions to this policy were able to steer public sympathies in certain directions, the secret of the Great Powers' 'real' intentions was still undiscovered.

We can state, with the aid of hindsight, that these intentions were in fact no secret; on the contrary, there was a flurry of projects, which was only made worse by the first confrontations of the cold war in its initial stages. The results of the first Italian opinion polls give us a valuable insight into public opinion at that time. The central element of any argument for or against the validity of the 'war alliances' with Italy was always the treatment the country would be given within the confines of a peace treaty, which was demanded time and again with the utmost urgency, so that Italy's international status would become clear. In this regard, it was the level of reparations which played the dominant role in the minds of the Italians themselves, concerned at the attitude of the British and French in particular. In the case of London, it was Winston Churchill's statement on 'the price of the ticket' Italy had to pay in order to be sure of returning to the democratic fold which made Italians fearful of negative decisions concerning Italy's eastern border and her colonies. In the case of France, it was de Gaulle's statements on the Alpine frontier and the colonies which added to Italian apprehension. The two 'positive' elements in this seemed to be the 'generous' policies of both the USSR and the USA; these were often evoked in an attempt to counteract the ambitions or lust for vengeance to be seen in London and Paris.

A whole series of important facts are lent a completely new light when linked to these hopes and fears. The cool nature of relations with the allied powers following the hectic phase of the military operations in Italy, and especially following the end of hostilities in Europe, can be directly linked to allied plans on the subject of Italy concerning her future status. This was still a contradictory mixture of vanquished enemy and sincere ally. The political forces in Italy, the parties and trade unions, recognised this contradiction and complained about it. They were, however, unable to make real changes to a situation which left precious little room for hopes of a generous allied policy towards Italy and her people.

Long before the cold war led to a division among them, the Italians were deeply split on the popularity and sympathy they showed towards those politicians personifying the various allied policies. According to one of the first public opinion polls, carried out in October 1947, in which the samples were asked which countries they thought were sympathetic towards Italy and thus positively disposed towards a peace treaty, the spread of answers was very revealing: 76 per cent voted for the United States and 9 per cent for the USSR. There were 8 per cent 'don't knows'. Lastly, the other allies: 5 per cent for Great Britain and 2 per cent for France.[2] These results are important in that they give us a clear picture of what Italians really felt during the postwar years following the political storms suffered by Italy during the Second World War. On the eve of the peace treaty Italians pinned their hopes upon the United States, whose policy was described as 'generous and unselfish'. They turned away from the USSR, but above all they rejected Britain and France because they thought these two wanted to wreak vengeance upon Italy. All this gave the policy of Prime Minister De Gasperi and his Foreign Minister Carlo Sforza a very clear character in its basic options: Rome would orient its general policy towards America in future, and also pin its hope of a peace treaty upon America, a treaty which was to be 'fair and equitable', without ruling out the odd sacrifice on Italy's part.

However, the treaty the allies imposed upon Italy turned out to be worse than the blackest visions with its concept of punishing the country: it was a totally unjust treaty and went completely against the notion of joint command upon which Italy had always relied. The correction of the Alpine border and the eastern frontier, the loss of Trieste and all her colonies, the payment of heavy reparations to the allies, the surrender to those same allies of most of Italy's naval fleet, and even most of the merchant fleet, the military restrictions placed upon the frontiers caused by the demilitarisation and destruction of important fortifications; all this turned Italian public opinion against the wartime allies in a period when international questions, particularly the start of the cold war, seemed to offer Italy a new role in a Western strategy.

In the case of Italy, as in the case of West Germany, it was the threat, real or imagined, posed by the Red Army which gave a sense of urgency to the idea of 'European defence' or the defence of the West, whereby Italy did not have a clear conception and, above all, did not see the solution in one sense or another in the present *status quo*.[3] Indeed, in spite of the great sympathy they felt towards the USA and their pro-American attitude, the Italians were fairly negatively disposed towards any form of alliance or commitment, even together with the United States, following the episode of the peace treaty. This document (signed on 12 February 1947) remained an obstacle to any form of solidarity with these allies, who were only then remembering that they were allies, after having imposed a punitive peace upon a democratic Italy, despite their many promises during the war.

What role in Western defence could Italy play, who had had nothing but disappointments in her recent dealings with these allies? Italian public opinion either failed to see, or did not see clearly enough, the part Italy should play in a defence of a West which had responded so badly to her problems and needs until now. It was not so much the military occupation and the resulting burden of military bases which the Italians found difficult to comprehend but also the problem of a 'new' alliance of three of the four Great Powers, which had already existed, and which had not had a favourable effect in Italy's eyes during the great discussions on peace and the difficult negotiations for her treaty.

On an international level, the failure of the Moscow meeting in March 1947 and the new Marshall Plan gave a sense of urgency to the Italian political leadership's basic options, and they put Italian diplomacy in a difficult position regarding options and their evaluation within a global diplomatic strategy, in which Italy played no part but to the consequences of which the country was subjected. The Italian ambassadors in the major capitals made every effort (as can be seen from their correspondence) to comprehend and evaluate the new dimensions of this international policy, of which the main elements were known but the future consequences of which seemed difficult to judge. The term

Italy

'cold war' was too new to be seen in its full light and with all its contradictions. There was much talk concerning the West and its defence, but what was 'the West'? What was the doctrine of a geographical term which was still controversial? The reports made by Quaroni in Paris and by Gallarati Scotti in London show us that the concept of 'the West' in no way implied a unanimous view of the most important international problems on the part of its members, which might have given this 'West' an initial structure. On the contrary, the views of, say, London and Paris were often different from those of Washington; sometimes, indeed, they were violently at odds. So what was one to think of this 'West'? The concept, a difficult one *per se* at the time, seemed even less easy to understand, even if the will was there, and Italian diplomacy had the will, to forget the peace treaty and its disappointments and to work towards Italy's interests in a more permanent sense. Above all towards her return to full membership of the international community, and especially her participation in the UN, which was still a matter for discussion.

The central theme of this analysis was, of course, always the problem of relations between the USA and the USSR and their development. It seemed clear that the other areas of diplomacy were merely secondary to these superpower relations, a global strategy in which Europe seemed to be relegated to a secondary level, one which deprived it, and especially London and Paris, of any initiative of their own. If we see Italian diplomacy in this light, we can understand the sadness felt by the diplomats, who were well aware that their views and ideas had no future, since it seemed that only those of the USA and the USSR counted. Italy, whose military structures and defences had been destroyed by the peace treaty, could hardly be under any illusions: Europe was defenceless and, in military terms, there was no other answer to Soviet aims at ideological expansionism than the US doctrine of a second liberation: a prospect which did nothing to reassure Europeans in general and Italians in particular.

Thus it was in a completely novel situation that Italian diplomacy asked itself what alliances had to be renewed and what relations had to be reopened; they had the peace treaty as a shining example of errors and hypocrisy, but political life in Italy had to orient itself towards the future and above all had to aim towards an internal situation which demanded a certain degree of consideration, even from the diplomats themselves. The cold war was above all a confirmation, for Italian diplomats, of the fact that the era in which Europe had been the centre of the world was over; and it was thus the start of a new era in which Europe found itself involved in comprehensive strategies, obeying only the global laws of equilibrium and compensation, laws over which Europe and the Europeans, of whatever nationality, had almost no control. Quaroni phrased this well in a letter to his minister, Sforza, from Paris, dated 22 January 1948: 'At a time in the distant past, in which the governments were less democratic but nevertheless more civil ... politics was a matter for Europe and Europeans. If one country saw another country, with which she wanted to have friendly relations or conclude an alliance, flirting with her enemy, she tried to win her over by offering her greater advantages. The Russians and Americans, each in their own sphere of influence, are pursuing a policy which might be more effective at this time, but which is certainly less seductive: the policy of power.'[4] We can add to this by summing up the views of this great diplomat as follows: they exploit their position as superpowers in order to impose the results of their reciprocal agreements upon the rest of the world. However, although this was the situation on the diplomatic level, from Italy's point of view, it was the internal situation which seemed to dictate or even impose choices.

With regard to public opinion, as well as that of the Italian military, the dominant theme was the question of which side Italy should choose. This led to the old quarrels concerning the need, or lack of it, to join alliances which, all in all, seemed meaningless to this Italy which was under attack from all sides. Even if some of the powers claiming to be democratic leaned towards the United States, this fact did not seem sufficient to counteract the animosity felt by France and Great Britain towards this new Italy, who was, against her will, being blackmailed due to her having been a member of the Axis, and whose democratic bona fides were constantly being questioned. Regarding relations with the Soviet Union, they were excellent; however, their direct internal consequences, in other words the Italian Communist Party, were the cause of the most violent opposition due to the PCI's political message and her 'revolutionary' plans, which the majority of Italians seemingly rejected from the start.

In the case of the military, which seemed to have been hardly affected by the propaganda in favour of an alliance with these 'allies', who had shown so little generosity towards the new Italy's military requirements by imposing the hard conditions of the treaty, the question of alliance with one side or the other had a clear third option – neutrality. This was the prevailing impression: while there was much sympathy towards the United States, the preferred position was that of equilibrium and thus neutrality.[5] However, one factor completely changed this original position, and that was the internal argument, which followed the fall of the anti-fascist government, concerning the recognition of the part played by the regular army in the war of liberation.

The left-wing parties – the PCI and the Socialist party – were still united in the form of a popular front. This was the result of the ideological meeting of minds during the anti-fascist struggle of the war and the postwar period, particularly between Pietro Nenni and Palmiro Togliatti; thus the left-wing parties maintained a climate of tough criticism of the regular army and its role in the resistance. They were happy to accuse those military structures of 'treason'. They also described the army's attitude towards the popular struggle against the fascist Italian Socialist Republic and the Germans as half-hearted. Apart from these outbursts, the military, who had already been unhappy about the former role of the army, according to which 'the army keeps out of politics', started taking an interest in Italian political life. As a reaction to criticism from the left, the general staff published documents recounting the Italian army's participation in both the 'regular' war in the South and the partisan war in the North, where it had often lent officers to the resistance and without whom it would never have been organised on a solid military basis. Among these works was the 'official' book by Col. Edoardo Scala on *The Renaissance of the army (La riscossa dell'esercito)*, a most positive balance of the army's military activities during the war of liberation, both in the North and the South. The results of these arguments between the military and the left are of great importance, since they show us more clearly than any other material the military's change of opinion from their initial neutralist positions in favour of a military and political commitment, contrary to the ideas defended by the left. Even before this argument and its consequences, a military observer, Demezio Zemaco, had emphasised in a very direct and interesting way the importance for the armed forces of not having an inferiority complex towards the political parties, who very often launched into polemics with the military in an attempt to become more 'popular'.[6] At that time (1945), the air force was accused of having been the breeding ground of the fascist regime, and of continuing to harbour right-wing diehards. Following this first statement on its political inferiority compared to the parties, particularly those on the left wing, the military (above all the former chief of staff, Admiral de Courten) had increasingly tended to keep out of the superpower struggle; this tendency was certainly strengthened by the peace treaty. However, the argument over the liberation gave a new impetus to this global examination of Italy's role in a worldwide system; the decision against the left became almost inevitable, despite the general reservations raised by plans for a 'second liberation of Europe', preached by certain military and political observers in the United States.

However, it was the internal political climate in which the argument between neutralism and military commitment in an alliance with the West showed up such a crass contrast between the views of the left and the centre-right. In an atmosphere of persistent intransigence, this rapidly led to the radicalisation of an argument which, at the beginning, had seemed so harmless. Never before had the options in favour of European integration led to such a crisis among the parties; an agreement made with the United States on 2 February 1948, 'of friendship, trade and navigation', seemed to left-wing observers to be proof that the government of De Gasperi was about to make a definite choice of basic Italian foreign-policy direction with this agreement, a clear anti-Soviet choice and active military participation by Italy in plans for a Western bloc. This seemed to be on the cards since the government was seeking rapprochement, especially with France (Turin meeting of 20 March 1948).

The left rejected Italian participation in any kind of military organisation or alliance, which, under the circumstances of the cold war and the cooling of East-West relations, could only be an anti-Soviet alliance. After the founding of the Cominform, it was the PCI which took the lead, organising, in September 1947, the campaign for the 'Defence of Peace', which meant adhering to Soviet theses against the 'imperialist intentions' of the United States. The party newspaper 'Rinascita' put it very clearly when it stated: 'Only he who staunchly defends peace, rejects without hesitation any accession (by Italy) to the imperialist bloc and refuses to serve their plans for expansion and exploitation, can say that he is pursuing a national policy. For Italy in particular it is only possible to defend national independence by defending peace. It must also be recognised that independence is an essential prerequisite for any national policy, for any defence of civilisation.'[7]

These arguments appealed to a section of the Italian public who were disappointed by the peace treaty they considered to be unfair, and who were not much inclined to recognise all the reasons given by the three Western powers for putting the blame for the international tensions and the cold war on the USSR alone. It would be wrong to think that tendencies towards absolute Italian neutrality in the cold war were only linked to the Socialists and Communists; on the contrary, there was a certain section of the Christian Democrats (including the future President of the Republic, Giovanni Gronchi) in which tendencies away from making military treaties with the Western powers were voiced. However, we must take into account the circumstances of their coming into being as much as possible: they were seemingly a 'moral' position rather than the result of political discussion. Such abstract, apolitical arguments were doomed to being ignored by the centre parties, and even by the people who raised them, who seemed to lose their cool when they found out that this standpoint was 'the' position of the left-wingers, whose influence and rise to power they feared.

Thus it was the two main left-wing parties, the Socialists and the Communists, who regained the initiative of coordinating Italy's neutralist efforts. From then on the struggle became more radical, turning into an election battle where the options of alliance with the United States or neutrality got lost in the mire of polemic arguments which were at the bottom of the rivalry between the left and the centre. The fundamental question soon became weighed down with the whole ideological baggage of the various parties, became merely a minor point in an election battle which, at the beginning of 1948, came as the moment of truth for those political forces which had come out of the war. Even the left, who had originally made the neutrality issue one of their major arguments, mentioned it right at the end of the last chapter of the Founding Charter of the Popular Democratic Front on 28 December 1947. In the election pact concluded between the two main left-wing parties the problem of the cold war and Italy's role in this struggle for peace is not mentioned until after all the other questions: structural reforms, agriculture, industry, the problems of southern Italy, democratic development, urban issues, cultural life, questions concerning the family, women, youth policy and so on.

It is certainly surprising to see this, since the question was an important one; however, it was perhaps an election tactic, as the left-wing experts probably wanted to concentrate on definite, populist policies, so as to achieve an election victory of such a size that the concrete problems, it was hoped, could be used to clear the way for neutralism: a concept which was certainly of less interest to the majority of Italians than the everyday problems contained in the Popular Front's manifesto.

In the other camp, in other words the centre coalition, and among the Christian Democrats in particular, the military problem and thus that of an alliance with the United States was presented as a comforting factor in Italy's future. She would only be able to defend herself against the Russian bear and his Italian helpers, whether intentional (i.e. the Communists) or otherwise (the Socialists), with America's help. Therefore the question of alliances was a part of the 'bulwark against Communism', the principal theme during the elections of 18 April 1948. The fact that the left-wing Front failed to win the voters over to its programme, but on the contrary saw the latter flock to the Christian Democrats, led to the idea of neutralism going under, together with the Front's political and social ideas.

After the elections (which the left lost), the Socialist leader Pietro Nenni insisted in vain upon the value of such a position, emphasising that 'our policy of neutrality was aimed at avoiding making our people put on once again the uniform of the Foreign Legion of capitalism.'[8]

According to the analyses made by the Socialists and Communists, there was one real danger for Italy: that a victory by the ecclesiastically moderate, conservative parties might cause the government (the fifth cabinet under De Gasperi, with Sforza still as Foreign Minister) to transform the economic and aid agreements concluded with the United States into a military-treaty package without really realising what they were doing.

Following the elections, the tone of political debate became still louder, but now it was a rearguard action: the voting figures told the story of how the left-wing line had been rejected, and thus the majority of the government's plans could be realised.

On the home front, the USSR's international position concerning Italy's admission to the UN, with constant Soviet vetoes in the Security Council, made it fairly difficult for the left, and the Communists in particular, to speak of Moscow's 'real, active' friendship towards Italy. The Socialist party began to present their themes under their own banner rather than that of the Front. On 31 October 1948, 'Socialist Peace and Neutrality Day', the critical analyses the party made at its Congress in Genoa (from June 27 to July 1) were made known to the Italian general public. Out of the three motions on the agenda, two examined the problem of world peace, together with a clear refusal to enter into any kind of alliance; thus Italian participation in any policy of commitment with the two blocs was rejected. The third motion was more overtly anti-American, naming capitalism as the only danger to peace. It might be of interest to examine these motions in more detail, but suffice it to say that 26 per cent of the votes in this Congress were evidence of a development, a change of ideas within the Socialist party itself, thus signalling the virtual end of the Popular Front. On 30 November, in the Italian Parliament, Nenni presented a motion on Italy's foreign policy which was the result of agreement between the Genoa motions. But the tone of the speech already revealed the vastly differing positions within his party.

De Gasperi and Sforza were able to go on to more extensive diplomatic measures, without much fear of being hemmed in: on the one hand, they committed themselves to working towards European agreements and, on the other, they envisaged agreements on Western military cooperation, which were already on the cards and which were announced in grand style on 11 March 1948. However, all this happened without great excitement: the Atlantic Pact was seen as an instrument to be used in Italy's attempts to have the peace treaty reviewed. In this regard, the Italian situation was anything but clear: on the one hand there were plans to rearm the country, but on the other, no one could make up their mind to do away with the treaty, in order to benefit from it, or to resolutely commit themselves in favour of Italy's admission to the UN. This did not happen until 14 December 1955, and it had, of course, a whole series of internal political repercussions, which had for too long been quietly ignored.

Notes

1. The exact figures, according to Italian military sources, are as follows: 70,011 dead, 18,528 wounded and 29,281 missing; total losses amount to 117,820. Ministero della Guerra, *Considerazioni relative all'esercito nei riguardi del Trattato di pace*, Rome, April 1946, p. 16.
2. DOXA Italian Polling Institute, *Il volto sconosciuto dell'Italia*, 2 vols., Milan, 1956.
3. Norbert Wiggershaus, 'The decision for a West German defence contribution', in *Western Security: The Formative Years: European and Atlantic Defence 1947–1953*, Olav Riste (ed.), Oslo, 1985, pp. 198–214.
4. P. Quaroni, letter dated 22.1.1948, in AMAE (unpublished).
5. There are plenty of examples of this, but the most interesting work is contained in the article by Gen. Nino Pasti (now a left-wing senator) in the *Corriere Militare* of June 1948. On the problem as a whole see Virgilio Ilari, *Le forze armate tra politica e potere 1943–1976*, Florence, 1978.
6. Demezio Zemaco, 'L'Aviazione ed i partiti politici', in *Rivista Aeronautica*, 1945, pp. 15–18.
7. On these problems see *La politica estera della Repubblica italiana*, 3 vols., Milan, 1967.
8. Pietro Nenni, 'Meditazioni su una battaglia perduta', in *Avanti!*, 1.5.1948. See also D. Ardia, *Il partito socialista e il patto atlantico*, Milan, 1976. Also the memoirs of Pietro Nenni, *Tempo di guerra fredda*, Milan, 1981; Alcide de Gasperi, *Il ritorno alla pace*, Rome, 1977; and Carlo Sforza, *Cinque anni a Palazzo Chigi*, Rome, 1952.

10
The Reluctant European: Norway's Attitude to Military Integration, 1948–1950

Olav Riste

Geographically located in the north-western corner of Europe, Norwegian security since the beginning of this century was regarded as resting on a dual foundation: a comparative remoteness from the centres of European conflict, and the implicit guarantee of protection seen in British sea power. The resulting neutralist/Atlanticist orientation produced a policy which, up to 1940, attempted to combine isolationism with friendly relations with Great Britain. The German invasion and occupation of Norway in 1940 exploded both parts of the dual-security basis, and the foreign policy reappraisal undertaken by the government during its exile in London resulted in an outspoken 'Atlantic policy', aiming to 'nail the Anglo-Saxon powers' – the United States included – 'to their responsibilities in Europe'. In regard to Europe, Norway's dilemma was summed up in a wish not to be isolated either with Europe or against Europe.

The first postwar years saw a gradual reaffirmation of the Atlanticist orientation under the shadow of the Soviet Union. But the remoteness of the United States put Britain in the forefront, and Bevin's idea of a European 'third force' between 'the red tooth and claw of American capitalism and the Communist dictatorship of Soviet Russia' found a ready audience among members of Norway's Labour Government. The assumptions were that such a 'third force' would be British-led; that it would have economic and political cooperation as its main emphasis; and that it would be backed up by the United States in the fields of defence and security. Norway had few illusions about the will-

185

ingness of the Continental states to concern themselves with the defence of Northern Europe, and increasingly doubted the ability of Great Britain to provide any form of security guarantee for the Scandinavian countries. During the crisis weeks of March 1948, therefore, Norway's questions about the possibility of military assistance went to Britain *and* the United States.[1]

For the same reasons, Norwegian membership of the Brussels Pact was not on the cards. In fact, although Scandinavian security problems were on Bevin's mind as he planned his pivotal statement to the House of Commons in January, he saw the point of his advisors that a mention of the Scandinavian countries would only lead to embarrassing questions about what Britain could contribute to their defence. Also, as later explained in a memorandum from the Foreign Office to the State Department, it was pointless to invite the Scandinavians to the Western Union talks since, even taken together, the Brussels Pact countries could not by themselves effectively defend that part of the world against pressure.[2] Evidently, everybody considered a trans-Atlantic security association as a *sine qua non* for the inclusion of Scandinavia in a Western defence pact.

Norwegian aloofness from the process that led to the Brussels Pact was therefore not so much a case of residual neutralism as a reflection of an almost instinctive feeling that the right framework had not yet been formed. Both public opinion and political positions in Norway seem to have taken a sharp westward turn during the winter of 1948. An increasing number of newspapers, including many of the Labour papers, called for a change of course for the nation's foreign and security policy. Some, and notably the main Labour party organ in Oslo, even advocated a Western military alliance with the participation of the United States. In the non-socialist opposition, criticism of the Labour government's unwillingness to take a strong public stand in favour of the principle of Western security cooperation in one form or another was increasing. And strong elements in the Labour party made similar demands in the inner circles of the party.[3]

One of the principal advocates of an open declaration of at least moral support was the party's Secretary General, Haakon Lie, and together with Prime Minister Einar Gerhardsen he succeeded in having a resolution passed by the council of the Oslo branch of the party on 3 February 1948. While the text of the resolution said nothing about cooperation in the defence or security field, and stressed the primary need for 'new and more practical forms of Nordic cooperation', the central message was clear enough: 'The initiative taken by the British Labour Government for extended economic and political cooperation must also have our support'.

Four days later, representatives of the Nordic social democratic parties gathered in Stockholm for one of their frequent high-level consultations. The Norwegian delegates apparently came with hopes that a decision would be made to explore the possibilities of economic, political and military cooperation, in the first instance within a Nordic framework, but without excluding an association with the Western powers. But as the delegates of the other three countries were opposed, the outcome was limited to a resolution of approval for the Marshall Plan and a call for intensified economic cooperation within Scandinavia.[4]

The Norwegian Government's dilemma during those weeks was reflected in the somewhat tortuous language used by Foreign Minister Lange in his statement to a secret session of the *Storting* in the beginning of April:

> It is perfectly clear that neither the British Government nor any other party to the Brussels Treaty plans to encourage the Nordic countries to adhere to this treaty unless we ourselves expressly wish to join. We know that strong reservations exist both in Sweden and in Denmark concerning such adherence. For Norway's part it would be more natural to think in terms of a direct association between the Scandinavian countries and Great Britain rather than an association with the Brussels Treaty ... If it were possible to obtain assurances that we would not be left standing alone in the unlikely case of being exposed to aggression, without binding ourselves to automatic involvement in every war in Western Europe through membership in the Western pact, then that would be the most favourable solution to our security problem, while being at the same time the solution least likely to complicate the preservation of intimate cooperation with the other Nordic countries.[5]

Leading members of the Norwegian Cabinet did toy with the idea of a British-Scandinavian defence union during the spring of 1948. In a secret memorandum, dated 4 April and addressed to four of his Cabinet colleagues, Defence Minister Hauge put forward the following proposals:

Norwegian foreign policy-makers should presently start quiet work on the outlines of a 'Northern Union' between *the Scandinavian countries and England* concerning economic, cultural, and military cooperation.

Once we are clear in our own minds about what a 'Northern Union' ought to be, *we should take the initiative both towards the Scandinavian countries and England.* It should not be impossible that such an initiative could lead to results in one form or another. The alternative of Scandinavian adherence to the Five-Power Treaty, which other parties may well decide to join, is less favourable and less realistic.[6]

However, it soon transpired that Hauge's idea of a 'Northern Union' was, in Haakon Lie's words, 'stillborn'. During the remainder of 1948, the question of a Scandinavian defence pact came to dominate the Norwegian political agenda. Accordingly, a Norwegian commitment to participation in a European defence context had to remain in abeyance until the formation of NATO.

Military Integration before 1949

It is of some importance to note that Norway's disinterest in the Brussels Pact, and her wary attitude towards a Scandinavian Defence Union, were related to the geographic limitations of the schemes and their inadequacy in terms of Norway's own defence needs, and should not be interpreted as scepticism toward military integration as such. In fact, the degree of integration as regards planning, forces and matériel foreseen by the Scandinavian defence committee, in its report to the three governments in early January 1949, in most respects went beyond that achieved by the Western Union or NATO in later years. An alternative model of a fairly loose pattern of military cooperation, which the committee's mandate had authorised the experts to consider, received only perfunctory attention.

In Norway's case, after all, military integration was nothing new. The years of the wartime alliance had given Norway, and presumably also the other governments-in-exile, ample experience of collaboration at several levels among allied forces. Proceeding from a pattern established during the summer and autumn of 1940, and formalised in Norway's case through the Anglo-Norwegian Military Agreement of 28 May 1941, units of the Norwegian army, navy and air force operated side by side with British units under allied – generally British – operational control.

Under the terms of the agreement, the two governments affirmed their 'determination to prosecute the war to a successful conclusion', and agreed 'that one of the objects of the war is the re-establishment of the freedom and independence of Norway'. For those purposes it was decided that the Norwegian armed forces in the United Kingdom 'shall be employed either for the defence of the United Kingdom or for the purpose of regaining Norway', and that they should be 'organized and employed under British command, in its character as the Allied High Command, as the Armed Forces of the Kingdom of Norway allied with the United Kingdom'.

In separate appendices to the agreement, detailed provisions were laid out for each service. In the case of the army it was stated that it should as far as possible 'retain the character of a Norwegian force in respect of personnel, particularly as regards discipline, language, promotion and duties', and units and formations would be commanded by Norwegian officers. Units of the Norwegian navy and air forces would be 'attached to the British navy and be under the operational control of the British naval authorities'. But they would be under the command of Norwegian officers and manned by Norwegian crews; they would operate under the Norwegian flag; and the internal administration of the units and their personnel would be the responsibility of Norwegian authorities.

Throughout the Second World War, those arrangements functioned with a remarkable lack of serious friction or jurisdictional conflict, even in instances where their practical application led to results hardly foreseen by the drafters of the treaty. One such instance occurred when, in 1944, the two fighter squadrons of the Norwegian air force were combined with one British squadron to form 132 (N) Wing, with a Norwegian Wing Commander – an arrangement which was maintained during the subsequent addition of another British and then a Dutch squadron. Similarly, the wartime history of the Norwegian navy records several instances where Norwegian naval officers commanded mixed allied naval forces.[7]

After the war was over, practical experience of military integration was extended to cover also the Norwegian army, as from

1947 a Norwegian brigade served with the British Army of the Rhine on occupation duties in Germany. Several different considerations motivated the Norwegian government's decision to contribute a major part of each year's intake of conscripts to the allied occupation of Germany. One of them was Norway's moral and political obligation to share in this common burden of the wartime allies. But the brigade also served as a symbol of Norway's adherence to the Western powers and her reliance on British support in future emergencies. Other major considerations were the advantages of joint training with British troops, and of acquiring – on favourable terms – British arms and equipment not only for the brigade in Germany but also for the armed forces at home.[8]

After the formation of NATO, the position of the Norwegian brigade in Germany took on a new dimension. Norway's NATO commitment had on the face of it made superfluous the brigade's role as a symbol of our links with the Western powers, even if the special link with the British remained potentially valuable. At the same time, within the NATO framework, Norway approached the principles of defence coordination and integration with considerable reluctance, from a fear that European security in a NATO context would translate into an essentially Continental defence concept. With Central Europe as the 'schwerpunkt' of NATO defence-planning, Northern Europe risked being relegated to the realms of oblivion. So, while Foreign Minister Halvard Lange soon became a firm adherent to the idea of an 'Atlantic community' with extensive cooperation in the political and economic spheres, Defence Minister Jens Chr. Hauge felt constrained to say, as late as May 1950, that: 'Joint defence and joint planning means to us that other and stronger countries prepare to use some of their military resources for the defence of our country and our part of the world.'[9] Subject to that overriding condition, however, and as always with the reservation that Norwegian military and naval bases would not be opened for utilisation by allied forces in peacetime, the Defence Minister for his part had no doubts about the practical implications of the 'common defence' requirement:

> When the defence of our part of the world and of our country is a common concern and requires cooperation, we must on our side adjust not only our strategic defence plans but also to a certain extent

our own defence organisation to conform with the cooperative concept. Joint planning will have implications in many areas. It may affect the balance among the services; it may influence our choice of types of naval vessels and of aircraft. The arrangement of the supreme military command in the region will naturally have to be taken into account in decisions concerning our central and local defence command arrangements. The joint defence plans may also influence the choice of location for our command centres.

At that time, although the term 'integrated defence' was being used to describe the goal of NATO's efforts in the military field, few appeared to take it seriously. The US Congress in October 1949 had attempted to make military assistance conditional on progress towards 'integrated defence', and NATO's Defence Committee in December obliged by giving the alliance's 'grand strategy' the name 'strategic concept for the *integrated* defence of the North Atlantic area'. The decision served its purpose, since it enabled Acheson to report to President Truman that this justified the release of military assistance with the condition imposed by Congress.[10] The terminology was retained in the bilateral agreements between the US and its allies on military assistance, Article 1 of which stated: 'Such assistance shall be so designed as to promote an integrated defense of the North Atlantic area'. But the Norwegians, in their version of the agreement, translated 'integrated' into 'samordnet' ('coordinated'), and thought no more about it.[11] Already, Norway's main concern in NATO was to get Great Britain and the United States actively involved in planning and reinforcing NATO's northern flank. And their reluctance to be so involved inevitably raised fears on Norway's part that any pooling of resources would gravitate towards the Continent, leaving the northern flank uncovered.

On most of those points, the outbreak of the Korean War signalled a turning point. For Norway as for the other European members of NATO, their first face-to-face meeting with the spectre of a truly integrated defence effort came during the Council of Europe's meeting in Strasbourg in August 1950, when Winston Churchill made his celebrated call on the peoples of Europe to unite against the danger and to create together a European Army. The Council responded by a strong vote in favour of recommending the immediate establishment of a common European army under a European Defence Minister. Most of the Norwegian delegates were among the one-fourth that abstained. Replying to criticism that Britain and Scandinavia were obstructing European unity, the leading member of the Norwegian delegation and chairman of Norway's parliamentary committee on foreign affairs, Finn Moe, declared:

> We have no intention of creating difficulties in the way of establishing regional agreements, be it a French-Italian union, a French-German union or an even larger federal union. We only ask that the Norwegian people may themselves decide if they wish to join such a union, considering the fact that we are all members of a more significant and essential community – the Atlantic Community.

He warned the delegates against assuming that Norway was hostile to European unity just because she believed in functional rather than federative solutions to Europe's problems, and ended his speech with a rhetorical question:

> Is it not a more meaningful task to integrate the defence of the whole democratic world than to create a European army which would be unable to defend Europe without support from the powerful democratic nation on the other side of the Atlantic? Let us be careful that European unity does not lead to European isolation.[12]

Norway's attitude to that 'more meaningful task' of Atlantic defence integration was soon to be put to the test, as the NATO Council meeting in the following month began consideration of the US package proposal for an integrated Atlantic defence of Europe under a US Supreme Commander, with West German participation, and backed by the commitment of US ground and air forces to be stationed in Europe. There were ample reasons to expect Norwegian hesitations towards the proposals. Reluctance at the prospect of German military units, so soon after we had been occupied by the Wehrmacht, was one of them. Small-state concern about a loss of sovereign control over the nation's defence and the disposal of its own military forces was another.

Most important, in the eyes of the Norwegian Government, was the question of whether the promised strengthening of Europe's defence would include the northern flank of NATO, or whether integration would mean centralisation to the Continent of NATO's still inadequate armed forces, and centralisation of decision-making to the Standing Group and the 'Big Three'.[13] When Norway voiced these concerns during the Council meeting in New York in September, Acheson had few answers. Lange then requested a recess for consultations with his government.

At a series of meetings in Oslo, in which consultations between the Cabinet and the parliamentary committee for foreign affairs had a prominent place, the Norwegian position was hammered out. In his presentation of the issues to a session of the full *Storting* on 22 September,[14] the Foreign Minister stressed the urgent need for the reinforcement of Europe's defence after the outbreak of the Korean War, and pointed to President Truman's declared intention to station the US troops in Europe as an important signal of American willingness to contribute to that reinforcement. On the European side the available forces were bound to remain limited in spite of efforts to increase them, so every effort had to be made to increase their effectiveness – hence the proposal to create 'an integrated, that is a joint, force under unified command'. Lange hastened to explain that this did not mean the dissolution of each country's national defence. 'The idea is that each country singles out the units it considers may usefully be made part of the common defence, and that those units are then joined together in a special force under separate command, thus becoming a key force in the defence of Western Europe.'

The second part of the Foreign Minister's statement linked the issue of integrated defence with the question of Germany as Western Europe's front-line state, and of its contribution to Europe's defence. He admitted that 'to all the peoples who have been subjected to German aggression and German occupation the mere thought of a rearmament of Germany calls forth sinister memories and fears about the possible consequences'. But West Germany's progress towards a stable democracy ought sooner or later to result in her reintegration into Western society, and the proposal for an integrated defence force provided an equitable means of achieving a German military participation without risking a revival of German militarism.

The third part of Lange's statement was devoted to Norway's special situation on the northern flank, whose security problem was particularly closely linked with the Atlantic. There was no doubt that the whole plan for an integrated common force was principally designed with a view to the central areas on the Continent, and the defence of the central front was of obvious importance to Norway. 'But our geographic position raises particular problems which necessitate close study of to what extent

Norwegian units should form part of the joint force.' The prospective organisational changes in NATO would in any event have an impact on arrangements in Norway, and there was need for clarification of the relationship between the joint force and the defence of Norway as well as between the unified command and the existing regional groups.

On the following day the Prime Minister summed up for a plenary session of the *Storting* the conclusions reached by the Cabinet after the consultations with the foreign affairs committee and the political parties, and obtained parliamentary sanction in principle for Norway's approval of the proposals before the NATO council.[15] Back in New York, Foreign Minister Halvard Lange on the last day of the Council session made a general statement of Norway's position on the issues. He expressed Norway's agreement with an integrated force as a realistic and necessary step to strengthen the alliance on the assumption that the Supreme Commander would have the task of organizing the defence of the whole of Europe, including the northern flank. He again urged the establishment of a separate regional command for Northern Europe, and stressed the expectation that, in an emergency, part of the integrated force should fall back on Denmark and Norway. Feeling reasonably assured on those major points, Norway agreed to the resolution of principle which established the command system and a joint force.[16]

It was clear that many questions remained to be solved, and many Norwegian demands remained to be met concerning the position of the northern flank in relation to the Central Front, after the NATO Council meeting of September 1950. A strong reminder that northern Europe was still at best a peripheral problem to some member states was Jules Moch's uncompromising advocacy of the Pleven Plan during the meeting of NATO's Defence Committee the following month. Together with Denmark, Norway reacted against the complete disregard for the security of the northern flank countries as revealed in Moch's statement.[17] However, at the Council Deputies' meeting at the end of November, the so-called Spofford compromise managed at least to paper over the differences. Norway supported the US proposal, and had kind words for the spirit of cooperation which was now forthcoming from France. The important thing now, the Norwegian Deputy concluded, was to get on with the immediate creation of a NATO integrated force, while continuing to study the more long-term objectives contained in the French proposal.[18]

The Spofford compromise, then, paved the way for the decisions of the NATO Council in December to proceed with the establishment of an integrated NATO force for the defence of Western Europe, under Eisenhower as Supreme Commander. In presenting these decisions for parliamentary approval in January 1951, Foreign Minister Lange stressed the advantages in terms of forward defence in Europe. A defence line so far east as to cover the land approach to Denmark would make 'a direct and exceedingly important contribution to the defence of Norway'.[19] On that basis, Norway also agreed to let the brigade we had committed to the occupation forces in Germany become part of the joint allied forces. Apart from that, the government assured parliament that there would be no question of Norway contributing sizeable forces to the joint forces in Central Europe. Nor, on account of the Norwegian bases policy, would there be any foreign armed forces stationed in Norway in peacetime.[20]

By the time Parliament came to debate the proposal, it was clear that Norway's demands for a regional command for Northern Europe were about to be met. This reduced the fear that defence plans for the northern flank would be left to simmer on the back burner somewhere on the Continent, even though the Norwegian government would have to continue their struggle to persuade both Britain and the United States to devote more attention as well as forces to the Norwegian part of the northern flank. Nonetheless, the parliamentarians seemed fully aware that the decision for an integrated defence was an historic one. As one supporter of the decision put it, they were asked to agree to 'something entirely new, and perhaps we should admit to ourselves that the military way of thinking has been somewhat alien to the Norwegian people during the last 150 years. What is put forward here is in some measure revolutionary.'[21] Thereupon Parliament approved unanimously the proposal for joint commands and integrated forces, and agreed to put the Norwegian Brigade in Germany under SACEUR command. Only on the final point, concerning West German participation in the defence of Western Europe, were four votes recorded in opposition.[22]

With hindsight, it could be said that Norway's approval of an integrated defence for Western Europe within the Atlantic framework squared the problem of the three interlocking circles which had beset Norwegian foreign policy and security planning ever since the Second World War. Torn between the Nordic circle, with its bonds of kinship; the European circle, with its economic, cultural and political ties; and the Atlantic circle, which in addition provided security, Norway for as long as possible tried to avoid having to make a choice which would mean severing any of those ties. Building bridges, while avoiding exclusive commitments, seemed to offer solutions to the dilemma. In 1949 the Nordic circle suffered a set back, as Sweden refused to consider a Scandinavian defence union with openings toward the west. Had the integrated defence of Western Europe been established on the basis of a European army on the French model, Norway would hardly have had any choice but to stay outside and forge more direct links across the North Atlantic. The US package plan from the autumn of 1950 made such an agonising decision unnecessary, and since then, while other choices have had to be made, such as non-membership of the EEC, Norway has managed to keep a precarious balance between the European and Atlantic components of her security calculus. However, as Ibsen's *Peer Gynt* experienced, a choice deferred tends to present itself at the next crossroads, and at the next. Norway may yet have to make that fundamental choice in the 1990s.

Notes

1. For more details on the historical background, see O. Riste, 'The historical determinants of Norwegian foreign policy', in J. J. Holst (ed.), *Norwegian Foreign Policy in the 1980s*, Oslo, 1985.
2. H. Turner, 'Britain, the United States, and Scandinavian Security Problems 1945–1949', (unpublished PhD thesis, University of Aberdeen, 1982) pp. 177–8.
3. For a thorough analysis, see K. E. Eriksen, *DNA og NATO*, Oslo, 1972, chaps. 2 and 3 in particular.
4. Haakon Lie, *Skjebnear 1945–1950*, Oslo, 1985, pp. 287–90.
5. Quoted in M. Skodvin, *Norden eller NATO*, Oslo, 1971, pp. 121–2.
6. Quoted in H. Lie (see Note 4), pp. 286–7.
7. For the wartime period see O. Riste, *London-regjeringa: Norge i krigsalliansen 1940–1945*, vols. I–II, Oslo, 1973–9.

8. An excellent study of the strategic and political role of the Norwegian occupation brigade is R. Tamnes, 'Kamp mot russerne på tysk jord? Tysklandsbrigaden og den kalde krigen 1947–1953', FHFS NOTAT no. 2, 1985.
9. Stortingsforhandlinger, 1950, 7a, p. 1170.
10. Lord Ismay, *NATO: The First Five Years 1949–1954*, pp. 24–7; FRUS 1950, III, pp. 1–2. A brilliant analysis is L. S. Kaplan, *A Community of Interests: NATO and the Military Assistance Program 1948–1951*, Washington, DC, 1980.
11. Stortingsproposisjon no. 23, 1950, p. 8.
12. Stortingsmelding no. 5, 1951, pp. 24–7.
13. See Rolf Tamnes, 'Norway's struggle for the northern flank, 1950–1952', in O. Riste (ed.), *Western Security: The Formative Years: European and Atlantic Defence 1947–1953*, Oslo and New York, 1985, pp. 225–30.
14. Stortingsforhandlinger, 1950, 7 b, pp. 1970–5.
15. Ibid., pp. 1975–6.
16. FRUS, 1950, III, pp. 330–2 and 349–52.
17. Ibid., p. 425.
18. Ibid., p. 492.
19. Stortingsproposisjon no. 20, 1951, p. 6.
20. Ibid., p. 7.
21. Stortingsforhandlinger, 1951, 7a, p. 403.
22. Ibid., p. 417.

11
Abandonment vs. Entrapment: Denmark and Military Integration in Europe, 1948–1951

Nikolaj Petersen

Introduction

When Denmark joined the North Atlantic Treaty she did so reluctantly and only after a dedicated attempt to create a Scandinavian Defence Union had failed. When Foreign Minister Gustav Rasmussen signed the treaty, neither he nor officials of his ministry had participated in the detailed negotiations which preceded the alliance. On the contrary, in order to concentrate all efforts on promoting a Scandinavian solution the Social Democratic government led by Hans Hedtoft had deliberately kept away from contacts with the Western Powers over the negotiations.[1] In contrast to the Norwegian government, whose foreign minister Halvard Lange had kept a close eye on these, the Danish government had only a broad idea of the concepts underlying the North Atlantic Treaty when it finally decided to join in March 1949.[2]

In his memoirs Dean Acheson relates his impression of Gustav Rasmussen when he arrived in Washington on a fact-finding tour in mid-March 1949:

> He brought irresistibly to mind a phrase in a letter from Abbé Bernard to Louis VII of France during the second crusade: 'Like a sparrow with careful watchfulness, avoid the snares of the fowler.' Rasmussen moved 'like a sparrow with careful watchfulness'; he had to, dependent as he was on a coalition government at home and an unstable environment abroad'.[3]

As Dean Acheson had predicted, the Danes would overcome their fears of being ensnared and join the alliance – but primarily out of another fear: namely the fear of being abandoned and isolated in an insecure world. Both these fears continued to play a conspicuous role in Danish security policy even after joining the alliance and were not stilled until the early 1960s. Here this theme is explored in an analysis of Danish alliance deliberations between 1948 and 1949 and of Danish attitudes towards military integration in the early years of the alliance which culminated in the American proposal of September 1950 to create a joint, integrated force including German contingents for the defence of Western Europe.

The 'Watchful Sparrow' and the Benefits and Perils of Alliance Membership

Glenn Snyder has made an interesting contribution to alliance theory which is highly pertinent to this problem. On the basis of a logic derived from game theory, Snyder analyses the determinants of national strategies in what is termed the 'alliance game', i.e. intra-alliance politics, and the 'adversary game', i.e. inter-alliance relations, respectively. In his view such strategies are interrelated in ways which involve highly complicated evaluations of the pros and cons of various strategies within the two games – or 'goods' and 'bads', as he terms them.[4]

In the Alliance game the principal bads are 'abandonment' on one side and 'entrapment' on the other, while the principal good of alliance participation is the possibility for reducing these risks. 'Abandonment' in Snyder's terminology means 'defection' by the ally and can take a variety of specific forms from abrogation of the alliance contract to a loosening or questioning of the alliance and captures the ever-present nervousness of allies as to the credibility of the alliance guarantee. The principal good at the other end of the spectrum from abandonment is therefore security based on a firm, credible commitment by the allies.

'Entrapment means being dragged into a conflict over an ally's interests that one does not share, or shares only partially'.[5] In an extended sense, 'entrapment' means losing control and getting involved in ventures one would have preferred to stay out of, such as losing freedom of action in international politics. The principal 'good' on this dimension is therefore freedom of action.

The two pairs of 'goods' and 'bads', furthermore, tend to vary inversely. It is normally not possible both to have a perfect alliance guarantee and at the same time to enjoy complete freedom of action; the guarantee will usually be predicated on a counter-guarantee, which in itself reduces the freedom of manoeuvre in a crisis, including the freedom to 'defect', i.e. to abandon the ally. On the positive side, 'abandonment' and 'entrapment' do not normally occur simultaneously, either. Rather it is 'security' and 'entrapment' which go together, and 'abandonment' and 'freedom of action'. A 'C' strategy (for 'cooperation') of alliance commitment may reduce the risk of abandonment (by increasing the alliance guarantee), but at the cost of reduced freedom of action, i.e. a degree of entrapment. Conversely, a 'D' strategy (for 'defection') may increase freedom of action by reducing the risk of entrapment, but at the potential cost of a weakened alliance guarantee and hence less security.

In sum, alliance politics involve difficult choices between often conflicting or even mutually exclusive goals. Such choices are further complicated by the fact that the 'alliance game' and the 'adversary game' are interrelated. Strategies designed for the manipulation of the adversary game may very well have unintended effects in intra-alliance politics; in the same way, strategies which are primarily designed for the alliance game, e.g. aiming at strengthening alliance cohesion, will normally have repercussions for the adversary game, e.g. by increasing the adversary's threat perception.

The issue of military integration which was brought up by the United States in NATO in mid-1950, affected most of the potential goods and bads of both the alliance and the adversary games. The US proposal of 15 September to create a joint European force (including a German contribution) was motivated by a sharply heightened perception of the Soviet threat after the Soviet A-bomb and especially after Korea; its primary goal was to increase the West's deterrent posture *vis-à-vis* the Soviets in the adversary game.

But the proposal also had an important alliance goal: namely to reassure the Europeans of the American commitment to their defence through the symbol of an American supreme commander and a firmer US commitment of ground-combat forces to the defence of Western Europe. The United States voluntarily offered to be 'entrapped' – much to the chagrin of some of her political and military leaders – but on condition that the Europeans should let themselves be similarly entrapped in a joint force. What was offered to the Europeans, then, was increased security, but at the cost of military and political 'entrapment' in NATO and a 'D' strategy of firmness towards the Soviet Union. To this was added the separate question of German participation in Western defence, where rational arguments about the necessity to tap the economic and manpower resources of west Germany became intermingled with psychological obstacles to cooperation with the erstwhile enemy so soon after the liberation as well as fears that this might further sharpen East-West conflicts.

In this situation the 'watchful sparrow' faced a choice between two alternative strategies: She might have chosen a 'D' strategy in the alliance game, i.e. opposed the American plan out of fear of being further involved in military integration, perhaps combined with a more pronounced 'C' (cooperative) strategy towards the East in order to reduce tension in the Baltic and Nordic region. This might, of course, have increased the risk of abandonment by the alliance, but on the other hand American strategic interests in the area might be sufficiently strong to guarantee a response in case of a Soviet aggression, irrespective of Denmark's alliance behaviour.

As a matter of fact, however, Denmark chose a 'C' strategy in the alliance game, went along with NATO integration despite certain misgivings about German rearmament, and relegated the potential negative effects in the adversary game to the background.

At least four factors impinged directly or indirectly on this choice of strategies:

1. The traditionally reticent Danish attitude towards involvement in international power politics, of which the 'watchful sparrow' is a very apt metaphor.
2. The acute feeling of insecurity which lay behind the Danish efforts, since the spring of 1948, to secure external guarantees and which were not sufficiently stilled by membership in the Atlantic Pact in 1949.
3. The German trauma in Danish politics which stems from the nineteenth century (the loss of Schleswig in 1864) and which was significantly reinforced during the German occupation from 1940 to 1945.

4. And, finally, the feeling of limited freedom of action in a question where overriding alliance interests, such as the American commitment to Europe, seemed to be at stake.

The interplay of these factors meant that the natural instincts of the 'watchful sparrow' were sufficiently stifled to permit a positive Danish reaction to the proposed European joint force in 1950.

Entrapment vs. Abandonment in the Decision to Join the North Atlantic Treaty

Denmark entered the postwar world with her traditional neutrality policy discredited for having failed to avert the German occupation in 1940, but with many of its underlying instincts intact.

Accordingly, Danish governments pursued a policy of reliance on the United Nations and of 'blockbuilding' between East and West during the first postwar years. This policy meant attempts to create more equal relations to the two sides, and soon became rather indistinguishable from old-time neutrality. As late as on 30 January 1948, Social Democratic Prime Minister Hans Hedtoft warned against placing Denmark in any bloc.[6] On the other hand, a natural bias to the West was perceptible in Danish foreign policy, and especially relations with Britain remained intimate, politically, commercially and militarily. Britain supplied weapons and training expertise to the Danish military forces, and from 1947 Denmark supplied a brigade (initially *c.* 4,000 men) to the British occupation forces in Germany. The brigade was integrated with the British Army on the Rhine, but only as far as occupation duties were concerned.

> Should the international situation in Europe develop in such a way that a danger could arise of great power entanglements, the Danish Government will give the brigade the necessary contingent orders, possibly by using its right to pull the brigade home, it being under all circumstances the Government's intention to prevent the brigade from being involved in such entanglement.[7]

Finally, in the spring of 1948, fears of entrapment gave way to fears of abandonment in Danish security policy. During the 'March crisis' the Danish government started its search for external guarantees to offset what it had come to see as the critical vulnerability of the country to a Soviet *coup de main* à la 9 April 1940.[8] Danish government officials from now on saw their country as possibly the most vulnerable in Western Europe, and this perception persisted long after Denmark had been included under the protective guarantee in NATO. In its search the Hedtoft government concentrated on the option of a Scandinavian defence union and with a preference for Scandinavian non-alignment (as Sweden demanded) rather than for limited alignment with the West which the Norwegians preferred. In this perspective, the final Danish decision to sign the North Atlantic Treaty represented only the third-best option on its scale of preferences. Fear of entrapment certainly played a role in its aloofness towards military cooperation with the West; decision-makers feared that membership in the pact might involve Denmark against its will in far away conflicts, and specifically it was feared that the Soviet Union might choose to attack Denmark, before the defences of the pact had been built up and its guarantee had become operationally credible. As one prominent Social Democratic parliamentarian used to say: 'Membership in the Atlantic Pact ensures immediate involvement in war, while a Scandinavian Pact might give at least a ten per cent chance of staying out of war.'[9]

But fears of abandonment also seemed to dispose Danish decision-makers to opt for a Scandinavian association, strangely as it may sound in retrospect. Fearing a surprise occupation, and not being well-versed in the novel and arcane concept of deterrence, they were particularly intent on receiving guarantees of prompt and effective assistance *in place*, were an attack to occur. The Western Powers could not conceivably promise such assistance because of distance and lack of available means, but the Swedes who were nearby and who had at the time one of the largest and most efficient military establishments in Western Europe might be able and willing to do so. The Scandinavian Pact aborted for other reasons, and so the Danish government was spared the realisation that its view of Sweden's military capability had been exaggerated. But its fears of abandonment in time of need persisted, even after she had learned about and internalised the basic, war-preventing strategy on which the Atlantic Alliance was originally built. These lingering fears came to play a major role in the formulation of Denmark's response to the proposed integrated force in Europe.

During the Scandinavian negotiations of 1948–9 many aspects of military cooperation and integration were discussed, especially in the so-called Scandinavian Defence Committee, a body composed of one military representative, one civil servant and two politicians from each country which was set up in October 1948 to investigate the possibilities for military cooperation between Denmark, Norway and Sweden. In its reports of 14 January 1949, the Committee noted that a prepared defence cooperation between the three countries would increase their collective effectiveness in war. Hence, a Scandinavian defence union whose members had declared and 'above all demonstrated in action its will to common defence against aggression' would have a certain – though not perfect – preventive effect.[10]

The details of the Committee's deliberations and proposals concerning the character and degree of military integration envisaged for a defence union are still classified, but subsequent political discussions, both in Denmark and in inter-Scandinavian meetings, leave the impression that both military leaders and politicians were thinking in terms of a fairly high degree of coordination between the military commands of the three countries and a high level of peacetime cooperation between their military forces (e.g. cooperation between intelligence services, weapons' standardisation and joint exercises) – if only the political preconditions for a union could be established. In Denmark, most supporters of a Scandinavian defence treaty seemed to envisage a fairly comprehensive and integrated alliance with equanimity and without fears of entrapment.

However, such fears surfaced on several occasions during the process of adjustment to membership in the North Atlantic Treaty after the breakdown of Scandinavian talks in January 1949 especially as a fear of being dragged into faraway conflicts. But in this respect, the vagueness of Article 5 (which had earlier nurtured the fear of potential abandonment) now came to be seen also as a safety valve against such contingencies.

During the fact-finding tour to Washington in mid-March 1949 Foreign Minister Gustav Rasmussen received assurances that in some circumstances (Rasmussen had asked about an attack against Alaska) 'it would be preferable for some parties not to declare war ... but to take other appropriate measures',[11] but that in case of an 'obvious' aggression (e.g. against Denmark) individual countries would presumably take action without waiting for the consultative machinery of the alliance to start.[12] Gustav Rasmussen also sought – and received – reassurance that the

United States would not demand military bases in Denmark.[13]

The decisive factor for Denmark's entry, however, was that she did not have much choice. Even if the fears of entrapment and abandonment were only partially stilled, joining the alliance was by far preferable to standing alone. Complete guarantees were not available, as Prime Minister Hans Hedtoft told the Parliamentary Foreign Relations Committee.[14]

IV. Denmark and the Alliance until Korea

As a consequence of the way in which Denmark entered the Atlantic Alliance, her politicians were even less prepared than their colleagues in other member countries for the political and military developments which in less than eighteen months transformed it into a highly integrated military organisation. Until the summer of 1950 military integration played only a minor role as a goal of NATO planning.[15] Danish attitudes towards the alliance in this early period were primarily shaped by reactions to the practical efforts to make the new organisation a going concern, for example the establishment of the regional-planning groups, the negotiation of military-assistance agreements and the formulation of the first joint contingency plans.

Compared to Norway the Danish government took a cautious and reactive approach to discussions in the alliance during this period. On most questions Danish and Norwegian attitudes did not differ much, but normally the Danes preferred to take the back seat and let the Norwegians do the running.

This passivity created considerable irritation in Norway and gave the impression that the Danes did not do enough to cope with their difficult security situation.[16] Like Norway, Denmark was in favour of the establishment of the North European Regional Planning Group (NERPG), covering Denmark and Norway, when military organisation under the North Atlantic Treaty came up for discussion in the autumn of 1949, presumably because this served to retain a certain Nordic identity within the alliance structure. At the same time, the two countries urged that Britain should participate fully in the NERPG and that the attachment of the United States to NERPG should not be inferior to its participation in the Western European planning group. The prime motivation for these demands was, of course, the wish to commit the Western powers as firmly to the defence of the region as possible and to prevent all their resources and attention from going into the force build-up and contingency planning for the central region. These efforts were later resumed in order to secure the maximum British and American participation in the command structure of the Northern Region when this question came up for discussion in late 1950 and early 1951.[17]

From the outset, Danish efforts were directed towards securing firm British and American pledges of reinforcements for Denmark in case of an attack, but with only limited success. In the summer of 1950 Defence Minister Rasmus Hansen complained that while a Danish-Norwegian agreement in principle had been reached in NERPG to consider Denmark and south Norway as one region where Danish and Norwegian forces should be used according to an overall plan, no comparable clarity had been reached as to 'the extremely important question' of utilising British forces in the Nordic area. Nor had it been possible to get any information from the United States on expected assistance in case of an attack; on the contrary a recent American memo to the NERPG had indicated that direct US assistance for the area was not contemplated for the first phase of an attack. In Rasmus Hansen's view this was highly unsatisfactory, as the defence of Denmark against a Soviet blitz attack was only feasible if effective assistance was available from other pact members simultaneously with the initiation of the attack. To have much meaning the concept of balanced collective forces (which was underwritten at the London meeting of the North Atlantic Council in May 1950) presupposed that in case of an aggression in Europe tactical forces should be immediately shipped east from America and that corresponding forces should at once be moved from the western parts of Europe and deployed towards the more vulnerable eastern areas.[18]

The last-mentioned concept referred to another source of Danish uneasiness over the trend of strategy discussions in the alliance: namely the geographical isolation of Denmark from the bulk of western defence in the central region. During the discussion before the decision to sign the North Atlantic Treaty, a Social Democratic politician had cautioned that if the Rhine were to be the main defence line, then Denmark would be on the wrong side.[19]

These concerns about the defence line in Europe and the Anglo-Saxon contribution were shared by the Norwegians and, in more general terms, by the other continental allies. From the start they objected to the American concept according to which the Europeans were to shoulder the responsibility for land and air defence in Europe while the Americans would be responsible for strategic warfare and trans-Atlantic communications.[20] In the overall strategic concept for the alliance adopted by the North Atlantic Council in January 1950 the European responsibility for continental defence was qualified by the insertion of the term 'initial' and of the obligation of other members to assist with the shortest possible delay in case of a Russian attack,[21] but it was not until after Korea that the Americans were willing to pledge additional land forces to the defence of Continental Europe.

The British were equally reluctant to commit themselves. In March 1950 they decided to earmark two infantry divisions for the Continent in case of an attack,[22] but their interests were focused on the central front and the Rhine line rather than on the Northern flank which was considered secondary and indefensible anyway.[23]

The main approach of allied contingency planning in this early period was hardly promising either, as seen from a northern perspective. The Medium Defence Plan adopted by the Defence Committee on 1 April 1950 was based on holding the Rhine-Ijssel line, i.e. a line well behind the approaches to Denmark.

In the north the Kiel Canal and northern Norway were to be held 'if possible' and certain key base areas in the region 'in any event'.[24] But this was hardly reassuring to the Danes, who felt acutely vulnerable, as long as there was no muscle behind the plan. In the spring of 1950 Denmark and (more actively) Norway fought to persuade the British to commit combat troops to the Kiel Canal line and to join the Danish and Norwegian occupation forces in Schleswig-Holstein in setting up a Jutland covering force. The British, however, had little faith in the possibility of holding the canal and actually foresaw a rapid withdrawal to and even evacuation from Denmark, if the Russians were to attack from the south.[25] Finally, in the summer of 1950, they gave in and promised to relocate an armoured-car regiment to the area,[26] but this was far less than hoped for by Denmark and Norway and clearly too little to make the Kiel line really credible, especially as the area from the canal and up to the demarcation line was virtually devoid of allied forces.

The failure to receive firm guarantees of allied reinforcements and the perception of lying on the wrong side of the defence line in Europe contributed to a bout of extraordinary frustration and pessimism which gripped the Danish government and especially Prime Minister Hedtoft during the first half of 1950. In June 1950 Norwegian Foreign Minister Lange (who had recently met Hedtoft at a meeting of Scandinavian Social Democratic leaders in Oslo) told the American counsellor in Oslo that the Danes were apprehensive of their exposed position and the difficulties of defending their territory, and that they lacked conviction as to British and American intentions to defend them. In general, the Danes had misgivings about the benefits they would derive from the Atlantic Pact and regretted that it had not been possible to organise a Scandinavian defence agreement.[27] A week later Prime Minister Hedtoft vented the same fears directly to Mrs Eugenie Anderson, the US Ambassador to Denmark, whose previous 'impressions of his doubts on effectiveness of NATO in meeting Denmark's security and defense needs were confirmed and deepened'. Hedtoft's anxieties seemed particularly to stem from the defence plans discussed in the NERPG and at the recent defence ministers' meeting in London which in his view did not provide Denmark with sufficient protection. The ambassador ended her telegram by warning that 'I believe his concern with Denmark's defense cannot be allayed unless he receives more positive assurances on assistance Denmark may expect or receive in event of emergency'.[28] By the summer of 1950 Danish policy-makers were thus in a sombre mood and plagued by severe second thoughts as to the wisdom of signing the Atlantic Pact a year earlier. A further element aside from concern with Denmark's own national defence needs were doubts as to the durability of American interests in Europe. In May, Hedtoft expressed both his hope that the United States would stay in Germany indefinitely and his anxiety that they would not, to Mrs Anderson.[29] In his view, there was only one way to redress the general weakness of Western Europe *vis-à-vis* the Soviet bloc, viz. that 'a Western European Community be developed into a much stronger association politically, economically and militarily to offset the Soviet menace, and that Western Europe must be able to look to US for spiritual leadership in the effort'.[30] But at the time he hardly dared to believe in this eventuality.

Nikolaj Petersen

US Initiatives and Danish Responses, July 1950 to February 1951

A few months later – after Korea – the United States started to exercise such leadership and found a rather more receptive attitude in Copenhagen than the pessisism which had prevailed till then would have suggested. In the view of Defence Minister Rasmus Hansen, Korea had 'galvanized' Danish public opinion and 'NATO thinking' had been enormously strengthened by the US/UN reaction.[31] In fact, the government reacted promptly to the US request of 25 July to the European Pact members to submit immediate statements on their proposed defence increases, by pledging on 5 August an additional defence effort over the next two years to the sum of Dkr. 300 million plus Dkr. 100 million for civilian defence purposes.[32] This initiative, which the American Embassy considered 'a dramatic response to aggression in Korea', was also received quite favourably in the State Department.[33]

But the government ran into domestic trouble over its covering proposal which included a progressive defence tax as well as a compulsory defence loan for the higher income brackets. While the expanded defence budget went through parliament on 9 August with the combined votes of the governing Social Democrats, the Liberals and the Conservatives, the debate showed such disagreement over the covering laws that the Hedtoft Government chose to dissolve the *Folketing* and to call for general elections for 5 September.

After the elections the Hedtoft Government continued on a somewhat weakened basis. But Denmark was still in a kind of political interregnum on 15 September, when the United States presented its proposal in the North Atlantic Council to establish a unified military force in Europe, to include a German contribution and to put it under an American supreme commander. The new Hedtoft Government was not formed until the same day and the newly elected *Folketing* was not scheduled to convene until the first week of October. Because of the uncertain domestic political situation, Foreign Minister Gustav Rasmussen had decided to stay home from the New York Council meeting, and his representative, Ambassador Henrik Kauffmann, was therefore caught in a delicate situation by the American initiative, which was sprung upon him in the council meeting of 15 September. Kauffmann reacted to this situation by aligning himself closely with the Norwegian Foreign Minister Halvard Lange, possibly on the strength of his general instructions for the council meeting. In the meeting on 15 September he pronounced himself in agreement with Norway and Belgium, both of which had urged caution on the question of German rearmament in their initial responses to the US proposal. Lange stressed the psychological and political problems involved in the use of German manpower and proposed that the alliance should begin studying the technical aspects of the problem.[34] The Belgian representative had an equally circumscribed attitude towards German rearmament, but also took a more positive line in urging a defence line as far to the east as possible and German participation in its own defence.[35]

When the question came up again in the council meeting on 18 September, Kauffmann briefly explained that the Danish and Norwegian positions were generally similar, which was why he preferred to speak after Halvard Lange, whose position he subsequently 'generally subscribed to'.[36] At this meeting Lange was more specific in his reservations on the American proposal, but also more positive towards it. On the one hand he asked several critical questions, which undoubtedly also covered Danish concerns: Would the proposed force cover the whole treaty area or only central Europe? Would the Supreme Commander have authority over the training of units which were not allocated to him? What would be the effect of the integrated force on the regional planning groups? And should the US proposal be considered a package proposal? But Lange also stated that he had been greatly impressed by the arguments in favour of an integrated force and that Norway would never wish to obstruct action which the Great Three and other alliance members were agreed upon.[37]

The reason for this more positive attitude can presumably be found in the reassurances which Acheson had given to Lange concerning his critical questions, and in which he *inter alia* stated that the US proposal was meant to cover the whole treaty area, even though he added that no one could tell at the moment how the defence was going to be, as this depended on the circumstances, including the forces available. Acheson also stated that the Supreme Commander would have no authority over forces intended for, but not yet allocated to, the integrated force, but that he should have an important voice in setting standards of training, etc.[38]

Nonetheless, it was clear that neither Lange nor Kauffmann were able to commit their governments without referring the problem home for domestic decision. As Secretary of State Dean Acheson wrote to President Truman on 20 September, both countries felt that:

> the implications of a united force had to be very carefully considered. Their geographic position made it clear to them that they will want to be sure how much of their own force would be retained for the defense of their own country and how much would be used for general operations on the continent. They also wanted to know to what extent the supreme commander would direct his strategy towards defending their particular countries. Of course, no one could answer this latter question.[39]

As a result the council meeting was recessed for a week, and the two governments promised to answer by then.

In the domestic discussions that followed, the two governments continued to keep in close contact with the Norwegians in the more active role. Thus on 22 September the Danish Embassy in Oslo was able to report home the preliminary American reaction to some further questions which the Norwegian government had posed. In a meeting with the Norwegian delegation in New York, Theodore Achilles of the State Department had confirmed that the supreme commander would be charged with the defence of all Europe. He also subscribed to the goal of moving the defence line so far east that Denmark could be covered, but did not fail to point out that this would depend on the availability of sufficient forces. Whether Denmark could be held would therefore depend on the circumstances, i.e. whether the supreme commander would have forces available for its defence, in case the defence line was broken. It was difficult to give commitments as far as Denmark was concerned.[40]

As will be discussed below, such strategic concerns were very much in the forefront of Danish deliberations on the American proposal. But the government had other worries as well. As mentioned, the newly elected *Folketing* was not scheduled to convene before early October, which meant that the Parliamentary Foreign Policy Committee (*Udenrigspolitisk Naevn*) where the government would normally seek its parliamentary backing, had not yet been elected. The government was therefore in a dilemma between calling in the *Folketing* for an emergency session, postponing its answer until October (which would be diplomatically very difficult) – or finding some other procedure for securing domestic support. The dilemma was exacerbated by the critical attitude of the Radical party, the government's normal parliamentary support. The Radicals had opposed Danish membership in the alliance in 1949 and now demanded a full-blown parliamentary debate and an extended deadline for the final decision.[41] Privately, *Politiken*, the leading Danish daily, threatened 'strenuous opposition' if the government were to go ahead without parliamentary approval.[42]

In the event, an informal procedure was found through consultations with the leaders of the so-called 'democratic' parties who then consulted their own parliamentary groups on an informal basis. On 23 September the parliamentary groups of the three major parties, i.e. Social Democrats, Liberals and Conservatives, gave their assent to the government's proposal to accept in principle the American package. The Radicals were opposed, arguing that acceptance of the integrated force would have even more far-reaching implications than the original decision to join the alliance, while the Justice Party argued that the decision should be made by parliament, and that only voluntary troops should be sent abroad to serve in the European army.[43] A few days before, the Communist party had claimed that a Danish acceptance would mean giving up Danish control over war and peace as well as violate the constitution.[44]

On this background Foreign Minister Gustav Rasmussen could state in the North Atlantic Council on 26 September that:

> Danes agree (1) defense as far east in Germany as possible and (2) integrated defense forces proposed by US. Danes understand each NAT government should as soon as possible indicate forces to be committed to integrated force and are studying this. However, due to geographic considerations Danish forces will be insufficient alone to defend Denmark and it is Danish understanding that one of tasks of integrated defense force is defense of all of WE including Denmark. Re German participation, Danes recognize need of utilizing all available forces for defence of WE and believe US proposal provides basis for German participation without reviving German militarism. Re NATO, Danes believe basic structure should remain unchanged and in particular Council should continue to exercise its authority as supreme NATO body.[45]

The Danish acceptance of the integrated force was sanctioned by the *Folketing* on 18 October with 112 members voting for, eighteen against and eleven abstaining. During the debate both Prime Minister Hedtoft and Foreign Miniser Gustav Rasmussen emphasised that the Danish acceptance was in principle only, and that the council resolution of 26 September was to be considered mainly as a framework to be filled out by the defence ministers and the military authorities in subsequent negotiations.[46] Consequently Danish politicians continued to be highly interested in the practical details of the proposed force.

Thus the Hedtoft Government reacted sharply to the French Pleven Plan of 24 October 1950. At the Defence Committee meeting in Washington at the end of October where the Pleven Plan and its American counterpart were given their first hearing, Defence Minister Rasmus Hansen started out doubting whether it was the right time to try to implement the French plan in view of the constitutional and other practical problems which it raised. On the other hand, he was authorised to support the American plan; even though German rearmament caused great political problems in Denmark, she could accept in principle both the inclusion of German units in the integrated force and German production for it. Hansen also reiterated the well-known Danish demand that NATO's line of defence must follow approximately the demarcation line in Germany; and as it turned out a few days later, when he spoke his mind on the French plan, this was also his principal objection to it. In a long attack on the French position 'he expressed disappointment "to use mild words" that all Fr[ench] statements and Fr[ench] plans reveal complete disregard [for the] security of Denmark and Norway ... [A p]ractical solution of Denmark's security problem must be found.[47]

Immediately before the Washington meeting the Hedtoft Government fell, to be replaced by a Liberal-Conservative coalition. The new government chose to tone down its criticism of the Pleven Plan, but without changing its fundamental sympathy for the American, rather than the French, approach. In a *Folketing* debate the new Foreign Minister, Ole Bjørn Kraft, lauded the Pleven Plan for its 'mixture of imagination, openness and logic' and as a contribution to the clarification of the issue. However, it was too complicated and too far-reaching to be implemented with the necessary speed, and Denmark would therefore support efforts in the alliance which could meet the immediate need for

Denmark and Military Integration

the creation of a unified European force including a German contribution.[48] As Denmark argued in the Deputies' Council, the proposed European Army would compromise a speedy German contribution to the defence of Western Europe and delay the creation of adequate defences at the zonal boundary in Germany. The Germans should therefore be taken directly into the NATO force under NATO supervision and safeguards.[49]

Eventually, the Danish government supported the compromise formula which was reached at the North Atlantic Council meeting in Brussels in December 1950. And in February 1951 the *Folketing* endorsed the Brussels resolution and the assignment of the Danish brigade in Schleswig-Holstein to the new Supreme Allied Commander Europe (SACEUR).[50]

The Main Determinants

Above it was hypothesised that Denmark's response to the proposals for military integration in Europe might be explained by four factors or determinants: (1) her need of security and fear of abandonment, (2) her need of freedom of action and fear of entrapment, (3) her attitudes towards German rearmament; and (4) her decision-makers' feeling of constraints in the decision-making situation. Below these four factors will be analysed, starting with the latter question.

Freedom of Decision

Danish politicians undoubtedly worked under severe constraints during their discussion of the American proposal in September. The government felt acute discomfort at having to make a decision under time pressure and under circumstances where the normal parliamentary consultation procedure could not be followed. This problem was exacerbated by the fact that parts of the Social Democratic party were only lukewarm to alliance membership,[51] and that the government's normal parliamentary support, the Radicals, were opposed to a positive response.

On one hand the government felt that it would give an unfortunate impression of unwarranted external pressure, if the *Folketing* were to be convened for an emergency session; on the other hand, 'it would have made a negative and deleterious impression if after a week Denmark as the only Atlantic Pact power should have declared itself unable to make a statement in principle, but had asked for time for further consideration'.[52]

Denmark also felt strong external pressures to assent to the American proposal. As Gustav Rasmussen told the party representatives: Denmark had a veto power in the North Atlantic Council, but it was formal rather than real.[53]

The freedom of manoeuvre of the Danish government was therefore severely circumscribed. However, this does not appear to be a sufficient explanation of the decision to accept the American proposal; it was probably not even a necessary condition for it.

The Demand for Security

As we have seen, by the summer of 1950, Danish policy-makers felt acute frustrations over the alliance guarantee, which even amounted to genuine fears of abandonment. These fears were based on the size and geographical proximity of the Soviet threat, on the failure so far to receive firm commitments of allied reinforcements in case of an attack, and on the fact of geographical isolation from the main alliance defence as long as the Rhine was the official forward-defence line. These concerns were summed up in Prime Minister Hedtoft's words to Ambassador Anderson: 'Denmark wants to be defended, not liberated.'

The possibility that a joint, integrated force in Europe might contribute to a solution of Denmark's delicate security was probably the single most important factor in the Danish decision to accept the American proposal.

The force was generally seen as an important strengthening of the alliance. According to Foreign Minister Gustav Rasmussen the prime consideration of the government had been 'the supreme importance that the Atlantic powers can really be defended'. The preservation of peace would, of course, be the best and surest means, but the government would be irresponsible if it discounted the possibility that Denmark could be attacked. In the government's view the American plan would strengthen the pact both politically and militarily. However, it wanted to receive specific assurances that the force would defend Denmark, too.[54] Consequently, in its reply of 26 September, the government expressly stated its view that the joint force should prevent any pact member being occupied and that it must have as one of its purposes the protection of Denmark. Specifically, it was emphasised that the defence line should be placed as far east as possible.

In September, these points were merely hopes or, at best, assumptions which might – or might not – be fulfilled at some later date. On the other hand, Danish policy-makers did not have much alternative to clinging to such hopes. As the parliamentary spokesman for the Social Democrats, Poul Hansen, told the *Folketing* on 12 October, Denmark's geographical position was so exposed that hardly any other country could have a larger interest in the joint force.[55] The government reacted so nervously to the Pleven Plan because they saw it as a French device to postpone German rearmament and to retain the Rhine as NATO's primary defence line. In November, former Defence Minister Rasmus Hansen told his parliamentary group that the adoption of the plan would constitute a 'significant change' in the underlying assumptions of Danish alliance membership. He also spelled out, more clearly than had been done in the public debate, that without a German rearmament there would be no possibility of moving the defence line eastward from the Rhine, which meant that Denmark and Norway would be uncovered.[56]

The parliamentary debate in early 1951 over the ratification of the Brussels decisions provided an opportunity for re-examining the original assumptions of the Danish response. Harald Petersen, the new Liberal Defence Minister, specifically referred to Gustav Rasmussen's remarks in October (see above), and asked rhetorically whether Denmark's special interests had been taken into consideration. In his opinion this had been the case. Thus he referred to General Marshall's remark at the end of the Defence Committee meeting in October 1950 that the defence forces should be deployed eastward, if alliance membership were to have any strategic meaning to Norway and Denmark and give them an effective guarantee. According to Petersen, the problem of the defence line had from the start been 'the central point' in the making of the alliance's defence plans. He conceded that its solution would naturally depend on the strength of the Western European defence force, but took the decision to partially rearm west Germany as an indication of a will to move in the direction indicated by General Marshall:[57]

> If we succeed in deploying the defence towards the east, whereby i.a. Northern Germany will be included in the defended area, it will be readily seen, that this provides cover for the Jutland peninsula, which would be of vital importance for the defence of Denmark. In this way, the land defence of Jutland can be pushed forward to the common front in Germany, whereby it would, of course, gain much in strength. This strategy furthermore entails the highly important advantage for the defence of Denmark, that a potential enemy is not given on beforehand coastal areas in the western part of the Baltic from where attacks could be mounted against the Danish islands and the Belts; in the same way a potential enemy will not be able to place air bases close south of the Danish border.[58]

This, in a nutshell, was the strategic rationale of the Danish acceptance of the integrated force. It was also the background for assigning the Danish brigade in Schleswig-Holstein to the new supreme commander in Europe.

Fears of Entrapment

Apart from the arguments of the NATO opposition and especially the Communists, fears that the joint force might involve unwelcome commitments played only a limited role in the public debate and in the political deliberations. After the decision to accept, spokesmen of the pro-NATO parties joined to assert that the force was a natural consequence of the alliance, and that international cooperation would always involve certain voluntary limitations of national sovereignty.[59] Hedtoft also pointed out that the Scandinavian Defence Union would have implied some amount of military integration.[60]

On the other side the very fact that Denmark – together with Norway – was the only country which felt it necessary to submit the American proposal to some scrutiny before accepting it in principle, is an indication that policy-makers did not feel it quite so natural to accept as was claimed afterwards, and that they felt at least some hesitation at entering the scheme. According to Foreign Minister Rasmussen one important premise for Danish participation would be that it would not commit Denmark to military measures which were deemed to be against Danish security interests.[61]

Other concerns also came up for discussion. One was whether participation in the force would be constitutional. Both Hedtoft and Rasmussen mentioned this as a problem to Ambassador Anderson,[62] and on 21 September the Permanent Secretary in the Prime Minister's Office, Andreas Møller, wrote a memo on the constitutional aspects of the proposal. Mr Møller did not see such a problem *per se*. But he also emphasised that the unified command must not abrogate the individual country's right to decide whether it would use armed power in case of an attack on another member country, that competent Danish authorities must retain administrative control over the Danish contingent to the force (e.g. with respect to call-ups), and that the joint command must be answerable to the individual member countries. Mr Møller found that these concerns were taken care of in the American proposal, and he especially pointed out that Danish participation in NATO organs would serve to enforce the principle that Danish forces should be used primarily to protect the homeland.[63]

This was another concern of the government, which argued that Denmark had so few resources and such an exposed geographical position, that she had very little with which to contribute to the defence of other than the national territory. In the decision of February 1951 to assign the Danish brigade in Germany to SACEUR it was therefore expressly stated that it should be used for the defence of Denmark's southern border.[64]

One final reservation was that the proposed arrangement must preserve some Danish voice and influence in the Alliance.[65] In the official reply of 26 September it was therefore particularly emphasised that the North Atlantic Council (because of its principle of unanimity) should remain the supreme organ of the organisation; in the Danish view, the establishment of a separate military system within the alliance must not lead to any loss of political control.[66]

On a number of points, therefore, Danish decision-makers had reservations as to the commitments which the new military organisation might imply; they were rather vague, however, compared to the perceived potential benefits with respect to increased national security. The fear of abandonment was considerably stronger than the fear of entrapment.

The German Trauma

A final Danish concern was the proposed rearmament of West Germany which revived the traumatic experiences of German occupation during the Second World War. Contemplating the resurrection of the Wehrmacht only five years after the war was psychologically and politically difficult, and in the Danish case, the German occupation had only been the culmination of a century-long security and national problem *vis-à-vis* Germany which went back to the Schleswig wars of the nineteenth century. Furthermore, this trauma had been nurtured in the postwar years by a Danish resentment over the less-than-liberal treatment of the Danish minority in South Schleswig by the German regional authorities.

There was therefore a deep-seated anti-German sentiment in Denmark which could be used – and was used, especially by the Communists – against the integrated force. In its official reply the government referred to its serious concern over any resurrection of Germany's military power, but at the same time conceded the urgent necessity to include all available resources in the Western defence, and also noted that the proposal would secure the necessary controls.[67] As the parliamentary committee argued in February 1951, the scheme did not imply a rearmament of Germany, but only the participation of German units in the joint defence force, and it was also noted that all other countries which had been occupied by Germany during the war had accepted this.[68] The crucial argument for accepting, and even welcoming, German participation, however, was its potentialities for strengthening the defence of Denmark. Only through the build-up of German forces would it be possible to establish the covering force of the southern approaches to Denmark which the Danish government saw as its main security object. Compared to this, other arguments were of lesser importance.

Conclusions

The Danish decision to accept the North Atlantic Council resolutions of September and December 1950 to create a joint force in Europe was made under circumstances of extreme domestic and external constraints which left decision-makers little room for manoeuvre. The main determinant, however, was the security benefits which the force might potentially entail, both through its basic premise to defend all of NATO Europe and the specific contribution to the defence of Denmark which would result from a movement of the forward-defence line from the Rhine to the Elbe – or to the demarcation line, as Danish politicians insisted.[69]

Danish decision-makers did not accept the steps towards military integration without some concern both for national freedom of action (fear of entrapment) and for the consequences of a German rearmament, but these concerns were not allowed to dominate the security interests involved. The fear of abandonment proved the stronger concern, as it had been since the spring of 1948.

In a curious way, the problems of the early 1950s repeated themselves towards the end of the decade. At this time the Bundeswehr was slowly gaining strength, and hence the question arose as to the forms of cooperation between Danish and German forces in the Baltic and in the Jutland peninsula.[70] Again, the Danish government was placed under considerable pressure with both the Federal Republic and SACEUR urging the establishment of a joint command for Denmark and Schleswig-Holstein and threatening a change of the boundary between the northern and central regions, if Denmark did not accept. Again, fears of entrapment arose because of potential German dominance within the joint command, and again the German 'bogey' was conjured up by opponents of the proposed arrangement. But once more, the need for security and the fear of abandonment proved the stronger motive. Throughout the 1950s, these fears had continued to plague the Danish governments, as it took an unexpectedly long time before the German contribution could begin to make itself felt, and because the allies refused to increase their meagre commitment to the defence of Denmark's southern approaches in the meantime; in 1953 the Norwegians even withdrew their force from Schleswig-Holstein, further exposing the vulnerable Danish flank. Only from about 1958 when the *Bundeswehr* and the *Bundesmarine* began to have some strength could the hopes for increased security which had originally inspired the acceptance of the integrated force back in 1950 begin to be fulfilled. In the Danish perspective, the BALTAP Command, which was finally established in 1962, put the final seal on the fear of abandonment which had been such a conspicious element in Danish security policy since 1948. And its smooth operation since then has served to still many of the fears of entrapment which intimate military cooperation with the Federal Republic had originally evoked.

Notes

1. Nikolaj Petersen, 'Optionsproblematikken i dansk sikkerhedspolitik 1948–49', in Niels Amstrup and Ib Faurby, (eds), *Studier i dansk udenrigspolitik tilegnet Erling Bjøl*, Aarhus: Forlaget Politica, 1978, pp. 199–236. Cf. Nikolaj Petersen, 'Atlantpagten eller Norden? Den danske alliancebeslutning 1949', in Carsten Due-Nielsen, Johan Peter Noack and Nikolaj Petersen (eds) *Danmark, Norden og NATO 1948–1962*, Copenhagen: Jurist- og Okonomforbundets Forlag, 1991, pp. 17–42.
2. Nikolaj Petersen, 'Danish and Norwegian alliance policies 1948–49: a comparative analysis', *Cooperation and Conflict*, XIV, 1979, pp. 171–92.
3. Dean Acheson, *Present at the Creation: My Years in the State Department*, New York: Norton, 1969, p. 279. Acheson was wrong about the coalition government, but otherwise gives a very apt characterisation of Gustav Rasmussen personally and of the delicate position of his government.
4. Glenn H. Snyder, 'The security dilemma in alliance politics', *World Politics*, vol. 36, no. 4, July 1984, pp. 461–95.
5. Ibid., p. 467.
6. Ministry of Foreign Affairs, *Dansk sikkerhedspolitik 1948–1966*, Copenhagen, 1968, vol. 1, p. 22.
7. Communication from Ministry of War to Maj. – Gen. R. Allerup, Chief of the Danish Brigade in Germany, 23 June 1947, *Records of the Danish Foreign Ministry* (UM) 13 D 25 a.
8. For most of the arguments for a Scandinavian alignment ans against membership in the atlantic Part, see a memo termed 'Some considerations for use *vis-à-vis* the Western Powers in the case it is decided to sign a Scandinavian defence agreement without commitment to enter an Atlantic Union' in *Danish Foreign Ministry*, 2 February 1949, UM 5 F 90a.
9. Julius Bomholt, Chairman of the Parliamentary Foreign Affairs Committee.
10. Concluding remarks of the Scandinavian Defence Committee Report, in *Danish Foreign Ministry*, vol. II, p. 55.
11. Dean Acheson, 11 March 1949. *Foreign Relations of the United States*, FRUS, 1949, vol. IV, p. 193.
12. Charles Bohlen, 12 March 1949. Ibid., p. 198.
13. Ibid., p. 194.
14. 2 March 1949. Records of the Parliamentary Foreign Relations Committee, UM 3 E 91 1.
15. Christian Greiner, 'Die alliierten militärstrategischen Planungen zur Verteidigung Westeuropas 1947–1950', in Roland G. Foerster, Christian Greiner, Georg Meyer, Hans-Jürgen Rautenberg und

Norbert Wiggershaus, *Von der Kapitulation bis zum Pleven-Plan. Anfänge westdeutscher Sicherheitspolitik 1945–1956.* vol. 1., München, Wien: Oldenbourg, 1982, p. 244.
16. Rolf Tamnes, *Kamp mot russerne på tysk jord?, Tysklandsbrigaden og den kolde krigen 1947–1953,* FHFS notat no. 2, 1985, p. 47.
17. Ibid.; Rolf Tamnes, 'Norway's Struggle for the Northern Flank, 1950–1952', in Olav Riste (ed.), *Western Security in the Formative Years: European and Atlantic Defence 1947–1953,* Oslo: Universitetsforlaget, 1985, p. 230. The Danish government did not support the Norwegian demand for an American chief, however, partly for fear that this might increase the pressure for additional defence expenditures. Ibid.
18. Message from Defence Minister Rasmus Hansen to Danish Liaison Officer at the Standing Group, 5 July 1950.
19. Gustav Pedersen in the Parliamentary Foreign Policy Committee, 23 February 1949, *Danish Foreign Ministry,* UM 3 E 91 1.
20. See Greiner (Note 16), pp. 230–53.
21. Ibid., p. 247.
22. See Tamnes (Note 17), p. 10.
23. Ibid., p. 45.
24. Kenneth W. Condit, *The History of the Joint Chiefs of Staff: The Joint Chiefs of Staff and National Policy,* vol. II: *1947–1949,* JCS Historical Division, 1976, pp. 405–6.
25. See Tamnes (Note 17), p. 38.
26. Ibid.
27. Lange also said that there was an undercurrent of Danish resentment towards Norway for having dragged Denmark into the Alliance. Tel. 549 from Oslo, 9 June 1950, FRUS, 1950, vol. III, pp. 120–1. According to US Ambassador Anderson Hedtoft had made some 'tentative overtures' (presumably concerning Scandinavian defence cooperation) at the Social Democratic meeting in Oslo. Desp. 322 from Copenhagen, 12 October 1950. National Archives and Records Service, Washington, DC, NARS, Department of State Records, RG 59, DS 759.13/10–1250.
28. Tel. 425 from Copenhagen, 15 June 1950. 740.5/6–1550, ibid.
29. Tel. 547 from Copenhagen, 30 May 1950. 740.5/5–3050, ibid.
30. Conversation with Ambassador Anderson 17 April 1950. Tel. 276 from Copenhagen 18 April 1950. 759.00/4–1850, ibid.
31. Tel. 37 from Copenhagen 11 July 1950. 759.5/7–1150, ibid.
32. Danish defence expenditures for FY 1949–50 amounted to a total of D.Kr. 310 million.
33. Tel. 171 from Copenhagen 10 August 1950. RG 59, 740.5/8–1050, NARS.
34. FRUS 1950, vol. III, pp. 309–10.
35. Ibid., p. 310. The eastern defence line was also heavily stressed by the

Dutch Foreign Minister. Ibid., p. 309.
36. Ibid., pp. 328, 330.
37. Ibid., pp. 329, 330.
38. Ibid., p. 330.
39. Ibid., p. 336.
40. Tel. from Ambassador Schön, Oslo, September 1950.
41. Letter from Jørgen Jørgensen and Bertel Dahlgaard, MPs, to Prime Minister Hedtoft 21 September 1950. Hans Hedtoft's Archives, box 46.
42. Tel. 318 from Copenhagen, 21 September 1950. RG 59, 759.00/9–2150, NARS. *Politiken* was affiliated with the Radical party, but had nevertheless supported Danish adherence to the Atlantic Pact in 1949.
43. *Avisaarbogen 1950*, 23 September 1950.
44. Ibid., 21 September 1950, Add.
45. FRUS 1950, vol. III, pp. 348–9. Official Danish text in Udenrigsministeriet, *Dansk sikkerhedspolitik 1948–66*, vol. 2, pp. 258–9.
46. *Rigsdagstidende*, 1950–51, Parliamentary Records, Folketingets forhandlinger, col. 207, 18 October 1950.
47. FRUS 1950, vol. III, p. 417, 425.
48. *Rigsdagstidende* 1950–51, Folketingets forhandlinger, cols. 1377–8, 5 December 1950.
49. FRUS 1950, vol. III, p. 492, 28 November 1950.
50. *Rigsdagstidende* 1950–51, Folketingets forhandlinger, cols. 1854f., 2046f, 30 January and 6 February 1951.
51. In May 1950 Hedtoft told Ambassador Anderson that he feared that about 200,000 out of 800,000 Social Democratic voters did not really accept NATO, and that this might cause him to lose the next election. Tel. 547 from Copenhagen, 30 May 1950, RG 59, 740.5/5–3050, NARS.
52. Gustav Rasmussen in the *Folketing*, 17 October 1950. *Rigsdagstidende* 1950–51, Folketingets forhandlinger, col. 213.
53. *Protocol of the Conservative parliamentary group*, 23 September 1950.
54. *Rigsdagstidende* 1950–51, Folketingets forhandlinger, col. 210, 17 October 1950.
55. Ibid., col. 69, 12 October 1950.
56. *Protocol of the Social Democratic parliamentary group*, 16 November 1950.
57. *Rigsdagstidende* 1950–51, Folketingets forhandlinger, col. 1856–57, 30 January 1951.
58. Ibid., col. 1858.
59. See e.g. Poul Hansen (Soc. Dem.), Erik Eriksen (Lib.) and Bjorn Kraft (Cons.) in the *Folketing*, 12 October 1950. Ibid., 68, 98 and 104–5.
60. Ibid., cols. 177–8, 17 October 1950.

61. Ibid., col. 210, 17 October 1950.
62. Tels. 318 and 322 from Copenhagen 21 September 1950. RG 59 759.00/9–2150 and /9–2250, NARS.
63. Memo from the Prime Minister's Office, 21 September 1950.
64. Report of *Folketing ad hoc* committee, 2 February 1950. *Rigsdagstidende* 1950–51, tillaeg B, col. 213.
65. Gustav Rasmussen, 17 October 1950, in *Rigsdagstidende* 1950–1, Folketingets forhandlinger, col. 210.
66. Memo to Ambassador Kauffmann, Washington, 23 September 1950.
67. Ibid.
68. See Note 65.
69. See Defence Minister Harald Petersen in the *Folketing*, 6 February 1951. *Rigsdagstidende* 1950–51, Folketingets forhandlinger, col. 1957.
70. Since the early 1950s Denmark and Schleswig-Holstein had belonged to NATO's Northern Region (HQ: Oslo), while the remaining part of the Federal Republic belonged in the Central Region.

PART III
Problems of Cooperation and Integration

12
Foundation and History of the Treaty of Brussels, 1948–1950*

Wolfgang Krieger

In his book on the early period of European reconstruction after 1945, Alan Milward points out that economic integration was primarily used by the Europeans to recreate their own national interests.[1] Does this also apply to military integration, and to what extent does this serve to explain the failure of the Treaty of Brussels?

Indeed, the foundation and development of this organisation offers a valuable glimpse into the national interests of the five signatories to the treaty (Great Britain, France, The Netherlands, Belgium and Luxembourg), their relations with the USA and how they rated the Soviet threat, as well as their view of Germany's future.[2] There are, however, a number of basic structural weaknesses to be considered which resulted in the treaty not reaching great historical age and importance. This rough sketch will go into this point in greater detail, using as its source material treaty files only recently made available. Questions of principle, which arise within military alliances between democracies, can only be touched upon here.

What were the historical conditions leading to the creation of the Treaty of Brussels? Three main factors were uppermost in politicians' minds at that time in Western Europe:

---

* I would like to thank Ambassador Dr Jürgen Diesel, who allowed me access to the files of the Brussels Treaty (on film in the Public Record Office in London, henceforth called: PRO/DG) and also the Faculty of Social Sciences at the Universität der Bundeswehr in Munich, which funded my journeys. Special thanks to Professor Dr E. Pikart, who first awakened my interest in postwar history.

(1) In view of the total defeat of Germany, and since the threat posed to Europe by Soviet power politics had not yet dawned on the Western European public, the governments of the liberated countries concentrated their efforts on the most pressing economic and social problems. In spite of this, one cannot overlook the fact that leading politicians in these countries were searching for new and effective instruments of national security policy after the shattering experience of the war. These instruments were to come in the shape of the UNO, bilateral treaties or a combination of the two. Thus the Benelux countries, on 5 September 1944, in other words before they were liberated, decided to form a new, primarily economic alliance. At the beginning of 1945, the Dutch Foreign Minister declared that their tradition of neutrality, which had lasted for almost a century, was out of date. Instead, he maintained, it was necessary to enter into alliances with other European states, which could, however, only be concluded by a newly elected government.[3] France and Czechoslovakia were among the countries which followed new roads in terms of security even during the war. They signed treaties with the Soviet Union.

(2) A certain degree of military integration was already present, due to the close contact between the European governments in exile in London, and also because of the incorporation of their soldiers into the allied armed forces, which made political and military cooperation after the Brussels and North Atlantic Treaties that much easier.[4] In certain cases military cooperation occurred, for example during the occupation of Germany, Austria and Trieste, where Great Britain, France and the USA granted each other transit rights, made joint use of some facilities and, finally, even came together over emergency measures and strategic plans. Apart from this, the British and the Americans continued their cooperation, at least as far as intelligence and weapons technology were concerned, in the Combined Chiefs of Staff (CCS), although (on the American side) there was no legal basis and, on top of this, no recognisable public demand.[5] We will consider this practical involvement of the USA in questions of European security, before the Atlantic Treaty was signed, later in this essay.

(3) As a whole the European governments aspired to a foreign policy (as in their home and economic policy also) which would restore the *status quo ante*, but also (if possible) with certain structural improvements. Despite great difficulties, they expressed the desire to regain control over their lost colonies.

How could a new security policy come about under these conditions? Apart from the UNO's task of maintaining peace, there were two models in existence. In April 1946, US Secretary of State Byrnes offered to conclude a twenty-five-year treaty with the other three occupying powers on the demilitarisation of Germany, which was to a large extent aimed at removing Soviet forces from Central Europe.[6] The Soviets laid down a variety of conditions and refused to put their name to such an agreement, at least at that time. France was more in favour of a bilateral system of alliances and thus had talks with Poland and Czechoslovakia.[7] She wanted to be seen as the 'third power' and independent of both the Soviet Union and the USA. Belgian Foreign Minister Spaak made the offer to France of concluding bilateral treaties with Paris and London, adding, 'If the Russians should object, Belgium would offer to sign a similar agreement with them.'[8]

The Treaty of Dunkirk, signed on 4 March 1947, brought no practical military cooperation. It served the purpose of stabilising the French government of the day, which was having difficulties at home. France was to be persuaded to give up her plans to cut off the Rhineland, on the eve of what promised to be decisive talks on Germany at the Moscow Foreign Ministers' Conference (March–April 1947), in order to have as united a Western policy on the German question as possible.[9]

There were no illusions in London about the limited value of a bilateral military agreement without the strategically important Benelux area and the USA. It seemed vital to give the Soviets an excuse to demand a similar alliance, perhaps in the shape of a revived Anglo-Soviet treaty as in 1942. Stalin had expressed an interest in this during his talks with Montgomery at the beginning of 1947.[10] Apart from this, the London government did not want to give the Americans the impression that they were no longer important for the defence of Europe. London's reason for entering into an alliance in Dunkirk, a possible German attack, was 'at that time fairly academic', as a senior British civil servant put it, and was merely for decorative purposes.[11] In any case, the British did not think of the unstable, Communist-riddled France as a serious treaty partner with whom one could cooperate in a military sense. Thus the Treaty of Dunkirk was not a true forerunner of the Treaty of Brussels.[12]

This becomes clear from the viewpoint of the Benelux states, which were offered a treaty on the lines of Dunkirk, but who rejected this as insufficient. Holland, interested as she was in a revival of trade with Germany, was particularly against an alliance directed against Germany. On the contrary, she demanded that the Benelux states be consulted in matters concerning both them and Germany, and that they be treated as equal partners in any alliance. Furthermore, the USA should agree to a 'Western Union', so as to maintain US commitment in Europe. A Byrnes agreement seemed further away than ever after the failure of the London Foreign Ministers' Conference in December 1947. Above all, however, the Western Powers, including the USA, were to regard an invasion of the Benelux states as a *casus belli*. Thus the Benelux countries wanted a regional pact, as was permitted under Article 52 of the United Nations Charter, with strong economic elements and excluding Italy, in order to keep the focus upon North-West Europe.[13]

The British offer of a 'Western Union', in Bevin's well-known Commons speech of 22 January 1948, came against the background of the failed Foreign Ministers' Conference. At this time the plan was to avoid stirring up Soviet mistrust by laying special emphasis on economic cooperation and the German threat.[14] In France there still seems to have been the hope of resuming talks with Poland and Czechoslovakia.[15] However, the Prague coup at the end of February 1948 created a new situation in which it was imperative to avoid a repeat of Prague after the Italian elections of 18 April 1948. One event followed another at such a rate that even in the few weeks since Bevin's Commons speech the plans had changed. Now the aim was a military alliance containing economic and political elements.

Negotiations began on 8 March 1948, and ended on 12 March after ten sessions.[16] Because of pressure from the Belgians and the British Foreign Office, the Rio Pact (Act of Chapultepec 1947) served as the model, as it stuck closely to the rules on regional security contained in the UNO Charter, and the new alliance was no longer solely directed against Germany. In particular, the phrases 'an attack upon one is an attack upon all' and 'each party shall take appropriate measures' – in other words, that there was to be no automatic military support – derived from the Rio Pact, and were also to be included in the North Atlantic Treaty later.

How was Brussels Treaty cooperation organised? On the same day as the treaty was signed, it was decided to create a Permanent Consultative Council, consisting of the five foreign ministers, which was to meet at least each quarter in one of the capital cities. A Permanent Organ, to which the ambassadors

Foundation of the Treaty of Brussels

accredited in London belonged, was to ensure constant contact. The defence ministers and their Chiefs of Staff, who also met about every three months, as well as a variety of other special committees (for economic, social and cultural matters) all reported to the Permanent Consultative Council. In London a Military Committee, also subordinate to this council, was created. Its Secretary-General, George Mallaby, had been part of the Military Secretariat in the War Cabinet between 1942 and 1945, and had worked as Assistant Secretary in the Ministry of Defence between 1946 and 1948. Thus he had a wide level of experience, not least in the field of Western military cooperation.[17]

During the foreign ministers' consultations, almost the whole spectrum of political themes was dealt with, from the Berlin crisis and the Italian colonies through to Palestine, but also problems of coordination within the Marshall Plan and, later, the North Atlantic Treaty, as well as financial matters. In many ways one could say that the Treaty of Brussels produced the kind of discussion and cooperation which had been expected to occur in the United Nations.

What was expected of the treaty in terms of security, and to what degree were these expectations realised? First of all we must consider relations with the USA, without whose support the Western Europeans felt insecure. As early as the end of the failed London Foreign Ministers' Conference, the three Western Allies were discussing the basic thrust of their future policy.[18] While it was true that the Americans, due to the prevailing wind in Congress, could give no assurances concerning alliances, they let it be known, at the final session leading to the signing of the Brussels Treaty, that they were doing all they could.

Indeed, the USA had been consulted over the details of the negotiations. Even before the treaty was signed, a date was fixed for the secret 'Pentagon Talks', which were conducted (at the time) only by the USA, Canada and Great Britain, and which formed the basis for the negotiations for the North Atlantic Alliance.[19] Again due to the attitude in Congress, the theme of military aid was detached from the Marshall Plan bill, although both sides were in favour of such a project. Some experts within the Truman Administration, notably George Kennan and Charles Bohlen, thought the USA should limit herself to military aid and not enter into a formal defensive alliance, as her presence was already formalised by the occupation of Germany.[20] Others, above all John D. Hickerson, regarded an Atlantic Alliance as vital and eventually pushed their plan through.[21] Apart from this, for the moment the Western Europeans also did not want the Americans at the negotiating table, because, as Bevin said to Bidault, 'they would be telling us what to do'.[22] For the same reason the Europeans wanted to have a certain breathing space before they invited an American observer into the Military Committee.[23] Running parallel to the talks on an Atlantic system of security, there were two other closely linked sets of negotiations. First, there was the Six-Power Conference on Germany, which was opened on 23 February 1948 in London, and, second, intensive consultations on the Marshall Plan Budget and organisation, which had been going on since the New Year.

One cannot over-emphasise how interdependent these three pre-Brussels Treaty negotiations were. On the one hand, the Western Europeans had to make Congress believe that they were interested in a policy of constructive rebuilding, and on the other they tried to use US support for their own national interests as far as possible. In this connection the German question was particularly important. The main aim was to dissuade France from her goal of isolating the Ruhr area, in exchange for assurances over German deliveries (especially of coal) concerning French national security.[24] From this situation, it became obvious that the Treaty of Brussels was to a large extent designed to coordinate these negotiations on a Western European basis, and thus lost much of its importance, after both the German question and the institutionalisation of the Marshall Plan were brought to some kind of a conclusion. Thus it was not merely the founding of the Atlantic Alliance which weakened the Brussels Treaty.

For the British, during the Brussels negotiations on strategy and armament, it was mostly a matter of appeasing France, while London herself, interestingly enough, only wanted to assume a very limited role in protecting the Continent. In fact, the beginning of 1948 saw a controversy within the British government over Britain's role in the defence of Western Europe. Prime Minister Attlee, Bevin and senior army officers regarded a slashing of the military budget and of the size of the armed forces as inevitable. The army was to be reduced from its wartime strength of about a million men to 713,000, which, of course, would have definite strategic consequences. 'We shall not in a future crisis initially send a land expeditionary force to the Continent.' The conclusion to this decision was, 'If this policy is maintained, and it is based on sound realism, we shall eventually either have to admit it to our allies or refuse to disclose our intentions.'[25] Bevin added, 'We do not want any more Dunkirks. I do not think that large armies on the Continent will be effective.' Britain wanted to reduce the size of the army and keep the air force and the navy in readiness, not least in order to increase her influence in the Middle East.[26]

This means that, despite all the talk of the Soviet threat and despite economic problems at home, the British wanted to strengthen their positions in areas best suited to consolidating (or regaining) her position as a world power.[27] There had been timely military preparatory work in only one area, which was the build-up of British air defence in France and the Benelux countries. Negotiations had taken place even before the signing of the treaty, with the aim of giving the British air surveillance, supply and landing rights.[28] Thus the Brussels Treaty was to be in many ways a substitute for a definite military guarantee of security for France; and at the same time a measure designed to build up an atmosphere of trust, together with the hope that such a Western European alliance would be armed and backed up by the Americans.

In spite of these British reservations, the basic doctrine of the Brussels Treaty had to be, 'We will defend on the Rhine or as far east as possible,' but how could this be achieved? At their first meeting, on 30 April 1948, the defence ministers and their Chiefs of Staff merely agreed to activate all available forces and weapons, and to draw up strategic plans and aims on this basis so as to coordinate rearmament.[29] However, the French urged that more substantial measures be taken. Since the autumn of 1947, they had tried to persuade the Americans actively to engage in military cooperation.[30] In the face of the Prague crisis, Foreign Minister Bidault put pressure on his British opposite number:

> since Russia knew that the West was really organising itself but was not yet strongly organised, this was the obvious moment for her to strike. He said that they would be mad if they let this opportunity pass.[31]

President Auriol expressed one constantly recurring fear held by the French government as follows:

> War with Soviet Russia would mean civil war in France, since the Communist Party would rise in conjunction with the enemy. Moreover, war with Russia would be even worse than with Germany

and might involve the destruction of the whole élite of the Nation, so that after two years nothing valuable might be left.[32]

On 20 May 1948, the French member of the Military Committee, Maj.-Gen. Ely, suggested that the three Western Commanders-in-Chief of the Occupation Zone meet at once with Belgian and Dutch officers in order to draw up emergency plans, to bring up reinforcements for the air forces from Britain, and to arrange US arms shipments. His British colleague rejected this idea, however, saying that there was already a degree of coordination in terms of planning, that the Brussels Treaty was not responsible for strategic missions, and that the US administration did not have the support of Congress.[33]

Interestingly enough, the US Military Governor and Commander-in-Chief, General Clay, took up the French idea and asked the Three Powers' military planners to meet him at his HQ in Wiesbaden – a delicate matter because Clay had a very bad reputation among the French Command where Germany was concerned.[34] It is also symptomatic that cooperation ended as soon as the Commanders-in-Chief Committee of the Brussels Treaty took over these tasks at the turn of the years 1948–9.[35]

The Western occupation forces in Central Europe, despite their military weakness, in fact gave some degree of protection, as a trip-wire in the event of Soviet aggression, which at that time was thought more likely to be in the form of Soviet-sponsored subversive activities than a large-scale attack.[36] Since the treaty was signed there had been joint efforts against Communist infiltration and subversion.[37] Dutch Foreign Minister Stikkers' proposed meeting of the heads of the various intelligence services, and the extension of these efforts to the colonies, were not wanted by the British[37a], on the one hand, probably, because they (at least) did not trust the French, and on the other because they were trying to keep overseas policy, and in this case particularly the 'Indonesian trouble', out of the Brussels Treaty. The idea of deciding upon a policy of active destabilisation in the Soviet zone of influence, supported by British Defence Minister Alexander, was rejected by his French counterpart Ramadier.[38]

What did the five nations have in terms of manpower for their plans? Here was the treaty's greatest weakness. While the British political leaders were speaking of reducing troop strength in early 1948, and also of their intention of not starting a new Dunkirk with a large expeditionary force, Montgomery was saying the exact opposite – Britain had to have enough troops in order to hold the Rhine line, and in any case it was necessary to involve the Germans in this.[39] At least the British had some combat-ready units. The Dutch, however, were practically defenceless in 1948 because almost all their troops were abroad, mostly in Indonesia.[40] During a three-day visit to Holland in January 1949, Montgomery criticised the navy, which was in his opinion too large and costly, and also the commitment of troops in Indonesia, where 120,000 men were stationed. His report to the Dutch Chief of Staff, General Kruls, pulled no punches: 'if the Dutch were not prepared now to meet their obligations, they had better withdraw from Western Union. ... he would then throw back his left flank from the River Yssel to the line of the Rhine-Maas to Rotterdam'. He added that 'General de Lattre de Tassigny had already advocated recently at a Chiefs of Staff meeting holding the Rhine-Maas line and abandoning three quarters of Holland to a Russian invasion'.[41]

Montgomery had not told the full story, however. In fact, a few days earlier, de Lattre de Tassigny had asked the British Defence Minister to station a British brigade on the Ijssel, as their symbolic effect would be enormous in this 'now completely defenceless area'. Alexander replied that the British armed forces were 'stretched and strained all over the world'. Britain was already making a large contribution to the treaty, and it was first necessary to ascertain what level of manpower was required in the long term for the defence of the Western European Union (WEU). In any case it was politically impossible to supply a replacement for Dutch troops which were being committed elsewhere in a questionable fashion.[42]

The British also had nothing good to say about the Belgian forces. They were not of high calibre: Belgium spent too little of her budget on defence – here one must add that she suffered the least damage during the war and thus was the first to recover afterwards – and her Defence Minister (Col. DeFraiteur) was weak.[43] France also had her best troops overseas, mainly in an attempt to reconquer Vietnam, and the increase of 80,000 reservists in November 1948 was meant above all to protect the government against a coup from either the left or the right.[44] Apart from light weapons the French were badly armed.

Ten months after the founding of the pact, Spaak expressed his disappointment at what had been achieved as follows: the allocation of functions was unclear; the main difficulty lay in the economic situation; almost nothing had been achieved on the military side. 'It was pointless to make vast plans if we had no armed forces.'[45]

In fact the few weapons they had could not even be shipped from one country to another because there were no rules governing payment transactions. Thus the British offered the French government sixty warplanes – 'the first tangible result of the pooling of Western Union resources', as Alexander wrote to his Defence Minister, but they refused to accept them due to the difficulties in payment.[46]

A sheer farce was the story of 600 tanks which the British had sold as 'surplus lend-lease' to a Belgian scrap-metal dealer, and which were then resold to Argentina. Finally the affair was brought into the open by the US State Department, and this did not exactly shed a good light upon Western European requests for US military aid. To cap it all, several of the tanks still stored in Antwerp were offered to the Belgians. Van Loo, the scrap dealer, 'must have made a very large profit on the tanks he had already sold to the Argentine', a British Foreign Office member commented.[47]

Speedy rearmament was also hampered by narrow-minded national economies and the fact that there was no weapons standardisation, except in those cases where US or British wartime equipment was still being used. Only after pressure from the Americans were efforts made to pool resources, arrange weapons transfer and, finally, put forward a strategic plan, which was the Americans' proviso for their support (as it was with Marshall Plan aid). The USA made the five treaty states promise to spend $325,000,000 during 1949–50.[48] As the British Defence Minister Shinwell said, in an effort to calm the other partners, most of this expenditure was going to benefit the civil infrastructure. In spite of this, however, the Dutch and the French complained that their high level of spending in Indonesia and Vietnam respectively, 'which also benefited the Brussels Treaty', was not sufficiently taken into account.[49]

The American 'milch cow' did not deliver the goods as quickly as the Five had hoped after the Truman speech of 17 March 1948. While US military aid had become official policy in July 1948, American military leaders had some doubts about the ability of

Foundation of the Treaty of Brussels

the US army budget to withstand arms shipments to Europe. Finally, the Western Union Chiefs of Staff failed to put forward the rearmament plan by the required date of 15 November 1948, not least because the Europeans feared that the rearmament efforts which the USA had stipulated would have a negative effect on the general economic reconstruction process.[50]

Another weak point, which this time had little or nothing to do with money, was the division of military command. After much argument it was agreed that an American was to be the Supreme Commander in case of war, with a British Air Marshal as his second-in-command, a Frenchman in command of the land army, an Englishman at the head of the air forces, and a French naval commander, as the supplies would mostly have to be landed in France. Using this command structure, a Committee of Commanders-in-Chief was finally created, with Montgomery as its Chairman, having the supreme command in wartime until he was replaced by an American.[51] General de Lattre was in command of the land army, Air Marshal Robb commanded the air forces and Admiral Jaujard was Naval Adviser. These were the committee members. A part of Château Fontainebleau was converted into the headquarters, while Montgomery was given a rearward HQ in Dover House in London. This committee was subordinate to the Western Union Chiefs of Staff Committee from the five countries, which often led to tension, as a Brussels Treaty officer (especially in the case of the British) was obliged to report to an officer of lower rank in the Western Union Chiefs of Staff.[52]

Beside the problem of military hierarchy, serious limits were placed upon the powers of the committee. For example, the chairman was definitely not responsible for air defence nor for the internal security of the member states. The occupation forces were also still under the command of the military governors (until such time as they were finally incorporated into the Brussels Treaty forces), which meant that operations orders had to be agreed to by them, and normally in advance.[53] French Defence Minister Ramadier was even of the opinion that in peacetime there could only be national command over individual units, an idea which his general, de Lattre, thought would be 'catastrophic' in wartime.

What a Foreign Office report termed Montgomery's 'robust attitude (which) had had a very heartening effect' on the treaty partners, also most likely played a certain role in such conflicts. But there were still open wounds left over from the war. De Lattre (and many others) believed that the British might not be so concerned with defending the Continent, thinking more of the subsequent new 'Battle of Britain'. This would not satisfy the Europeans, however, and they needed a guarantee that 'their own defence on the continent will be all out'. These reservations, according to de Lattre, would not be fully dispelled even with an American as Supreme Commander.[54] Nevertheless, he wanted to make it clear that in a crisis he would be ready to serve under Supreme Allied Commander Montgomery as a 'loyal subordinate'.[55]

The question of where and by what means the Brussels Treaty states were to be defended was a great strain on all military consultations. Montgomery's orders read as follows: 'The aim in war will be to hold the enemy in Europe as far east as possible in order to defend the home territories of the Western Union and to give depth to their air defence.' Until a strategic plan was drawn up, he was to make preparations on the basis of the available forces and compare notes with the planners of the Allied Military Joint Planning Staff in Wiesbaden. He could work on the assumption, they told him there, that US occupation forces were to be placed under his operational command in a war situation.[56] How they were so sure of this, however, is not all that obvious. What is clear is how dependent the practical military planning of the Brussels Treaty was upon the USA. From the start there was no way that the Europeans could plan and act on their own in this field.

When the Chiefs of Staff Committee, at the end of March 1949, put forward a 'Short Term Plan', General Huebner, representing General Clay, confirmed that US troops would be transferred, but also put strict limitations on this. Not until the Military Governor had evacuated US civilians and had been relieved of his responsibility for the government, and not until the US forces west of the Rhine had reached their combat positions, could US troops be placed *en masse* under the command of the Western Union. Of course, the President had to give the appropriate order first.[57]

At the same time as they gave news of their plan, the Chiefs of Staff Committee had to admit 'that in their view, the forces available ... are insufficient for the defence of Western Europe'.[58] A table put before the Permanent Consultative Council by Colonel

Foundation of the Treaty of Brussels

Mallaby put a figure on the necessary elements and their armament. At the outbreak of war eighteen divisions would be needed, which would have to be increased to fifty-six divisions with a total of 4,200 aeroplanes for the tactical air force within four weeeks. As Foreign Minister Spaak remarked, these facts were not exactly going to win the trust of the general public.[59]

A heated debate arose as this plan was about to be passed by the defence ministers on 23 November 1949. The Dutch representative complained that the planned Rhine-Ijssel defensive line would leave a quarter of his country's territory open to invasion. At the same time, 50,000 German auxiliaries would be evacuated, and would also have priority over Dutch civilians. British Defence Minister Alexander replied that these were workers under contract to the allies. His Belgian colleague confirmed that the Treaty of Brussels could not guarantee the security of its members despite great financial efforts. Even so, the 'Short Term Plan' was passed together with a Naval Emergency Plan, and thus became operative.[60] By this time, however, there was already a move towards the North Atlantic Alliance, which had been concluded in the meantime, with the following aim, 'The defence of Western Europe must be insured in depth east of the Rhine – i.e. the battle should be fought not *on* the Rhine but *for* it.'[61] It became clear from the North Atlantic Pact talks just how much the Western Europeans wavered between wanting to have their own security policy and the need for a US commitment. The French even considered this future alliance to be a poor second choice under the circumstances. For them two factors were decisive. Only the US troops in Germany provided a 'real guarantee'. Also, the administration in Washington was urged by Paris that what was needed was speedy rearmament of the French army rather than long-term programmes.[62] For this reason the French tried to build up bilateral relations with the USA, hoping to get weapons' shipments and close cooperation with the Joint Chiefs of Staff. However, this privilege was only granted to the British, and there were second thoughts in Washington concerning arms' shipments, which had been asked for time and again over a period of years, because France had been expending the main part of her military effort on regaining her colonial empire in South-East Asia. In spite of all this, General Clay was told on 16 September 1948 to give matériel to the French divisions stationed on German soil.[63]

What meaning would the Brussels Treaty have after the signing of a treaty with the USA? Foreign Secretary Bevin argued in the Permanent Consultative Committee in July 1948 that the Europeans had to 'lead the Americans' to a US guarantee for the Five Nations Pact, for the North Atlantic Pact would be tailored above all to American security interests. Finally, he said, an American guarantee was not sufficient on its own, and thus he demanded that the five Treaty Powers work together whenever possible, and that no other European states be involved in the negotiations at present.[64] From the British point of view, the Five ought to act as a consortium in negotiations – led by the British themselves, of course. This means that the British wanted to retain the Brussels Treaty in order to strengthen their position at the bargaining table.

After the North Atlantic Treaty was signed, and due to the founding of the Council of Europe (5 May 1949), the Treaty of Brussels was pushed on to the sidelines of international affairs. As late as November 1949 Bevin and Schuman suggested a 'more intense publicity plan'.[65] But there were still awkward questions, such as: should the military staff remain separate from the corresponding NATO facilities? In particular, should the supply organisations be kept apart? At the time there was probably a desire to maintain a degree of Western European sovereignty.[66] The reorganisation of security policy following the outbreak of the Korean War made a change in this situation inevitable. The planning staff and the Western Union Command were incorporated into NATO's organisations. It is true that on 20 December 1950 Bevin informed the Permanent Consultative Council about talks in the North Atlantic Council on German rearmament. However, this difficult subject was clearly a matter for NATO.[67]

Germany's future role in the West's policy of containment had been a millstone around the neck of the Brussels Treaty since it was founded. At the same time Germany had sat at the negotiating table like Banquo's ghost, whether it was the question of the formal anti-German stance after the Dunkirk model, or regarding the pitiful treaty forces, which would have sorely needed the help of the Germans: an idea still politically unthinkable. In the heat of the Berlin crisis, in September 1948, for example, the Military Committee had suggested that a sub-committee deal with the question of German armed forces, but this subject was dropped like a hot potato.[68] The possible German aggression mentioned in

Article 7 of the pact had never played a part in military planning – the only threat recognised by all was that emanating from the Soviets.

A special kind of German threat, however, was seen in the possibility of the Soviet Union gaining the use of German resources or even West German territory. Thus the Permanent Consultative Council looked several times at the Berlin crisis and the creation of a West German state.[69] As the Soviets let it be known that they intended to lift the blockade, the West reacted with amazement – 'It had seemed surprising that the Russians had not seemed to want to make political capital out of the problem of Germany' – as Schuman said after the Four-Power Conference at the Palais Rose in May/June 1949. Bevin spoke of the danger of the Soviets making the Germans a great offer, especially in terms of trade, which might undermine the Federal Republic's ties to the West.[70]

On three specific points one could already foresee the future conflicts on the German contribution to defence:

1. In Article 4 of the treaty, an attack on the occupation forces stationed in Germany was defined as a case for the alliance. The somewhat vague wording in the pact was specifically applied to this case by the Permanent Consultative Council, whereas there was a more precise definition in the North Atlantic Treaty (Article 6). According to this, West German territory (including West Berlin and the areas of Austria under Western occupation) *de facto* belonged to the sphere of influence of the Western Alliance.
2. This fact did not, of course, mean that there was an obligation to defend Western Germany. However, this was not something which could be mentioned to the public, although it was laid down in strategic plans. 'The Germans might otherwise think we are no longer interested in their fate,' warned Defence Minister Alexander in a speech to the Permanent Consultative Council.[71]
3. The three Western Powers did not make any statement in the Occupation Statute for the Federal Republic about a permanent German demilitarisation. This must be left for a peace treaty, they said. In reality, however, they expressly wanted to keep the door open for a future German contribution to defence.[72] In spite of this, the Five-Power Pact was a failure,

mainly because it was too weak on its own to incorporate Germany into Western containment policy.[73] Without the USA this problem seemed to be insoluble.

What conclusion can we draw from this historical sketch of the Brussels Treaty? Nowadays military strategists are trying to lessen the dependence upon the USA which is still predominant today[74]; one need only cast one's mind back to the military regulations contained in the WEU treaty and the Franco-German Treaty of Friendship. What opportunities lie herein is a matter for debate, but the Brussels Treaty avoids the question of an independent European foreign and security policy, for even when it was created the intention was to get the Americans involved in the Western European security alliance on a long-term basis.

In any case, there was a marked reluctance on the part of the Five to undertake major military efforts. Their individual security policy, however, shows definite signs of national or even imperial priorities.[75] There is a lot to be said for the theory, mentioned at the start of this essay, that the Western Europeans tried to involve the USA in Western Europe's security policy simply in order to keep their own forces free to follow their own national and imperial aims. Thus Geir Lundestad describes the US role as an 'empire by invitation'.[76] One must not forget, however, that it is at the very least questionable whether it would have been possible to deter the Soviets from attacking the West without US support, even using all available forces. But even if the USA had been slightly less active in Europe, it would probably not have been quite so easy for the colonial powers to delay the break-up of their overseas empires for so long. One of the 'unspoken assumptions' (James Joll) held by the politicians of the day was: How can we rebuild and safeguard the nation following the humiliation and losses of the war? In this respect, the efforts at integration were aimed above all at making good specific economic and political deficits in the individual countries, preventing the superpowers from having all the say and basically creating the necessary breathing space for a new national consensus.

In the end, the treaty did not play a great role as a receiving and allocating body for US military aid either, although this was supposed to have been the main purpose. The American Military Assistance Programme started operating only after the signing of the North Atlantic Treaty, and did not just apply to the five

Brussels powers but to all the other European Alliance partners.[77] Looking back historically, one could also imagine a straight line leading directly to the North Atlantic Treaty, missing out the Western Union pact, although this cannot be proved, for without the relevant assurances from the USA, France would have found it hard to agree to the creation of the Federal Republic of Germany. The Washington agreements on Western Germany were in any case concluded in tandem with the signing of the North Atlantic Treaty.

Thus we are left with the Brussels Treaty as a doubtful instrument for deterring the Soviets, and as a way of increasing the Western Europeans' sense of security, as an 'assurance' (Michael Howard). But how can a body which had almost no military 'teeth' have had such a calming effect? It is precisely this question which makes the Brussels Treaty such an interesting subject for anyone researching into Western security policy.

Notes

1. Alan Milward, *The Reconstruction of Western Europe 1945–51*, Berkeley, 1984, p. 494; *passim*; As a general introduction: Hans-Peter Schwarz, 'Die europäische Integration als Aufgabe der Zeitgeschichtsforschung, Forschungsstand und Perspektiven', in *VfZG*, vol. 31, 1983, no. 4, pp. 555–72; On the problems of military integration: Stephen M. Walt, 'Alliance formation and the balance of world power, in *International Security*, vol. 9, no. 4, 1985, pp. 3–43; On the general history of Western security policy: Alfred Grosser, *Das Bündnis: Die westeuropäischen Länder und die USA seit dem Krieg*, Munich, 1982 (enlarged paperback edn.), esp. pp. 122–39; there is as yet no exhaustive history of the Brussels Treaty.
2. Cf. the individual essays on the member countries in this book.
3. H. A. Schaper, 'The security policy of The Netherlands 1945–1948', in *The Foreign Policy of The Netherlands*, J. H. Leurdijk (ed.), Alphen, 1978, pp. 89–116, here pp. 89–92; see also Jan Schulten, 'Die Aufstellung des königlich-niederländischen Heeres nach 1945', in *Entmilitarisierung und Aufrüstung in Mitteleuropa 1945–1956*, mit Beiträgen von Alexander Fischer, Christian Greiner, Klaus A. Maier, Ulrich de Maizière, Wilhelm Meier-Dörnberg, Georg Meyer,

Manfred Rauchensteiner, Jan Schulten, Hans-Erich Volkmann, Norbert Wiggershaus, Herford, Bonn, 1983 (*Vorträge zur Militärgeschichte*, Bd. 4), pp. 209–23.
4. Michael Howard, 'Introduction', in *Western Security: The Formative Years. European and Atlantic Defence 1947–1953*, Olav Riste (ed.), Oslo, 1985, pp. 11–22, here p. 17.
5. On this point as a whole: John Baylis, *Anglo-American Defence Relations 1939–1980. The Special Relationship*, London, 1981.
6. Text of the draft treaty in *Foreign Relations of the United States*, Diplomatic Papers, 1945–60, Washington, 1967–1980, FRUS. 1946, II, pp. 190–3.
7. Wolfgang Krieger, *General Lucius D. Clay und die amerikanische Deutschlandpolitik, 1945–1949*, Stuttgart, 1987; FRUS, 1947, III, p. 713f.
8. Schaper (see Note 3), p. 102.
9. Sean Greenwood, 'Ernest Bevin and Western Union: August 1945–February 1946', in *European History Quarterly* 14, 1984, pp. 319–38; Greenword, 'Return to Dunkirk: the origins of the Anglo-French Treaty of March 1947', in *Journal of Strategic Studies*, vol. 6, 1983, no. 4, pp. 49–65.
10. *The Memoirs of Field-Marshal the Viscount Montgomery of Alamein*, London, 1958, pp. 446–56; in this context, the British informed the Kremlin in December 1945 and again in April 1946 of their intention to conclude a treaty with France: PRO, FO 371/73045, FO Minute by Hogg, 19.1.48.
11. Greenwood, 'Return' (see Note 9), p. 61.
12. Alan Bullock, *Ernest Bevin: Foreign Secretary, 1945–1951*, London, 1984, p. 357f.
13. Schaper (see Note 3), pp. 96–9, 108–12.
14. PRO, CAB 129/24, CP (48)46. Bevin's report to the British Cabinet on 10 February 1948: 'I think it is important that there should be some reference to Germany if we are to avoid misunderstanding on the part of Russia.'
15. PRO, FO 371/73051, Teleg. 190 Harvey to FO, 1.3.1948.
16. On this point in general see the British files: PRO, FO 371/73046–51. Cf. Bullock (see Note 12), pp. 526–30. Bullock deals neither with the Dunkirk nor with the Brussels negotiations in more detail.
17. Between 1950 and 1954 George Mallaby (1902–78) was Under-Secretary in the Cabinet Office and from 1957 to 1959 High Commissioner in New Zealand. After this he was a teacher in Oxford and wrote several books on William Wordsworth. His memoirs were published in *From My Level*, London, 1965, and *Each in His Office*, London, 1972.
18. FRUS, 1947, II, pp. 811–30.
19. Bullock (see Note 12), p. 530; Escott Reid, *Time of Fear and Hope, The Making of the North Atlantic Treaty 1947–1949*, Toronto, 1977, *passim*; FRUS, 1948, III, p. 1f. Talks began on 22.3.1948.

20. PRO, FO 371/73069, Minute of Conversation by Balfour, 4.5.1948; FRUS, 1948, III, pp. 61–4 and *passim*.
21. FRUS, 1948, III, p. 40f. and *passim*.
22. PRO, FO 371/73057, Minute of Conversation by Roberts on Bevin-Bidault talks, 16.4.1948.
23. See PRO, FO 371/73070, Minute of British COS Meeting, 26.5.1948. Apart from the American there was also a Canadian observer. Both participated for the last time in July 1949, as in the meantime the bodies of the North Atlantic Treaty had begun operating.
24. On this point in general: Krieger (see Note 7), chap. 11.25. PRO, FO 371/73045, Memo by Kirkpatrick, 9.1.48; Bullock (see Note 12), pp. 523–5.
25. PRO, FO 371/73045, Memo by Kirkpatrick, 9.1.48; Bullock (see Note 12), pp. 523–5.
26. PRO, FO 371/73045, Memo by Bevin, 12.1.1948; in general see Michael Howard, *The Continental Commitment: The Dilemma of British Defence Policy in the Era of the Two World Wars: The Ford Lectures in the University of Oxford*, London, 1972; Cameron Watt, *Succeeding John Bull: America in Britain's Place 1900–1975: A study of the Anglo-American relationship and world politics in the context of British and American foreign-policy making in the 20th century*, Cambridge, 1984.
27. David Dilks, 'The British view of security: Europe and a wider world, 1945–1948', in *Western Security* (see Note 4), pp. 25–9, here p. 35.
28. Cf. PRO, FO 371/73051, FO Minute by F. D. W. Brown, 1.3.1948.
29. PRO, Brussels Treaty Organisation: (PRO, DG) 1/5, Def. Min and COS Meeting, 30.4.1948.
30. FRUS, 1947, III, p. 818f.; Memo by General Albert C. Wedemeyer 'Strategic planning ... French Military Combat Effectiveness', 26.12.1947, incl. appendices National Archives and Records Service, Modern Military Branch, Washington DC (NA, MMB), Record Group (RG) 319, P&O 091 France tS sec I case 1/2.
31. PRO, FO 371/73955, FO Minute by Frank K. Roberts, 17.3.1948.
32. PRO, FO 371/73057, Record of Conversation Bevin-Auriol on 17.4.1948 by Harvey, 22.4.1948.
33. PRO, FO 371/73070, Brit. Minutes/Military Staff Committee, 20.5.1948, dated 21.5.1948.
34. Details on US strategic planning and cooperation with France and Great Britain: Krieger (see Note 7), chap. 14.
35. PRO, DG 1/5, FC (48)29, Memo by COC Committee, 7.1.1949.
36. PRO, DG 1/5, Memo FC(48)31 COS Committee, 15.11.1948.
37. PRO, FO 371/73054, Record of Conversation five Foreign Ministers, 17.3.1948.
37a. PRO, DG 1/10/53, Report of the COS Committee FP(48)49, 6.10.1948; PRO, DG 1/1, Perm. Cons. Council, 25./26.10.1948.

38. PRO, DG 1/5, Memo FC(48)29 by COC Committee, 7.1.1949.
39. Bullock (see Note 12), p. 523.
40. Schaper (see Note 3), p. 93.
41. PRO, FO 371/79248, 2667 G. Report on Montgomery's visit to Holland, 15.–17.1.1949.
42. PRO, FO 371/79248, Record of Conversation de Lattre-Alexander, 11.1.49.
43. PRO, FO 79249, Aide Memoire by Min. of Defence, 26.1.1949.
44. J. Femeaux and A. Martel, 'French defence policy 1947–1949, in *Western Security* (see Note 4), pp. 92–103, here p. 95.
45. PRO, DG 1/1, Perm. Cons. Council, 28./29.1.1949.
46. PRO, FO 371/73075, 26781 G, Alexander to Stafford Cripps, 12.8.1948.
47. PRO, FO 371/73076, 27270 G, Lawrence (FO) to Gabbett (MOD), 9.9.1948.
48. PRO, DG 1/9/52, Gladwyn Jebb to Douglas, 14.5.1948; Harriman memo in PRO, DG 1/12/62, Metric Doc. No. 243, 3.3.1949; PRO, DG 1/1, Perm. Cons. Council, 14./15.3.1948 with Finance and Defence Ministers present.
49. PRO, DG 1/1, Perm. Cons. Council, 16./17.4.1950 with Finance and Defence Ministers present.
50. Lawrence S. Kaplan, *A Community of Interests: NATO and the Military Assistance Program, 1948–1951*, Washington DC, 1980, pp. 20–6, *passim*.
51. PRO, DG 1/5, Record of meeting Defence Ministers and COS, 27.9.48.
52. Mallaby, *From My Level* (see Note 17), pp. 150–168, *passim*.
53. PRO, DG 1/9/52, Draft Directive with Annex I FP(48)41 30.9.1948.
54. André Kaspi, 'Prelude to NATO: two examples of the integration of military forces', in *NATO after Thirty Years*, Lawrence S. Kaplan and Robert W. Clawson (eds), Wilmington, 1981, p. 196.
55. PRO, FO 371/79248, Record of Conversation de Lattre-Alexander, 11.1.1949; PRO, FO 371/79247, 2105 G, FO Minute, 24.12.1948.
56. PRO, DG 1/9/52, Draft Directive with annex I FP(48)41, 30.9.1948, quotation.
57. PRO, DG 1/5/32, Memo by Defence Committee, 23.3.1949; MD(49)8 (28.3.1949). The plan itself is not in the file as it was not yet declassified at the time of writing.
58. Ibid.
59. PRO, DG 1/1, Perm. Cons. Council, 16./17.6.1949.
60. PRO, DG 1/5, Def. Min., 23.11.1949. At the meeting of the Perm. Cons. Council on 16./17.4.1950 it was suggested that the plan be tested in two exercises in May and October. See PRO, DG 1/1, Perm. Cons. Council, 16./17.4.1950.
61. PRO, DG 1/5/34, Report MD(49)30, 11.11.1949; emphasis in original.
62. FRUS, 1948, III, p. 218; PRO,DG 1/1 Perm. Cons. Council, 19./20.7.1948.

63. FRUS, 1948, III, pp. 253, 664–82; as a whole see Krieger (see Note 7), ch. 17.
64. PRO, DG 1/1, Perm. Cons. Council, 25./26.10.1948.
65. PRO, DG 1/1, Perm. Cons. Council, 7.11.1949.
66. PRO, DG 1/5, Def. Min., 23.11.1949.
67. PRO, DG 1/1, Perm. Cons. Council, 20.12.1950.
68. PRO, DG 1/6/37, Milit. Committee, 8.9.1948.
69. PRO, DG 1/1, Perm. Cons. Council, 19./20.7.1948, 25./26.10.48.
70. PRO, DG 1/1, Perm. Cons. Council, 16./17.6.1949.
71. PRO, DG 1/1, Perm. Cons. Council, 14./15.3.1949.
72. PRO, CAB 128/13, Cab. Minutes 81(48), 15.12.1948; on US policy see Krieger (see Note 7), *passim*.
73. Lawrence S. Kaplan, 'An unequal triad: the United States, Western Union and NATO', in *Western Security* (see Note 4), pp. 107–77, here p. 121. The rivalry between Britain and France over military command is proportionately less important, or rather it follows from the insufficient military potential, which leads one back to the German problem.
74. Howard (see Note 4), p. 22.
75. A very instructive book on this subject is Scott L. Bills, 'The United States, NATO and the Colonial World', in *NATO* (see Note 54), pp. 149–64.
76. Geir Lundestad, 'Empire by Invitation? The United States and Western Europe, 1945–1952', in *SHAFR Newsletter* vol. 15/3, 1984, pp. 1–21.
77. FRUS, 1949, IV, pp. 285–8; Kaplan (see Note 50), p. 32f.

13
Foundation and History of NATO, 1948–1950

Wichard Woyke

The Soviet Threat and Western European Security

The dramatic worsening of East-West relations in 1947 led to an increased subjective feeling of danger among the governments of those countries whose foreign policy had assumed more of a 'wait and see' stance concerning bloc membership (especially France,[1] Belgium and The Netherlands).[2] Thus Belgian Foreign Minister Paul-Henri Spaak told the Russian delegate Vyshinsky, during a session of the UN Assembly in 1948, 'Do you know the basis of our policy? It is fear, fear of you, your policy, your government ... The truth is that your foreign policy today is more audacious and more ambitious than that of the Tsars themselves.'[3]

Soviet policy was seen in the West as highly expansionistic, and fears were openly expressed that the USSR wanted to extend her territory, using military force if necessary.[4] Indeed, it was possible for the Soviet Union, with Stalin at the helm, to bring the governments in Budapest, Bucharest, Sofia, Warsaw and Prague under her control during the period 1947–8.[5] Thus 1947 became a turning-point, not only in relations between several European states and the USSR, but also between the USA and the USSR, where sweeping changes made themselves felt in the attitude and the actions of the Americans. While the Western Europeans had reason to believe they were *directly* threatened by the proximity of the Soviet sphere of influence, the USA's primary concern was the middle- and long-term threat to their leadership in international politics. 'They were, moreover, anxious to safeguard regions both militarily and economically, regions which were to be stable anti-Communist elements on the periphery of the new Soviet empire.'[6] The Truman Doctrine of March 1947 is, therefore, the clear starting-point for an indirect offensive policy towards the USSR.

At first, the US stabilisation policy in Europe was to involve economic aid for Greece and Turkey, two states threatened by the USSR, which was to be followed by the Marshall Plan: in other words, financial support of the Western European countries as a whole. To the USA, who now also viewed the East-West conflict as a kind of 'cold war', Europe represented an area of strategic security, which had to become economically stable in order to prevent Communism gaining a hold. In addition, Europe became an essential part of America's own security concept, so that Western Europe, at least, had to become a bulwark against Communism. However, the prerequisite for the allocation of Marshall Plan funds was internal agreement among the relevant European states on how to distribute this US aid. This was achieved by the creation, in 1948, of the Organisation for European Economic Cooperation (OEEC).[7] Thus the Americans were able to put into effect both their 'short-term aim of socio-economic stabilization'[8] in 1948 and also, later, the long-term aim of increasing strategic security.

Western Europe's acceptance of Marshall Plan aid meant that their economic security was tied to that of the USA, and it also meant the preliminary stage of a military security partnership. After structural steps were taken to ensure economic integration, military union would follow.

From 1945 onwards the French had been suggesting a military partnership between the USA and Western Europe. The Chief of the French General Staff, Révers, and General Billotte had been pressing for a formal union during talks with the US ambassador in Paris.[9] On the political front, it was British Foreign Secretary Bevin in particular who was hoping to achieve the aim of tying the USA more closely to Europe. By means of this policy, the Labour Foreign Secretary, as the representative of a victorious power, albeit a somewhat toothless one, hoped to gain not only the close support of the USA but also, as a representative of Western Europe, to get British ideas put into practice.

Foreign Secretary Bevin was convinced that a military-aid programme, on the lines of the Marshall Plan, would not be sufficient, but rather that a close military connection, if possible in the form of a treaty between the USA and Europe, was needed.[10] Thus, since 1945, the British Ambassador in America, Sir Oliver Franks, had been urging the USA to commit themselves militarily in Europe.[11] Bevin told his American opposite number Marshall concerning a Euro-American union, 'We must invent a kind of Western-democratic system which includes the Americans and even France, Italy and of course the Dominions ... not a formal union but rather an agreement on the basis of power, money and decisive action ... a sort of spiritual federation of the West.'[12]

In the USA, in March 1947, there were also public expressions of support for a military union between Western Europe and America. The chairman of the Senate Foreign Affairs Committee, Arthur Vandenberg, had pushed for a pan-American regional pact, and had said on this point, 'I am not certain ... that it would not be worth looking at the possibility of regional alliances with a view to Europe ... I am firmly of the opinion that security is at the heart of the difficulties we are faced with.'[13]

On 18 December 1947, Bevin told his US colleague Marshall, 'I am convinced that the Soviet Union will not for the time being be prepared to negotiate reasonably with the West, and that the future of the West will depend on the creation of a kind of formal or informal Union in Western Europe, which is supported by the United States and the Dominions, and on a mobilisation of moral and material power such that it will give rise to trust and energy within and respect elsewhere.'[14]

The European-American union, which had now been talked about at length and in many variations, had to be preceded by steps towards European union. After Bevin had received support in principle from his US colleague Marshall for his security concept,[15] he suggested in the Commons, on 22 January 1947, the founding of a Western Union. This led to the signing of the Treaty of Brussels on 17 March 1948.[16] This was seen by the British government as a first important step on the road to a defensive alliance in the Atlantic area, as a pact 'which is to achieve the defence of "free Europe", on a collective basis, by including the military and economic capacity of the USA as a decisive element'.[17]

Foreign Secretary Bevin could be fairly certain of support for his efforts to create an Atlantic alliance, judging by what

President Truman had to say on the day of the signing of the Brussels Treaty: 'Rapid changes are occurring in Europe which impose limits upon our foreign policy and our national security. Nations which are concerned to retain a form of government which guarantees their citizens their freedom are being increasingly threatened. The United States are deeply anxious to preserve the freedom of these nations. It is vitally important that we act now in order to guarantee conditions under which we can achieve a lasting peace based on freedom and justice.'[18]

The French government was now equally keen to have a military alliance with the USA in 1948, not least in order to achieve their other foreign-policy aim – to be safe from attack by Germany. Immediately after the events in Czechoslovakia in February 1948, and before the signing of the Treaty of Brussels, Foreign Secretary Bidault sent his US counterpart a message which read: 'The time has come for closer cooperation, political and, as soon as possible, military cooperation between the New and the Old World, united as they are in their duty towards the only civilisation worth living in.'[19] According to Bidault the European countries were not strong enough and did not possess the necessary military potential to successfully defend themselves against a Soviet attack.[20] 'The French Foreign and Defence Ministers demanded that US military planning be based on the defence of Western Europe. Taken as a whole, the French aim was, not only for the Western Union but also for a European-American agreement, 'a strong military alliance (against a Soviet attack) with an exact commitment to do certain things under certain circumstances'.[21]

The Atlantic Treaty Negotiations

As early as 22 March 1948, a few days after the signing of the Brussels Treaty, secret talks began between the ambassadors of Great Britain, Canada and US State Department officials on the North Atlantic Treaty, in order to have a basis in this small group for later talks with the other participants.[22] On 11 April 1948, the first meetings on security in the Atlantic theatre were held among the US foreign affairs élite, i.e. Secretary of State Marshall, Defence Under-Secretary of State, Lovett, and the two Senators, Vandenberg and Tom Connally.[23] Ever since the end of 1947 the

Deputy Director of the European Department, John Hickerson, and his subordinate Theodore Achilles had been fighting, against stiff State Department resistance, for a North Atlantic Treaty.[24]

In April/May 1948 the State Department and the National Security Council prepared the US position for the negotiations with the Europeans. Within the State Department there were violently conflicting opinions, as two important decision-makers, George Kennan and Charles Bohlen, warned against signing such a treaty because, on the one hand, Congress would not feel able to enter such an alliance in an election year and, on the other, the USSR might see a provocative act in the creation of such a pact.[25]

The idea of a formalised Atlantic defence community was openly discussed for the first time on 28 April 1948, as Canadian Prime Minister Saint Laurent put forward to the Lower House the suggestion of a single defence system based upon mutual assistance, which was to include both the two North American states and the members of the Brussels Treaty, thus making the latter obsolete.[26] The question of US commitment was to be decisive. Thus State Department officials and representatives of the National Security Council worked on ways in which the USA could contribute to this pact. The only point was that they could no longer slip back into their isolationist ways. The USA had made it clear, by concluding the Rio Pact in 1947, that they were prepared to enter military alliances, at least in their own hemisphere. Thus the State Department officials, using Article 51 of the United Nations Charter as a guide and sticking closely to the Rio Pact, formulated the following rules for the treaty:

1. It was to be based upon self-help and mutual aid.
2. It was to strengthen the resolve of the free nations to resist aggression decisively and in concert, and improve their capability of doing so.
3. It was to keep to the basic framework of the Rio Pact, assuming that an armed attack upon one member was to be seen as an attack upon all.
4. Each member was to decide for itself whether an aggressive act had occurred and what action it wanted to take, until there was agreement on joint measures.[27]

The treaty was to run for ten years. The treaty area was to include North America, Continental Europe and the areas occupied by members' armed forces in the North Atlantic theatre.

The striking element of these American proposals was that they sought to avoid an automatic commitment at all costs. Therefore a solution had to be found which would involve the Americans, for only through them could Western Europe receive effective help,[28] and which would also tie the Europeans together, offer them protection and at the same time give the USA the choice of how much they were to commit themselves. 'The Americans had to be sure that their enormous efforts would be rewarded by the continuing readiness of the Europeans to work together on defence and the relevant level of joint policy. The Europeans had to be sure that they could count on the protection and help of the USA. At the same time, the Soviet Union had to be shown what it could expect if it threatened the central US security zone.'[29]

Apart from the political aspect, great importance was to be attached to the strategic side of the new Atlantic Alliance. In December 1947 the Joint Chiefs of Staff considered a Soviet attack unlikely in the next five to ten years. After the Prague crisis of February 1948, however, this became a distinct possibility, especially after General Clay, the Military Governor in Germany, had sent his famous telegram to Washington.[30] Clay who also thought war unlikely in the medium term, saw a sudden change in the Soviets' behaviour. Clay's telegram had no little effect on the decision-making process at the highest foreign and security policy levels in the USA. Among the Joint Chiefs of Staff there was a perception of the Soviet danger and the recognition that defence of US security interests had to begin on the Elbe. The military command also wanted at all costs to keep the initiative and not be trapped in an automatism. This is confirmed by the statement of General Gruenther, GSO 1 of the Joint Chiefs of Staff, on 29 March 1948: 'It must be made quite clear that a commitment to come to the aid of a state under attack should not be taken to mean that the assistance must be rendered locally. We must be free to conduct operations against an aggressor according to (our) strategic conception.'[31]

After the Brussels Treaty was signed, the American Chiefs of Staff prepared a memorandum in which they recommended the immediate creation of a 'Committee of Commanders-in-Chief',[32] which was to be headed by a US general in wartime. The US Chiefs of Staff and some European countries wanted a unified armed force, which had its tentative beginnings in the summer of

Foundation and History of NATO

1948, and thus had a definite influence on the later shape of military integration within the Atlantic Alliance. As early as 20 July 1948, the US military delegation led by Maj.-Gen. Lemnitzer, and also a delegation of Canadian officers, took part in meetings of the Brussels Treaty.[33] When Field-Marshal Montgomery, who argued for Western Europe's defence to be as far east as possible, finally set up his headquarters at Fontainebleau in September 1948, there were American observers present and strategic plans were being coordinated.[34]

Now it became clear on the political front that a form of military alliance between the USA and Western Europe had to be found. The problem for the USA was the change in foreign policy: in other words, that alliances had to be forged against former tradition. But before this could happen the public, still used to centuries of isolationism, had to be convinced. In addition to this, it was an election year, and President Truman had to think very hard about whether he could give up this isolationist position and be re-elected. In order to be able to enter into alliances at all, the Constitution had to be amended. The initiative came from Senator Vandenberg and Under-Secretary Lovett, and crystallised into the Vandenberg Resolution. On 11 June 1948, the Senate voted sixty-four to six in favour of this resolution, among other things for the 'participation of the USA by constitutional means in regional and other collective organisations which are based upon lasting and effective self-help and mutual support, and which affect US security interests'.[35] After President Harry S. Truman had given his approval to this resolution on 2 July 1948, formal negotiations could begin between the Europeans and the Americans.

National Interests and the Atlantic Treaty

The NATO Treaty negotiations must be divided into two sections. First of all there were 'exploratory talks on security' between the USA, Canada and the Brussels Treaty states, which were held in Washington from 6 July 1948 to 15 March 1949, and which were mainly conducted by the ambassadors of the states concerned and State Department officials.[36] During the second, shorter phase, from 15 March to the signing of the treaty on 4 April 1949, Italy, Portugal, Denmark and Norway joined the negotiations. They were to deal with the following specific problems:

(1) Membership, i.e. which countries would be subject to the treaty.
(2) The question of territorial applicability: in particular, whether the overseas territories of the European colonial powers were to be included in the treaty.
(3) The question of guarantee, i.e. whether there should be a clause as in the Brussels Treaty providing for automatic assistance, military or otherwise.
(4) The question of the lifetime, i.e. whether the pact should be valid only in the short term, for ten years, or, like the Brussels Treaty, last for sixty years, and
(5) The question of military cooperation.

While the USA, but also Canada and Great Britain, were trying to achieve the greatest possible degree of political and military freedom of action, the Europeans were looking for a way of tying the USA to Europe in military terms as closely as they could. For France, in the second half of 1948, the difficult part was not so much the formal commitment to an Atlantic pact as, above all, the delivery of equipment from the USA and 'a US commitment to participate in containing a Soviet attack on Western Europe as far east in Germany as possible'.[37] At that time, France was only prepared to accept the Atlantic treaty under the following conditions: 'Immediate unification of command; immediate shipment of US matériel to France; immediate commitment of US troops to France'.[38]

However, the USA were not prepared to agree to such radical demands at that time. In the Vandenberg Resolution they had aired the possibility of close political ties, but the US chief negotiator, Under-Secretary Lovett, working on a suggestion made by British Foreign Secretary Bevin, said that the political, military, economic and intellectual resources of Western Europe had somehow to be combined into a union 'behind which the USA would stand'.[39] Initially the USA wanted to play the role of a promoter of European military integration, who would provide political support but who did not want to be committed militarily. The talks were hindered by the coming Presidential elections, since any new formal military ties had to be confirmed by Congress, which was also up for election. The Europeans, and

Foundation and History of NATO

especially the French, tried to persuade the USA time and again to make a greater European commitment by painting a picture of the Continent under threat, as this threat was seen by the French as being far greater than the Americans would accept. A typical example of this is the analysis made by the then French Prime Minister Henri Queuille who, when the talks were at the critical stage, told a US news agency: 'The United States must never allow Russia to invade France and Western Europe as Germany did. But France cannot hold out alone as the outpost of Europe. If there are enough forces available to keep the Russian army from crossing the Elbe, then the civilization of Europe will be saved. Two weeks after an invasion it will be lost.'[40]

When it became clear from the negotiations that an alliance between the Europeans and the North Americans, in whatever form, was on the cards (not least because of the pressure placed on the governments to produce something, caused by the Berlin blockade, which the USSR had kept up since June 1948),[41] there had to be an agreement on who would take part in the alliance. Since the talks started, both the Americans and the Western European Union had agreed 'that Norway, Denmark, Sweden and Iceland would be welcome and useful partners'.[42] It was known that Sweden, due to its traditional neutrality, would hardly be able to join, but it was hoped, in spite of this, that Sweden would accede to the new organisation, as it was a democratic state. The membership of the Scandinavian countries was desirable, not just because of their deeply-rooted democratic systems, but more so due to their extreme strategic value. As the aircraft then in service had only a limited range, it was necessary to make intermediate landings when crossing the Atlantic, and so it was vital to have Iceland and Greenland, and hence Denmark as alliance members, in order to be able to transport supplies to Europe in case of war. The same problem existed in the southern sector of the North Atlantic, which meant that the Azores were needed. Thus the USA also pressed to have Portugal as a member, although the political system under the dictatorship of Salazar was unable to produce the evidence of a democratic structure required by the new alliance. While the parties to the talks had invited Ireland along, it first of all demanded the return of Ulster, and so, due to the British veto, did not take part.[43] Although there were doubts about Italy's qualification, as it was not strictly speaking an Atlantic state, France was especially keen

259

to include Italy, saying that the latter should not be placed in a worse position than Norway. 'For this reason Italy was a member of the Alliance from the beginning, and the alternative, a Mediterranean pact, in which Italy might have had a leading role, and which it had vaguely touched upon, was thus put on ice.'[44]

There was talk of including Greece and Turkey, but this was turned down on the grounds that there had already been special relations with these countries since the start of the Truman Doctrine in March 1947. Spain was, of course, also vitally important strategically, but it could not be included in negotiations on account of its dictatorial Franco regime. So the question of members was resolved, but there was still the problem of the territorial limits of the new alliance since the European colonial powers wanted guarantees for their overseas territories.

The USA tried to have the treaty area strictly limited to the North Atlantic, but the other members agreed, under French pressure, to include the Algerian *départements* in the treaty. Since the USA was completely isolated on this issue and France had threatened to withdraw its membership of the pact, and since she was necessary both for strategic and political reasons, the USA finally agreed to this solution.[45] The Belgians, French, Dutch and British overseas territories were not included in the guarantee, on the one hand because their geographical situation was not comparable to that of Algeria, and on the other because such a far-reaching guarantee would not have found support in the US Senate.[46] However, Article 4 of the NATO Treaty, 'the parties shall consult each other if, according to one of them, the territorial integrity, political independence or security of one of the parties is threatened', was taken to be a substitute for this guarantee, and thus expressed regional military validity in political terms.

The most important bone of contention between the negotiating parties was the mutual-assistance clause. The Benelux states and France wanted the same kind of automatic mutual-assistance clause as was contained in the Brussels Treaty, but the USA and also Great Britain would have none of this. The USA wanted to avoid an automatic commitment to military assistance at all costs, and preferred to keep their freedom to decide if and what military aid they might give. The chairman of the Senate Foreign Affairs Committee, Tom Connally, declared to the Senate on 14 February 1949:

> Do what you want, don't worry, if something happens we'll come over and fight your battle for you ... The United States cannot blindfold themselves to the truth and promise today to enter every war which might break out in the next 10 years, to send our boys and matériel to Europe and fight. We cannot act like Sir Galahad, rushing headlong into war and taking sides every time we hear a shot, without knowing what we're doing and what we're fighting for. There are many people – we've found them in the government and elsewhere – who argue in favour of an automatic entry into war, which would mean that we would leave it to the European countries to declare war, and they would leave it up to us to fight it.[47]

The USA were afraid of automatically being dragged into a war in which they had no interest.

This argument was to give General de Gaulle an excuse, sixteen years later, to pull France out of the NATO military organisation for good, although there was a tacit automatism, which was not included in the treaty itself. The USA wanted to be able to decide for themselves whether they should get involved in a conflict, and whether and by what means they should then support the Europeans. The US delegation's aim during the talks was to make sure the mutual-assistance clause clearly stated that each of the allies were to decide for themselves what measures to take in the event of war. Both British Foreign Secretary Bevin and his French opposite number Schuman did not give this form of support much chance of getting off the ground.[48] The Canadian government also sharply criticised the US attitude, when it communicated to the State Department through its ambassador that:

> the aim of the treaty will not be achieved by an undertaking which is so watered-down that it does not even represent a moral duty to effective action, but rather something the United States gives out of a sense of charity. This reduces the planned North Atlantic Treaty almost to the level of the Kellogg-Briand peace treaty. If the treaty contains no satisfactory commitment, and if it is simply looked upon by the Senate as a way of keeping the European countries out of trouble which does not directly concern the United States, then its value is greatly reduced.[49]

There were three different versions up for discussion, prepared by a working group of ambassadors in Washington, elements of the US Senate and by Senator Connally.[50] The ambassadors' version was the most radical and proposed that all partners would be bound to take 'military and other measures' in the event of an attack on any one treaty member. In the second version, which emerged in the US Senate, an attack on one ally was taken to be an attack on all, but the phrase 'military and other measures' was not included. The third version, which Bevin thought Senator Connally had put forward on behalf of the State Department, contained the weakest mutual-assistance clause. 'In this version, not only the words "military or other measures" had been cut out, but also the concept that all partners were committed to act if one of them were to be attacked.'[51] Especially worrying for Bevin, however, was the intention that the measures to be taken by an ally in the event of an attack on another were to be purely a matter for the respective allies themselves. That meant that there would be merely a political and moral duty to take military steps.

When it became fairly clear to the Western European negotiating parties that they were not going to take away the USA's freedom of decision, they finally agreed on Article 5 of the NATO Treaty, in which it is left up to the partner to decide what aid he wants to render another. In the important passage of the article it says: 'whereas each [nation] of them for himself and in collaboration with the other parties forthwith takes measures, including the use of armed forces, which he considers necessary in order to restore or maintain the security of the North Atlantic areas'. 'From the atomic bomb to "benevolent neutrality" as reactions to an attack on the European treaty area, the whole range of possibilities were open to the USA.'[52]

On the one hand, the Europeans had to accept this article for lack of an alternative, but on the other they saw a way of using this phraseology to get closer to their aim of tying the USA to Europe. Bevin explained that persuading a government to enter a war in support of an ally depended on there being common plans, and not on mere paper commitments.[53]

The fourth problem was the lifespan of the treaty. The French government wanted the agreement to be binding for fifty years, as in the Brussels Treaty,[54] while Great Britain, Canada and the other European states were in favour of a twenty-year agreement at least. On this point a compromise was reached. While Article 13 of the treaty provided for a period of twenty years before a partner was able to opt out, it was, however, agreed in Article 12 that the parties could demand a review of the treaty text after ten years. Thus the USA had the option of 'leaving the agreement when European defence, as planned, had become practical using purely European forces, after an initial phase of American aid'.[55] After the problems had been sorted out by the North Americans and the Brussels Treaty countries, Portugal, Italy, Denmark, Norway and Iceland were, in March 1949, invited to take part in the treaty negotiations,[56] without, however, being able to make far-reaching changes to the text.

This text describes NATO specifically as a political alliance, as there was no agreement to set up a military organisation. There is merely provision for a Foreign Secretary's Committee and a Defence Committee, which was, however, seen primarily as a political body and which, contrary to French ideas, was not supposed to draw up 'military plans'.[57] The USA saw themselves as political guarantors, and they took part in the meetings of the Western Union Military Committee as an observer, but at the same time refused to allow the Western Europeans a say in military matters.

After the diplomatic talks had solved the political and legal problems between the Europeans and the Americans, at least for the time being, the representatives of the USA, Canada, and the ten European countries (Belgium, The Netherlands, Luxembourg, France, Great Britain, Italy, Portugal, Iceland, Denmark and Norway) signed the North Atlantic Treaty in Washington on 4 April 1949. It came into force on 24 August of that same year, after the individual countries had ratified the treaty (without too much enthusiasm in certain countries, but on the whole a smooth process)[58] and after the documents of ratification had been sent in. Thus the West had a military bloc as well as an economic one, consisting of the two North American countries and ten Western European nations. The USA had given up their isolationism, in the form of an official treaty, and had accepted the continent of Europe as their central strategic security zone. But the moral and political US commitment to assist Europe in case of war was stronger than the formal one, which still left the USA with their freedom of action and decision. The signing of the North Atlantic Treaty demonstrated to the Soviets, particularly in view of the Berlin crisis (which was still going on as the treaty was being signed), that the USA had gained a foothold in Europe in military as well as in political and economic terms. Not least the presence of US occupation forces in Germany was a guarantee of this American commitment in Europe.

Wichard Woyke

The Organisation of the Alliance

After the North Atlantic Treaty came into force, on 24 August 1949, the treaty partners found themselves faced with the task of giving the alliance an organisational structure, and of agreeing on a joint defence policy. The NATO Council met for its first session, under the chairmanship of US Secretary of State Dean Acheson, on 17 September 1949 in Washington, and made a number of important decisions. First, the Council decided to have a regular annual conference, with more meetings if necessary. According to Article 4 and Article 5 of the treaty, an extraordinary general meeting was necessary if one partner demanded it. In accordance with Article 9, the Council set up a Defence Committee, consisting of the defence ministers of the member states. Its task was to draw up coordinated defence plans for the treaty's territory. This committee was also to meet annually.

During the session of 18 November 1949, the NATO Council decided to create a committee for financial and economic matters. This committee, consisting of the finance ministers of the member states, had the task of working out general financial and economic guidelines for defence programmes, in conjunction with the Military Committee and the Standing Group. In addition to this, it was to gauge the financial and economic effects of rearmament plans put forward by the Military Production and Supply Committee or by the Military Committee, and to take other decisions concerning the financial aspects of military policy. 'The Military Production and Supply Committee is to promote coordinated arms production, standardisation and arms research.'[59]

As it soon became clear that the NATO Council was out of its depth when it came to gaining the upper hand over and supervising the alliance's civilian and military bodies, it decided, in May 1950, to create a new administrative organ – the Council of Deputies. This body, consisting of the Deputy Foreign Ministers, was to be based in London and was charged with the task of coordinating the activities of the civilian and military authorities within the alliance, and of serving as a forum for regular political discussions among the member states.

Foundation and History of NATO

The Military Organisation

Since there had been thoughts about the structure of the military organisation as early as 1948, both in the Western Union and in the United States, as well as meetings of military advisors on the subject of the joint defence concept,[60] it was obvious that the alliance's military steps would be implemented after NATO had been successfully founded.

This process started when the NATO Council created the Military Committee during its first session, on 17 September 1949. This consisted of the chiefs of staff of the member states (Iceland was allowed to send a civil servant as its representative as it had no armed forces). The purpose of the Military Committee was to advise the NATO Council on military matters. The Executive Committee of this body was the Standing Group until France left NATO's military organisation. This group consisted of the Chiefs of Staff of France, Great Britain and the USA. Its task was to draw up strategic guidelines for the treaty area. So as to make fast and efficient joint defence planning a possibility, and also in order to divide the responsibility between the member states, the Council formed five military Regional Planning Groups. This decentralised planning structure was thought up by the Americans, and was designed to prevent the USA becoming automatically involved, as well as taking the burden of sole responsibility for the whole area away from the USA.

The Northern European Regional Planning Group consisted of Denmark, Norway and Great Britain; for Western Europe: Belgium, Luxembourg, The Netherlands, Great Britain and France; Southern Europe/Western Mediterranean Planning Group: France, Italy, Britain; the North American Regional Planning Group, consisting of the USA and Canada; and finally, the North Atlantic Ocean Regional Planning Group, consisting of all the member states apart from Luxembourg and Italy.[61] This form of organisation was in accordance with the American plans of June 1949.[62] On the one hand the USA wanted to secure a commanding military role, but on the other it wanted to keep their freedom of action within the proposed military organisation as far as possible, with the result that a regionalised planning-group structure arose in the form of the five groups. This meant that there was to be no central planning and no central command, at the express wish of the USA. 'Worldwide planning and strategy were the exclusive province of the USA, and they wanted bilateral talks with the necessary Alliance partners to this end.'[63] The Europeans tried to have this plan changed, but were unsuccessful.[64]

There has also been detailed discussion between the prospective alliance partners concerning future defence concepts from as early as 1948. Without massive US military assistance, however, Europe's defence could not be organised, even though President Truman wanted this aid to be reduced to the lowest practicable level on the very day the NATO Treaty was signed.[65] US military assistance was supposed to enable the Western Europeans to mobilise their own armed forces capable of repelling a limited attack. Financial aid was meant above all to give psychological support to the Western Europeans' sense of security and also serve as a boost for the reinforcement and armament of their own armed forces.

On 6 October 1949, President Truman put his name to the mutual-defence programme, aiming to spend $1 billion on the NATO countries.[66] During the discussions, time and again the USA urged that European armed forces be mobilised as quickly as possible in order to contain an attack as far east as possible. The American position was, 'Every effort is to be made to persuade the Regional Planning Group to develop and accept the following plans:

(1) Short-term defence plans using only the resources of the European countries, and, at the same time, acceptance of an "alternative military strategy" for Western European defence. This "alternative military strategy" had the aim of creating a "substantial bridgehead" in Western Europe which can be further extended when additional military forces are mobilized. This is intended to prevent the Soviets occupying the North Atlantic area on a long-term basis.
(2) Long-term defence plans, which take into account the constantly-increasing likelihood that the European countries as a unit will be in a position to defend their territories against conquest and occupation.'[67]

The American goal was to consider the defence of Continental Europe, whether in the short or the long term, as a matter for the Europeans themselves. Thus the Europeans had to provide the

Foundation and History of NATO

'hard core' of the land forces, as well as troops for air defence and ground support. On 1 December 1949, the NATO Defence Committee agreed on a strategic plan for the 'integrated defence of the NATO area', and passed a preliminary programme for the production and supply of arms and equipment.[68] According to this plan, the aim of the alliance was to prevent war by means of deterrence, and, failing this, the coordination of all military and economic resources for common defence. The above-mentioned division of roles was confirmed by this concept. At the signing of the document, together with the bilateral military treaties, President Truman explained the division of roles as follows:

> First, the United States will be charged with the strategic bombing. We have repeatedly recognized in this country that the first priority of the joint defense is our ability to deliver the atomic bomb. Second, the United States Navy and the Western naval powers will conduct essential naval operations, including keeping the sea lanes clear. The Western Union and other nations will maintain their own harbor and coastal defense. Third, we recognize that the hard core of the ground power in being will come from Europe, aided by other nations as they can mobilize. Fourth, England, France, and the closer countries will have the bulk of the short-range attack bombing and air defense. We, of course, will maintain the tactical air force for our own ground and naval forces, and United States defense. Fifth, other nations, depending upon their proximity or remoteness from the possible scene of conflict, will emphasise appropriate specific missions.[69]

NATO's defence concept thus conformed fairly closely to US ideas and can be seen as a concept of national specialisation, in which parallel, and thus doubled efforts were to be avoided. The USA had the main responsibility for strategic forces and, together with Great Britain, had to guarantee the defence of the Atlantic sea lanes. The Continental Europeans were therefore given the job of supplying the hard core of the ground forces and also the support forces for ground warfare and air defence. This concept of division of labour, which did not meet with the approval of all European countries, was, at that time, the only feasible joint defence plan.

Now that the basic strategic plans had been agreed upon, it was the turn of the short and medium-term plans to be realised by the alliance. But the defence plans which were drawn up by the Military Committee, the Standing Group and the Regional

Planning Groups and which were passed on 1 April 1950, were economically totally unworkable. The outbreak of the Korean War on 25 June 1950 was to become the greatest factor influencing international politics and was to have an effect on the development of the Atlantic Alliance.

Conclusion

The founding of NATO was preceded on the one hand by military cooperation between the Benelux countries, Great Britain and France, and on the other by economic cooperation between Western Europe and the USA. It was above all the Western Europeans who pressed for close military cooperation with the USA and thus a greater US military commitment in Western Europe. Differences in the conception of how this European-American union should look were the basis for the Atlantic Alliance talks.

The perception of increasing Soviet pressure on Western Europe by the political leaders in the West finally led to the founding of NATO after the Vandenberg Resolution had created the preconditions for its creation required by the US Constitution.

The negotiations on the alliance officially began on 6 July 1948 (after talks between the USA, Canada and Great Britain on such a pact had begun immediately following the signing of the Brussels Treaty in March 1948) between the two North American states and the Brussels Treaty powers. Not until March 1949 were the other European countries involved in the negotiations, and they had no influence on the contents of the treaty.

The problems dealt with included membership, the territorial applicability of the treaty, the question of guarantee, the lifetime of the treaty and the question of the military organisation. The USA managed to put the majority of their ideas, both political and military, into practice during the talks. The ratification of the NATO Treaty went without problems in the individual member states, but also with no great enthusiasm in some cases.

During the initial phase the alliance gave itself a political and military organisational structure and produced a defence plan mainly based on US ideas. However, the Korean War, which broke out on 25 June 1950, was to have a strong influence on NATO development.

Notes

1. Cf. above all Klaus Hänsch, *Frankreich zwischen Ost und West. Die Reaktion auf den Ausbruch des Ost-West-Konflikts 1946–48*, Berlin, New York, 1972 (*Beiträge zur auswärtigen und internationalen Politik*, vol. 5).
2. On this point cf. Wichard Woyke, *Erfolg durch Integration – Die Europapolitik der Beneluxstaaten 1947 bis 1969*, Bochum, 1985.
3. Paul E. Smets, *La pensée européenne et atlantique de Paul-Henri Spaak 1943–1972*, Brussels, 1970, vol. 1, p. 154.
4. Cf. for example: Paul-Henri Spaak, *Memoiren eines Europäers*, Hamburg 1969, p. 195f.
5. Quotation from *NATO – Facts and Figures*, Published by NATO Information Dept., Brussels, 1990.
6. Ernst-Otto Czempiel/Carl-Christoph Schweitzer, *Weltpolitik der USA nach 1945. Einführung und Dokumente*, Opladen, 1984, p. 37.
7. Cf. Hugo Hahn/Albrecht Weber, *Die OECD: Organisation für wirtschaftliche Zusammenarbeit und Entwicklung*, Baden-Baden, 1976 (*Schriftenreihe europäische Wirtschaft*, vol. 44).
8. Martin Geiling, *Außenpolitik und Nuklearstrategie – Eine Analyse des konzeptionellen Wandels der amerikanischen Sicherheitspolitik gegenüber der Sowjetunion 1945–1963*, Cologne, Vienna, 1975, p. 48.
9. Cf. Georgette Elgey, *Histoire de la IVe République*, vol. 1: *La république des illusions 1945–1951*, Paris, 1965, p. 380.
10. Cf. Geiling (see Note 8), p. 50.
11. Cf. Lawrence S. Kaplan, *A Community of Interests. NATO and the Military Assistance Program 1948–1951*, Washington, 1980, p. 17.
12. Op. cit. Wilfried Loth, *Die Teilung der Welt 1941–1955*, Munich, 1982 (*dtv-Weltgeschichte des 20. Jahrhunderts*, vol. 4020), p. 213; Engl. edn.: *The Division of the World 1941–1955*, London, 1988.
13. Op. cit. Ernst-Otto Czempiel, *Das amerikanische Sicherheitssystem 1945–1949: Studie zur Außenpolitik der bürgerlichen Gesellschaft*, Berlin, 1966 (*Beiträge zur auswärtigen und internationalen Politik*, vol. 1), p. 402.
14. Op. cit. Theodore Achilles, 'Die Rolle der Vereinigten Staaten bei den Verhandlungen über das Atlantische Bündnis', in *NATO-Brief* 4/79, pp. 11–14, here p. 11.
15. Cf. Kaplan (see Note 11), p. 17.
16. Cf. AdG of 17.3.1948, p. 1422f.
17. Geiling (see Note 8), p. 57.
18. AdG of 20.7.1948, p. 1575.
19. Claude Delmas, 'Frankreich und die Entstehung des Atlantischen Bündnisses', in *NATO-Brief* 4/80, pp. 23–27, here p. 24.
20. Cf. Elgey (see Note 9), p. 382.
21. Christian Greiner, 'Die alliierten militärstrategischen Planungen zur

Verteidigung Westeuropas 1947–1950', in *Anfänge westdeutscher Sicherheitspolitik*, vol 1: *Von der Kapitulation zum Pleven-Plan*, von Roland G. Foerster, Christian Greiner, Georg Meyer, Hans-Jürgen Rautenberg, Norbert Wiggershaus, Munich, Vienna, 1982, pp. 119–323, here p. 152f.
22. Ibid., p. 153.
23. Cf. *NATO – Facts and Figures* (see Note 5).
24. Cf. Escott Reid, 'Die wundersame Geburt des Nordatlantischen Bündnisses', in *NATO-Brief* 6/80, pp. 14–20, here p. 18.
25. Ibid., p. 15.
26. Cf. *NATO-Facts and Figures* (see Note 5), p. 23.
27. Op. cit. Greiner (see Note 21), p. 153f.
28. Cf. Daniel Yergin, *Shattered Peace: The Origins of the Cold War and the National Security State*, New York, 1977.
29. Czempiel (see Note 13), p. 398f.
30. Cf. Loth (see Note 12), p. 218.
31. *Foreign Relations of the United States*, FRUS, Diplomatic Papers, 1945–1950, Washington, 1967–1980, 1948, III, p. 70; cf. Greiner (see Note 21), p. 155.
32. Cf. Geiling (see Note 8), p. 57f.
33. Cf. AdG of 20.7.1948, p. 1575.
34. Cf. Robert E. Osgood, *NATO – The Entangling Alliance*, Chicago, London, 1966, p. 34.
35. Op. cit. *NATO – Facts and Figures*, NATO Information Dept., Brussels, 1990.
36. Cf. Greiner (see Note 21), p. 155.
37. Reid (see Note 24), p. 16.
38. Ibid., p. 17.
39. Greiner (see Note 21), p. 156.
40. Op. cit. Delmas (see Note 19), p. 26.
41. Cf. on this point Dieter Mahncke, *Berlin im geteilten Deutschland*, Munich,Vienna, 1973 (*Schriften des Forschungsinstitutes der Deutschen Gesellschaft fur Auswärtige Politik*, vol. 34), p. 44.
42. Achilles (see Note 14), here: Part 2, in *NATO-Brief* No. 5/79, pp. 16–19, esp. p. 16.
43. Ibid.
44. Alexander M. Rendel, 'Der Nordatlantikvertrag stand bis zuletzt auf des Messers Schneide', in *NATO-Brief* 2/80, pp. 17–21, here p. 20.
45. Cf. Greiner (see Note 21), p. 45.
46. Cf. Achilles (see Note 42).
47. Op. cit. Reid (see Note 24), p. 16.
48. Ibid.
49. Ibid.
50. Cf. Rendel (see Note 44), p. 17f.
51. Ibid., p. 18.

52. Greiner (see Note 21), p. 158.
53. Rendel (see Note 44), p. 19.
54. Cf. Delmas, Frankreich (see Note 19), p. 25.
55. Greiner (see Note 21), p. 158.
56. Cf. on this point Lord Ismay, *NATO: The First Five Years 1949–1954*, Utrecht, 1954.
57. Cf. Greiner (see Note 21), p. 157.
58. Cf. Alfred Grosser, *Das Bündnis: Die westeuropäischen Länder und die USA seit dem Krieg*, Munich, Vienna, 1982, p. 128f.
59. *NATO-Tatsachen und Dokumente*, NATO Inf. Service, Brussels, 1976, p. 30.
60. Cf. Osgood (see Note 34), p. 40.
61. Cf. *NATO: Final Communiqués 1949–1970*, NATO Inf. Service, Brussels, p. 31f.
62. Cf. Greiner (see Note 21), p. 231.
63. Ibid., p. 232.
64. Ibid., p. 233ff.
65. Cf. Osgood (see Note 34), p. 41.
66. *Die Organisation des Nordatlantikvertrages*, Section de L'Information (ed.), Paris 1958, p. 23.
67. National Archives and Records Service, Modern Military Branch, Washington DC, (NA, MMB), Record Group (RG) 218, Geographic File (GF) 1948–1950, Western Europe (3–12–48), Sec. 30, Memorandum for the Secretary of Defence, Subject: Guidance for the United States Military Representative appointed to the Military Committee and to the Standing Group of the North Atlantic Treaty Military Organisation, 30.9.1949, op. cit. Greiner (see Note 21), p. 241.
68. *Die Organisation des Nordatlantikvertrages* (see Note 66), p. 28.
69. Osgood (see Note 34), p. 376.

14
The Military Situation and the Idea of Threat

Eberhard Pikart

The position of US and Allied troops, and of the USSR's forces, at the end of hostilities was to be vitally important for international developments after the Second World War. Due to the war, and afterwards, the United States had assumed a 'global' position.[1] From 1946, however, after her forces had been demobilised, the USA had only a relatively small amount of manpower available with which to consolidate this position, or, to put it another way, only limited forces were made available, mostly for financial reasons.[2] While this was sufficient for the occupation of Germany, Austria, Trieste, Japan and so on, there was a noticeable lack of suitably trained elements, as well as air forces, up to about mid-1950.[3] Also, US atomic weapons, up to the beginning of the 1950s, had not yet taken on the military and strategic importance which one rightly assumed that the public and also, most likely, the Soviet military planners perceived. The US forces did not receive atomic weapons before the Korea crisis, and there were wildly contrasting opinions on their optimum size, number and military employment.[4] At the onset of the Berlin crisis, but also at the start of the Korean crisis, the Americans were forced to improvise, as there were definite operational plans at that time.[5] Thus it is difficult to imagine the USA as a serious military threat to the Soviets up to the Korean War, if one discounts the fact that the mere presence of the USA's military globalism was taken as a threat by the Soviets.

With a view to the military situation during the period 1948 to 1953, however, it must be said that the USA had entered other wars with relatively little military preparation, but had been able to build up an overwhelming matériel, armament and economic potential within one or two years of entry into a war. Even after the end of the Second World War, US strength lay not so much in her military might (disregarding atomic weapons) as in her economic power, her belief in the value of her political views, in her unbroken and undamaged civilisation, and in her extraordinary international esteem. The Soviets had to be careful not to challenge this potential again.

Thus, after 1945, there seemed to be more of a military threat from the Soviets than the United States. Would they or could they provide the acid test for this relatively thinly spread, militarily ill-secured and partially overstretched US 'globalism', by military or other means? Would they or could they attempt to exploit the relative weakness of Western Europe for their own political or military purposes? Would they then run the risk of placing the territorial gains of the Second World War and the increase in her sphere of influence (the Eastern bloc) in jeopardy? Would they dare to do this, in view of the fact that the Soviet Union was weakened by losses and destruction to a far greater extent at the end of the war than the United States? However, the West did not take much notice of the obvious Soviet weaknesses and paid little attention to them when estimating the Soviets' military strength or their military intentions. Thus, after the Second World War, the Soviet Union appeared to the West to be a well-armed, threatening, expansionist state, strangely violent in her aims and methods.[6]

This threatening impression was reinforced by the fact that the Soviet Union showed herself to be uncompromising ideologically, politically and diplomatically, without the will to cooperate with others in order to solve the many problems of the postwar years. Soon it also became clear that the means of resolving conflict (cooperation between the superpowers, joint efforts in the United Nations, conference diplomacy) in which the USA above all had placed her trust since the Second World War were almost totally ineffective.[7] The talk was soon of the 'cold war', a state of affairs which was neither war nor peace. The international problems of the time are well known. If it was not possible to solve these in a cooperative way, would this not inevitably lead to a war, considering that the USA and the Western Europeans could justifiably blame the Soviets for making a cooperative solution impossible?

In spite of this the Americans and the West in general as well as (presumably) the Soviets hesitated to use the ultimate weapon, war, as the solution to their problems. In his memoirs George F. Kennan writes: 'War, despite the evil shadow of Soviet power, would be neither inevitable nor an appropriate solution.'[8] Thus we note, even in the two time periods examined here, 1948 and the Korean conflict, that there was a decision to avoid starting a war in spite of certain thoughts to the contrary: a war which we must see as a global struggle between the two mightiest world powers since 1945, the USA and the USSR.

The Danger of War and the Threat to the West in 1948

The spring of 1948, from March to June, brought forth a variety of events of great regional or international importance – the crisis in Czechoslovakia, the Italian elections, the start of Western Europe's joint security policy, the beginning of the Berlin crisis, the announcement of the creation of a West German state, the break between Yugoslavia and Moscow (events outside Europe, such as in China, cannot be dealt with in detail here). Many of these events, or rather the results of these, could have led to a war, possibly or necessarily, under different and earlier historical circumstances. In 1948, however, a war did not break out. But, and this can be clearly seen from the files, the fear of war gripped the Western European states (apart from West Germany, which had other problems), and everywhere one could point to a possibly acute threat from the East. At this time Clay wrote his famous telegram, in which he pointed out that a war could break out with 'dramatic suddenness'.[9] I can only make a list here of many other clues to and proof of this fear of war – statements by Auriol, Truman, Hervé Alphand, Bérard, as well as by Norwegian, British and Canadian politicians.[10] What were the reasons for this fear of war, this concept of threat, which becomes so evident in 1948?

George F. Kennan reports, in his memoirs, a statement made by John Foster Dulles in either 1948 or 1949, in which he said that the French felt naked, i.e. the Western Europeans began to see clearly, in 1947–8, that militarily they were totally inferior to the Soviets, especially just after the outbreak of a conflict.[11] I will not go into the question of comparative military strength, as it is already well known. Also well known is the fact that the British left their army of the Rhine in Germany partly because it was cheaper to have them there than in Great Britain. The total numbers of French and British troops available for employment are very open to question as, first, a large proportion were involved in the occupation; second, because very large military administrations were maintained after the Second World War, to deal with the consequences of war, and last, because the Western Europeans' best troops were overseas in the colonies rather than in Europe. Also, the US combat-ready elements in Europe were fairly weak (about one and a half divisions at the start of the Berlin conflict, about two divisions at the outbreak of the Korean conflict). The combat efficiency of the regular units was relatively low due to the large turnover of personnel, the lack of manpower necessary for fighting strength, the lack of training and so on.[12] This does not even mention the weaponry of the European forces. Churchill said, concerning Western military strength, which was not exactly impressive: 'It is indeed a sad thought that there is nothing to protect Europe from an overwhelming attack except the extraordinary resources of the United States in this awful weapon.'[13] In fact no single European country and not even all the Western Europeans together were successfully able to take on the military might of the Soviets, and thus they had to rely on the help of the USA.

When one considers this fear of war, it also becomes obvious that it was expressed more often by politicians than by the military (apart from General Clay, that is). But Western military leaders, in particular the Americans, had their worries. They also believed that a Third World War was possible, if not inevitable.[14] However, apart from this insecurity concerning the USSR's intentions, apart from the professional precautions to be taken against a possible 'blitzkrieg', there was also the political use of the fear of war, pointing to their own military weakness as a way of forcing a level of rearmament appropriate to the Soviet threat, including the expected completion of the Soviet atom bomb.[15] But, just at the time of the Berlin crisis of 1948–9, the fear of a sudden outbreak of war began to recede. The danger seen in the first half of 1948, that, as Hervé Alphand put it, the Russians might think it better to start a war immediately than to wait for US rearmament, was seemingly no longer as great.[16] (We shall not deal with Western estimates of the motives for Soviet warlike intentions (preventive war or imperialist war) in this essay.)

In 1947, and especially in 1948, everything depended upon Soviet plans, and the West asked herself time and again how she could know what the Russians had in mind. There was more guesswork than facts involved in Western plans, guesswork about Soviet military intentions and strength.[17]

Particularly threatening for Europe seemed to be the heavy concentration of Soviet troops in the Soviet zone of occupation in Germany and in the western zones of the Soviet Union itself. There was little knowledge of the degree of Soviet disarmament at the end of the war, and little was known about how Soviet soldiers were being employed in the reconstruction of the country. A danger seemed to be the concentration of forces in what is now the GDR. Thus the military situation appeared to be good for the Soviet Union, taking into account the weakness of the Western European states and the lightweight US presence in Europe. Also, the situation was totally lop-sided, and it was this asymmetry which Western Europe suddenly perceived as being threatening in 1948 as this was based on recognition of their own weakness. I will not bring in the statistics showing the actual strength of the Soviet forces at this point, although they have since been published.[18] It must, however, be said that at this time the Soviets developed a secretive attitude to their military and general statistics (perhaps in order to have a counterweight to the US atom bomb), and they kept this up, with the result that Western nations were sometimes almost forced to make errors of judgement, to exaggerate or to simply guess wrongly.[19]

In fact the Soviet Union was in a dilemma. On the one hand she needed a strong military force in order to make the Eastern bloc into a Communist stronghold and to keep it that way – and unfortunately the best and most suitable base for the Soviet forces, from a military and/or tactical control point of view, it had to be admitted, was the Soviet occupation zone of Germany.[20] Of course, these Soviet troops would also be a deterrent for the West, so as to prevent the West exerting an influence upon the instability of the Eastern bloc. Thus a threatening situation was created, which forced the West, in 1948, to look for and develop new forms of security organisation and new security measures. This could also be construed as a threat by the East. The West's military development before the Korean conflict was not really so great a threat to the East in any case. I only wish to hint at the fact that, while the West reacted quickly to Soviet mulishness in the UN both politically and economically, the military reaction was much slower, and thus there was little or no threat to the Soviets. NATO itself was, for the sake of argument, no serious threat to the Soviets in 1949 either. It was only the Korean crisis and the German contribution to Western defence, apart from US atomic weapons development, which made NATO a military tool worth taking seriously.

When one takes these considerations into account, one can safely say that there was neither a threat in the military sense nor in the political sense in 1948. One could also say that the perceptions of threat were a way of adapting to the world political climate. This statement requires some qualification, however.

In 1948 everything pointed to three crises coming to a head, even if these crises did not get to that stage. The first crisis situation was caused by the Prague Spring of 1948. What would have happened if the Czech Communists had used Soviet troops to take over control of the country (from 1946 onwards Czechoslovakia was no longer under Soviet occupation)? It is possible that General Clay had this crisis in mind when he wrote his telegram. Perhaps the West would not have intervened. One can only speculate upon the following: what would have happened if the crisis had spread from Czechoslovakia to other Eastern bloc states?

The second flashpoint in the spring of 1948 was Italy. Again the speculative question: what would have occurred had a Communist or Popular Front government come to power? George F. Kennan had worries in this respect, which, however, proved to be groundless as soon as the results of the general election were known.[21] Doubtless US security interests would have been affected had the course of events been different. Moreover, at this time, while the Western politicians were voicing their misgivings about Soviet military intentions toward the West, the Soviets themselves were discussing the question of Yugoslavia.[22] Did the Russians have plans to solve this conflict within the Communist camp by military means? We do not know the answer to this, but we do know that Yugoslavia was able to follow the road to Communist independence without the Soviets becoming involved. We can, however, assume that the West feared Soviet military action against Yugoslavia.

We need only look quickly at the Berlin crisis in connection with conflicts which might have ended up in war. It seems that there was a definite effort, in contrast to the Korean crisis, to steer the situation along so carefully that it was not necessary for either side to issue an ultimatum. Of course, the main feature of this particular crisis was that Soviet and US interests directly collided in Berlin.

One other factor must be mentioned here, which probably played a big part in the background during the conflicts or near-conflicts of 1948 and the following years. When the European states entered the First World War in 1914, no one knew what a 'world war' really was. In 1948, after two world wars, it was clear what such a war involved. The Soviet Union had not yet recovered from the rigours of war, but she had come out of the war as a recognised, feared world power. If we look at the effort needed by the British and Americans to beat Hitler, then we can say that the military in particular, but also the economists, both in the USA and in the Soviet Union, all knew very well what a new 'global war', a real world war, would mean. The Second World War was also an ideological war, and it was well known how difficult it was to end such a war in an internationally acceptable fashion. Was the aim of this war simply 'debellatio', total occupation, re-education, liberation?

Experts pointed to the extreme effort needed for the victory over Hitler. But what would happen if the enemy was of the order of magnitude of the Soviet Union of China? US Senator Vandenberg said on this point, in the debate on China staged by the Senate Foreign Affairs Committee on economic problems: 'We cannot deal with the Chinese economy in the same all-enbracing way as we did with the ERP (European Recovery Program). China is too large...The problem is too complicated.' He went on to talk about military considerations and said, 'No matter what we might want to do, any such attack over so great an area would be impossible.'[23] Was conventional warfare not going beyond the bounds of what was feasible when applied to campaigns against China or even the Soviet Union, as the West should have imagined?

Thus it seems that the great hesitation in considering a third world war in 1948–9, and also a factor in the Korean conflict, was borne out of the Second World War experience. When one speaks of deterrence, therefore, one must always point out that there was and still is a pre-atomic deterrence: in other words, conventional deterrence, which had and has its basis in the experience and the magnitude of the Second World War as a total, ideological and global war. However, alongside this statement, that the experience of the Second World War perhaps had the effect of preventing the third, we must also state that the events of the period 1947–9 are proof of a definite growth of mistrust. And events were to prove that there was seemingly no alternative to both sides modernising their armed forces, to rearmament, the development of atomic weapons and a mainly military-based alliance policy.

The Korean Conflict

The Korean conflict (25.6.1950 to 27.7.1953) probably ushered in a new era in security-policy history. In Europe, NATO began to function, and there were talks on the Federal Republic of Germany's contribution to military security. The doctrine of 'massive retaliation' put an end to the differing concepts of US employment of atomic weapons. The Soviet Union also possessed atomic weapons from 1949 onwards, and they were ready for military use in the 1950s. US 'globalism', which appeared to have 'little back-up' in the period to 1950, became more tangible, not least due to the reorganisation of the armed forces.[24]

But let us tear ourselves away from these things, which look to the future, in order to come back to the burning question: was there a danger, between 1950 and 1953, that a direct struggle between the Americans and the Soviets, in the language of that time a Third World War, might have occurred? This would have meant that the Korean conflict would have had to spread and involve Europe. Basically, this 'local' or 'limited' conflict was a combination of highly complicated diplomatic and military problems. Let us, however, limit ourselves to a few questions and answers.

First, why did the United States get involved, although she did not regard her military presence in Korea as one of the essential factors in her Far East policy, and thus kept only a relatively small force in South Korea? (Western Europe, including the Federal Republic, West Berlin and particularly the Ruhr, but also Japan, all belonged to the 'essentials'.) The Americans did not even strengthen South Korea, militarily or strategically, after Mao's victory over Chiang Kai-shek. South Korea's regime was not a great favourite of the USA, and the country was militarily speaking not very important.[25]

The Military Situation and the Idea of Threat

There were no military or geo-strategic motives for the USA's becoming immediately involved. The decisive factor was that North Korea's attack, most probably ordered to be carried out by the Soviet Union, or at least agreed to and scheduled by her, went against the recognition of the Containment Doctrine, now firmly rooted in public opinion both in the USA and in Western Europe (especially in West Germany). By attacking, the North Koreans, as representatives of the Soviets, had overstepped a sensitive line. This attack in the Far East was seen as breaking the rules of the cold war.[26] This had the same effect on public opinion in the United States as it did in Europe or Japan, where the mood was pessimistic. This confirmed what people had expected of the Soviets. The Americans viewed it as a provocation, which it probably was, while the Europeans saw a threat to themselves, which was more than likely unjustified. Fears, considerations and guesswork also led to the United Nations soon identifying themselves with US military retaliatory measures, at least during the initial phase of the conflict. This offence against the doctrine of containment, this attempt by a substitute of the USSR to make a quick attack on the USA's seemingly ponderous military machine, caused the latter to act quickly, although the Americans were unprepared, and although they had only limited manpower available at the time.

In the USA there was uncertainty over how the Soviet Union would react to an American intervention. Now we know that the Soviet Union did not become involved. The North Koreans were left to fight for themselves after the Soviet 'advisers' were pulled out. There was little danger of the conflict spreading during this initial phase. Had the Soviets wanted a full-scale war in 1950, she could have started one in another location, and would have had more chance of success. Finally, one can say after the event that the USSR did not even react militarily to the 'rearmament' of West Germany, considering that the German question was so much more important for the Soviets than the Korean problem.[27]

The danger of the conflict spreading was much greater at the end of the initial successful phase of the war, after the crossing of the 38th Parallel and after the South Korean troops (and behind them the Americans) had reached the Yalu River. Here they came upon a great number of regular Chinese forces, and they were again unprepared for this. A critical situation arose, in which the obvious questions were asked: should they try to cut off the

Chinese supply lines on Chinese territory itself, should they follow Chinese warplanes into Chinese airspace and fight them there, would it be possible to employ Nationalist Chinese troops against North Korean or Chinese forces, and was it feasible to use atomic weapons against certain Chinese targets? The risk of war, declared or otherwise, between the USA and Red China was a definite one, and there were US military leaders ready to run the risk. Of course, there was the even more serious question of whether the Soviet Union would stand by and watch such a war, or become involved at a time which suited her interests, and whether this involvement would be diplomatic or military. In any case, the European allies got nervous, and particularly the British advised against such an expansion of affairs, which would be hard to keep under control, and which would have disastrous consequences. We know that Truman, after some deliberation and after much wrangling and infighting among his personal advisers, decided not to take the risk. This seemed to be 'the wrong war at the wrong time in the wrong place'.[28] It seemed to the Administration to be a better idea to consolidate Europe. During this conflict the Americans began to recognise the danger of having a majority of her armed forces embroiled in long-drawn-out struggles. Also, it was doubtful whether the use of atomic weapons would have the same effect of ending a war quickly as it had against Japan (the discussion about atomic weapons had begun). In short, there was no reliable and obvious idea of how to end the conflict quickly and successfully. The Third World War was avoided, but so was the solution to the Korean problem. A ceasefire was concluded in 1953, again under Eisenhower's threat of atomic weapons. Korea remained divided.

Notes

1. The locations of global, i.e. extra-American, commitments and conditions are shown by a list of bases used in US security strategy, put together and annotated by the Joint Chiefs of Staff. The rights to these bases were secured by treaties which were not always without problems in respect of both diplomacy and finances, see *Foreign*

Relations of the United States, Diplomatic Papers, 1945–1950, FRUS, 1946, I, pp. 1112–17 and 1174–7. Factors other than these historical and geographic reasons for US globalism cannot be dealt with here. Cf. on this point James F. Schnabel, *The History of the Joint Chiefs of Staff: The Joint Chiefs of Staff and National Policy*, vol. I, *1945–1947*, Wilmington, 1979, p. 141: 'Geographic location would no longer afford the United States the security and protection it once had.' See also David A. Rosenberg, american atomic strategy and the hydrogen bomb decision, in *Journal of American History*, vol. 6, 1979, p. 79, where he points to 'the wide gap now existing between our international military commitments and our military capacities'.

2. The defence budget passed by the US Congress in 1946 totalled $40,132,674,031, and in the following year it was $7,304,542,400; see Elias Huzar, *The Purse and the Sword, Control of the Army by Congress through Military Appropriations, 1933–1950*, Ithaca, 1950, p. 140. In literature on the subject there is often a great discrepancy regarding the figures of the defence budget. On the demobilisation of the US armed forces see *American Military History*, Maurice Matloff (ed.), Washington DC, 1973, p. 529f. On the demobilisation of the Soviet forces see Mathew A. Evangelista, 'Stalin's postwar army reappraised', in *International Security*, vol. 7, 1982; 8, 1983.

3. Harry R. Borowski, 'Air force atomic capability from V-J Day to the Berlin blockade – potential or real?' In *Military Affairs*, vol. 8, 1980, pp. 105–10, here p. 106: 'Within weeks after Japan's surrender, American combat capability began eroding. Even military planners understood that demobilization would follow the war, but few anticipated the extent and the devastating results.' Borowski goes on to say that the Strategic Air Command (SAC) was not reorganised until the summer of 1948. Also Harry R. Borowski, *A Hollow Threat, Strategic Air Power and Containment before Korea*, Westport-London, 1982. For example the troops stationed in Japan were also badly trained in 1950, see also James F. Schnabel, *Policy and Direction: The First Year*, Washington DC, 1972 (*US Army in the Korean War*), p. 44f.

4. David A. Rosenberg, 'The origins of overkill', in *International Security*, vol. 7/4, 1983 and 'US nuclear stockpile, 1945–50', in *Bulletin of the Atomic Scientists*, 38, 1982. Also Wolfgang Krieger, 'Die Amerikanischen Atomwaffen und der Kalte Krieg, 1945–1950', in *Neue Politische Literatur*, vol. 28/2, 1983, pp. 209–18.

5. In other words specific plans for possible local conflicts e.g. Berlin or Korea. This does not mean the contingency plans for the evacuation of personnel in crisis situations, or the basic plans for a possible struggle with the USSR. Cf. on this point: *Anfänge westdeutscher Sicherheitspolitik 1945–1956*, Bd. 1: *Von der Kapitulation bis zum Pleven-Plan*, von Roland G. Foerster, Christian Greiner, Georg Meyer, Hans-Jürgen Rautenberg und Norbert Wiggershaus, Munich/Vienna 1982,

particularly Teil II: Christian Greiner, 'Die alliierten militärstrategischen Planungen zur Verteidigung Westeuropas 1947–1950', pp. 119–323.
6. US public opinion reacted violently between 1945 and 1948 to two areas of Soviet postwar policy above all: first, to the brutal policy of bringing the Eastern Bloc states into line (particularly referring to the Czech crisis of 1948); second, to the lack of willingness to compromise shown by Soviet diplomats in the UN as well as during the many postwar conferences. US diplomats observed very carefully how strong the Communist parties were in the countries of Western Europe and Scandinavia. The following passage from the Churchill speech 'Sinews of Peace' of 5.3.1946 typifies the European opinion: 'A shadow has fallen upon the scenes so lately lighted by the Allied victory. Nobody knows what Soviet Russia and its Communist international organisation intends to do in the immediate future, or what are the limits, if any, to their expansive and proselytising tendencies.'
7. The US diplomats accused the USSR of having a 'non-conciliatory attitude', both in the UN and during the various postwar conferences; also, that she only agreed to solutions which lay in her closest interests, and the interests of other states were not considered; Soviet policy was limited only by her own economic situation, and by the borderline of what she thought of as the highest risk factor, i.e. that open war with the USA had to be avoided. Cf. for example Marshall's statement of 1947 concerning the London Foreign Ministers' Conference: 'As regards Germany ... three of the delegations agree that boundary commissions be at once established to examine all frontier questions. The Soviet Union rejects this proposal ... The Soviet Union has refused to furnish vitally necessary information with respect to reparations removals ... The Soviet delegation has refused to agree to the relinquishment of property interests unilaterally seized under the guise of reparations ... The Soviet practices in eastern Germany have prevented Germany from playing its part in the recovery of Europe ...The Soviet Union demands reparations for itself and Poland/which would imply/the establishment of an economic power so comprehensive that it would be in reality a power of life and death over any German government.' Op. cit. *Documents on Germany Under Occupation 1945–1954*, Beatrice Ruhm von Oppen (ed.), London, New York, Toronto, 1955, pp. 261–3.
8. George F. Kennan, *Memoiren eines Diplomaten (Memoirs 1925–1950)*, Stuttgart, 1988 (orig. edn 1967), p. 365.
9. *The Papers of General Lucius D. Clay, Germany 1945–1949*, Jean Edward Smith (ed.), London, 1974, vol. 2, p. 568f.
10. Escott Reid, *Time of Fear and Hope: The Making of the Atlantic Treaty 1947–1948*, Toronto, 1977.
11. Kennan, (see Note 8), p. 399. I will not go into the strategic consider-

ations connected with this. The raid-like opening to the war made by Hitler and the Japanese had played a role in strategic plans both in the USA and in the USSR, and for the Soviets, but also for the French. There was also the fact that the war was fought on their own territory, among other factors.
12. See above, Note 3.
13. See also Churchill's speech of 9.10.1948: 'Nothing stands between Europe today and complete subjugation to Communist tyranny but the atomic bomb in American possession.' Winston S. Churchill, *Europe Unite, Speeches 1947 and 1948*, London, Toronto, Melbourne, Sydney, Wellington, 1950, p. 413.
14. Cf. the introduction to the 'HALFMOON' strategic plan drawn up by the Joint Chiefs of Staff on 21.7.1948, in particular: 'There is a possibility that war will occur at any time as a result of miscalculation by the USSR as to the extent that the United States or other western Powers would or could resist their present expansion policy. It is also possible that the active opposition of the Western Powers to Soviet expansion policy may induce the Soviets to believe that it would be advantageous or even mandatory for them to anticipate any increase in this opposition by starting a war themselves. Such a war would come with little or no warning.' Op. cit. *Containment: Documents on American Policy and Strategy 1945–1950*, Thomas H. Etzold and John Lewis Gaddis (eds), New York, 1978, p. 315.
15. Cf. the OFFTACKLE strategic plan by the Joint Chiefs of Staff of 26.5.1949, three months before the explosion of the Soviet atom bomb. They assume that 'atomic weapons will be used by the USSR if available'. Op. cit. *Containment* (see Note 14), p. 326. About one year later, in Security Program NSC 68 of 7.4.1950, we read: 'We do not know accurately what the Soviet atomic capability is but the Central Intelligence Agency estimates ... assign the Soviet Union a production capability within the following ranges:

By mid–1950	10–20
–1951	25–45
–1952	45–90
–1953	70–135
–1954	200

This estimate is admittedly based on incomplete coverage of Soviet activities and represents the production capabilities of known or deducible Soviet plans. If others exist, as is possible, this estimate could lead us into a feeling of superiority in our stockpile that might be dangerously misleading, particularly with regard to the timing of a possible Soviet offensive.' Op. cit. FRUS (see Note 1), 1950, I, p. 251.
16. Hervé Alphand, *L'étonnement d'être. Journal 1939–1973*, Paris, 1977.

17. Here one would have to check the US strategic plans to see their estimation of Soviet military strength and capability. In spite of all their doubts about Soviet logistic capability, they considered it feasible for the Soviets to gain 'blitz-like' results in Western Europe. The knowledge of their own momentary inferiority was possibly a greater factor in dictating the scenario than the knowledge of their potential enemy's opportunities and worth.
18. Peter Gosztony, *Die Rote Armee: Geschichte und Aufbau der sowjetischen Streitkräfte seit 1917*, Vienna, Munich, Zurich, New York, 1980.
19. Cf. Zbigniew K. Brzezinski, 'How the cold war was played', in *Foreign Affairs*, vol. 51/1, 1972, pp. 181–209, partic. p. 183: 'For political reasons, the Soviet Union chose to keep its demobilization a secret. As a result, contemporary Western estimates of Soviet military strength were considerably higher than reality.'
20. On the strength of the Soviet armed forces in the Soviet-occupied zone of Germany cf. Norbert Wiggershaus, 'Bedrohungsvorstellungen Bundeskanzlers Adenauers nach Ausbruch des Korea-Krieges', in *MGM*, vol. 1, 1979, pp. 79–122, particularly p. 99f.
21. Cf. Reid (see Note 10), p. 20: 'Soviet control over Italy or Norway ... would result in a strategic situation which would in the long run be intolerable to the interests of the United States and which would greatly increase the chances of war (Kennan) or which would result in a slow deterioration of the western position until the western powers were forced to resort to war (Bevin).'
22. Milovan Djilas, *Jahre der Macht: Kräftespiel hinter dem Eisernen Vorhang. Memoiren 1945–1966*, Munich, 1983; Wolfgang Leonhard, *Die Revolution entläßt ihre Kinder*, Cologne, Berlin, 1955.
23. Cf. on this point also Albert C. Wedemeyer, *Der verwaltete Krieg*, Gütersloh, 1960, p. 309; he points out that General Marshall had expressed his 'dislike' of 'empire-builders' (regarding the Chinese mission); see also Hans Speier, *German Rearmament and Atomic War*, Evanston, New York, 1957, Rand Corporation R–298, 15.2.1957 (Reprint Univ. Microfilm International, Ann Arbor, London, 1980), p. 53: 'One knows from history that China cannot be defeated militarily.' The 'China factor' seems also to have been a leading force in Stalin's Chinese plans, Djilas (see Note 22), p. 1919: 'A decisive factor in Stalin's attitude concerning China was certainly as much reluctance to enter a conflict with the West, and particularly the USA, as probably also unease at the rise of a revolutionary state which, due to her innovations, her size and her independence, could turn into a successful, invincible rival for the Soviet Union.'
24. Matloff (see Note 2), p. 572f.
25. Cf. William Whitney Stueck, Jr., *The Road to Confrontation, American Policy towards China and Korea 1947–50*, Chapel Hill, 1981.
26. For example Konrad Adenauer, who feared a Soviet preventive war

immediately after 1950, spoke of the date of the North Korean attack on South Korea as a 'black day'; see Hans-Peter Schwarz, *Adenauer: Der Aufstieg: 1876–1952*, Stuttgart, 1986, p. 867.
27. Schnabel (see Note 3), and Rosemary Foot, *The Wrong War: American Policy and the Dimension of the Korean Conflict, 1950–1953*, Ithaca, 1985.
28. Foot (see Note 27), p. 23: the statement came from General Omar Bradley, Chairman of the US Joint Chiefs of Staff.

15
Europe and America 1948–1950: An Unequal Relationship

Pierre Melandri

'L'Europe ne peut pas se défendre seule avant longtemps ou avant très longtemps ... Sans la sécurité que la Communauté atlantique peut donner aux Européens, ceux-ci ne pourront pas faire l'Europe et il n'y aura pas d'Europe.'

('Europe will be unable to defend herself for a long time, a very long time ... Without the security the Europeans can gain from the Atlantic Community, they will be unable to create a united Europe and it will not come into being.)

René Meyer in his report on the Atlantic Alliance before the French National Assembly.[1]

'It is possible that the historian may judge that the Economic Recovery Act and the Atlantic Pact were the two things which prevented a unity in Europe.

John Foster Dulles during the US Senate hearing on the Alliance.[2]

Between 1948 and 1950 Western Europe discovered both her powerlessness and her dependence. The Marshall Plan alone could ensure the success of economic reconstruction, and it seemed that only the creation of an Atlantic Alliance could restore Western Europe's confidence. In other words, the Old World was forced to rely on the United States both for their security and for their very survival. This loss of status on the part of a Europe which, at the start of the Second World War, still seemed to dominate the globe obviously led to a sense of defiance and envy. Indeed, several Old World leaders wondered whether the United States was mature enough to assume the mantle of power destiny had offered her. Sometimes they voiced their annoyance at the strict conditions their new 'leader' placed upon her economic and strategic assistance. However, their desire or their need to link themselves firmly to the United States was sufficiently great to put these worries into the background in the end. In any case the balance of power between themselves and the new superpower was more subtle. Although America was firmly in the driving seat, her partners knew how to get their own way from time to time.

Strangely enough, the most important result of the unequal nature of these relations at that time was not the one which gave rise to the most controversy. Although Europe, aided by America, began to lay the foundations for her own reconstruction as well as her economic independence, between 1948 and 1950, she gave up her say on strategic affairs and based her identity upon a new Atlantic system. This change, which began in the winter of 1950, reached its zenith as a result of the Korean War. On 21 March 1951 Eisenhower announced that he would take command of the Atlantic area on 1 April, and that the Chiefs of Staff Committee of the Brussels Pact would cede responsibility to him on 31 March at 23.59 hours.[3] However, even though this meant that the alliance between Western Europe and America was formalised, the United States had by no means done more to achieve it than her allies.

During the period 1948–50 American superiority was crushing and her influence turned out to be dominating. Not only were the Europeans under no illusions concerning their inferiority in terms of matériel to their future ally, but they also made more and more pleas to the USA for aid.

In fact, during this period, America had a kind of monopoly of power in strategic terms. Until September 1949, in military terms, she also had a monopoly in nuclear weapons. In ideological terms she was seen as the champion of democracy. With more than 50 per cent of world industrial production, a massive trade surplus and gold stocks totalling two-thirds of all international reserves, the USA was the uncontested world economic leader. The privileged status enjoyed by the US dollar both sanctioned and reinforced this position. In fact at this time the dollar was valued more highly than gold itself, as only dollars could buy the goods vital to the reconstruction of the Old World. Thus it was the 'dollar gap', the lack of dollars held by the European states compared to their immense requirements, which led to their becoming so dependent upon the Americans. In the winter of 1946–7 it became clear that, if America did not come up with a massive aid plan for the ruined Old World countries, the social and economic fabric of Europe was in danger of disintegrating. On 5 June 1947 Secretary of State Marshall announced a plan aimed at helping them overcome their plight. However, at that time, the situation of some states was so desperate that a short-term 'interim aid' programme was necessary in order to avoid the coming chaos.

Meanwhile, on 17 December, the very day on which the interim aid plan was finally approved, Marshall found himself faced by another European demand. After a meeting with his French colleague Georges Bidault, Foreign Secretary Ernest Bevin admitted to Marshall that he saw no other alternative for the West but 'some western democratic system comprising the Americans, ourselves, France, Italy, etc., and of course the Dominions'.[4] Though he gave an evasive answer on 17 December, it was clear that Marshall would have to decide and soon. On 13 January his colleague sent him a memorandum which pulled no punches: 'The Soviet Government has based its policy on the expectation that Western Europe will sink into economic chaos and they may be relied upon to place every possible obstacle in the path of American aid and of Western European recovery.'[5]

When, on 4 March 1948, he received a letter from his French counterpart imploring him 'to restore the cooperation between the Old and New Worlds in the political and (as soon as possible) the military fields, a relationship which is so intimate due to their common attachment to the only worthwhile civilisation',[6] the Secretary of State had laid down the general size of the response the United States was willing to give to the demands made of her. From 1948 to 1950, therefore, one rule was to be applied time and again: the Europeans had first of all to provide *proof of their willingness to help each other* before America would help them. They had to openly avow their determination to 'cooperate'.

As, at the beginning of 1948, negotiations began on a guarantee of security, this model was really nothing novel. It developed together with Marshall Aid. This is because the failure of the first attempts at reconstruction had convinced the US administration that two conditions had to be fulfilled at all costs: a) Germany had to be allowed to participate in the economic recovery, as without her such a recovery would be a Utopian one; and b) the Europeans had to do away with customs and currency restrictions, and pool their resources, in order to overcome their difficulties.[7]

Thus, during the summer of 1948, Congress literally adopted this concept as its own, with the result that the State Department had to intervene in order to slow down the speed with which Congress wanted to push it along. But, to be honest, this was not the only condition Congress placed on the granting of economic aid.[8] However, Congress' frequently expressed wish that Europe should be 'integrated' in a gradual manner was reaffirmed, more strongly with each passing year, both in the preamble and in the text of the European Recovery Programme (ERP).

In addition, as the problem of a security guarantee arose, the administration's reaction seemed to be well founded: US policy was always to be dependent upon the evidence of goodwill which the Europeans would have to present beforehand. They could not get round this proviso, not least due to the fact that their request for aid was causing massive uncertainty on the part of both US administrative officers and Congress itself. Indeed, at the beginning they seemed a little stunned by the reaction. At the turn of the years 1947–8, the strategic threat posed by the other side did not appear to them to be the principal danger, and the concept of an Atlantic Alliance seemed far removed from the official prevailing opinion at the end of the war. At the beginning of 1948, the United Nations system was still dear to the hearts of both public opinion and Congress.[9] As early as 17 February, Deputy Secretary of State Lovett reminded the British ambassador of this fact.[10]

The Joint Chiefs of Staff, on the contrary, were more worried than overjoyed about the prospect when they were asked for advice. Would military assistance, something certain countries, France in particular, were thinking of, not tempt potential allies to raise a claim on already-limited US resources? Would committing America to protect a Europe which was feeble compared to the other side not mean plunging the USA into a venture costing more than the present budget allowed her to spend?[11]

As a result of this, from the beginning, the conviction gained ground that the Marshall Plan could be threatened if the Europeans' subjective fear were not lessened. Thus Marshall's reply was no surprise: Europe should first of all begin by 'helping herself' and by demonstrating her own capacity to unify herself. Bevin's 'European' speech of 22 January 1948 and the conclusion of the Brussels Pact less than two months later can be seen as directly linked to this demand for progress towards unity. On the other hand, President Truman, on 17 March, the very day of the signing of the Brussels Pact, thought it wise to welcome this conclusion and to let it be known that the United States would do everything in her power to ensure that the new allies were successful. Thus the process which was to end in the Vandenberg Resolution got under way. However, before this could really begin, there was another American demand which had to be met first: the Europeans not only had to install the Consultative Committee foreseen by the new treaty but, in addition, a secretariat and a Permanent Military Committee.

In the course of the summer, when the secret talks on the conclusion of a security agreement were finally under way, the same process could be seen. It is true that on 1 July 1948, NSC-14, which foresaw the granting of massive military assistance, was adopted, and that on 23 July General Lemnitzer arrived in Europe to check on how this aid could be distributed, but soon all this was again dependent upon one main proviso: that progress was made by the new allies in working out a supranational defence plan.[12] Thus, on 22 September, the Europeans created a permanent organisation in order to set up a *joint* defence policy and to deal with difficulties concerning the production of matériel for this purpose. This body was to comprise command elements of the army, navy and air force and be under Field Marshal Montgomery as its permanent military 'chairman'.[13]

However, this did not mean that the USA stopped raising conditions. The demands sent by the Western Union to the United States on 11 March 1949 were merely a catalogue of national requirements, and there was no mention of how the aid was to be used. Congress was unimpressed by this. When, in early October 1949, the *Mutual Defense Assistance Program* (MDAP) was passed, there was a clause in it which specified that 90 per cent of the billion dollars allocated could not be transferred until 'the President of the United States approves recommendations for an integrated defense of the North Atlantic area which may be made by the Council and the Defense Committee to be established under the North Atlantic Treaty'.[14]

On 14 December, the Atlantic Alliance defence ministers were thus obliged to agree upon a 'strategic concept': in other words, upon a package of basic guidelines instead of a proper plan. According to these, no European state was to try to create a complete military force, but rather each was to make the best possible contribution to the newly formed alliance.

The same procedure was applied to those decisions which had been shelved due to the events in Korea. The Americans refused to commit themselves to the creation of an integrated Atlantic armed force and the appointment of one of their generals as Commander-in-Chief until the Europeans, at least in theory, agreed to a German contribution to this Atlantic force.[15]

Thus it was clear that the Americans were in the driving seat during these events. Two facts emphasise this even more strongly: in March 1948, in the greatest secrecy, they, together with the Canadians and the British, had laid down the main points of the treaty which was to be 'negotiated' during the coming summer; the Americans were also largely to blame for the long delay in the realisation of the already-conceived plans: this was due on the one hand to the fact that the plans depended upon the agreement of Congress, but also because the old party hands in the administration could not reach agreement.[16]

As we might have guessed, this US domination could also be found in the new foreign relations. Thus, from the start, according to the wishes of the United States, what was initially an Anglo-French plan, namely to extend the Dunkirk Pact to include the Benelux states, was radically changed to form a new treaty (that of Brussels). In this regard the German question was at the centre even of these matters of security. At the end of 1947, during the Four-Power Conference in London, the break was finally made with the opposing camp. A West German state was created quickly, in order to protect the population of the Western zones from the pressure Moscow might exert on them towards reunification on her terms. So as to calm the fears which were bound to arise among Germany's neighbours, France in particular, concerning this new state, as well as limiting the discrimination to which it would doubtless be subjected, the Americans saw only one solution: to integrate it into 'the community of Western

European nations'. It was clear that, for the time being, this objective was out of reach. At least they could make sure that this solution was a practical proposition in the future. As early as 20 January 1948, Kennan had warned his colleagues of the potential danger involved in the initial Anglo-French plan: 'The general adoption of a mutual assistance pact based squarely on defense against Germany is a poor way to prepare the ground for the eventual entry of the Germans into this concept.'[17]

We should not be surprised to learn that the Americans finally got their way. After all, the US factor was omnipresent during the Anglo-French negotiations: What did Washington think? How was Washington going to react? The French were obsessed with the fear of becoming alienated from their potential ally. Since Couve de Murville, Directeur-général des affaires politiques (Director General of Political Affairs) in the Quai d'Orsay, was against the suggested changes, it was Jean Chauvel, Secretary-General in the Quai d'Orsay, who was sent by the French to negotiate the new treaty on their behalf.[18] The signed document finally contained just two references to the German threat, while Article 4, the key clause, no longer specified the aggressor against whom the signatories were to render each other automatic armed assistance.

The progression from the original pact to the Atlantic Treaty, during the next few months, leaves us in no doubt of the effectiveness of American influence. From 1 April 1948 onwards, the end of the secret talks with the Canadians and the British, this could clearly be seen.[19] Indeed, from the beginning, the Americans had stated the fact that *only* an organisation larger than that containing a combination of the United States and Canada with the Brussels Pact would be a workable proposition.

This line was maintained throughout the summer, to the horror of the French, who were kept in the dark concerning the preceding talks. In the eyes of Bidault, who described the project, on 19 July 1948 in The Hague, as 'a monster as fabulous as the unicorn',[20] an 'Atlantic Pact' would only serve as an excuse to suppress the real priority: an American guarantee of security coupled with military assistance to those European countries who were particularly weak in military terms. However, the US diplomats surrendered even less as their position was supported by Congress: in the Vandenberg Resolution, an American association was only mentioned concerning those agreements 'as are based upon continuous and effective self-help and aid, and *as effect its national security*'.[21] From the word go Lovett was skilled in reminding the other delegates of this fact.

Under these circumstances Washington's influence weighed yet more strongly upon the result of these negotiations. Thus it was at the insistence of the United States that Article 4 was included, as early as the spring of 1948, in spite of British reservations.[22] At the same time Article 5 did not contain the degree of automatic reaction the Europeans would have liked. To comply with their wishes would have gone against the right to declare war which the US Constitution conferred upon Congress.[23] The question had given rise to differences of opinion between the Americans and the British since March. In the version of 24 December 1948, Article 5 foresaw that each party 'will assist the party or parties so attacked by taking forthwith such *military or other* action ... as may be necessary'.[24]

Unfortunately Congress' vigilance had been forgotten. In 1949 this vigilance had been strengthened due to the change in the majority and the resulting Democratic regaining of power over the GOP (Grand Old Party, i.e. Republicans). On 14 February, according to Secretary of State Dean Acheson, a catastrophe had barely been avoided: Senators Vandenberg and Connally had demanded 'that it must be made clear in Article 5 that there was no obligation, moral or otherwise, to go to war'.[25]

In addition to this senators made use of military aid in order to impose a certain number of conditions upon their allies. 'Bilateral' agreements, which the partners were forced to sign according to Article 402 of the Mutual Defence Assistance Programme (MDAP), subjected their utilisation plans to the supervision of American advisory teams,[26] which were sent to each capital city, and who asked the beneficiary states to provide concrete proof of 'reciprocity', which meant the opening of bases and other facilities.

The way in which the Americans went about squeezing agreement to German rearmament out of their allies, especially the French, can be seen as an unparalleled example of how they were able to impose their will, even if their decisions were most contested. However, Lawrence Kaplan is right when he states that the Americans, during the years following the Korean War, fulfilled their commitments more quickly and faithfully than the countries of the Old World.[27] Their domination however, was by no means always as crushing.

As one could expect, the US demands were not always to the liking of their European counterparts, and during this period they raised a variety of pointed objections. However, to be fair, the 'conditions' imposed by Washington were never unacceptable when compared to the advantages which the aid and the US guarantee meant to the Old World countries. In any case, they also had one or two trump cards up their sleeves.

The conditions the USA placed on their assistance had already led to a certain mistrust on the part of the other future members of the alliance. For example, when the French foreign minister learned of the terms of the bilateral agreement which the recipients of Marshall Aid had to sign, he thought 'one must wonder if they are in keeping with the independence of nations'.[28] As a result of this, French civil servants reacted to certain demands in an irritated way, such as the requirement that new financial efforts be undertaken, or the long-winded process which forced them to enter into 'complex negotiations' and 'give reams of information over and over again' whenever the other side had to be persuaded to give up his cherished point of view.[29] Apart from this certain states were annoyed at the American demands for cooperation and economic integration, as they feared the loss of their sovereignty.

Finally and above all it was obvious that the Europeans constantly suspected US favouritism of the Germans. As early as 11 July 1947, the new directive JCS 1779 had affirmed that: 'An orderly and prosperous Europe demands the economic contribution of a productive and stable Germany.'[30] In fact the announcement of the Marshall Plan had immediate effects, in particular Paris' unwilling decision to accept the Robertson-Clay Agreement. 'American policy is really unjust and frivolous,' protested French President Vincent Auriol, clearly affected.[31]

This problem was obviously at the heart of the entanglements by means of which the Atlantic Treaty was to be created. If, at the beginning of 1948, the British and French were so anxious to get a guarantee of security, it was only because they wanted to achieve Western unity, whereas the Americans had practically decided that a West German state was to be created. This was dangerous in two ways, according to the French in particular. In the short term one could not rule out a violent reaction from the opposing camp – the blockade of Berlin was to strengthen this fear. In the longer term a reconstituted Germany, with all her power, was the danger against which certain countries wanted to be protected. Because of this some started to think that the Americans should take on some of the risks which they continually brought into being. However, on the contrary, the Americans linked the guarantee asked of them to further European progress along the road they had drawn. Thus, four days after the signing of the Atlantic Treaty, the Washington Agreeements were signed. But pressure was being placed upon the French even before agreement had been reached on the 'London recommendations'. On 8 June, the American Ambassador in Paris, Jefferson Caffery had again pointed out that a rejection of the 'London recommendations' by the French Parliament would have 'disastrous' effects on US public opinion and on that of Congress.[32]

The way in which the US administration never stopped quoting the goodwill of the American public as a decisive factor was clearly a source of concern and uncertainty for the Europeans. However, there were those who wondered if the elected Congressmen were not an excellent pretext behind which the government tried to hide when promoting its most unpopular ideas. This was especially true in the case of colonial questions. Without doubt it was the problem of decolonising the French Empire, a few years later, which made matters worse. Nonetheless, there were already signs of complaints and worried reactions. One serious incident divided Americans and Dutch. As Dirk Stikker, the Dutch Foreign Minister, recalls: 'This was the occasion when Averell Harriman ... informed me that no military aid under the new treaty would be contemplated by the United States for countries which, like the Netherlands, had not resolved their colonial problems ... If this threat had become reality I would never have sought nor have obtained authority to sign the North Atlantic Treaty on behalf of Holland.'[33]

But on the other hand, above all, the Europeans could not help remembering what became of the Treaty of Versailles! Seen as a whole, the final phase of the talks on the Atlantic Treaty, as well as the brutal way in which Congress, during the summer of 1949, refused seriously to consider the original programme passed to them by the government (Military Assistance Programme), show that they were by no means prepared to surrender the rights accorded them by the US Constitution. This did nothing, however, to prevent certain countries from expressing their annoyance at the possible threat to their sovereignty posed by US demands for bases and other facilities, or at the loss of their independence due to an integrated defence plan.

These feelings of inequality were made even stronger by the outbreak of the Korean War, since this event emphasised another fundamental difference between the USA and most of her allies: she was far more powerful and had far wider interests. The Europeans said time and again, with a real sense of anxiety, that their problems could not always be the Americans' top priority. Although they were happy to see the Americans firmly opposing aggression in the Far East, they were worried about the effects of a policy over which they had no control. As a Canadian document of 1951 expressed it: 'The greatest strain has probably resulted from the Far Eastern crisis (because of the danger that a general war in Asia would leave Western Europe defenceless).'[34]

Apart from this reorientation of US policy towards other regions, the Europeans also feared having to suffer the consequences of American policy in the zone outside the treaty against their will. When, at the end of 1950 in particular, it looked as if nuclear weapons might be used in Korea, with the agreement of the French government, Prime Minister Attlee took the next plane to Washington to express his concern. Here the main problem concerning alliance relations could be seen: inevitable differences in their concept of a threat to peace and in the policy to counter it. To be sure, these differences would not come to the fore until after June 1951, as Moscow let it be known that she would support a ceasefire in Korea. However, there had been arguments even during the preceding years. In May 1948 the Soviets had cunningly revealed that the Americans had proposed 'summit meetings'. The allies, who were not consulted on this, were disconcerted.[35]

During the whole summer, the French were irritated by the devil-may-care attitude with which their future ally treated all risks of immediate attack on the part of the Russians. In the spring of 1950, on the contrary, it was the Americans who thought the Europeans might be taken in by the idea of becoming a 'third neutral force'. Conversely, European public opinion tended to take a harder line with the Americans than with the opposing camp. And as early as 15 March 1950 the Dutch Prime Minister, Willem Drees, was able to underline the fact that 'the weaponry of the USSR and her satellites was seen by many as proof of the peaceful intentions of these countries, while there was no hesitation in speaking of agressive intentions when the other nations tried to increase their defensive potential'.[36]

In reality the European leaders were more concerned the less they knew about America's capacity to protect them. Since the spring of 1948 the rumour had spread that the US generals did not think they were able to defend Europe north of the Pyrenees, if at all. It was no use the Americans assuring privately that the atom bomb would put a stop to an attack by the Soviets within forty-eight hours;[37] the allies were no longer completely sure of this. Of course, the explosion of the atom bomb in the Soviet Union seemed likely to change the whole situation once more. At the beginning of 1950 Jean Chauvel declared to the French president: 'We joined the Atlantic Alliance for our military security and, at that time, the Americans were able to give us immediate assistance; they had a head start of five years on the Russians with regard to weapons and the atom bomb ... Thus we had five years to prepare ourselves to defend Europe ... This is no longer the case today.'[38]

On 3 April 1950 Charles Bohlen, Counsellor of the US Embassy in France, was still able to note that: 'The words "security" and "successful defense" have different meanings here and in Western Europe: in the US, that we will ultimately win a war; in Europe, that we can either prevent a war or, if forced into it, hold off Russian penetration.'[39]

In spite of this, at that time, an effort had been made and the Americans had let themselves be persuaded that the drawing-up of military plans which merely confirmed how weak the allies were was not the best method of galvanising the forces necessary for reconstruction. The decision had been taken to prepare a Medium Term Plan (MTP) which envisaged the installation of a defensive system on the Rhine in four years' time. But this by no means removed all the obstacles. Dirk Stikker recalls that he received a 'shock' when he found out on checking the MTP 'that the northern provinces of the Netherlands and all of Germany east of the Rhine were to be abandoned'.[40]

However, one fact could not be denied – at the height of the Korean War, after the initial shock had died down, the Europeans obtained the best guarantee they could have hoped for: apart from four extra US divisions for their protection, they managed to persuade their grand ally to confirm that she would commit herself to intervene against an attack by the Soviets, thanks to the creation of the integrated armed force. In other words, taking everything into account, the main and vital European priorities had been achieved, and for this reason they did not, all in all, consider the price to be too high. But this statement reflects another reality. If what seemed to be a plot hatched out by Bevin and Bidault, to bind the United States to the Old World, was successful, then only because the Americans had no real way of resisting the pressure placed on them by their new allies. This suggests that the latter were not always helpless when it came to defending their interests.

From 1947 onwards, indeed, the United States found herself faced with a simple but inevitable alternative: either assume her responsibilities as a superpower, whatever the cost, or see her national experiment endangered. We can see that the President was prepared to pay a high price to rescue the Old World from the great political risk he was also prepared to take. In 1946 Harriman, at that time Trade Secretary, noted that his countrymen thought about nothing else but 'going to the movies and drinking Coca-Cola'. In November of the same year they elected a Republican Congress which was bent on cutting the budget. However, the catastrophe which might stem from the 'loss' of Western Europe seemed such a threat that Truman had no qualms about risking losing his popularity. And as the Europeans demanded a security guarantee, the Americans were soon forced to admit that they could not refuse them without placing their entire policy in jeopardy.

Since, from then on, the Americans could not really stand by and watch Western Europe fall, their future allies were not lacking in trump cards. They played their aces, whether this meant pointing out the risks involved in some US demands for their own security, or conjuring up the spectre of an incident of such gravity that it would destroy the whole system Washington was trying so hard to create. In the spring of 1948 Bidault was able to make use of the fact that certain of his colleagues in the French government were wondering if the 'Alliance' with the United States was such a good idea after all. In their eyes, as, on the one hand, France was incapable of maintaining her own armed security, and as, on the other hand, the Americans did not seem capable of protecting her for the moment, would it not be advisable not to rush things, to negotiate until France had regained her military power?[41]

In this way Bidault might succeed in speeding up the Senate vote on the Vandenberg Resolution. As early as 23 April, Bevin had reminded the Americans in an ultra-secret telegram that 'an Atlantic security system was probably the only way in which the French could be brought to agree to a rebuilding of Germany'.[42] On 3 June Lovett laid out the problem before the Senate Foreign Affairs Committee. Although agreement had been reached in London, it was not yet all over because Bidault feared he would face 'a very difficult time' getting it past his MPs: 'I want to emphasise this again: they still want a security guarantee from this country. They still want, if possible, some form of alliance with respect to Soviet aggression.'[43]

These pressures designed to force the Americans to act in their turn could be found in all the 'Atlantic' talks during this period. As early as 27 April 1948 Lovett had explained to Truman, Marshall and Dulles, Truman's foreign policy adviser, that the Europeans had gone as far as they possibly could and that only a gesture by the Americans could persuade them to think of further progress.[44] And, in the summer of 1948, Paris made no bones of the fact that she was going to hesitate to join the Atlantic Alliance until she was better informed on exactly what level of *assistance* she could expect from the Americans. In June 1949, during its sixth session, the Consultative Council of the Brussels Pact decided once more that any substantial action on its part would depend upon an agreement on the US aid question.[45]

Apart from this, the history of the treaty negotiations was not, however, that of a constant submission, as an over-hasty analysis might lead us to think. At that time many of the 'successes' of US diplomacy were only won with the help of certain European nations, or were only possible as a result of a consensus among the allies. Although the initial Anglo-French project had been easily transformed, this was doubtless due to the fact that the Americans could count on the support of Belgium's Prime Minister Spaak. He had very quickly come round to their way of thinking, partly because these ideas seemed to have caused less hostility on the part of the British than of the French, and partly because they gained unexpected support from the opposing camp. The 'Prague coup' was indeed to put an end to Paris' unwillingness to agree to an idea which might 'disconcert' her. At the same time, the March 1948 talks were very quickly coming round to an Atlantic Treaty, which was already among the three propositions placed on the agenda by the British.[46] And Defence Minister Ramadier, who had raised the most objections to the risks involved in Article 4,[47] was obliged to admit that one of the main reasons for the creation of the treaty was the threat of Communist subversion with the backing of the Soviet Union.

Above all, the Europeans sometimes succeeded in pushing certain ideas through. Article 5, in spite of opposition from certain Congressmen, mentions the 'use of armed force'. The inclusion of Algeria was clearly the result of Paris' threat to pull out of the treaty if this demand was not met. As well as this the Europeans managed to get the examination of Germany's and Spain's relationship to the new treaty put off for the moment.

The Americans had just as little success with the economic-aid lever as using the military-aid lever. Not only did the Europeans object to the military efforts demanded of them, not only did they succeed in getting all clauses placing controls upon East-West trade left out of the bilateral agreements they had to sign, but the Dutch also showed that they did not feel defenceless in the *hors traité* zone, that not covered by the treaty. Congress' initial plan, linking the allocation of aid to a change in Dutch policy on Indonesia, had to be abandoned. In addition to this, in the spring of 1950, the French insisted that US aid could not be denied them in the war they were fighting against Communism in Indochina. Above all, the Americans were never really able to persuade the Europeans to 'unify'. This is perhaps the most fascinating and at the same time most paradoxical aspect of the strange relationship which arose between Europe and America.

During this period, indeed, the real problem was the Old World's failure to work out the basics of a defence which could one day be, if not totally independent, at least independent of the USA. European integration and the Atlantic Alliance were soon to fall into a strange relationship, that of complementing each other on the one hand and of being rivals on the other. This situation can best be illustrated by the later history of the EDC.

We cannot ignore the American part in the change from a European defensive system to an Atlantic Alliance. It was the United States, as we have shown, who demanded the widening of the zone covered by the Treaty and who rejected the idea of a simple combination of themselves and the recently created Brussels Pact. It was they who, before rendering the assistance asked of them, demanded the signing of *bilateral* agreements, thus depriving the Western Union of some of its responsibility and therefore its power. It was they who made closer relations between themselves and the Continent dependent upon the rearmament of Germany and thus launched European integration on to a military expedition in which it had to suffer one of its greatest setbacks. Finally it was the United States who often did not hesitate to divide and rule: in September 1950 she brilliantly succeeded in isolating the French when they sat on the fence instead of agreeing to German rearmament as they had been requested to do. Moreover, as early as the spring of 1948, she rejected Britain's request that Paris be allowed to send representatives to the Three-Power Talks, doubtless because, among other things, she wanted to reach agreement with the United Kingdom before raising the question with the French, whose opinions were reportedly far removed from those the Americans wanted to see put into practice.[48]

Does this mean that the weakening of the European position regarding the military plan had been the *sole* result of a *deliberate* decision taken by her new partner? There are many reasons to believe that such a conclusion would be a shaky one. It was not just that the Americans themselves were divided on the policy to be followed, as the permanent high-level rivalry between the American Committee on a United Europe (ACUE) and the Atlantic Union Committee (AUC) shows,[49] but apart from this their decisions seem to have been dictated above all by the attitude of their future allies.

After all, one cannot help thinking that the Americans sincerely wanted to see a new European unit get off the ground: one which would have been capable of organising itself so as to guarantee its own security in the long term. On 21 January 1948 Hickerson, a leading official in the State Department, emphasised that he 'had envisaged the creation of a third force which was not merely the extension of US influence but a real European organization strong enough to say "no" both to the Soviet Union and to the United States' The Americans, he added, 'would be willing to take our chance in dealing with any such organization of freedom-loving nations confident that we could settle any differences with them'.[50] And the Europeans would surely agree that the Americans had made real efforts to convince them to organise themselves. During this whole period, conversely, the European tendency had been to accuse them of the opposite: that they made too many demands for European unity without giving adequate guarantees in their turn.

This is, in fact, the origin of the problems which were later to shake the alliance to its foundations. From 1948 to 1950, to the surprise of many of the leading American politicians, the Europeans were most concerned with matters of security, and they seemed to regard their armed force mainly as a way of obtaining an American guarantee, without which their efforts would have been pointless. 'The most important thing,' noted Massigli, Ambassador in London, concerning Bevin's and Bidault's priorities in December 1947, 'was to act quickly and to make American "commitment" easier.'[51]

Despite American moves to bring the French and the British closer together, they did not hesitate to wash their dirty linen in public. These differences were to culminate in the quarrel over how to continue the programme of European reconstruction in the summer. On 19 and 20 July 1948, in The Hague, Bidault proposed the creation of a European Assembly and an Economic and Customs Union. However, this suggestion met with icy indifference from his British counterpart. The events which followed suggest that the hopes placed by some Americans in the rise of a united Europe turned out to be shaky to say the least.

On the contrary, everything points to the fact that only America could supply an answer to Europe's problems. Indeed, Europe's powerlessness was never better illustrated than by her wish to see, as early as 1948, an American general at the head of her own security system. Not only did the British military chiefs suggest General Clay, US military governor in Germany and Supreme Commander of US forces in Europe, as the best man for the job; but the French saw this as the perfect opportunity to avoid a British Supreme Commader. As Massigli put it: 'Our military leaders saw red' at the mention of Montgomery's name; 'either no Supreme Commander or an American'.[52] The French General Staff had, in reality, no real supranational European feelings,[53] but the Quai d'Orsay was willing to listen, as the opinion there was that an Englishman might only want to protect his national territory to the detriment of the other allies. When, under pressure from the USA, it became clear that there was no getting round the appointment of Montgomery, some hoped that the creation of an Atlantic Alliance 'might present us with an opportunity to rid ourselves of Field-Marshal Montgomery in favour of an American Supreme Commander'.[54]

Under such circumstances, there were only two options open. The first was hardly feasible, even if the French preferred it: the greatest possible US commitment, together with massive aid, to a Brussels Pact which would nonetheless remain a free agent. Under such a scenario, the Americans would not only be forced to renounce all control over the assistance they rendered – something out of the question, if only because of the watchfulness of Congress – but they would also have to guarantee a system which was *a priori* doomed to failure!

Thus the most acceptable alternative was a treaty unifying the Canadians, Americans and the members of the Brussels Pact, *but also* including other countries judged to be vital to the security of the United States. To be sure, another solution might have been considered: that of a treaty between two 'spheres' (Kennan, Chief of Policy Planning Staff at the State Department, called it the 'dumb-bell principle'), one side containing America and Canada and the other the Brussels Pact and other European nations. However, the Canadians had doubts about their status in such an arrangement. The Brussels Pact countries refused to water down their unity in a system containing too many divergent elements, and also refused to extend guarantees to other countries which they already felt incapable of maintaining for themselves.

In the system which was finally adopted, the Brussels Pact kept, at least in principle, certain elements of their original concept and tried, as we know, to play a special role. But this very quickly became lost due to the Europeans' incapability to give even a semblance of credibility to their wish to do so.

Apart from the mistrust of the French, one essential reason was doubtless the refusal on the part of the British to give up their 'special relationship' or their links to the Commonwealth in favour of greater progress towards unity. As Bohlen was forced to say: in the OEEC, since the spring of 1948, the number of British delaying actions, if not to say filibusters, had been impressive. During the Strasbourg meeting it was again the British who had put up resistance. With regard to Western Europe, British participation had been reduced to nought by obvious British doubts about the possibility of seriously defending Western Europe.[55]

From this moment on the French, fearful at the thought of finding themselves left alone to face the Germans on the

Continent, obstinately refused to take the next step. In the summer of 1949, therefore, an almost-desperate suggestion by Kennan, that the Atlantic system be reorganised to form a new version of the 'dumb-bell', with the Anglo-Saxons on the one side and a supranational Continental union under the leadership of the French on the other, was to lead to a shocked reaction from Ambassador Bonnet and the Quai d'Orsay.[56]

At that time everything seemed to point to the fact that only an Atlantic framework could speed the formation of a united Europe if it was one day to come about. The change of opinion of John Foster Dulles is explanatory in this regard. Initially he had been opposed to the idea of an Atlantic pact as it would slow down efforts towards unity. But, in January 1950, he was to express less severe reservations in a letter to his brother: 'In my opinion there is no need for conflict between the two ideas (European and Atlantic). I think some form of union is indispensable for a solution to the German problem, but the European countries might fail to do this due to being scared to deal with this problem in an audacious and effective way, unless they had protection which should be given by some form of Atlantic union including the United States.'[57]

During the spring of 1950, the administration also seemed to be convinced that no great successes could be expected from European efforts towards unity and that only the build-up of an Atlantic 'Community' could overcome the difficulties. As a top official was to note: the US could no longer push the Europeans towards integration, they had to lead them there.[58]

Finally, French Foreign Minister Schuman, apparently dissatisfied with the overconfidential character of the course of events, attempted to quicken the pace by recommending, on 16 April, the creation of an 'Atlantic High Council'. With this dramatic gesture he risked raising the suspicion which Acheson would have preferred to have dealt with by diplomatic means: 'A Plan to Submerge America in Europe', read the headline of the *Chicago Tribune* a few days later.

The impasse seemed to have been overcome by the announcement, on 9 May 1950, of Schuman's plan for a European Iron and Steel Community: did the French not, for the first time, want to enter into an adventure with the Germans and without the British, and did they not in doing so set their former enemy on a completely-equal footing? In short, one could get the impression that the US presence could allow Europe to stabilise after all [59] and to put the past behind her.

However, the Korean War made a nonsense of all this and the imbalances came to the surface. Once again the mounting of strategic tensions made the European nations painfully aware of how vulnerable they were, that they were no more than medium-sized powers. This was one of the constant factors during these years: every time the threat seemed to increase, whether in the summer of 1948, during the Berlin blockade or in the winter of the same year, with the North Korean attack, the Europeans had no other priority but to secure the assistance of the Americans. And the more they became dependent upon their grand ally, the more each of the Old World countries became tempted to sacrifice the cause of unity to those enterprises and efforts which would, in their opinion, allow them to play the starring role with this partner. From the beginning, as early as the start of 1948, the British would have loved to have seen the United States conclude the first bilateral agreement with the United Kingdom, and of course they tried to exploit to the limit the advantages they could gain from their 'privileged relations'. Conversely, the French were fairly obsessed by the wish to receive military aid on a privileged basis and to benefit from special treatment in the same way as they saw London doing so. As early as 29 June 1948 Bidault requested US Ambassador Caffery that France be included in the Anglo-American Military Committee, which had been based in Washington since the end of the war. Finally, it was Bohlen who suggested the basics of the *Standing Group* as a future compromise: 'to give France full membership in whatever was the real controlling body from the military point of view of the Pact, but at the same time confine the functions of any of the organizations under the Pact to the immediate question of the implementation of the Treaty'.[60]

Of course, the Korean War brought this process to a head. Attlee's *démarche* at the end of that year has already been mentioned. But we need to remind ourselves of another gesture: In 1951, the French government twice, without success, requested the creation of a 'three-power consultative body (with Britain) to coordinate policy on a world-wide basis'.[61]

Indeed, France has never been more Atlanticist than during the months following the outbreak of the Korean War. In two notes, sent on 5 and 18 August, she went so far as to ask for the establishment of common policy and a common budget within the framework of the Treaty.[62] In short, the European idea was hardly relevant at that time to matters of security. However, it was there that the process was to develop; the demand for German rearmament forced the French to the most daring programme of military integration imaginable: the European army, which was soon transformed into the European Defence Community (EDC).

To what degree would the disastrous failure of this idea lead in turn to every other new plan for military unity being dropped? The answer to this question is all the more difficult, as military integration was just as much blocked by insoluble problems connected with the European say in the decision concerning atomic weapons. But the EDC can make a partial contribution to our understanding of the strange legacy which those years have left to us. While Europe finally learned to secure her autonomy and solidarity in economic terms, her efforts to do the same in military terms have remained at the good intentions stage. Because of this the alliance, born out of the aftermath of war, has since the 1960s found itself in a dilemma which it has never found a way out of and which has been the cause of so much argument and difficulties: how can it reconcile the economic *status quo*, which has been reached in the meantime, with the role, but also with the great responsibilities, which the United States continue to assume within the alliance itself?

Notes

1. Quoted from René Massigli, *Une comédie des erreurs, 1943–1956*, Paris, 1978, p. 140.
2. Senate Committee on Foreign Relations (SCFR): North Atlantic Treaty, Hearings, 81st. Cong., 1st sess., p. 368f.
3. Massigli (see Note 1), p. 133.
4. Foreign Relations of the United States. Diplomatic Papers, 1945–1950, Washington, 1967–1980, FRUS, 1948, III, p. 1; Massigli (see Note 1), p. 105.
5. FRUS, 1948, III (see Note 4), p. 3f; Harry S. Truman, *Memoirs*, vol 2: *1946–1952, Years of Trial and Hope*, New York, 1965, p. 280.

6. Quoted from Georgette Elgey, *La république des illusions, 1945–1950*, Paris, 1965, p. 382.
7. Pierre Melandri, *Les Etats-Unis face à l'unification de l'Europe, 1945–1954*, Paris, 1980, pp. 87–145.
8. Details in Harry B. Price, *The Marshall Plan and its Meaning*, Ithaca, 1955, p. 67.
9. On this problem see esp. Lawrence S. Kaplan, *The United States and NATO: The Formative Years*, Lexington, 1984, pp. 30–48.
10. FRUS, 1948, III, (see note 4), p. 22.
11. Kaplan (see Note 9), p. 69.
12. Ibid.
13. Massigli (see Note 1), p. 125.
14. Quoted from Dean Acheson, *Present at the Creation: My Years in the State Department*, New York, 1969, p. 352.
15. On this point see Norbert Wiggershaus, 'The decision for a West German defence contribution', in *Western Security: The Formative Years: European and Atlantic Defence 1947–1953*, Olav Riste (ed.), Oslo, 1985, pp. 198–214; Pierre Melandri, 'Les Etats-Unis et le plan Pleven, octobre 1950-juillet 1951 in *Relations internationales* 11, 1977, pp. 201–29; Jules Moch, *Histoire du réarmement allemand depuis 1950*, Paris, 1965. On the American decision itself: Lawrence W. Martin 'The American Decision to Rearm Germany', in *American Civil-Military Relations. A Book of Case Studies*, Harold Stein (ed.), Birmingham, Alabama, 1963.
16. Pierre Melandri, *L'Alliance atlantique*, Paris, 1979, pp. 40–6.
17. FRUS, 1948, III (see Note 4), p. 7f.
18. See on this point Maurice Vaïsse, L'échec d'une Europe franco-britannique ou comment le pacte de Bruxelles fut créé et délaissé, in: *Histoire des débuts de la construction européenne (mars 1948-mai 1950)/Origins of the European Integration (March 1948-May 1950), Actes du Colloque de Strasbourg 28–30 novembre 1984*, sous la direction de/ Raymond Poidevin (ed.), Bruxelles, Milano, Paris, Baden-Baden, 1986, pp. 369–89.
19. FRUS, 1948, III, (see Note 4), p. 73.
20. See Vaïsse (see Note 18).
21. Barton J. Bernstein and Allen J. Matusow (eds), *The Truman Administration: A Documentary History*, New York, 1966, p. 274f.
22. Cees Wiebes and Bert Zeeman, 'The Pentagon Negotiations, March 1948: The Launching of the North Atlantic Treaty', in *International Affairs*, vol. 59, 3, 1948, p. 359.
23. A series of analyses made by Henri Bonnet, the French Ambassador, shows how closely and tensely Paris followed the debates. Archives diplomatiques françaises (= ADF) Série B-Amérique, 1944–1952, Etats-Unis, vol. 114, 8.3.1948–30.7.1949.
24. FRUS, 1948, III (see Note 4), p. 335.

25. FRUS, 1949, IV (see Note 4), p. 109.
26. Kaplan (see Note 9), p. 130.
27. Ibid, p. 27.
28. Vincent Auriol, *Journal du septennat*, vol. II: *1948*, Paris, 1974, p. 281.
29. See Archives de France, Paris, F 60 to 378, fonds du Secretariat Général de Coordination interministérielle (= SGCI); P.P. Schweitzer, Report on a conversation with Tomlinson dated 2 December 1948, also F 60 to 357, SGCI 49/no. 814, 19.4.1949 (these documents were kindly supplied to me by Gérard Bossuat).
30. Alfred Grosser, *Les Occidentaux*, Paris, 1978, p. 87.
31. Auriol (see Note 28), vol. I: *1947*, Paris, 1970, p. 409.
32. ADF, B-Amérique, vol. 114, Telegrams, 2195 to 1298, Washington to Paris, 21.5.1948, and conversation by the American director with Jefferson Caffery, 8.6.1948.
33. Dirk Stikker, *Men of Responsibility: As Seen through the Memoirs of a Participant in Years of World Crisis*, New York, 1966, p. 285. See also FRUS, 1949, IV, pp. 163, 165, 178f., 251f., 259f.
34. Public Archives Canada, Record Group (RG) 2, Privy Council, 18, vol. 243, C-10-9, 1947–1951: 'A survey of relations between Canada and the US', 20.6.1951.
35. FRUS, 1948, III (see Note 4), p. 860; ADF, B-Amérique, vol. 114, Bonnet's note dated 24.5.1948. See also George Kennan, *Memoirs, 1925–1950*, New York, 1969, (paperback edn), p. 364f.
36. ADF, Europe-Généralités, 1949–1955, Etats-Unis-Europe, vol. 18, The Hague to Paris, 15.3.1950.
37. ADF, B-Amérique, vol. 114, conversation European director with Caffery, 8.6.1948.
38. Vincent Auriol, *Mon septennat, 1947–1954*, Paris, 1970, p. 256.
39. FRUS, 1950, III, p. 1369f.
40. Stikker (see Note 33), p. 297.
41. Auriol (see Note 28), pp. 174–80.
42. Truman (see Note 5), p. 282.
43. The Vandenberg Resolution and the North Atlantic Treaty, Hearings held in Executive Session, US Congress, SCFR, Historical Series, made public August 1973, p. 76.
44. *Dulles Papers*, I, Princeton University Library.
45. Kaplan (see Note 9), p. 124.
46. Wiebes and Zeeman (see Note 22), p. 353f.
47. Auriol (see Note 28), p. 602.
48. Wiebes and Zeeman (see Note 22), p. 356.
49. See Kaplan (as in Note 9), p. 132f.; Melandri (see Note 7), p. 179f.
50. FRUS, 1948, III (see Note 4), p. 11.
51. Massigli (see Note 1), p. 105.
52. See chapter 3 by Lawrence Kaplan in this book and Massigli (see Note 1), p. 124.

53. Vaïsse (see Note 18).
54. Ibid. Pierre Guillen confirms this impression in 'Les chefs militaires français, le réarmement de l'Allemagne et la CED: 1950–1954', in: *Revue d'histoire de la deuxième guerre mondiale*, 129, 1983, pp. 13–33.
55. Bohlen to Kennan, 29.10.1949, Kennan Papers, Box 7, Princeton University Library.
56. See Kennan (as in Note 35), p. 474f. FRUS, 1949, IV, pp. 469–72; Kennan to Bohlen, 12.10.1949, Kennan Papers (see Note 55).
57. John F. Dulles to Allen W. Dulles, 19.1.1950, *Dulles Papers*, Additions of 1971 (see Note 44).
58. Joseph M. Jones to George Elsey, 2.3.1950, Foreign Policy Planning, Folder 2, Subject File, Elsey Papers, Truman Library, Independence, Missouri.
59. See Josef Joffe, 'Europe's American pacifier', in *Foreign Policy*, 54, 1983, pp. 64–82.
60. FRUS, 1949, IV, p. 256.
61. Acheson (see Note 14), p. 552. See also FRUS, 1951, III, p. 495, 567.
62. See Hervé Alphand, *L'étonnement d'être, Journal, 1939–1973*, Paris, 1977, pp. 217–21 and Alphand, *L'année politique*, Paris, 1951, p. 180f.

16
Strategic Concepts for the Defence of Western Europe, 1948–1950

Christian Greiner

According to one of many definitions, security policy has the aim of preventing war and of preserving political freedom of action.[1] Military strategy is 'the whole concept, according to which (an) alliance and its individual members...make use of military potential in pursuing security policy goals'.[2] This concept consists of estimating a military threat, making plans in order to meet this threat, and laying down and securing the financial, economic and military resources necessary to carry out these plans. From the start, the Western 'security community's'[3] strategy was of a defensive nature, one which at the same time had the political aim of deterrence.[4] As long as this deterrence, and therefore the avoidance of war, seemed to be accepted and thus ensured by all the alliance members, the importance of strategic planning was often lessened. This is especially true of the period I wish to examine in this essay, 1948 to 1950, a period in which US nuclear and economic potential was seen as a sufficient deterrent to prevent the Soviet Union mounting an attack on Western Europe. Thus my presentation of military plans for the defence of Western Europe after deterrence fails seems to be of merely academic interest. But on the other hand the generally accepted fact 'that there can be no single military strategy in the narrow sense of the term in an Alliance of sovereign states, but rather recognisably national variations within the plan itself',[5] is confirmed in the early stages of Western defence Alliances. This is why historians today avoid using the term 'military strategy', preferring 'strategic concept'.[6] Thus I shall attempt to present the Western European concepts of the most important NATO and Brussels Pact member countries, using the categories 'threat', 'plans' and 'resources', and also to judge the success of the efforts made within the alliances to harmonise these national variations.

Today, as in the period 1948–50, the problem of differing views is mostly connected with the attitudes of the larger members of the Western Alliance – the USA, Great Britain, France and the Federal Republic of Germany. There are two reasons why I include German politicians and military leaders among the Western protagonists. Since 1946 there were certainly relations (albeit a little one-sided) both of an official and of an unofficial nature, in which an exchange of military strategic opinions could occur between former enemies and future allies.[7] Even if the three Western zones (and later the Federal Republic) were not yet members of the Western Alliances, their potential and their territory were of great importance for all Brussels Treaty and NATO defence plans. Consequently, I would like to look at the German concepts a little more closely, as they have remained relatively unknown, in contrast to those of the Western Allies and their defensive alliances.

Estimating the Level of Threat

There was a large measure of agreement in the West concerning the level of military threat posed by the Soviet Union and the Eastern European states, which were seen as more or less dependent satellites.[8] Above all the opinion was that the Communist bloc was a closed, monolithic system. This convergence of opinion in the estimation of the level of threat was based on the fact that there had been close cooperation in the field of military intelligence since the spring of 1948, at least between the British and the Americans. The data also often came from the same sources. For example, the Gehlen Organisation worked both for the Americans and German military experts. There was also the tendency among the various military staffs to agree on the worst possible scenario, and also to exaggerate rather than underestimate Soviet capabilities. They were also agreed that defence budgets should be at least protected against the efforts of politicians to cut them. The former German army officers had a clearer perception of military threat, first due to their experience of the Soviet armed forces during the Second World War, second due to Germany's position just in front of the Iron Curtain, and last due to the feeling that Communist ideology and its expansionist aims could be seen at work everywhere.

Constant factors in this threat perception remained Western Europe's close proximity to the continental landmass of Eurasia, and the great numerical superiority of the Soviet armed forces compared to the Western Allied forces on the continent of Europe. The picture was darkened still more by the large presence and offensive structure of the Soviet land forces and above all their spearhead in the Central and Eastern European satellite states. Faced with this might, the forces of the Western Allies, stationed as occupation troops in the three Western zones of Germany, appeared to be fairly ineffective. It was this 'military vacuum' in Western Europe, as one German officer put it, which might tempt the USSR to launch a speedy military action.[9]

The result of such an analysis of the level of threat was the assumption that the Soviet Union was capable of overrunning and occupying the Continent in a short period of time. Within this totally conventional scenario the fate of the British Isles was unclear. There were doubts about the effectiveness of Soviet submarines in the event of another battle in the Atlantic. The Soviet air force had at best tactical and operational importance. Thus the continent of Europe alone seemed to be threatened by military destruction or occupation more or less without a fight. American experts tended to see in this the USSR's first step towards a global struggle with the USA. Due to the rearmament in the Soviet Zone, the West Germans feared a German civil war, as it was almost impossible to interpret the attitude of the Western occupying powers in this case. The basic political intention behind the USSR's military capability was always a matter of agreement. The final aim of Soviet policy was the creation of a Moscow-controlled global empire. The political and military conquest of all Europe seemed to be the prerequisite for this. The views about whether the Soviets were prepared to risk military conflict to achieve their goals changed according to the USSR's political actions. It was agreed that the Soviet Union would engage in a world war if the situation were favourable. In 1947 both the Americans and the British thought there would be a ten to fifteen-year period of peace in which Soviet expansionism would occur by peaceful means alone. The coup in Czechoslovakia and the Berlin blockade in 1948, however, led to a kind of 'war in sight' feeling, particularly among US officers in Europe.

In spite of the changing perception of threat, the Western Allies' strategic planning for Europe during the period dealt with here remained based on deterrence and defence against a large-scale conventional attack by the Eastern bloc, as could be expected in the event of war. This was, of course, especially true for the Continental Europeans, who were closest to the front line. Planning was still very closely based on the Second World War strategic and operational concepts, but did have some differences, both in Europe and America, as well as among German officers.

US Strategic Plans

The increasing gravity of the international situation, typified by the Czech crisis in the spring of 1948 and the restrictions the Soviets were starting to impose upon the overland route to Berlin, led to a speeding-up of planning in the USA for a possible war with the Soviet Union.[10] Work on the HALFMOON strategic plan began in the spring of 1948 without political guidelines. There was little difference between this plan and fragmentary versions from the period 1946 to 1947, when one considers both the concept as a whole and the part dealing with Europe. Western Europe would still be surrendered while a massive atomic strategic air offensive would be fought against the USSR from bases in Great Britain, Okinawa and in the Cairo-Suez or Karachi areas. Only these Strategic Air Command (SAC) bases were to be defended, while the US occupation troops would be evacuated from ports in France and Italy after a short period of resistance on the Rhine. Although the Joint Chiefs of Staff recognised that the greatest failing of this plan was the lack of support for the Continental countries, they had no other alternative due to lack of resources. HALFMOON was taken as a base for planning by the Chiefs of Staff on 19 May 1948, and was meant to be the basis for a military intervention on the part of the USA during the Berlin blockade.

In November 1948 the National Security Council formulated the long-term policy which the USA wished to pursue against the USSR. Concerning Europe, it was decided, with the approval of the President, that 'Soviet domination of the potential power of Eurasia, whether achieved by armed aggression or by political subversive means, would be strategically and politically unacceptable to the United States'.[11] General Eisenhower, from February 1949 onwards military special advisor to President Truman and his Secretary of Defence, until August 1949 also Chairman of the Joint Chiefs of Staff, laid the foundation for a new plan for a war with the Soviet Union, introduced in the spring of 1949. The Europeans should be given the ability to defend the Rhine at the earliest opportunity. Alternatives to the plan were either the defence of a substantial bridgehead in Western Europe or measures aimed at the fastest-possible return to the Continent.

Although there was a willingness to employ US occupation troops to hinder the Soviet attack and not, as before, withdraw them more or less without engagement, and although there were hopes that nuclear and conventional air strikes against the USSR would slow down the advance of Soviet troops, only the defence of southern Spain, Great Britain and the Mediterranean could realistically be included in the final planning. A reconquest of Continental Europe was not envisaged until two years after the start of the war. It was clear to the Chiefs of Staff that, despite being part of NATO, it was not feasible to support the Continental partners in the defence of their territories, as the USA did not have the available land forces.

Cuts in the defence budget for fiscal 1950, ordered by the President himself, meant that only the Strategic Air Command and forces for the defence of the necessary bases around the Eurasian continent could be maintained. Since there had been three groups (wings) of B-29 strategic bombers stationed in Britain from July 1948, the Continental Europeans thought that the plan only included the defence of the British Isles. Even the defence of the Mediterranean was in jeopardy.[12] In spite of this fact, this OFFTACKLE plan, which was adopted by the Joint Chiefs of Staff on 8 December 1949, took into account any potential US commitments in the North Atlantic Alliance (at least according to the Americans themselves), and was destined to be the American basis for NATO planning.

All this was only known to Canada and Great Britain. In April 1948 there were consultations on HALFMOON and in September/October 1949 on OFFTACKLE. Both nations agreed to make the US plans the basis of their national planning. Both could accept the US proposals without hesitation, as the defence of their countries was envisaged in the plans, with the support of the USA.

US military strategy was determined, up to the time when planning was carried out within NATO, by her global policy and by the limits on her resources. This global view of a possible war with the USSR, and the fact that the only effective means of combating the enemy was the Strategic Air Command (SAC), led to the concept of a total war which had to end in defeat for the Soviet Union. The deterrent effect was based on the retaliatory character of the threat of greater damage inflicted upon the USSR in the event of an attack on Western Europe. Within this scheme Europe, and the continent in particular, were only of regional importance. Only the European SAC bases and the bases of European dependencies in the Atlantic (Greenland, Iceland and the Azores) were significant. Thus, there was at best a peripheral, indirect European defence, if the deterrent effect of the SAC and its nuclear potential were to fail. For the Americans, direct (and above all conventional) defence on the Continent was of minor importance, or rather a matter for the Europeans themselves.[13]

European Concepts

Great Britain sought to maintain her status as a great power after the Second World War. Thus she had a 'special relationship' with the USA, so as to gain her support for the build-up of Britain's national nuclear arsenal. She tried to hold her colonial empire together as a power base in the form of the Commonwealth. British military strategy was therefore a worldwide one, as was that of the USA, but with much smaller resources.

For this reason the main points of interest in British security policy were Great Britain herself, the sea routes and the Near or Middle East. Thus the European continent played a mere supporting role in British planning. To lose the Continent in wartime was no great loss to the British, if by doing so both Britain and the sea-lanes were successfully defended. Time and again the British government refused to reinforce her troops in her zone of occupation either in peacetime or in wartime. In any case, only the already-present forces of the 'Army of the Rhine' were to be involved in direct conventional defence. Any other decision would have been totally unworkable due to the Spartan reserves both in Great Britain and worldwide. On top of this, a decision on strengthening troops on the Continent depended upon the attitude of the Americans. In close cooperation with the USA, Great Britain tried to increase her nuclear potential and the necessary means of delivery so as to be able to take part in the strategic air offensive against the USSR. Therefore the conventional forces were also neglected in the long term, and so demands from the Continentals that Britain commit herself more to the defence of the mainland were bound to be refused. This made the Continentals sceptical, and memories of Dunkirk in 1940 came to the surface. Not least in order to avoid increasing this mistrust, British military leaders tried to keep Anglo-American plans (some of which were drawn up by the committees of the wartime 'Combined Chiefs of Staff', which had been recreated in 1946) secret from their Continental European partners.[14]

While *France* was also anxious to retain her power base (her colonial empire), she was forced by her geographical position to concentrate her strategic efforts on defending her own territory and thus on direct, conventional defence on the European continent. The deterrent effect of the corresponding plans, which were also taken up by the smaller Western European states, consisted of demonstrating to the Soviets the futility of military action against Western Europe. The 'Battle of Europe' was thus at the centre of all French planning. The aim was successfully to defend France on her 'natural borders', particularly on the Rhine. The survival of France was bound up with the existence of all Europe in the opinion of French military leaders. If Europe were lost, they said, then the war was lost for the Americans also. From this premise came the demand that France and her North African hinterland be made the 'natural centre' of Western European defence. In addition to this the French demanded full support, particularly from the USA and Great Britain, because her own forces were on the one hand too weak and on the other hand mostly in the Far East, in Indochina. In this connection the French were more interested in US military aid and troops than American nuclear potential, which threatened to destroy France and indeed Europe itself in the event of war.[15]

Christian Greiner

German Considerations

Despite the Allied Control Council having forbidden any form of German military activity, there were some ways for German military experts to participate in defence plans for Western Europe from 1945 onwards.[16] I need only remind the reader of the German officers who worked for the Historical Division of the US Army, the German 'Naval Historical Team' of the US Navy, the Gehlen Organisation which worked for the USA, and the officers involved with German organisations such as the 'Deutsches Büro für Friedensfragen', or who were working for individual politicians such as Konrad Adenauer. In some cases German officers wrote memoranda 'by special request' for the US Command in Europe (EUCOM).[17]

From 1948 onwards planning concentrated on the defence of the three Western Zones, while earlier plans tried to safeguard all four by international guaranty, either by the UN or by the four Occupying Powers. At the same time there were meetings with leading politicians of the future Federal Republic. Among the German strategic brains, two Lieutenants-General of the former Wehrmacht, Heusinger and Speidel, stood out from the rest. They had not been so deeply involved in Nazi politics and also had good contacts, both abroad and with German politicians.

German planning can basically be divided into two alternatives, which we will call 'Rhine Defence' and 'Elbe Defence'. The first alternative was initially the dominant one. A German memorandum, which was circulated among the US Chiefs of Staff, recommended that Western forces withdraw to the Rhine as quickly as possible and defend bridgeheads on the eastern bank. The Soviet military machine thus halted on the Rhine was to be weakened by air strikes on the USSR itself and forced to capitulate.[18] The suggestion for a 'Rhine Zone Defence' came from the German officers at the US Historical Division. This 'Rhine Zone' was to be an area west of the Rhine up to a line running between Antwerp, Namur, the River Meuse and Upper Moselle to the Vosges Mountains. While the plan was to fight a delaying action east of the Rhine using large battle groups, trying to gain time without losing too many men, and while it was thought that there would be merely a short battle on the Rhine itself, the decisive phase of the defensive battle was to take place west of the Rhine. In this 'Rhine Zone' the Soviet attack was to be halted by a 'highly mobile' defence, so that the mass of the Soviet armoured force was prevented from gaining a theatre of operations in France. If it was possible to contain a Soviet attack between Rhine and Meuse in this way, then it would be feasible to put into practice the 'fundamental strategic concept that the great counter-offensive to the East would have to go into operation sooner or later – in other words, that the West will have to defend herself by mounting a military offensive'.[19] This offensive, however, was not to start from terrain still held by the West but, on the contrary, would hit the USSR in her most 'sensitive' spot from the Mediterranean. The target would be the southern industrial zone of the USSR, while at the same time links to the factories east of the Urals would be cut. The USSR would thus be obliged to withdraw from Western Europe and to go into battle on a southern front while at the same time production, weapons, supplies, lines of communication, but also land forces would all be subject to attack by the West's strategic air force. The main point of the action was relentless air battle. By means of a war of 'air and supplies' the Soviet Union was to be forced to give up her aggressive aim and would be subdued both militarily and politically.

Heusinger himself developed plans for a 'Rhine Defence' on behalf of American military authorities from 1948 onwards. The Rhine was to be defended from Lake Constance up to the Zuider Zee. It was also necessary to maintain the area from the Alps to the Rivers Danube and Traun, as well as as Schleswig-Holstein, down to a line between Hamburg and Lübeck. Heusinger wanted to engage in a delaying battle in front of the 'Rhine Defence' using three German divisions. Here again, the halted Soviet forces were to be cut off from their supply lines and deprived of a matériel base.[20]

Western Germany's defence concept, which was recommended by all the military experts, was based on the static defence of geographically suitable areas and a mobile defence between these areas, with the aim of defeating the attacking Soviet forces. In the opinion of the German planners this concept was best suited to geographical conditions and the country's capabilities. It seemed capable of thwarting the ambitions of the Soviet commanders, who were not considered to be so adept at mobile warfare. The three Soviet Army Groups generally thought to be allocated to the Western zones were to be engaged between two strong 'cornerstones' south of the River Main and in the Bremen-Hamburg-Lübeck region, according to the German defence plans, and defeated individually by means of mobile warfare. For this purpose it seemed necessary to have three allied groups in the Bamberg and Göttingen-Brunswick areas as well as east of the Nord-Ostsee-Kanal.

Of course the manpower necessary for these plans could not be supplied by the Western Powers' present armed forces. Thus the Germans demanded that the allies increase their presence in the Western Zones. The Rhine was to be defended by US, British, French and Swiss divisions. From 1948 onwards the German military experts were of the opinion that 'a German (political) representation is duty-bound to suggest means of self-defence or of assistance in the defence of the heart of Europe'.[21] Care was taken to impress upon the Americans that such ideas were not intended to serve any kind of military interest but were rather borne out of the pure conviction that this problem had to be dealt with soon, and that this would also be in the USA's best interests. Germany's contribution to Western European defence, deemed vital by all German military experts, was based on German defence concepts as to structure and strength of forces. Heusinger recommended fourteen German divisions for his 'Rhine Defence', to be employed south of the Danube, east of the Rhine itself and in Schleswig-Holstein.[22] Speidel, however, was of the opinion that fifteen divisions would be a suitable German defence contribution, some as defensive elements for the above-mentioned 'cornerstones' and the rest as armoured divisions for mobile warfare. The plan was to have an American Commander-in-Chief, German divisional commanders and a German presence in all staff headquarters above division. Other demands were for the latest equipment and weapons, as there was no wish for the Germans to serve as mere cannon fodder, as well as 'organic allocation of air force units' to the German land forces. Somewhat different was the suggestion put forward by the Historical Division. The ten to twelve German divisions envisaged as support for the Allied units in front of the 'Rhine Zone Defence' were to be recruited as 'auxiliary or border patrol units' on a voluntary basis and would be under the command of allied officers.

The Western Union's Plans

Military strategic planning on the part of the Treaty of Brussels (or the Western Union, as the British and Americans called it),

Concepts for the Defence of Western Europe

founded on 17 March 1948, was slow getting off the ground.[23] On the one hand there was a lack of organisation, and on the other the USA was expected to play an active role. However, there was no doubt about the Western Union's strategic goals. The five defence ministers informed the USA in April 1948 that, 'In the event of an attack by Russia, however soon it may come, the Five Powers are determined to fight as far east in Germany as possible ... Their preparations are therefore aimed at holding the Russians on the best position in Germany covering the territory of the Five Powers in such a way that sufficient time for the American military power to intervene decisively can be assured.'[24] Immediately prior to talks with an American military delegation, a strategic concept 'for the defence of Europe as far east as possible in Germany against the background of a global strategy' was being debated in the Military Committee of the Western Union. As she had already stated to the USA, the Western Union decided to defend herself as far east as possible in the medium term, and to build up an 'impenetrable' defence on the Rhine as a short-term measure. The French members of the Western Union Military Committee even went so far as to refuse to even consider withdrawing operations west of the Rhine.[25]

Both in the short and the long term, however, the members of the Brussels Treaty lacked the resources to realise such plans. The 'Rhine Defence' was to be effected with one division per 100 kilometres.[26] There was a lack of manpower, not only because the partners had difficulty in obtaining economic backing for the assembly of new units after 1945, but also because France, The Netherlands and Great Britain had large parts of their armed forces stationed abroad. Thus the plans were put into operation, but were at the same time seen to be unworkable.[27]

Military aid and additional troops were therefore expected from the USA. She also had to adapt her military strategy to the needs of direct conventional defence in Continental Europe. Therefore the Continental members of the Western Union tried to make the USA accept a global strategy and to make the strategic air offensive, as practised by the British and Americans, immediately feasible for Rhine Defence purposes. There was, however, little trust in the effect of the atom bomb.

On the West German glacis in front of the 'Rhine Defence', the Western Union reacted in a way which smacked more of generosity toward German needs than consideration of them. Much destruction and extensive terrain changes were necessary in order to contain or funnel the Soviet attack. The German refugees were to be the West German Federal Government's worry. At an early stage the thought emerged of 'using Germans in the Western Union's plans'. While the Military Committee developed a plan on the basis of this, the member states' chiefs of staff and the political committees considered any decision and all measures over-hasty.[28]

Anglo-American Reactions to Western Union Plans

Barely a month after the foundation of the Treaty of Brussels, on 17 April 1948, France and Great Britain invited the USA to take part in the military-planning discussions.[29] The American delegation, which arrived in London on 21 July 1948 accompanied by Canadian officers, had been instructed by their political and military superiors to cooperate merely in a very limited sense with the Western Union. They took part in Western Union committee discussions on a 'non-membership' basis without any commitment on the part of the USA. Their aim was to prevent the USA's strategic freedom of action being limited by demands from the Brussels Treaty states for military aid or even direct military support in the event of war. The Western Union's Continental members received no clues about Joint Chiefs of Staff war planning; they were merely told that the USA had no concrete strategic plan for a war with the USSR but rather a variety of options. In the case of a 'major conflict', there was agreement on the commitment of US occupation forces in Europe, the SAC and other US forces outside Western Europe and on the sea routes, together with the mobilisation of US arms potential as an arsenal for her allies.

The reaction of the US Joint Chiefs of Staff to the Western Union's strategic planning was limited to blocking all global plans, preventing any foreign influence upon the employment of the SAC, and merely agreeing to the employment *en masse* of US occupation forces under Western Union command west of the Rhine. They refused the Brussels Treaty request for an American Commander-in-Chief for the Continental theatre. The planned 'Rhine Defence' was criticised as being unrealistic, but only at a meeting with the British chiefs of staff.

The British representatives in the Western Union were basically on the American side. Neither were they willing to let the Continental partners get a glimpse of strategic air-war planning, nor did they agree to reinforce their troop presence without a similar move by the USA. Both the British and the Americans said that the Continentals should first of all make efforts to help themselves and exploit their own resources before looking for help from outside.[30]

Thus neither did the Western Union succeed in tying the USA into direct defence, nor did the USA succeed in convincing the Continentals of the worth of their peripheral defence. Both concepts collided with one another. The American plans had the advantage that they took account of the available resources, while the European version was unrealistic and Utopian as regards available manpower. Therefore, the newly-founded NATO (4 April 1949) had to make efforts, within its own strategic planning, to bring these varying ideas into some kind of agreement.

NATO's Proposals

However, the USA remained reticent, not to say uncooperative, even as the leading member of NATO.[31] This could be seen as early as the planning stage of the military organisation, which on the one hand was designed to ensure that the USA kept her 'strong military leader role', but on the other hand also to give her 'the greatest possible freedom of action'. She wanted to prevent the Continentals gaining too much influence over the highest permanent body, the Standing Group. For this reason it was based in Washington, and while France was included in this body, she was still excluded from the 'global strategic planning' done by the British and the Americans. Due to the creation of five geographically fixed Regional Planning Groups, which were meant to do the real military planning work, the treaty area was 'regionalised' and thus divided into separate areas of responsibility. The USA was only really responsible for the USA-Canada and Atlantic areas. She was, however, not a full member of the North, West and South Europe Planning Groups, but rather merely agreed 'to participate actively in defence planning as appropriate'.

In a short time (from October 1949 to January 1950) NATO succeeded in drawing up a basic strategic concept for the defence of the treaty area. However, the Europeans found themselves under considerable pressure, as US military aid, which had in the meantime been approved by Congress, could to a large extent only be given after the President had agreed to an integrated NATO defence plan.

Thus a programme of role-sharing which had been devised by the USA, and which had also been discussed by the Western Union, was accepted by the Europeans after having been passed by the Senate during the military aid debate. The USA's task was to conduct strategic air war with all available resources, including nuclear weapons. The Continentals were to supply the majority of the land forces for the defence of their territories and thus the Continent itself. The only change the Europeans managed to achieve was that they would be responsible for their own defence only at the *beginning* of a conflict, and that the other partners, particularly the USA and Great Britain, were to come to their aid as soon as possible. As the basic concept had deliberately been left open, so as not to risk a breach of security during the military aid negotiations, the differences of opinion between the USA and her Continental partners did not appear to be so crass.

They did, however, disagree sharply in the matter of short- and medium-term defence plans for Western Europe. The US members of the various NATO committees had received clear instructions on how these plans were to be developed:

> Every effort should be made to encourage the development and acceptance by the regional planning groups of:
>
> (1) Short term defence plans envisaging reliance by the European nations on their own defence effort, recognizing at the same time that an alternative strategy for the defence of Europe must be adopted. This alternative strategy will point toward the retention of a substantial bridgehead in Western Europe, which could be expanded if additional military forces are mobilized, with a view toward preventing the long time overrunning of the North Atlantic territory by the Soviets.
> (2) Longer term defence plans envisaging progressively greater likelihood that the free nations of Europe will collectively be able to deny their territories to conquest and occupation.[32]

The American basis for NATO medium-term planning was to be OFFTACKLE, particularly regarding US troop employment.

Concepts for the Defence of Western Europe

Thus there were to be immediate, marked differences between NATO intentions and US plans. Even using the forces available up to 1 July 1954, the Joint Chiefs of Staff considered it only possible to defend the Rhine, a 'Scandinavian bastion' and Italy. First of all an attempt was made to find a compromise formula by means of the North Norway-Nord-Ostsee-Kanal-Rhine/Ijssel-Alps/Isonzo defensive line, but in the end European NATO managed to push through her demand for a defence as far east as possible. The main NATO effort was to be placed upon the 'first phase of the defence of Continental Europe'. As early as the planning stage this idea started to look somewhat doubtful: 'It will be necessary to make a maximum initial effort with all available resources even though it may not be possible to sustain this effort, provided by so doing, sufficient delay may be achieved to allow for reinforcement, and for the strategic air offensive to take effect.'[33] The USA was neither prepared to make concrete promises about reinforcements for employment in Europe, to say nothing of assembling these forces in peacetime, nor were the Americans certain of the effect which the strategic air offensive against Russian territory would have on the Soviet troops attacking Western Europe.

The Joint Chiefs of Staff were particularly critical of the figure of ninety divisions said to be necessary for the defence of European NATO. Conversely, great discrepancies remained between the US OFFTACKLE plan and NATO's medium-term defence plan, since the Joint Chiefs of Staff omitted to align the medium-term NATO plan to their strategic intentions. They merely wanted to re-examine the manpower plans with the aim of reducing the figures.

By laying down short-term defensive aims, the USA wanted to persuade the Western Europeans to accept an 'alternative military strategy', i.e. the defence of a 'substantial bridgehead' in Spain or on the Atlantic. This plan failed mainly because of France, who succeeded in getting her 'Rhine Defence' concept accepted in both the Western Union and the Western European Regional Planning Group. In a spirit of resignation, the Joint Chiefs of Staff stated: 'However, it has been impossible to plan for withdrawal to successive defence lines because of the refusal of the French to consider anything other than to ... stand on ... the Rhine and defend to the last man. The French position, as stated by themselves, is based on psychological and political reasons.

However, the end result is a completely unrealistic short term plan for West Europe.'[34]

The Joint Chiefs of Staff reacted by instructing their Commander-in-Chief in Europe that the 'Rhine Defence' was only valid for the initial operations. Western Europe was to be defended 'in successive positions'. They failed to persuade the European NATO defence ministers to undertake a 'realistic revision'. The short-term defence plan was agreed on by these ministers on 28 October 1950. Thus, before the outbreak of the Korean War, NATO did not succeed in developing a single, short- and medium-term defensive plan for Western Europe. The main reason for this must be seen in the fact that the Europeans were planning a defensive concept for which resources were not available, and thus they expected the USA to supply them with these resources. In this regard the Europeans were less eager to have the Strategic Air Command with the atom bomb, which was looked on with mistrust mixed with the fear of the destruction of Western Europe, but conversely wanted US troops directly to defend their territories.

However, due to the parlous condition of the land forces in particular, the USA was unable to fulfil the above demand. She wanted a defence plan oriented towards European resources, but this would have meant the loss of large areas of Western Europe in the short term. For the time being, the differing military strategies within NATO were overshadowed by the deterrent, war-preventive effect of US nuclear potential.

The German Attitude to the Western Union and NATO

The Western Union's intention, both in private and in public, of choosing the Rhine as a 'feasible and secure' defensive line prompted renewed German considerations.[35] This plan was rejected on the grounds that Western Germany, Austria, Switzerland and the routes to Italy and Scandinavia would be surrendered. Thus, according to Lieutenant-General (ret.) Speidel, Western Europe was lost in the long run, since the Soviet divisions on the Rhine or even on the Atlantic would be a different matter altogether to those 'mostly third-rate Home Guard divisons ... which had defended the propaganda mock-up called the Atlantic Wall'.[36] The success of another 1944-style invasion thus seemed questionable.

As a whole the Western Union's political unity and military effectiveness were judged sceptically if not very critically. In order not to have to depend on this insecure West European Security Alliance, Speidel demanded a 'security or defence guarantee' from the USA, backed up in military terms by the stationing of fresh US divisions on the Continent. US support 'in all areas and in all three dimensions' was vital. With the forces of the USA and the Western Union, West Europe and Western Germany were to be defended 'decisively' and not as a 'delaying tactic' on the Elbe line, 'which in some cases has first to be taken', or at least on the line running between Vienna, Passau, the Bohemian Forest, the Fichtelgebirge Mountains, the River Main, Spessart, the Taunus Mountains and the River Weser.

The conclusion of the North Atlantic Treaty, and also the 'Rhine Defence', under NATO command, forced the Germans to make a further statement. Speidel saw with regret that the Atlantic Treaty had nothing to say about what was to happen to the terrain east of the Rhine. To surrender the Western Zones as a military no-man's land, or to use it as a marshalling area, did not mean any kind of defence in Speidel's opinion but would rather tempt the USSR into making an attack. Thus the founding of NATO, according to the German line, did not mean any change in West Germany's security situation. In spite of this, Speidel and Heusinger, in an 'interim statement', which they made in a memorandum in April 1950, came to the conclusion that West Germany would have to be completely equal in both political and military terms, and would also have to be admitted to NATO itself, before she could make a contribution to Western European defence.

Despite all their criticism of NATO's military weakness, the Germans were aware that only entry to and equal say in this alliance could offer security and give Germany the opportunity to develop and plan a defence suited to her needs in the event of war.

Konrad Adenauer recognised this at an early stage, and he declared his support for the 'Elbe Defence'. After having received memoranda from Speidel in November and December of 1948, he announced as early as 30 January 1949 that a 'guarantee for West German security' was needed, as well as defence on the Elbe rather than on the Rhine. Apart from the hope that the Western Security Alliances would be effective in preventing wars, the German political and military leaders made the wish for a 'say in the decision-making process concerning West European defence', their future watch-word in order to ensure that the Federal Republic was defended.

However, the Chancellor had little success with his official request for a guarantee of the Federal Republic's defence and for an increase in allied troop strength in the country. The foreign ministers of the three Occupying Powers, in their reply of May 1950, pointed to the relevant articles of the Brussels and NATO Treaties, according to which an attack upon the occupation troops would cause a reaction by these alliances.[37] Thus the defence of the Federal Republic seemed to them to be assured, apart from the deterrent effect upon the USSR. In view of the weakness of the allied forces stationed on the Continent this last element was questionable to say the least.[38]

The Increasing Level of Threat in 1949–50

The events of the years 1949 and 1950 changed the threat situation markedly.[39] The Soviet Union had had the atom bomb since the autumn of 1949, even if the number and the necessary means of delivery were obviously still limited. At the beginning of 1950 China became part of the Communist bloc. In June 1950 Communist North Korea attacked the Western-oriented southern half of the Korean peninsula.

The Soviet atom bomb added a nuclear threat to the conventional one. At the same time Great Britain and the North American sub-continent were endangered. The USSR's conventional superiority became increasingly important, since she had a nuclear 'umbrella', albeit a thin one. Western intelligence agencies disagreed on which part of the newly created North Atlantic Alliance was more threatened. Was Continental Europe only under a conventional threat, or was there also a nuclear one? Was Britain threatened by an 'atomic blitz'? Or would the USSR use her nuclear potential to destroy the North American base of Western Europe's defence as much as possible, so that she would have an easier task of defeating the Europeans on the Continent itself? For the Western Allies it was obvious that they had to arm themselves against both conventional and nuclear dangers.

The Communist People's Republic of China threatened the position of the USA and France in the Far East. She obliged both of them to divide their political interests and military potential between Europe and the Pacific.

The Korean War, behind which the West thought were the USSR and China, pointed to the Communist bloc's readiness to make use of local and possibly even global military resources in order to realise their political aims. Some saw the war as the prologue to a Third World War or as the preliminary stage of a military conflict in Europe. The Federal Republic saw definite parallels to the situation of South Korea. It seemed obvious that the same fate could befall her.

US nuclear potential had proved itself insufficient to deter the USSR from this conventional action. It showed itself to be incapable of being employed militarily in the Korean theatre of war, one purposely limited by both sides. Clearly there was the danger that the USSR's and the USA's nuclear weapons would cancel each other out. Then the Russians would still have their conventional superiority.

Fear of war and war hysteria, whether really present or 'manufactured', spread through the West following the outbreak of the Korean War. After the situation in Korea had stabilised, it was Soviet nuclear potential which served as a barometer for her war capability. The prophecy was that the next years would be 'years of the greatest danger', in which it was vital to prepare the West's armament. 1954 was seen as one of these years, but after the shock of Korea in the USA the crisis was put forward to 1952. It took a long time for the realisation to sink in that the political confrontation between East and West would be a lengthy affair, and that the West always had to be prepared in case a political conflict suddenly changed into a military one.

US-European Rapprochement

The start of the Korean War proved how doubtful the effect of the USA's strategic nuclear potential was in deterring a conventionally led attack and in defending within a conflict which was limited in terms of geographical location and employment of resources.[40] Despite the fact that there was a war in the Far East, US and thereby NATO strategic interests remained fixed on Europe, as it could not be ruled out that a similar Communist bloc action would occur in this much more important region. The

USA's strategic ideas concurred with those of her Continental NATO partners on this point, and she tried to bring the existing alliance plans closer to fruition by increasing its military resources.

The USA's first military duty was recognised as being the defence of the whole treaty area. Most important was the defence of Western Europe. In order to accommodate earlier European requirements, the USA promised to participate in direct defence on the European continent, by means of more military aid, additional troops stationed in peacetime, by agreeing to speedy reinforcements in the event of war and by a stronger role in a new military organisation, which would now have an American Commander-in-Chief. This was possible due to an extensive US rearmament programme, which had seemed necessary even before the outbreak of the Korean War, but had only become a priority after this dramatic event. Up to 1952, for example, the US arsenal was to be supplemented by eight divisions, four aircraft carriers, forty-eight destroyers and twenty-five air force wings. The plan was to increase the nuclear potential as a whole, and to have resources for any kind of situation, from nuclear warheads for the combat zone to hydrogen bombs for large-scale strategic destruction. These US efforts were accompanied by demands to the Europeans: namely that they build up their own conventional forces and that they allow German armed forces into NATO as soon as possible.

The NATO reaction to the new military strategic thinking in the USA was very swift, and the US positions were laid down in agreements and decisions. In August 1950 the list of tasks seen as of 'first-rate importance' for Western European defence was drawn up. The first priority was to keep the enemy pinned down as far east in Europe as possible. The strategic air offensive against the USSR and the strengthening of direct defence in Europe came second. In December 1950 the NATO Council defined for itself what was to be meant by defence as far east in Europe as possible. It was known as 'forward strategy', i.e. to begin defence as close to the 'Iron Curtain' as possible.

The change from the former planning body into a command organisation was also unproblematic. The Regional Planning Groups were renamed 'command areas' under a NATO Commander-in-Chief for Europe (Supreme Allied Commander Europe–SACEUR). The Atlantic Region also received its own

Commander-in-Chief (SACLANT). The alliance members were put under pressure by the USA to allocate the troops planned for defence to these commanders in peacetime. Only the Canadian United States Regional Planning Group retained its name (CUSPRG for short). All these areas were subordinate to the Standing Group. An American, General Eisenhower, took over the responsibility for the defence of Western Europe, thus tying the USA even closer to Europe. Field Marshal Montgomery acted as his second-in-command. He made sure that Europe kept her role in strategic planning and also that Britain was still involved on the Continent. However, Eisenhower kept command of Central Europe for himself, pointing to its 'paramount importance' for the whole alliance. An American was also to be in command of the Atlantic area. The general feeling of military renewal required its figureheads and found them in the organisers of the 1944 invasion and the victors over the German Reich in the West.

At about the end of 1950, after military planning and NATO's military organisation had been brought to a pleasing and harmonious conclusion, at least in the medium term, it only remained to specify the numbers of troops required. The North Atlantic Alliance still wanted to complete the build-up of her armed forces by 1954, planning to have thirty-two divisions in place in the Central European Area, twenty-two more to be mobilised within thirty days, and fourteen within ninety days. Thus sixty-eight divisions were seen as being necessary in order to realise 'forward strategy'. Initial responses from the alliance members involved revealed a gap of thirteen divisions. While the inclusion of German armed forces was the subject of a serious alteration between the USA and France in the second half of 1950, this gap already shows how many divisions the Federal Republic would have.[41] The same was true of 'forward strategy', which was impossible without the use of German territory and the active participation of the Federal Republic. Conversely, the aim of 'forward strategy' was to protect Western Germany and her potential, and thus also a sign of goodwill toward a future ally.

German Alignment to NATO's Military Concept

In the Federal Republic itself there were preparations for cooperation with and within NATO by the drawing-up of official strategic plans. There was a marked similarity between alliance planning and German ideas in the fields of threat perception, military plans and in the use of military resources. This was not only the result of a similar grasp of more or less constant factors, such as geographical location, the balance of power and the aims to be reached, but also a conscious effort at alignment on the part of the Germans.[42] According to Heusinger, who had formulated the relevant passages in the memorandum written on behalf of the German Chancellor, success depended upon 'above all a joint strategic plan of how defence is to be effected. This plan must specify the military expenditure of the countries of Europe ... as well as US military support. Using these figures, the various countries' armed forces have to be calculated, mobilised and equipped.' NATO had done precisely this since the autumn of 1949 and had developed her basic concept, her medium and short-term defence plans and her armed-forces plan up to the end of 1950. The statement that 'German defence must be adapted to this plan' surely only had this alliance planning in mind. If one considers the wording of the important sentences and the identical nature of the main facts, one could almost be forgiven for thinking that the German military experts had known the NATO plans in advance. West German territory, as NATO also thought, had to be 'defended as far east as possible'; this was the uppermost aim. Added to this, however, was the intention to 'conduct hostilities on east German territory as soon as possible', which was in Germany's interest. The 'Elbe Defence' had come to the fore in German planning. Emphasis was expressly placed on the following: 'German territory must not be seen as the forefront of a main defence planned on the Rhine.'

As in all previous German memoranda, the primary aim was to 'bring the Russian attack to a halt on land'. Air attacks also served this purpose. At the same time, however, the USSR and her raw-material supply areas had to be attacked with the 'atomic weapon'. The struggle between the Elbe and the Rhine was to be conducted using fifty-five divisions. The twelve German divisions were to be activated by 1952. In this respect the Germans came closer to the American timetable than that of NATO.

The almost-complete agreement, or rather alignment, of German plans to those of NATO was surely also the expression of the hope that West Germany would soon be an 'equal' partner, or at least be 'integrated' into the organisation. However, at the

Concepts for the Defence of Western Europe

same time there was no mistaking Germany's demands for a 'forward strategy' in the shape of the 'Elbe Defence'. Here Heusinger used very clear terms in his dicussions with the US authorities. The Elbe Defence also lay in the best personal interests of the USA's strategic plans. As he wrote: 'The USA seems to be relying upon the strategic air force and the atom bomb. It should not, however, be forgotten that these cannot be successfully employed without the use of Western Europe. For this reason also Western Europe's defence must be based upon the Elbe on a long-term basis.'[43]

If we look back at the reasons for the differing concepts of 'Rhine' and 'Elbe Defence', we can only make guesses. The closer someone was to allied organisations, or if he actually worked for them, the more prepared he was to follow their intentions, whether known or conjectured. In such cases German interests receded into the background and adapted themselves to allied ideas. The 'Rhine Defence' and the 'Rhine Zone Defence' used Germany as the foreground, as did the Western Union and NATO, without considering how to protect her territory. Plans and ideas meant for German politicians or for public consumption tried, of course, to save German territory, as much as possible, from the fate of becoming the battlefield. This was the origin of the idea that the Elbe was to be defended. For even using a mobile defence on the border to the eastern zone, large parts of the Western zones would have to be surrendered. There was not sufficient manpower for a static defence along a front of around 800 km., and the terrain of the border area was not as suitable as that of the Rhine. Finally, both concepts tried, using a strong offensive element, whether in the air or on land, to remove hostilities from German soil sooner or later, or to end the war at the earliest opportunity. After the outbreak of the Korean War the Elbe Defence became the official German concept as an offensive variation of NATO's planned 'forward strategy'.

An Integrated Military Strategy for Western Europe?

If there had ever been a universally accepted alliance strategy, then this must surely be in the NATO Council decisions of December 1950 and in the aim behind these.[44] Belgian Foreign Minister Paul van Zeeland wrote the following, on 19 December

1950, as Chairman of the NATO Council: 'If peace is to be secured, we must draw three conclusions from the tragic events of the last weeks (i.e. the Korean War):

> (1) The Atlantic Community must be strong and must restore the balance of power.
> (2) The NATO states must remain united and must have the same goals.
> (3) The planned NATO armed forces will only be in a position to secure peace if they are activated without delay.'[45]

British Foreign Minister Bevin declared: 'It is granted to few men to fulfil their dreams. I know that I was close to death three times in the last year. But I am still alive because I wanted to see this North Atlantic Alliance put on the right track. This has happened today'.[46]

The harmony of plans, aims and intentions between the Americans, Europeans and Germans, proclaimed with such emotion, very soon fell apart when faced by the harsh reality of unavailable and unfeasible resources. Eisenhower, who retired from his NATO post in April 1952, said he was disappointed at Europe's performance. Out of twenty-seven divisions planned for 1951, only twenty were activated. The Europeans were solely to blame for the missing men, as the USA had stationed four additional divisions on the Continent in 1951. Thus there was still no chance of mounting a real resistance east of the Rhine barrier.[47] NATO made a new attempt to build up conventional armed forces approximately matching those of the USSR in Europe. The plan was to have ninety-six divisions and 4,000 aircraft available. Thirty-five to Forty of these divisions were to be present, and the rest were to be mobilised at different rates.

NATO's strategic guidelines, newly written in December 1952, were based on the armed-forces programme decided upon in February of the same year, and demanded:

> (a) defence in Western Europe as far east as possible with all resources, also supported by 'unconventional operations';
> (b) the carrying-out of strategic air attacks using 'all kinds of weapons';
> (c) the protection of all bases and air and sea routes necessary to carry out these operations; and
> (d) the preparation of subsequent offensive missions.

The further development of the basic strategic concept, accepted in December 1949, towards a greater emphasis upon conventional, direct defence remained. As had been decided in August 1950, conventional defence was the highest priority, supported, however, by 'unconventional', i.e. nuclear missions.

This 'nuclear option' came more and more to the fore in NATO's strategic concepts from 1953 onwards, because the conventional forces situation was still as it was before the outbreak of the Korean War. But the general situation had worsened. The predictable lack of success of direct defence was accompanied by increasing doubts about the deterrent effect and the success of the indirect effect. For the USSR was increasingly in a position to answer strategic blows against her territory by mounting similar attacks upon Western European and American soil. Nuclear weapons in the tactical sense and for employment on the battlefield only gave rise to a (very temporary) comforting feeling of superiority. Then the USSR caught up once more. Since 1945 the conventional inbalance has remained in Western Europe with all its negative consequences. This fact shows how little common strategy there has been for Western Europe since 1948, at least in the field of the allocation of resources. In the end the lack of resources had a negative impact on individual conventional plans and on the judgement of threat. Thus there was a great deal of wishful thinking, which can surely be no basis for an alliance's military strategic concepts. Even if these concepts have a different starting-point according to the different countries, they should be feasible in crisis and war situations.

Notes

1. Ernst Lutz, *Lexikon zur Sicherheitspolitik*, Munich, 1980, p. 236.
2. Robert E. Osgood, 'NATO, problems of security and collaboration', in *The American Political Science Review*, LIV/1964, pp. 106–29, here p. 106.
3. Karl W. Deutsch et al, *Political Community and the North Atlantic Area*, Princeton, 1968, p. 5f.
4. Amt für Studien und Übungen, *Militärpotentiale NATO/WP, 1949–1984*, Teil 1: *Nukleare Potentiale*, Bergisch Gladbach, 1985, p. 18.

5. Ibid.
6. Ibid.
7. Christian Greiner, '"Operational History (German) Section" und "Naval Historical Team": Deutsches militärstrategisches Denken im Dienste der amerikanischen Streitkräfte von 1946 bis 1950', in *Militärgeschichte: Probleme – Thesen – Wege*, Im Auftrag des MGFA zum Anlaß seines 25 jährigen Bestehens ausgewählt und zusammengestellt von Manfred Messerschmidt, Klaus A. Maier, Werner Rahn und Bruno Thoß, Stuttgart, 1982 (*Beiträge zur Militär- und Kriegsgeschichte*, vol. 25), pp. 409–35.
8. Cf. on this section: Christian Greiner, 'Die alliierten militärstrategischen Planungen zur Verteidigung Westeuropas 1947–1950', in *Anfänge westdeutscher Sicherheitspolitik 1945–1956*, vol. 1: *Von der Kapitulation bis zum Pleven-Plan*, von Roland G. Foerster, Christian Greiner, Georg Meyer, Hans-Jürgen Rautenberg and Norbert Wiggershaus, Munich, Vienna, 1982, pp. 119–323, here pp. 197–205 and 287–92; Greiner (see Note 7), p. 416f, Greiner, 'The Defence of Western Europe and the Rearmament of West Germany, 1947–1950', in *Western Security: The Formative Year: European and Atlantic Defence 1947–1953*, Olav Riste (ed.), Oslo, 1985, pp. 150–77; Norbert Wiggershaus, 'Bedrohungsvorstellungen Bundeskanzler Adenauers nach Ausbruch des Korea-Krieges', in *MGM* 1/1979, pp. 79–122. Indispensable for any study of security policy and military strategy during this period are the following: *The History of the Joint Chiefs of Staff. The Joint Chiefs of Staff and National Policy*, vols. 1–4, 1945–1952, Wilmington, 1979–80 and *Foreign Relations of the United States* (= FRUS), *Diplomatic Papers*, 1945–1950, especially vols. 1948, III, 1949, IV, and 1950, III, Washington DC, 1967–1980. The US documentation used here is in part reprinted in *Containment: Documents on American Policy and Strategy 1945–1950*, Thomas E. Etzold and John L. Gaddis (eds), New York, 1978.
9. The American-Soviet Problem in Europe and the Near-East, November 1948 (Heusinger and co-workers), p. 25 (MGFA, Befragungsmaterialien, Depositum General a.D. Adolf Heusinger).
10. Cf. on this section Greiner, 'The Defence' (see Note 8), p. 150f.
11. FRUS, 1948, I, p. 667.
12. Greiner, 'Alliierte militärstrategische Planungen' (see Note 8), p. 193f.
13. Rudolf Hecht, *USA/NATO-Sowjetunion: Entwicklung der strategischen Doktrinen, 1945–1952/3*, Vienna, 1983, p. 103f; Lawrence S. Kaplan, An unequal triad: the United States, Western Union and NATO, in *Western Security* (see Note 8), pp. 107–27, here p. 115.
14. Greiner, 'Alliierte militärstrategische Planungen' (see Note 8),p. 213f. Public Record Office, London (PRO), CAB 129/37/3C.P.(49) 245, Defence Estimate 1950–1951, Memorandum by the Prime Minister,

8.12.1949.
15. Greiner, 'Alliierte militärstrategische Planungen' (see Note 8), p. 215f; Jean de Lattre, *Ne Pas Subir, Ecrits 1914–1952*, Elisabeth du Réau (ed.), Paris, 1984, p. 388f.
16. Cf. on this section Greiner, 'The Defence' (see Note 8), p. 160f.(quotation p. 160 f.); Greiner, 'Operational History' (see Note 7), p. 417f; Roland G. Foerster, 'Innenpolitische Aspekte der Sicherheit Westdeutschlands 1947–1950', in *Anfänge westdeutscher Sicherheitspolitik* (see Note 8), pp. 403–575, here p. 405f.
17. The American-Soviet Problem in Europe (see Note 9), p. 1: 'It is forwarded on special request of EUCOM'.
18. National Archives and Record Service. Modern Military Branch, Washington DC (NA, MMB), Record Group (RG) 218, CCS 319.1: 'A War between the West Powers and USSR in Europe Theater' (2–27–47), Joint Chiefs of Staff, Memorandum for Information No. 526, Report entitled 'A War between the Western Powers and the Soviet Union in the European Theater' by Lt. Gen. Jodl, retired, German Army, 27.2.1947, p. 9f. The study dates from August 1946.
19. Here and in the following sections: Greiner, 'Operational History', (see Note 7), p. 42.
20. Adolf Heusinger, The Defence of Western Europe, 1949–50, p. 12f. (MGFA, Befragungsmaterialien, Depositum General a.D. Adolf Heusinger); see also Heusinger, Die Bedeutung des Alpengebietes im Fall eines kriegerischen Ost-West-Konfliktes, 1949, idem.
21. The American-Soviet Problem in Europe (see Note 9), p. 65.
22. Heusinger, The Defence (see Note 20), map Annex 6.
23. Cf. on this section Greiner, 'Alliierte militärstrategische Planungen' (see Note 8), pp. 210–30; Greiner, 'The Defence' (see Note 8), p. 152f; de Lattre, *Ne Pas Subir* (see Note 15), pp. 426–51.
24. FRUS, 1948, III, p. 125f.
25. PRO, Brussels Treaty Organisation, DG 1/6/36, Minutes of Meetings of the Chiefs of Staff Committee, F.C.(48), 6th Meeting, 15.12.1948, fol. 87.
26. Ibid., F.C.(48) 7th Meeting, 17.12.1948, fol. 97.
27. Ibid., F.C.(50) 1st Meeting, 16.2.1950, fol. 264 and F.C.(50) 2nd Meeting, 20.6.1950, fol. 303. The question was even asked if British Field Marshal Montgomery would take over command at all in case of war (ibid., fol. 303).
28. Ibid., F.C.(48) 1st Meeting, 26.8.1948, fol.7 and F.C.(48) 2nd Meeting, 8.10.1948, fol. 57. The document bears the title 'Employment of Germans for the Defence of Western Europe' (F.P.(48)32).
29. Cf. on this section Greiner, 'Alliierte militärstrategische Planungen' (see Note 8), p. 221f; Greiner, 'The Defence' (see Note 8), p. 154.
30. PRO, Brussels Treaty Organisation, DG.1/6/36, Minutes of the Meetings of the Chiefs of Staff Committee, F.C.(48) 3rd Meeting,

27.10.48, fol. 65; F.C.(48) 6th Meeting, 15.12.48, fol. 87f.
31. Cf. on this section Greiner, 'Alliierte militärstrategische Planungen' (see Note 8), p. 252f; Greiner, 'The Defence' (see Note 8), p. 152f.
32. NA, MMB, RG 218, Geographic File (GF) 1948–1950. Western Europe (3–12–48), sec. 30, Memorandum for the Secretary of Defence, Subject: Guidance for the United States Military Representatives appointed to the Military Committee and to the Standing Group of the North Atlantic Treaty Organisation, 30.9.1949, p. 4.
33. NATO HQ, Brussels, International Staff, Central Registry, (NISCA), 7/1, DC 13, North Atlantic Treaty Organisation Medium Term Defence Plan, 28.3.1950, p. 61.
34. NA, MMB, RG 218, GF 1948–1950, Western Europe (3–12–48), Sec. 65, JCS 2073/106, Report on the Western Europe Regional Short Term Plan, 28.12.1950, p. 754.
35. Cf. on this section the literature for Note 16.
36. Hans Speidel, 'Ergänzung für ein Gespräch', in Speidel, *Aus unserer Zeit: Erinnerungen*, Frankfurt, 1977, p. 466.
37. Cf. on the discussion within the Brussels Pact on the validity of Article 4 also in the case of an 'aggression in Germany': PRO, Brussels Treaty Organisation, DG 1/6/36, Minutes of the Meetings of the Chiefs of Staff, F.C.(48) 6th Meeting, 15.12.48, fol. 85 discussion on the Standing Military Committee's paper, F.C. (48) 18, 'Aggression in Germany' and DG 1/5/31 Conference of five defence ministers and chiefs of staff, M.D.(49) 1st Meeting, 17.1.1949, with the final passage reading: 'Agreed to recommend to the Consultative Council that it would be desirable to decide that any armed attack directed against an occupation authority must automatically be construed as an attack against occupying countries and must immediately set in motion the machinery of the Brussels Treaty'. (fol. 14).
38. Greiner, 'Alliierte militärstrategische Planungen' (see Note 8), p. 261f.
39. Cf. on this section the literature for Note 8.
40. Cf. on this section Greiner, 'Alliierte militärstrategische Planungen' (see note 8), p. 287f; Hecht, *USA/NATO* (see Note 13), p. 88f.
41. Norbert Wiggershaus, 'Die Entscheidung für einen westdeutschen Verteidigungsbeitrag 1950', in *Anfänge westdeutscher Sicherheitspolitik*, vol. 1 (see Note 8), pp. 325–402.
42. Cf. on the following: Hans-Jürgen Rautenberg, Norbert Wiggershaus, 'Die 'Himmeroder Denkschrift' vom Oktober 1950: Politische und militärische Überlegungen für einen Beitrag der Bundesrepublik Deutschland zur westeuropäischen Verteidigung', in *MGM* 21/1977, pp. 135–206, here p. 171f.
43. Adolf Heusinger, Notizen betreffend Brief Oberst John R. (Lovell), 12.6.1950, p. 4 (= MGFA, Befragungsmaterialen, Depositum General a.D. Adolf Heusinger).

44. Cf. on this section *Westeuropäische Verteidigungskooperation*, Karl Carstens and Dieter Mahncke (eds), With a foreword by Helmut Schmidt, Munich, Vienna 1972, pp. 56–71; Thomas H. Etzold: 'The end of the beginning...NATO's adoption of nuclear strategy, in *Western Security* (see Note 8), pp. 285–314; Robert C. Richardson, 'NATO nuclear strategy: a look back', in *Strategic Review* 2, 1981, pp. 35–43; Greiner, Nordatlantische Bündnisstrategie und deutscher Verteidigungsbeitrag, 1954 bis 1957', in *Entmilitarisierung und Aufrüstung in Mitteleuropa 1945–1956*, with contributions by Alexander Fischer, Christian Greiner, Klaus A. Meier, Ulrich de Maizière, Wilhelm Meier-Dornberg, Georg Meyer, Manfred Rauchensteiner, Jan Schulten, Hans-Erich Volkmann, Norbert Wiggershaus, Herford, Bonn, 1983, pp. 116–1943 (*Vorträge zur Militärgeschichte*, vol. 4).
45. NISCA, North Atlantic Council, Summary Records, C6-R/2, 19.12.1950, p. 5.
46. Franz-Wilhelm Engel, *Handbuch der NATO*, Frankfurt, 1957, p. 78. Bevin, who regarded the initiation of the Western Union and NATO as his 'greatest triumph', died on 14 April 1951 (*Encyclopaedia Britannica*, vol. 3, London, 1964, p. 559).
47. Greiner, 'Alliierte militärstrategische Planungen' (see Note 8), p. 314.

17
Economic Aspects of the Creation of the North American-Western European Alliance System (1948–1950)

Manfred Knapp

Alliance Policy and Economic Relations

From the beginning there were a variety of considerable economic problems connected with the creation of the North American-Western European security and alliance system. It had its forerunner in the Brussels Five-Power Treaty signed on 17 March 1948, and a firm basis in the North Atlantic Treaty signed on 4 April 1949. Historical and politico-logical studies of the initial development of this comparatively new community of the most important Western industrial nations, in the sense of both military and security policy, have more or less completely covered some of the central economic prerequisites and the subsequent difficulties of the creation of the alliance.[1] Seen as a whole, however, too little emphasis has been placed by researchers[2] upon economic factors conditional to the North Atlantic Alliance which arose during the first few years, as well as the resulting political and economic questions. It is worth doing so, particularly as we can get a better insight into the themes dealt with here from documents and files recently published or made available for research.

The following essay is intended to focus on some economic aspects and the related problems of the early phase of the Western security system, i.e. from the founding of the Brussels Pact in the spring of 1948 until (after the outbreak of the Korean War in June 1950) the negotiations in the autumn of 1950 on the institutional establishment of the North Atlantic Treaty to an integrated military organisation.

The creation of a transatlantic security alliance raised a variety of important economic questions for all the partners, to say nothing of the basic political questions. For example, the United States was faced with the problem of how to fit her leading role in the Western Alliance and security system (something totally new for her foreign-policy tradition) into the pattern of her postwar foreign and trade policy. On the other hand, the European partners in this security community had to realise that the North Atlantic Treaty was more than merely a 'skeleton' agreement, with which it would be easier to obtain the requested guarantees of security and military aid from the rich and powerful Americans. All the NATO members basically had to settle the issue of how this new transatlantic cooperation, having begun with various US economic assistance programmes after 1945, could be extended to include the sensitive area of military security. It was also unclear what relationship the individual aspects of economic and military cooperation would have, and what kind of institutional framework would have to be developed for this purpose. Finally, seen in the light of reason, there could be no illusions as to the fact that great strain would be placed upon member states' budgets, even if joint efforts at defence and rearmament were increased, and possibly also pressure upon their internal economic and social policy, as well as on their balance of payments.[3] Moreover, the assumption that the close security-policy cooperation aimed at both sides of the Atlantic would lead to intrusions into traditional national rights of sovereignty and disposal, especially in economic matters, was to be proved correct in the near future.

Yet at the same time, in theory, the idea of a transatlantic alliance was also promising in economic terms. Due to the contractually binding commitment to assistance and particularly the possible combining of the military and economic potential and resources of the individual alliance members, it was possible to create an effective and, under favourable circumstances, also a very 'economical' security arrangement for all the partners against the presumed enemy, i.e. the Soviet Union. In the end no alliance partner, not even the United States, considered herself capable of guaranteeing her own external security alone.

Meanwhile, great problems quickly arose concerning the practical realisation of the transatlantic security alliance, the largest of which also had an economic background. From the beginning the NATO partners were faced with the question of the economic reconstruction of the war-ravaged industrial nations of Western Europe, which were just getting off the ground and, therefore, would be endangered by the possibly over-eager creation of a military alliance and the resulting inevitable expenditure on weapons and military infrastructure. Foreign-affairs experts such as George Kennan,[4] Director of the Policy Planning Staff at the State Department, among others, had made a point of recommending that the economic consolidation of the European countries be given top priority, and that the mechanisms of economic exchange between them would have to be restored before one could start to think about such a far-reaching and binding military and political community, if at all. On the other hand, the supporters of NATO considered the immediate, i.e. simultaneous, creation of a transatlantic security system to be vital in the face of the worsening East-West conflict. They won the upper hand.

Secret US-Anglo-Canadian talks on the chances of a security arrangement between the Western industrial nations on both sides of the Atlantic were held as early as March 1948: in other words, before the US Foreign Assistance Act regulating the execution of the Marshall Plan had even come into force. After the corresponding 'Economic Cooperation Act' (Title I of the 'Foreign Assistance Act of 1948') had become law, on 3 April 1948, and after the first aid shipments under the auspices of the large-scale 'European Recovery Programme' (ERP) had been sent out to their European recipients, the negotiators of the five Brussels Treaty states sat down together with their American and Canadian counterparts in Washington to start drawing up a new treaty, which resulted, after a year of negotiations, in the treaty creating NATO.

Even during these treaty negotiations, in which the US Senate's foreign-policy experts, Senators Vandenberg and Connally, also played a large role,[5] a number of basic politico-economic problems came up, which have occupied the Alliance's committees in countless variations ever since:[6] how was it possible to make sure that the members of the Alliance each provided a sufficient proportion of their economic resources to achieve the joint-military and security-policy aims without endangering their economic reconstruction and the subsequent stability of their national economy and the achievement of their internal economic goals? From the very start there was the old conflict of priorities between butter and guns, between economic stability and prosperity on the one hand and military security on the other. Apart from this, for the founders of the Western Alliance, the well-known problem arose of how they could gain the highest possible security with a certain available amount of funds, so that they could avoid the uneconomical use of resources and the waste of scarce funds to the greatest possible extent. Finally, again during the initial phase of the North Atlantic Alliance, the key question arose of how the costs and burdens of jointly guaranteeing outer security were to be fairly shared among the alliance partners. This has been a basic problem for the alliance, which led to a crisis at the beginning of the 1950s and which has since become worse under the heading of 'burden sharing'.[7]

Apart from military policy and armaments requirements, other economic-policy questions arose during the initial phase of NATO. Thus, in Article 2 of the North Atlantic Treaty, the alliance partners set out their intention 'to eliminate conflict in their international economic policies and will encourage economic collaboration between any or all of them'.[8] But it became clear, in the early stages of the alliance, that the structure of the joint security alliance was only of very limited value for conducting and sponsoring civilian transatlantic economic relations. Since there were already a variety of other organisations and institutions in the field of international economic relations (OEEC, International Monetary Fund and World Bank, GATT), the alliance partners were faced with a multitude of unclear rules about who was responsible for what, which often led to niggling and inertia. The early refusal to have the 'Atlantic Community' of NATO states made into a kind of economic community was, however, to lead to tension in transatlantic relations. After Schuman set out his plan in May 1950, and after the European Coal and Steel Community was founded, a problem became noticeable within the above-mentioned structure of North American-Western European relations, i.e. that military- and security-policy structures were not the same as economic ones. A tense relationship developed between the transatlantic security alliance and the organisations concerned with Western European economic integration which has remained until the present day. We must keep these problems in mind as we go on to consider the economic problem areas during the initial phase of NATO.

From the Brussels Five-Power Pact via the North Atlantic Treaty to the Beginnings of NATO

The architects of the North Atlantic Treaty were conscious of the fact that the creation of a North American-Western European security system would inevitably give rise to fundamental questions concerning economic cooperation, both between North America and Western Europe and within Western Europe itself. As the prehistory of NATO and the relevant treaty negotiations reveal, there were three main problem areas. The first was to decide what relationship the North Atlantic Treaty would have to the European Recovery Programme, and, further, to the whole organisational structure of transatlantic economic relations. Second, the alliance partners had to try to clarify the basic principles of mutual assistance, particularly the economic and financial questions arising from the build-up of defence potential. Third, it had to be decided whether the planned North Atlantic Treaty was to include not only military and armaments cooperation but also non-military cooperation, especially of an economic nature. All three problem areas were, of course, very closely linked.

When British Secretary of State for Foreign Affairs Bevin, after the failure of the London Four-Power Conference in December 1947, attempted to put his ideas concerning the consolidation of Western security into practice by suggesting the formation of a 'Western Union', and at the same time to gain the support of the United States, he got a cautious reaction from the US Administration.[9] Nevertheless, US Secretary of State Marshall admitted that 'Recovery and security are obviously interrelated.'[10]

Immediately following the signing of the 'Treaty of economic, social and cultural collaboration and collective self-defence'[11] between the United Kingdom, France and the Benelux countries in Brussels on 17 March 1948, Washington was prepared to enter into exploratory talks on security with representatives from Great Britain and Canada. During these meetings, held in Washington from 22 March to 1 April 1948, and whose results were written down in the 'Pentagon Paper', one of the subjects on the agenda was the 'possibilities of a military ERP'.[12]

During the promulgation of the law governing the Marshall Plan, which was just in the closing stages, Congress and administration had both decided against including a military component in the Foreign Assistance Act for Western Europe at the present time. Despite this, however, the idea of modelling the planned security association of North America and Western Europe on the ERP[13] was retained. The Americans in particular were eager to point out that the same basic principles of multilateral cooperation and mutual assistance were to govern the possible transatlantic security alliance as those applying to the ERP. The Western Europeans could not expect American support until they had first mobilised their own armed forces and had proved that they were prepared to work together on a long-term basis.

This fundamental principle was then laid down in the decisive Vandenberg Resolution passed by the US Senate on 11 June 1948, which paved the way for US entry into a collective defence alliance, and led the Senate to agree to the North Atlantic Treaty.[14] The Senate decision contained, among others, the statement that any US participation in a regional or other system of mutual defence had to have constitutional backing, and was to be 'based on continuous and effective self-help and mutual aid'.

The principles contained in the Vandenberg Resolution played a large role in the subsequent negotiations between the United States, Canada and the Brussels Treaty countries concerning the constitutional foundation of the security alliance. Thus the basic principles of guaranteeing mutual aid and assistance were laid down in the 'Washington Paper', the final document, at the end of the second round of talks, which took place at ambassadorial level in Washington from 6 July to 10 September 1948.[15] One can find them again in the subsequent draft texts during the third round of talks, which led to the draft treaty of 24 December 1948.[16] They were finally laid down in the treaty signed by the twelve founding members of the North Atlantic Pact on 4 April 1949.[17]

Apart from the general declaration of principles in the preamble, we should be most interested, in this essay, in Article 3 of the North Atlantic Treaty, in which the signatory states declare that they 'separately and jointly, by means of continuous and effective self-help and mutual aid, will maintain and develop their individual and collective capacity to resist armed attack'.[18]

The above-mentioned assistance formula 'by means of continuous and effective self-help and mutual aid' has, since the founding of the North Atlantic Treaty, been seen as the main source of the political duty to render mutual military and economic support in order to help create defence capability.[19] The American originators of NATO in particular saw this principle as an essential condition for the allocating of US military aid as urgently requested and expected by the Western Europeans.[20]

However, from an economic point of view, we can also consider as being relevant those treaty regulations governing the non-military cooperation agreed by the alliance partners. Some of the representatives of the founding nations, notably Canada, spoke out strongly in favour of the future North American-Western European Alliance being more than simply a classical military alliance, and that its aim should be the encouragement of civilian, economic, social and cultural cooperation between the partners.[21] The British government in particular argued against extending the area of competence into economic relations, stressing that there were already international (economic) organisations in existence in Western Europe (Brussels Treaty, OEEC), and pointing out that an extension of the transatlantic alliance's responsibility into the field of non-military cooperation would mean an unnecessary clash of interests, and could jeopardise the process of Western European unity.[22] Yet it was Great Britain who was not prepared to participate in any more intensive efforts at uniting Europe, to say nothing of supranational communities in Western Europe, because of her overseas connections and responsibilities (the Commonwealth) and her ostentatious claim to world-power status.

The differences of opinion on NATO's non-military function were patched over for the time being by a compromise ruling which led to the formulation of Article 2 of the North Atlantic Treaty. Here the partners declared their intention, among other things, to create the conditions for internal stability and prosperity in their states, and to be prepared to remove conflicts in their international economic policy, as well as encouraging economic cooperation between either individual states or all partners.[23]

At the end of the process of ratifying the NATO Treaty in the various member states (the treaty entered into force on 24 August 1949), the subsequent creation of the North American-Western European alliance system very soon proved that joint defence efforts also depend upon economic and financial conditions, and also mostly have far-reaching economic consequences. In order to solve this problem, the Brussels Pact committees immediately developed a certain activity, with US observers in attendance, writing reports on the necessity of pooling resources, pointing

Table 17.1 Basic Data on present level of defence effort of selected countries

Country	Population (in millions)	National income — Net national income at factor cost[1]	National income — Per capita national income in US dollars	Total Government expenditures	Budgetary revenue	Percent of revenue to total Government expenditures	Military expenditures[2]	Percent of military expenditure to national income	Percent of military expenditure to total Government expenditure
	(1)	(2)	(3)	(4)	(5)	(6)	(7)	(8)	(9)
Western Hemisphere Atlantic Pact countries (for comparison):									
United States	146.6	$224,400	$1,530	$41,858	$40,985	98	$14,268	6.4	34
Canada	12.9	12,800	992	2,300	2,800	122	262	2.0	11
Western Union countries:									
United Kingdom	50.0	40,300	806	15,419	15,475	100	3,063	7.6	20
France	41.8	24,764	592	7,204	5,483	76	1,203	4.9	17
Belgium	8.5	5,933	698	1,643	1,529	93	192	3.2	12
Luxembourg	.3	183	610	87	71	84	2	7.7	3
Netherlands	9.9	4,826	487	1,602	1,245	78	377	7.7	23
Total	110.5	76,006	688	25,955	23,803	92	4,837	6.4	19
Non-Western-Union Atlantic Pact countries:									
Italy	46.4	9,257	200	2,347	1,663	71	586	6.3	25
Portugal	8.4	[4]1,000	119	227	172	76	48	4.8	21
Norway	3.3	1,821	552	477	503	105	83	4.5	17
Denmark	4.2	3,230	769	466	513	110	63	2.0	14
Iceland	.14	[4]154	110	33	37	121	(5)	(5)	(5)
Total	62.4	15,462	248	3,550	2,888	81	780	5.1	22
Non-Atlantic-Pact military assistance programme countries:									
Greece[6]	8.0	(7)	(7)	392	242	62	116	(7)	30
Turkey	19.5	[4]2,500	128	489	447	91	198	7.9	40
Iran	15.0	(7)	(7)	336	239	71	63	(7)	19
Republic of Korea	21.0	(7)	(7)	437	373	85	31	(7)	7
Philippines	19.7	(7)	(7)	146	152	104	50	(7)	34
Total	83.2			1,800	1,453	80	458		18

[1] Most recent estimate availabe; 1948 actual or 1949 estimate. [2] In general, expenditures on internal security forces are included; veteran's benefits and nonmilitary functions of military departments are excluded. [3] May include some nonmilitary items. [4] Roughly estimated order of magnitude for Portugal, Iceland and Turkey, which have no national accounts figures. [5] Negligible. [6] Fiscal year 1948–49. [7] Not available

Source: US House of Representatives, Committee on Internation Relations, Selected Executive Session Hearing of the Committee, 1943–50, vol. V: Military Assistance Programme, Part I, Mutual Defence Assistance Act of 1949, Washington 1946, p. 532.

out the advantages of coordinating armaments' production and arguing in favour of standardising military equipment.[24] The relevant ministers, on the other hand, were already unable to hide their worries concerning the high costs of mobilising and equipping armed forces, and complained once again that their countries were financially weak.[25] Thus they had to admit a little sheepishly, for example, that delays had arisen in the setting-up of a military infrastructure programme.[26] In addition to this there was the burden of various overseas conflicts, in Malaya (Great Britain), South-East Asia (France) and Indonesia (The Netherlands).[27]

The economic conditions appeared to be no better within the larger framework of NATO. The economic potential of the so-called 'stepping-stone countries',[28] i.e. Norway (Spitsbergen), Denmark (Greenland), Portugal (the Azores) and Iceland, was comparatively low. Finally, one could also not expect great things from Italy, whose entry into NATO was highly controversial at the start, considering that the peace treaty concluded with Italy in 1947 had forced demilitarisation upon her in certain areas as well as limits on weapons.[29]

The European treaty partners looked at the situation and came to the conclusion that the build-up of their military potential agreed in the transatlantic alliance was impossible without outside help. As things stood (see the balance of power as presented in Table 17.1) this could only be obtained from the USA (and, to a lesser extent, from Canada). Across the Atlantic, the Truman Administration had great problems persuading Congress to pass the 'Mutual Defence Assistance Act' (6 October 1949). This law created a legal basis so that the Western European NATO states were able, under certain conditions, to receive US military aid as well as aid under the auspices of the Marshall Plan.

This did not mean, however, that the economic problems during the initial phase of the North Atlantic Pact had been solved. Realising that the economic and financial difficulties arising from a joint defence policy were worthy of greater attention, the NATO Council, during its second meeting in Washington on 18 November 1949, set up a committee for financial and economic issues and a military production and supply committee.[30] The 'Defense Financial and Economic Committee' was, at the beginning, concerned with preparing comparative surveys of individual member states' military budgets. When the committee staff

Table 17.2 Total defence expenditures of NATO countries 1949–1953

Country	Currency Unit	1949	1950	1951	1952	1953
Belgium	Million Bel. Frs.	7,653	8,256	13,387	20,029	19,901
Canada	Million Can. $	372	495	1,220	1,875	1,960
Denmark	Million Dan. Kroner	360	359	475	676	889
France	Milliard Fr. Frs.	479	559	881	1,297	1,451
Greece	Million Drachmae	1,630	1,971	3,345	2,470	2,767
Italy	Milliard Lire	301	353	457	521	480
Luxembourg	Million Lux. Frs.	112	170	264	436	489
Netherlands	Million Guilders	680	901	1,060	1,253	1,330
Norway	Million Nor. Kroner	370	357	572	831	1,067
Portugal	Million Escudos	1,436	1,530	1,565	1,691	1,975
Turkey	Million Lire	721	693	763	860	1,080
United Kingdom	Million £ Sterling	779	849	1,149	1,561	1,689
United States	Million US $	13,300	14,300	33,216	47,671	49,734
AREA						
NATO Europe	Million US Dollar equivalents	4,831	5,413	7,605	10,312	11,227
NATO North America	Million Dollars	13,672	14,795	34,436	49,546	51,694
TOTAL NATO	Million US Dollar equivalents	18,503	20,208	42,041	59,798*	62,773*

Note:
These figures are on the basis of the NATO definition of defence expenditures, and respresent actual payments made during the calendar year. They may differ considerably from the amounts given in national budget, which frequently relate to budgetary classifications differing more or less widely from the NATO definition, and which in some countries include substantial amounts which may be carried over for actual expenditures in subsequent years, in accordance with varying national budgetary practices. The figures are not limited to expenditures for the support of NATO forces, but include other defence expenditure as well.

Figures for the United States and Canada include expenditures for the procurement of military equipment to be furnished as end-item aid to European NATO countries. Figures for European NATO countries do not include any allowance for the value of this equipment.

Economic and defence support aid is not included in the defence expenditures of the United States. The national currency counterpart of US economic and defence aid, to the extend used for defence purposes, is included in the defence expenditure of the recipient countries.

The Table contains the figures as they were known on July 1st, 1954. Since that date, the figures for some countries have undergone slight modifications

*Expenditures financed from US Special Military Support are included in the figures for both the United States and France. These amounts to 60 million dollars (21 milliard Frenc francs) in 1952 and 148 million dollars (52 milliard French francs) in 1953. The 'TOTAL NATO' figures have been adjusted to eliminate double counting of these amounts.
Source: NATO (see Note 1) p. 111.

tried to find a yardstick by which to judge the relative amount of the actual military expenditure by its relationship to the economic capacity and financial strength of each member state, in accordance with the treaty, they immediately stumbled upon a sore point in Western Alliance politics – and could go no further.[31] From the beginning this was a source of internal wrangling within the alliance itself.

When, in April 1950, the NATO Defence Committee passed the draft version of a plan for the integrated defence of the North Atlantic Area, the so-called 'Medium Term Plan', the Europeans obviously had trouble pulling their financial weight.[32]

The readiness on all sides to take on higher defence burdens increased noticeably, however, when the Korean War broke out on 25 June 1950 (see Table 17.2). In spite of this, one can see that the United States had considered, and even made preparations for, large-scale rearmament and mobilisation plans as early as the spring of 1950 (NSC 68!).[33] During the internal talks on the levels of military expenditure and defence efforts, there was an increasing tendency to use a procedure which has become standard practice within the alliance – the Americans said that they were prepared to contribute additional material and financial resources in order to increase the alliance's ability to defend itself, but with the proviso that the Europeans were also ready to carry 'their full share',[34] i.e. to make greater efforts of their own.

Charles M. Spofford was given instructions along such lines by the US administration on taking up his post as chairman of the newly formed 'Council of Deputies Committee', consisting of deputies to the foreign ministers of the member states, which met for the first time in London on 25 July 1950.[35] Another of Spofford's instructions is worthy of consideration in view of the title of this essay: he was told to persuade carefully the representatives of the other NATO members to accept the idea of using West Germany's industrial capacity to reinforce and increase the West's defence measures.[36]

Thus a fundamental goal of US alliance policy gradually came to the fore; this issue became both a central and controversial negotiating point within the alliance from the second half of 1950 up to the mid-1950s: the United States was strongly pressing for the Federal Republic of Germany to be integrated into the West, both in military and defensive terms.[37] Although the founding of the North Atlantic Pact, according to the tacit intentions and expectations of its main founding members (the USA, Great Britain and particularly France), was to help among other things to solve the problem of security *against* Germany,[38] the inclusion of West Germany would now decisively improve the West's security situation. Thus the Federal Republic's economic defence contribution paved the way for her military integration into the North American-Western European alliance.[39]

The US administration's first move in this direction, as is well known, was not long in coming. US Secretary of State Acheson, who had taken over in January 1949, set out his famous package of suggestions during talks with his British and French counterparts, Bevin and Schuman, and also at the North Atlantic Council meeting in New York in September 1950. According to this, the United States was prepared to participate in the creation of an integrated NATO military organisation and to increase the number of her troops stationed in Europe, as well as topping-up her financial contribution towards the joint defence programme and providing an American Commander-in-Chief for a future NATO Command in Europe. The condition, however, was that the Western European NATO states also increased their defence efforts and, above all, that they agreed to a military contribution from the Federal Republic of Germany, which the United States wanted and which would be monitored by NATO itself.[40]

Even during the founding and the initial stages of the North Atlantic Alliance, important political and economic developments had taken place in the entire structure of the alliance. These can be seen particularly well in the changes in the relationship between the European Recovery Programme and NATO, as well as in the creation and execution of the US military aid programme. For this reason we will analyse these two aspects in the following two chapters.

On the Relationship between Economic Reconstruction (ERP, OEEC) and the Creation of a Security System (Brussels Treaty, NATO)

In January 1948, during a meeting with the British Ambassador in the USA, Lord Inverchapel, US Under Secretary of State Lovett pointed out that the passage of the European Recovery Programme through Congress might be endangered if someone

Economic Aspects of the Alliance System

came along at the same time with plans for military arrangements connected with Bevin's suggestions for the creation of a Western Union.[41] Immediately following the successful conclusion of the legislative process for the ERP, Senator Vandenberg seems to have felt that he had been placed under pressure by the 'boys in the State Department', as he said in a conversation with a senior official in that department. After he had just managed to get the law for the Marshall Plan passed (using, among others, the argument that this would lessen the danger of war in Europe), he was now faced with the far-reaching request of agreeing to a security pact with Europe.[42]

Indeed, the plans for the formation of a transatlantic alliance did not only meet with approval in the United States. Above all, many experts were concerned that the creation of a military pact would place limits on the ERP, which had barely been created, and would use up much of the resources required for this. Kennan, the Director of the Policy Planning Staff (PPS), was among those who warned most strongly against too great a reliance upon military security measures. In a PPS statement on the conclusion of a North Atlantic Security Pact, on 23 November 1948, he said, among other things:

> A North Atlantic Security Pact will affect the political war only insofar as it operates to stiffen the self-confidence of the Western Europeans in the face of Soviet pressures. Such a stiffening is needed and desirable. But it goes hand in hand with the danger of a general preoccupation with military affairs, to the detriment of economic recovery and of the necessity for seeking a peaceful solution to Europe's difficulties ... we should have clearly in mind that the need for military alliances and rearmament on the part of the Western Europeans is primarily a *subjective* one, arising in their own minds as a result of their failure to understand correctly their own position. Their best and most hopeful course of action, if they are to save themselves from communist pressures, remains the struggle for economic recovery and for internal political stability.
>
> Compared to this, intensive rearmament constitutes an uneconomic and regrettable diversion of effort.[43]

Kennan's warnings did not go unheard, at least for the moment. British Defence Minister Alexander also voiced his doubts in September 1948, during the first meeting with his Brussels Pact counterparts, saying that consideration had to be given to a country's economic situation and strength when allocating the available resources: 'It would be fatal to cripple the economic stability of the Western Union by devoting resources to defence beyond what could be afforded.'[44]

The State Department in Washington, seeing the beginnings of a conflict of interests between economic stabilisation and military security measures, decided that the execution of the European Recovery Programme and the measures started to rebuild the European economy, as well as the continuing economic cooperation between the participants in the Marshall Plan, all had priority over any demands made in connection with the establishment of the North Atlantic Treaty. When Harriman, in his capacity as representative of the Economic Cooperation Administration (ECA) in Paris, wrote to Secretary of State Marshall asking for definitive information on the aims pursued by Washington with the ERP, OEEC and the North Atlantic Treaty,[45] he received a detailed reply from Lovett. In this most illuminating document[46] of 3 December 1948, Lovett pointed out that the United States was still duty bound to the 'idea' of fostering European integration, and wanted to pursue this goal during the next three or four years along four main lines:

> (1) on a fairly broad but practical economic base through the OEEC;
> (2) on a geographically more restricted but probably even more concrete mutual security basis through the Brussels Pact and the North Atlantic Pact;
> (3) on a broad political base, probably vague in form at least in the immediate future, such as the British proposal for a 'Council of Europe' [...];
> (4) through a series of more limited sub-regional groups such as the Benelux Union, a closer drawing together of the Scandinavian countries and a possible French-Italian Customs Union.[47]

Lovett took the view that the United States was really working with two overlapping and complementary concepts, whose most important institutions and instruments were the ERP and the OEEC on the one hand and the North Atlantic Security Alliance on the other. Within this double strategy, he saw the OEEC, 'at least at the present time', as an apolitical, non-military organisation, whose exclusive aim was European economic reconstruction and the fostering of economic integration. On the subject of the relationship between economic recovery and rearmament, he writes 'we feel strongly that economic recovery must not be sacrificed to rearmament and must continue to be given a clear priority'.[48]

This choice of priority in favour of giving preference to European recovery (for the moment at least) can also be found in several other official statements and administration and Congress internal papers from 1949.[49] In an official statement made by the State Department on the occasion of the North Atlantic Treaty's publication, NATO is described as a 'necessary complement' to the comprehensive economic cooperation taking place under the European Recovery Programme. Although there were no formal ties between the two, both institutions would complement each other in the creation of a peaceful, prosperous and stable world. At the same time, the US administration, in conjunction with the founding of NATO, announced the preparation of a military aid programme in which the United States would be able to contribute to the fulfilment of the concept of mutual assistance, as described in Article 3 of the pact, in a 'logical' fashion.[50]

Due to the further development of the 'Military Assistance Programme' in the second half of 1949, it became more and more difficult to keep apart the two US aid programmes for Europe, i.e. economic aid and military aid. The arguments over the relationship between the two were not just a question of rivalry and hierarchical problems of two differing aid programmes, but were rather symbolic for the debate concerning the whole political, economic, military and alliance policy structure of North American-Western European relations, together with the aims and interests at the base of this structure.

The priority conflict between the demands made by economic recovery and the calls for the creation of a transatlantic security system was finally laid to rest, for the time being, by an increasing tendency to favour military and alliance policy requirements, which began with the initial decisions in the autumn of 1949. Several factors played a decisive role in this process.

First, there was the growing fear in the West of the Soviet Union's military potential. As it became known that the United States had lost her lead in atomic weapons, the Western European states, and particularly the US herself, felt that the potential danger presented by the Soviets had increased. The US's uncertainty was increased still more by the defeat of the Nationalists, whom they had supported for years, in the Chinese civil war, and the subsequent foundation of the People's Republic of China. These threat perceptions seemed to be vindicated by

Western interpretations of the outbreak of war in Korea in the summer of 1950. The West saw the conflict as proof of the aggressive nature of Moscow-led world Communism.

However, we must also consider the level of Western European cooperation at that time. The Americans had always stressed that this was to be steered towards economic and political 'integration' by means of the Marshall Plan. In the autumn of 1949 the Americans were most unsatisfied with the results achieved under the European Recovery Programme, and especially with the continuing difficulties the Europeans were having breaking down the trade barriers between them.[51] They particularly complained about the obvious weakness of the OEEC, although they were the ones who had helped prevent it becoming a clearing-house for independent Western European efforts towards integration. The sterling crisis, which had led to a drastic 30.5 per cent devaluation against the US dollar in September 1949, and which had resulted in a general wave of devaluation, proved once again that Britain's position of power and influence in the postwar world was severely shaken.[52] For this reason Washington was annoyed at the British Labour government's cool attitude towards European efforts towards integration. In a sharp exchange of notes at the end of October 1949, Acheson let it be known to his British counterpart that he would have welcomed a somewhat more positive attitude from London towards this fundamental question, so important for the future of the Western world.[53]

In view of the changed balance of power between East and West, and the increased need for security in the West, but also due to her disappointment over the lack of, or (as the US saw it) slow pace of European integration, the Americans sought a new direction in their European policy. They needed a concept which would give the US administration a better chance of steering the course of events in a direction suited to US interests. It was obvious that the various, often uncoordinated transatlantic economic and security relations had to be brought together under a military and security umbrella put up by the US herself. From her point of view this plan had the advantage that the United States, as the leading Western Alliance power, could demand and expect more loyalty from the Western Europeans, pointing to the seemingly indisputable need to cooperate on security matters.

It was Harriman who voiced such ideas during the meeting[54] between the foremost US ambassadors accredited in the

Economic Aspects of the Alliance System

European capitals, held in Paris on 21 and 22 October 1949, and who therefore put together a new US foreign-policy strategy. Regarding the well-known British attitude to European integration and the OEEC, he pointed out:

> that the approach of the US to this problem might best be made not from the purely economic or the purely political standpoint but from the standpoint of security which was the most important thing both with us and to the Europeans. Much could be done by the US under the security umbrella but the ways and means require careful consideration. In the first place, the security organization must not be considered simply a military problem.[55]

Elsewhere in the documentation, Harriman reiterated this view with the following suggestion:

> The Atlantic Pact concept should be the umbrella under which all measures agreed upon should be taken; that security, and not economic or political integration, should be the point of departure of our policy.[56]

World events and a certain over-eagerness on the part of some government agencies in Washington and Western Europe led to Harriman's outline concept being put into effect the very next year, possibly far more quickly and rigorously than he might have contemplated, in the form of a comprehensive 'militarization' of transatlantic alliance relations. When, during the fourth session of the North Atlantic Council, which ended on 18 May 1950, the Economic and Finance Committee of NATO was charged with finding out how funds for additional military expenditure could be raised, it was asked to consider not only the prevailing economic and financial conditions but also the necessity of an increased defence demand.[57]

A few weeks before this, the Pentagon had made the suggestion that the US economic and military foreign aid programmes be combined to form a single effective instrument.[58] Within the ECA in Washington, too, there had been thoughts on how best to use the economic capacity of the most important participants in the Marshall Plan (including West Germany) in order to speed the build-up of Western military and defensive potential.[59] Then, as the Korean War broke out on 25 June 1950, the relationship between economic reconstruction and rearmament was defined anew within a short period of time, with the latter gaining the upper hand, as well as quickening the pace of NATO's formation. Only four weeks or so after the alarming events in the Far East, the US embassies in Europe were being instructed by the State Department to comply with and put into effect the new security-policy aims.[60] At the same time the Consultative Council of the Brussels Pact discovered that its earlier decision to give priority to economic reconstruction no longer met the requirements of the new situation.[61] The European Recovery Programme was, therefore, being increasingly transformed into an aid programme for the military build-up of the North Atlantic-Western European alliance system.

The forced pace of change in favour of increased rearmament and the build-up of the North Atlantic Pact, caused by the war in Korea, also had an obvious effect on the still-unclear relationship between the OEEC and NATO. After the Brussels Pact institutions had also tried from the beginning to examine their links with the OEEC, but without success, the new priorities forced both bodies to attempt to 'solve' the problem of hierarchy by more or less giving the OEEC a subordinate role as an aid organisation.[62] Since the OEEC existed as a catalyst for European integration, a necessary body in itself, the US administration reasoned internally that the member states not (as yet) in NATO were also able to make a silent contribution to Western defence efforts. This pragmatic attitude, however, could not hide the fact that no convincing overall solution could be found to the problem of organising economic- and security-policy cooperation between North America and Western Europe during the initial phase of NATO.

The Significance of US Military Aid

The basic economic-policy problems within the NATO alliance also came to the fore when drawing up and conducting US military aid programmes for the Western European members of NATO. In the United States the question had been asked, since 1947, whether the US administration should not support countries whose inner stability or outer security were seen to be endangered by means of military aid programmes. While President Truman, in his famous Congress speech of 12 March

1947, pointed out that aid to be given by the US to 'free peoples' was to consist mainly of economic and financial support, the bulk of the $400 million allocated to Greece and Turkey was used for military purposes.[63]

In 1948 sections of the US administration were becoming increasingly sure that there was no way the US could avoid meeting the strong demands from various Western European states for material support for their armies and for military equipment. At the beginning of July 1948 the US National Security Council made a positive recommendation in this respect (NSC 14/1).[64] From then on it was a *fait accompli* that the formation of a transatlantic security alliance would be dependent upon the provision of US military aid.

Throughout the negotiations on the North Atlantic Treaty, and even afterwards, the Washington administration did not miss an opportunity to make clear to their European partners that military aid would not be without conditions, and that it would be dependent upon demonstrably increased efforts from the Europeans themselves. When Paul Nitze, then Deputy of the Assistant Secretary of State for Economic Affairs, returned from a fact-finding mission in Paris and London concerning the 'Military Assistance Programme', in January 1949, and reported that there had been no noticeable efforts on the part of the Western Union countries to increase their military budgets,[65] more pressure was placed upon the future allies. Nitze favoured a kind of 'carrot and stick' policy, whereby the Europeans would only be offered aid if they could prove that they had increased their self-help measures. Therefore the Brussels Pact states were advised to present the US with a jointly agreed and reasonable application, in which the principle of mutual assistance was taken into account. In other words, the US was not prepared to begin a new 'lend-lease' programme, but rather was thinking of real 'mutual aid'.[66] This principle was also explained by the Americans in that Washington expected the right to use military bases, transit rights and the provision of certain services by individual recipient countries in return for military aid.[67]

After talks between the countries involved, it was agreed that the Europeans were to put their official aid claim to the US immediately after signing the North Atlantic Treaty, which they did on 5 April 1949.[68] Prior to this the Brussels Pact countries had, after long negotiation, agreed to augment their military expenditure for the fiscal year 1949–50 to the equivalent of $200 million in total, and that Great Britain was to contribute $105 million, France $55 million, Belgium/Luxembourg $30 million and The Netherlands $10 million. For 1950–1 they planned to double this amount to a total of $400 million.[69]

On Acheson's advice, President Truman did not present Congress with the draft plan for the military-aid bill until after the ratification of the North Atlantic Treaty was completed on 25 July 1949. After difficult and controversial debates in both Houses of Congress, Truman was able to promulgate the 'Mutual Assistance Act (1949)' on 6 October 1949.[70] The Act provided for a total of $1 billion of military aid to the NATO states in fiscal year 1950 (title I); in addition, Greece and Turkey (title II) and, furthermore, certain other non-European countries (title III) were also to receive military aid on a smaller scale.[71]

The funds allocated to the NATO states however, were bound by the condition that only $100 million of this sum was available at that time. The remaining $900 million was not to be released until the US President had given the go-ahead for recommendations on an integrated defence of the North Atlantic Treaty area, which were to be decided upon by the North Atlantic Council and the NATO Defence Committee.

Because of this built-in barrier on the use of the funds, the NATO states felt even more obliged to develop a basic policy concept for a common defence as soon as possible. After the NATO Council had passed such a concept during its third session on 6 January 1950, President Truman accepted this defence plan on 27 January 1950 and released the $900 million of military aid for the NATO states.[72]

The proviso for the shipment of military equipment from the United States, made possible under this law, and also for other US involvement in the costs of military rearmament and infrastructure programmes (including so-called offshore procurement requests)[73] was the conclusion of bilateral treaties between the United States and each recipient country. These treaties, formulated under the auspices of the 'Mutual Defence Assistance Programme' (MDAP), were also signed on 27 January 1950 by eight NATO countries.[74] Washington's insistence on bilateral treaties caused some doubts even within the US administration itself. Thus Harriman, for example, considered negotiations on a bilateral basis to be somewhat at odds with the publicly pro-

Economic Aspects of the Alliance System

Figure 17.1 US economic and military aid

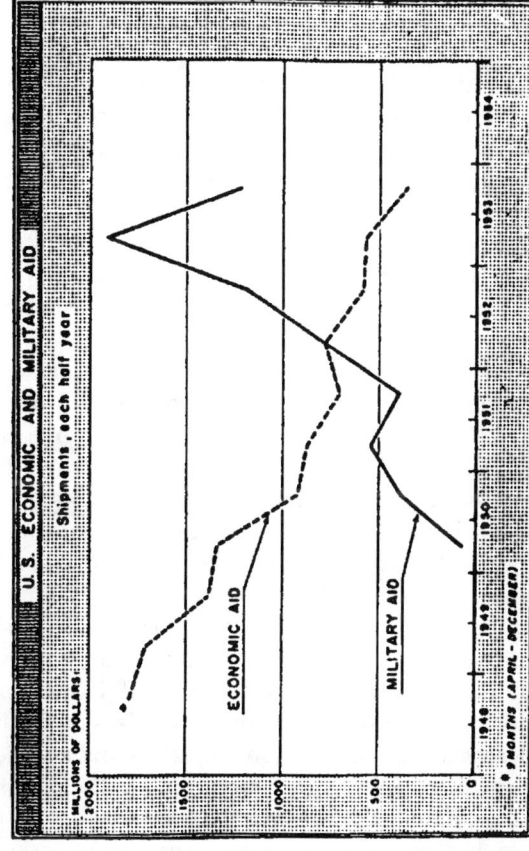

Note
ECONOMIC AID – Value of shipments of food, fuel, industrial raw materials, fertilisers, machinery and equipment, etc., plus $ payments for industrial development projects, technical assistance, contributions to the European Payments Union, and other forms of economic and financial aid to European NATO countries; does not include Intermediate Type Aid.
MILITARY AID – Value of weapons, ammunition and other military equipment supplied to European countries; does not include Intermediate Type Aid or training programmes. Includes relatively small amounts for non-NATO countries in Europe, Near East and Africa.
Source: Ismay, NATO (see Note 1), p. 137

claimed concept of partnership and equality between the Brussels Pact states and the US. However, his view that the US should have the final say on her foreign aid concurred totally with the prevailing opinion at the top of both administration and Congress.[75]

In any case, the above process was not exactly designed to support European efforts toward unity, which had hitherto been so favoured and encouraged by the United States. Also, the US military advisors sent to each recipient country to supervise the military aid only served to strengthen the impression shared by many that NATO and MDAP had really just become symbols of Western Europe's far-reaching dependence on the United States.[76] Critics on the left saw the alliance, equally kept alive by military aid, as mainly a system whereby the US plan to dominate the Old World was thinly veiled by the concept of partnership. Even smaller NATO, allies meanwhile, had fought bitterly against what they saw as US interference in their affairs, even if they were clearly wrong, as Holland was in the Indonesian question.[77]

At the same time, of course, the European NATO states were extremely interested in additional US military aid, and finally accepted almost all of the conditions imposed upon this.[78] However, when (after the outbreak of the Korean War in 1950) the sum of around $1 billion allocated to the NATO states for the second year of the programme was topped up by an additional claim, presented on 1 August 1950, for no less than $4 billion (of which the Europeans were to receive $3,504,000,000), the negative side to the military build-up being pushed forward by the US became clear. The hectic rearmament programmes and the massive increase in military expenditure (see Table 17.2) led within a short time to shortages of raw materials, price rises and other inflationary indicators, balance-of-payments crises and a variety of other economic difficulties, from which some of the affected countries had a long, hard task to recover.[79]

It is no surprise that, because of massive rearmament and militarisation, as well as an exorbitant increase in the military-aid programme, the civilian Marshall Plan for Europe receded more and more into the background. The preamble to the 'Mutual Defence Assistance Act' of 1949 still read 'that economic recovery is essential to international peace and security and must be given clear priority',[80] but, as a result of the Korean conflict, the already noticeable change in favour of a strengthening of military assistance and build-up plans seems to have been unstoppable. Due to increasing changes of plan, priorities or simple misuse of civilian economic aid, the US military foreign aid programmes soon gained the upper hand (see Figure 17.1).[81] In the end not even the former supporters of the ERP raised any objections to the economic and military sides of US foreign aid being merged into one single programme. The corresponding 'Mutual Security Act of 1951' came into effect on 10 October of that year.[82]

Summary and Conclusion

The mere fact that military expenditure was such a large part of each alliance partner's budget in the year in which NATO was created (in the United States it was 34 per cent of the budget, and in Western Europe it averaged 20 per cent), makes it clear that the formation and completion of a collective defence system had to have a great effect upon the plans made by each individual economy, as well as upon economic relations between the allied states. From the beginning the partners had great difficulty trying to develop ways and means of deciding how much of a defence contribution each country should make on the basis of her economic capabilities. The alliance bodies charged with this task had still not come to any decision by the end of 1950. The activities of the Defence Production and Economic and Finance Committees, which, between 1950 and the start of 1951, had either been renamed or newly formed, gives yet another indication of how hard it was to come to grips with this problem within the bounds of an integrated security policy.

Although the United States played a major role both in the economic reconstruction of the industrial states of Western Europe and in the creation of the North Atlantic Alliance, she did not succeed in building up a corresponding transatlantic economic organisation. From the beginning it was not possible to make NATO into a comprehensive 'Atlantic community', as was mentioned in Article 2 of the North Atlantic Treaty. The lack of correspondence between the security and economic systems resulted in great strains in relations between the United States and Western Europe even during the initial phase. This did nothing to lessen the US' supremacy within the Western Alliance, however. With her comparatively huge economic and financial power, together with her superior military potential, the United States was at all times able to impose her views on any obligations to the alliance to which she might have agreed.

The foreign policy of the United States with respect to NATO and European politics did not stem from some prior master plan. It was certainly determined by fairly constant basic interests, but was often pursued in a 'trial and error' fashion and was sometimes full of inconsistencies. Often the United States would demand favours or actions from her alliance partners which she was not prepared to perform herself. This was especially true in the case of the attempt to persuade the Europeans to give up their national right to decide how to use their resources in favour of strengthening a joint defence policy. Washington's use of bilateral treaties in allocating economic and military aid was also inconsistent with her attempt to push her Western European partners towards the creation of an integrated economic unit in Europe.

However, it was mainly due to the Europeans themselves that the many attempts to achieve European unity during the period covered by this essay had only limited success. They obviously had great problems in trimming their foreign policy and foreign trade interests to definite Western European cooperation, and also at the same time to a transatlantic security partnership with the USA and Canada. In view of their obvious economic weakness, they pinned their hopes rather too much upon the US' generosity. In doing this they often failed to reconcile their own security interests with the necessary wish to cooperate and the capacity to persuade both the USA and themselves. The persistent refusal of Great Britain to make a serious contribution to Western Europe's attempts to form a community, the timid delaying tactics employed by France in the urgent solution of the German question, or The Netherlands' injured reaction to the US' demand that she end Dutch colonial rule in Indonesia: all these simply increased the dependence of the European NATO partners upon the United States.

During the initial phase of the Western Alliance, the alliance partners on both sides of the Atlantic made efforts to keep a balance between the economic reconstruction and stabilisation aims of the ERP and the steps taken by both the Brussels Pact and NATO towards a system of military and alliance security policy. This delicate balance between 'Economic Recovery' and 'Military

Security' fell apart in favour of the latter as the US, with the general approval of her partners, made the build-up and integration of NATO and increased rearmament the foremost aims of the alliance as a result of the Korean War. The accompanying overemphasis on security requirements was an attempt and, at the same time, a temptation to use an inflated military policy as a way of integrating the North American-Western European alliance system. However, the events of the Korean crisis also show that such a policy can lead to a worrying overloading and weakening of the alliance partners' economies and thus to a dangerous undermining of the alliance's economic base.

Notes

1. In this essay I mostly draw on the following important works on the creation of the North American-Western European alliance system: Lord Ismay, *NATO: The First Five Years 1949–1954*, Utrecht, 1954; Ernst-Otto Czempiel, *Das amerikanische Sicherheitssystem 1945–1949. Studie zur Außenpolitik der bürgerlichen Gesellschaft*, Berlin, 1966; Escott Reid, *Time of Fear and Hope: The Making of the North Atlantic Treaty 1947–1949*, Toronto, 1977; Alan K. Henrikson, 'The creation of the North Atlantic Alliance, 1948–1952', in *Naval War College Review*, 32, 1980, pp. 4–39; Timothy P. Ireland, *Creating the Entangling Alliance: The Origins of the North Atlantic Treaty Organization*, London, 1981; Lawrence S. Kaplan, *The United States and NATO: The Formative Years*, Lexington, 1984; as well as: *The Private Papers of Senator Vandenberg*, A. H. Vandenberg Jr. (ed.), with the collaboration of Joe Alex Morris, Boston, 1952; George F. Kennan, *Memoirs 1925–1950*, Boston, Toronto, 1967; Dean Acheson, *Present at the Creation: My Years in the State Department*, New York, 1969; Charles E. Bohlen, *Witness to History 1929–1969*, New York, 1973.
2. Among the older studies on this subject, I refer to the following: Lincoln Gordon, 'Economic aspects of coalition diplomacy – The NATO experience', in *International Organization*, vol. 10, 1956, pp. 529–43; Ronald S. Ritchie, *NATO: The Economics of an Alliance*, Toronto, 1956. On the problem of burden-sharing, see Gavin Kennedy, *Burden Sharing in NATO*, London, 1979. A special examination of the US aid programme in the light of the development of the entire alliance was provided by: Lawrence S. Kaplan, *A*

Community of Interests: NATO and the Military Assistance Program, 1948–1951, Washington, 1980 (Office of the Secretary of Defence, Historical Office). Almost all historians tending towards the revisionist approach to research have covered more or less comprehensively the economic problems connected with the build-up of NATO. As an example of several other studies in this field see Joyce and Gabriel Kolko, *The Limits of Power: The World and United States Foreign Policy, 1945–1954,* New York, Evanston, San Francisco, London, 1972.
3. Cf. Ritchie, *NATO* (see Note 2), p. 97.
4. A note from Kennan to the Secretary of State dated 20.1.1948 reads (among other things): 'Military union should not be the starting point. It should flow from the political, economic and spiritual union – not vice versa.' In *Foreign Relations of the United States,* Diplomatic Papers, 1945–1950, Washington 1967–1980, FRUS, 1948, III, p. 7; Cf. also ibid., p. 7f., 108f., 283–9, especially p. 285.
5. Details concerning the 'architects' of the North Atlantic Treaty, and the role of the two Senators in Reid, *Time of Fear and Hope* (see Note 1), pp. 62–9, 87–98.
6. On this point cf. Gordon, *Economic Aspects* (see Note 2), p. 531.
7. Ibid., p. 537f.; Ismay, *NATO* (see Note 1), p. 28, 39–48.
8. *NATO – Basic Documents,* NATO (ed.), Information Service, Brussels, 1981, p. 10.
9. Cf. on this point the extensive documentation in FRUS, 1948, III, p. 1f.
10. The Secretary of State to the Embassy in France, 27.2.1948, ibid., p. 34.
11. English text in *American Foreign Policy 1950–1955: Basic Documents,* Department of State (ed.), vol. I, Washington, 1957 (Department of State Publication 6446), pp. 968–71.
12. Minutes of the Second Meeting of the United States-United Kingdom-Canada Security Conversations, held at Washington, 23.3.1948, in FRUS, 1948, III, p. 64f., quotation p. 65; 'Pentagon Paper', ibid., pp. 72–5.
13. Memorandum of Conversation, by the Under-Secretary of State (Lovett), 27.4.1948, ibid., pp. 104–8; the Director of the Policy Planning Staff (Kennan) to the Under Secretary of State (Lovett), 7.5.1948, ibid., p. 116f.; Report by the National Security Council, 28.6.1948, ibid., p. 140f.; memorandum by the Director of the Joint Staff (Gruenther) to the Director of the Office of European Affairs (Hickerson), 16.7.1948, ibid., pp. 188–93; memorandum of conversation by Bohlen to the Secretary of State, 6.8.1948, ibid., p. 206f.
14. Senate Resolution 239, 11.6.1948, text ibid., p. 135f. Also the following hearings: The Vandenberg Resolution and the North Atlantic Treaty, hearings held in executive session before the Committee on Foreign Relations, US Senate, 80th Cong., 2nd sess., on S. Res. 239 and 81st Cong., 1st sess., on Executive L, The North Atlantic Treaty, Washington 1973 (Historical Series).

15. 'Washington Paper' (9.9.1948), in FRUS, 1948, III, pp. 237–48, esp. p. 244, 246.
16. Ibid., pp. 333–43.
17. Text of treaty in FRUS, 1949, IV, pp. 281–5.
18. *NATO – Basic Documents* (see Note 8), p. 293.
19. Cf. on the treaty duties prior to the *casus foederis* Knut Ipsen, *Rechtsgrundlagen und Institutionalisierung der Atlantisch-Westeuropäischen Verteidigung*, Hamburg, 1967, p. 35f.
20. On this point see below, paragraph on 'The significance of US Military Aid'.
21. FRUS, 1948, III, p. 226, 245, 316f., 337; FRUS, 1949, IV, p. 85f.; FRUS, 1950, III, p. 116. On this point see also Reid, *Time of Fear and Hope* (see Note 1), p. 57, 68, 82, 133–42, 167–84.
22. FRUS, 1948, III, p. 226.
23. Cf. on the interpretation of Article 2 also Ipsen, *Rechtsgrundlagen* (see Note 19), p. 33f.
24. Brussels Treaty Organization: Minutes and Documents of the First Meeting of the Ministers of Defence, Paris, 27 September 1948, DG 1/5/30, ditto on the second meeting of the defence ministers on 14.1.1949 in Brussels, DG 1/5/31, ditto for the third meeting on 7.4.1949 in The Hague, DG 1/5/32, where the last document contains extensive information on the build-up of the Brussels Pact armed forces (all files and documents on the activities of the Brussels Five-Power Pact in the period from April 1948 to December 1950, which have been made available for inspection since 1981 or 1984 in the Public Record Office, London (PRO), were provided by Colonel Dr Norbert Wiggershaus of the Militärgeschichtliches Forschungsamt (Military History Research Office) in Freiburg, to whom I am most grateful).
25. PRO, Brussels Treaty Organization: minutes and Documents of the (4th) Meeting of the Ministers of Defence, Luxembourg, 15 and 16 July 1949, DG 1/5/33, pp. 3–6.
26. PRO, Brussels Treaty Organization: minutes of the (6th) Meeting of the Ministers of Defence, London, 5 September 1950, DG 1/5/35, p. 1.
27. PRO, Brussels Treaty Organization: minutes and Documents of the 4th Meeting (see Note 25), p. 6.
28. The term was first used by Kennan and referred to those states which because of their geographical position could have the function of a take-off point in the event of a war, FRUS, 1948, III, p. 226f., 304.
29. 'Treaty of Peace with Italy, 10 February 1947 (Summary)', in *A Decade of American Foreign Policy: Basic Documents 1941–1949*, Department of State (ed.), revised edn: Washington 1985 (Department of State Publication 9443), pp. 402–9.
30. Ismay, *NATO* (see Note 1), p. 25f.

31. Draft Report on Progress in Implementing the North Atlantic Treaty, 27.4.1950, in FRUS, 1950, III, pp. 72–5.
32. Memorandum for the Secretary of Defence (Johnson), 13.7.1950, ibid., p. 133f.
33. Text of NSC 68 (14.4.1950) in FRUS, 1950, I, pp. 234–92; for the origins of NSC 68 see Paul Y. Hammond, NSC 68: 'Prologue to Rearmament', in Warner R. Schilling, Paul Y. Hammond and G. H. Snyder, *Strategy, Politics, and Defense Budgets*, New York, 1962, pp. 267–378.
34. As in FRUS, 1950, III, p. 134.
35. Memorandum of conversation by the Secretary of State, 21.7.1950, ibid., p. 136f.
36. The Secretary of State to the Embassy in France, 1.8.1950, FRUS, 1950, III, p. 172f. This policy had been followed by the US administration since the spring of 1950: e.g. circular telegram from Acheson: the Secretary of State to Certain Diplomatic Offices, 27.3.1950, ibid. p. 34, and: The Ambassador in the United Kingdom (Douglas) to the Secretary of State, 14.4.1950, ibid., p. 50f. Also: the Secretary of State to the United States High Commissioner for Germany (McCloy), at Frankfurt, 18.10.1950, ibid., p. 389f.t
37. A top secret memorandum by the US Secretary of State concerning a meeting with the President on 31.7.1950 states among other things that: 'The question was not whether Germany should be brought into the general defensive plan but rather how this could be done without disrupting anything else we were doing and without putting Germany into a position to act as the balance of power in Europe,' in FRUS, 1950, III, p. 167f.
38. FRUS, 1948, III, p. 34, 80, 122, 138, 142, 308f., 327; FRUS, 1949, IV, p. 109, 490; FRUS, 1950, III, p. 60.
39. On this point Norbert Wiggershaus, Überlegungen und Pläne für eine militärische Integration Westdeutschlands 1948–1952', in *Kalter Krieg und Deutsche Frage: Deutschland im Widerstreit der Mächte 1945–1952*, Josef Foschepoth (ed.), Göttingen-Zürich, 1985, pp. 314–34.
40. FRUS, 1950, III, pp. 285–610, 1188–301. The events are analysed in detail by Norbert Wiggershaus, 'Die Entscheidung für einen westdeutschen Verteidigungsbeitrag 1950', in *Anfänge westdeutscher Sicherheitspolitik 1945–1956*, vol. 1: *Von der Kapitulation bis zum Pleven-Plan*, von Roland G. Foerster, Christian Greiner, Georg Meyer, Hans-Jürgen Rautenberg und Norbert Wiggershaus, Munich, Vienna, 1982, pp. 325–402.
41. FRUS, 1948, III, p. 13. Cf. also memorandum of conversation by the Director of the Office of European Affairs (Hickerson), 7.2.1948, ibid., p. 22.
42. Reid (see Note 1), p. 89.

43. FRUS, 1948, III, p. 285 (italics in original).
44. PRO, Brussels Treaty Organization: minutes and documents of the First Meeting of the Ministers of Defence, Paris, 27 September 1948, DG 1/5/30, p. 3.
45. FRUS, 1948, III, p. 283.
46. Ibid., pp. 300–10.
47. Ibid., p. 302.
48. Ibid., p. 305.
49. As in e.g. FRUS, 1949, IV, p. 111f., 147f.
50. Ibid., p. 240f.
51. The Administrator for Economic Cooperation (Hoffman) to the United States Special Representative in Europe (Harriman), 6.10.1949, ibid., pp. 426–9; the Secretary of State to the Embassy in the United Kingdom, 14.10.1949, ibid., p. 429f.; the Ambassador in the United Kingdom (Douglas) to the Secretary of State, 18.10.1949, ibid., p. 430f. The Ambassador in the United Kingdom (Douglas) to the Secretary of State, 26.10.1949, ibid., p. 435f. See also on this point the speech made by the Adminstrator of the ECA, Hoffman, to the OEEC Council on 31.10.1949 in Paris. The text is contained in *A Decade of American Foreign Policy* (see Note 29), pp. 852–5, also FRUS, 1949, IV, pp. 438–50.
52. On the background to the difference of opinion between the US and Britain on the subject of the latter's role in the postwar international system, and the ambivalent attitude of the US to London: R. B. Manderson-Jones, *The Special Relationship: Anglo-American Relations and Western European Unity 1947–56*, London, 1972, here esp. pp. 56–63.
53. FRUS, 1949, IV, pp. 346–9.
54. Documentation of these very interesting ambassadorial talks on the political situation in Europe, ibid., pp. 469–96 and 342f.
55. Ibid., p. 489.
56. Ibid., p. 494.
57. Kaplan, *A Community* (see note 2), p. 88, 94f.; the Secretary of State to the President, 18.5.1950, in FRUS, 1950, III, p. 123f.
58. FRUS, 1950, III, pp. 43–8.
59. See the secret ECA study entitled 'The Potential Military Contribution of the ERP Countries to the Common Defense of the West and its Cost to the United States', 22 May 1950, in National Archives and Records Service: Modern Military Branch, Washington DC (NA, MMB), Record Group (RG) 286, Box 2, Agency for International Development, ECA, Office of the Deputy Administrator, General Subject Files of the Mutual Security Program, 1950–51.
60. The Secretary of State to Certain Diplomatic Offices, 22.7.1950, in FRUS, 1950, III, pp. 138–41.

61. PRO, Record of the Ninth Session of the Consultative Council, The Hague, 1 August 1950, DG 1/1/2, p. 16.
62. Concerning the strained relations between the OEEC and NATO see e.g. FRUS, 1950, III, p. 324f., 659–72, 682–91.
63. Kaplan, *A Community* (see Note 2), pp. 6–9.
64. The Position of the United States with Respect to Providing Military Assistance to Nations of the Non-Soviet World, 1.7.1948, in FRUS, 1948, I, Part 2, pp. 585–8.
65. FRUS, 1949, IV, pp. 54–9.
66. The Secretary of State to the Embassy in the United Kingdom, 16.2.1949, ibid., pp. 110–13, and memorandum by Ambassadors Caffery and Harriman to the French Minister of Foreign Affairs (Schuman), 3.3.1949, ibid., p. 148f.
67. The Ambassador in the United Kingdom (Douglas) to the Secretary of State, 2.3.1949, ibid., pp. 136–9.
68. Ibid., p. 285f., and the US Government's answer of 6.4.1949 to the aid request by the Brussels Pact states, ibid., p. 287f.
69. PRO, Minutes of the Fifth Session of the Consultative Council, held in London, 14–15 March 1949, DG 1/1/1.
70. Important background material can be found in *US House of Representatives, Committee on International Relations: Military Assistance Programs*, Part I, Mutual Defense Assistance Act of 1949, Selective Executive Session Hearings of the Committee, 1943–50, vol. V, Washington, 1976 and ——, Part 2, Extension of the Mutual Defense Assistance Act of 1949 (...), vol. VI, Washington, 1976.
71. The text of this act is printed in Kaplan, *A Community* (see Note 2), pp. 214–22; excerpts also in *A Decade of American Foreign Policy* (see Note 29), pp. 957–63.
72. FRUS, 1949, IV, pp. 352–6; FRUS, 1950, III, p. 1f., 12.
73. In the case of so-called offshore procurement contracts, the USA bought arms and other equipment from the European allies and offered them to the same or other member countries at no cost.
74. On 27.1.1950 bilateral treaties were concluded with Belgium, Denmark, France, Italy, Luxemburg, The Netherlands, Norway and the United Kingdom as part of the MDAP.
75. FRUS, 1949, IV, p. 247f.; cf. also the opinions of US Ambassador Douglas, ibid., p. 250f.
76. On this point cf. Kaplan, *A Community* (see Note 2), pp. 60–5.
77. The US administration emphasised several times that military aid to The Netherlands could be dependent upon their resolving the Indonesian conflict according to the decisions made by the UNO Security Council: FRUS, 1949, IV, p. 163, 178f, 258–61, 267f. Cf. also Kaplan, *A Community* (see Note 2), p. 29f.
78. However, following a request by the Europeans, the clauses in the bilateral MDAP treaties governing the controls on the export of war

matériel and other strategically important goods (Article 7 of the draft treaty) were dropped, although the premise was that another method would be devised in order to keep checks on this form of East-West trade. On this point see Kaplan, *A Community* (see Note 2), pp. 62–5; FRUS, 1950, III, p. 9.
79. On the recovery from the Korean crisis in the case of the Federal Republic of Germany: *Die Korea-Krise als ordnungspolitische Herausforderung der deutschen Wirtschaftspolitik: Texte und Dokumente*, Mit Beiträgen von Karl Carstens, Otmar Emminger et al., Stuttgart, New York, 1986 (this book is based on a symposium held by the Ludwig-Erhard-Stiftung on 7.11.1984 in Bonn).
80. Kaplan, *A Community* (see Note 2), p. 214.
81. On this point cf. Imanuel Wexler, *The Marshall Plan Revisited: The European Recovery Program in Economic Perspective*, Westport, London, 1983, p. 69.
82. The text of this act can be found in Kaplan, *A Community* (see Note 2), pp. 224–39.

18
The Problem of West German Military Integration, 1948–1950[1]

Norbert Wiggershaus

Towards the end of 1947 Ernest Bevin, the British Foreign Secretary, formulated ideas on an Atlantic-European defence system for the US State Department. In this connection, he considered the later entry of Spain and Germany into the system, in spite of the latter being *de facto* divided, since he thought 'no Western system can be complete' without them.[2] Taking up this suggestion, Foreign Office officials included Spain and Germany's entry into a West European defence system in their Green Paper, 'as soon as the circumstances permit'.[3]

These words, spoken two and a half years after the end of the Second World War, were extremely courageous, if not daring, even if they were not for public consumption. This is especially true when one considers the plans to totally demilitarise Germany for decades, if not permanently; the measures taken against the danger of renewed German 'militarism'; and also in the face of the countless war victims and the vicious material and psychological wounds suffered by countries under German occupation.

These words were undoubtedly the immediate result of the now obvious 'cold war', the seemingly inevitable division of Europe,[4] and the opposing bipolar system of postwar relations, which had by then assumed the shape it was to retain for forty years. Seen in the long term, developments and considerations in this respect indeed pointed towards the likelihood of including West Germany in a European-Atlantic military alliance. There was the political integration of West Germany into the Western world, which had already begun, the American plans for a West German defensive bulwark against increasing Soviet influence (a key element in the success of the Marshall Plan)[5] and, finally, the intention of continually making sure West Germany stayed in the Western camp. This last point turned out to be of 'great importance',[6] as it was thus possible to counteract any possible Soviet-German overtures.[7]

The tricky question of a German contribution to the defence of Western Europe first came to the fore during secret Western military talks.[8] However, the crises during the East-West conflict soon drew the attention of the international press. The open discussion reached its first climax at the end of 1948 because of the Berlin blockade. In the face of the successful Soviet atomic bomb test in the autumn of 1949 and the potential stalemate between East and West in atomic terms which made it more necessary to have conventional armed forces and to strengthen these before the West's atomic lead disappeared, and with it the element of deterrence, politicians made a growing contribution to the discussion.[9]

In many cases this discussion was based upon a precise and sober estimate of the threat posed by Soviet military might. On the one hand, the peacetime Red Army strength of 175 divisions, with twenty two of them between the Rivers Elbe and Oder, had to be seen as threatening in itself, if one compared it to the twelve or thirteen combat-ready Western divisions. Thus Western strategic plans would have had to envisage the beginning of an adequate defence of Europe on the Rhine or even in the Pyrenees. On the other hand, there were no immediate signs of Soviet expansionist intentions or preparations, and none were expected in the immediate future (apart from subversive activities and political and economic pressure). Thus Lieutenant-General (retired) Adolf Heusinger, among others, was convinced that the Soviet Union would be fully cognisant of the risks involved in a preventive war against Western Europe, and thus thought it unlikely that they would attack. His reason for this was the United States' atomic superiority which he believed deterred the Eastern superpower, together with the need for a massive presence on both flanks (Italy and Scandinavia) in order to cover an assault on the central and Western European area. In Heusinger's opinion the Russian line during the final phase of the Berlin crisis of 1948–9 was a moderate one. It is true that many Western politicians and military observers, considering the developments in Soviet power politics in her East European forward zone, thought that the Kremlin would, in the long term, make offensive use of her military potential when the time was right. As far as can be seen from the available sources, the Soviets' own security requirements were not taken into consideration at that time.[10]

Public discussions up to the end of 1949 encompassed almost the full spectrum of opinions and possibilities for the inclusion of West Germany in Western Europe's defence plans.[11] The military's main argument was that Soviet conventional superiority could only be balanced out by the addition of West German forces.[12] The politicians argued that the main issue was the intention to tie West Germany to the West on a long-term basis. From the economic point of view this was important because it meant that the Western Allies could, on the one hand, reduce their own spending and, on the other, put pressure on Germany as a potential trade competitor.

However, there were also negative reactions to this proposal. The arguments against a West German defence contribution were mostly of a political nature, ranging from concern about a renewed German threat to world peace, via the argument against making the division of Germany permanent, the resulting worsening of the cold war and the worries about conflict within the alliance, to fears about West German democracy taking a wrong turn as a result of rearmament.

Since even the initial phase of West Germany's economic and political integration into the Western camp followed the basic principles of supervised, gradual progression, and since there were strong objections to West German rearmament, any future German military contribution to the containment of the Soviet Union was only feasible under the strictest supervision.

Indeed, almost all suggestions concerning West German rearmament started from the assumption that the country would contribute as a fully-'integrated' member of the alliance. In addition, at the base of all these plans was the unspoken proviso that the German military potential would never be fully exploited.[13]

The international public debate on West Germany's defence contribution in 1948–9 was already moving along the same lines. Those presenting possible ways of including West Germany in a military sense were convinced of the need to take measures to prevent this military force from being abused. It was unanimously agreed that a national German armed force and German independent arms production were to be rejected. Thus planning concentrated, on the one hand, upon German divisions or a contingent within an international army, and on the other on using Germans as mercenaries, or even limiting the German contribution to a joint defence posture to a financial and economic role. In mid-1949, long before the question of German elements was raised at cabinet or international conference level, the Dutch government issued a warning on the subject. We may assume that this was a reaction to repeated statements made by senior officers within the Brussels Treaty military organisation. For example, Field Marshal Montgomery, Chairman of the Western Union Standing Defence Committee, voiced the opinion that West Germany should be admitted to the Western Union, and later to NATO itself.[14] French officers on the Brussels Treaty military staffs were of like mind, and even US representatives at Western Union headquarters brought up the question of a German contribution in the Standing Committee.

In the end it took the political committees to stop the Military Committee from having a sub-committee examine the matter.[15] In any case The Netherlands sent a memorandum[16] to the Brussels Pact Organisation, in which the reconstruction of Germany was described as a risk and as an additional danger to European security. Two wars had been proof enough of the deadly threat posed by an undivided Germany. Based on a historically manifest German tendency to orient herself towards the East, the Dutch authors conjured up the danger of an agreement between the Germans and the Soviets. The Hague recommended that, in order to guard against unpleasant developments, the occupation of Germany should be maintained until Western Europe's military and political position had been sufficiently strengthened, as well as suggesting that armed forces and war matériel production on German soil be banned. At the same time, the planned West German state should be integrated as closely as possible into the Western democratic system.

The Dutch lead definitely played a role in West German rearmament not becoming an official subject for discussion within the Brussels Treaty military organisation. It was inevitable that the West Germans would also take up the question brought to them from outside. This was due to the fact that their status was sensitive to the conflict between East and West. West Germany would be the first potential battleground in any war and, in addition to this, she could not and indeed was not to be defended at that time. On the political side, it was above all Konrad Adenauer who had devoted his time and energy to this politically and militarily important object since the beginning of 1948. Basing himself on a clear link with the West as a foreign policy maxim, that of 'acting in concert with the allies' in the Western camp, as well as on the consistent policy of integration into the West by means of the preparatory and stabilising act of final reconciliation with France, Adenauer rightly sought security within the alliance. Even before he became Chancellor, Adenauer took up a position based upon the Western demand for security against Germany. This read as follows: rejection of a national army in favour of a German contingent within an international or supranational army.[17] The fact that he also linked rearmament to the goal of extending West Germany's room to manoeuvre does not detract from the impression of an idea adapted both to the situation at the time and to the future.

Adenauer's military advisers were ever-conscious of the need for a self-imposed limit upon Germany's power and of the inevitability of her being supervised by her future partners, in spite of their hints that a German contribution to the defence of Central and Western Europe was essential. The military experts were mostly against the resurrecting of the Wehrmacht, but wanted to include divisions, a Corps or a contingent in an international army. This deliberate qualitative limitation of Germany's national sovereignty was joined by quantitative limits on the size of German forces, caused by Western anxieties and estimates of capabilities. It was accepted that this force would be subordinate to strategic and operational control, and was to be under the command of alliance bodies.[18]

After the Federal Republic of Germany was constituted in September 1949, the three Occupying Powers made a variety of statements against arming the new state. This was in reply to public remarks made by Chancellor Adenauer in which he had reiterated that he was in favour of West Germany sharing the responsibility for future Western European military security. He had made this standpoint especially clear in an interview in December 1949. In addition, this period saw the beginning of the Western Allies' policy of disarmament and demilitarisation in the Federal Republic, particularly by means of institutionalised supervision (Military Security Board), contractual obligation (Petersberg Protocol) and legal limitation (Laws 16 and 24 passed by the Allied High Commission on 16 December 1949 and 8 May 1950).

The Western statements, with their clear rejection of German rearmament, resulted in a damping-down of public discussion for a while, and Adenauer was obliged to restrict himself to demanding a guarantee on security (not, however, without giving vent to the opinion, now and again, that it might be jumping the gun to bind his homeland to the West before their guarantee was on the table).[19]

In March 1950 public debate, obviously stimulated by NATO discussions on a medium-term defence plan, took on renewed vigour. Retired French General Pierre Billotte, former French Prime Minister Paul Reynaud, former US Military Governor Lucius D. Clay and the British Leader of the Opposition Winston S. Churchill, in their different ways, worked towards a West German contribution to the defence of Western Europe.[20] Their speeches and writings had one thing in common (apart from the fact that their authors no longer held military or government offices). This was that the German contribution was to be clearly limited and supervised. Thus Churchill, in a speech in the House of Commons on 28 March, rejected the idea of a national German army, seeking instead a German share in an integrated system.

Moves by these formerly highly placed and well-known personalities once again forced the three Western Powers to reject the inclusion of German armed forces in the defence of Western Europe. In the Federal Republic of Germany the occasional public debates and suggestions from abroad met with a negative response from almost all political parties. Heinrich von Brentano, chairman of the CDU/CSU group in the German Bundestag and a member of Adenauer's own party, declared, after hearing of Churchill's suggestions, that he was against any form of rearmament in Germany.[21]

Official statements made by the Western Allies proved to the Chancellor that the time had not yet come for a real discussion of the problem. However, he allowed his security adviser, former Panzer General (General der Panzertruppe) Gerhard Graf von Schwerin, to embark upon 'silent' rearmament in the form of a federal police force.[22] Such plans were not only the result of the presence of paramilitary Kasernierte Volkspolizei elements in the GDR. On the contrary, the British High Commissioner in Germany, General Sir Brian Robertson, made no bones about telling the Chancellor that he was in favour of temporary solutions.[23] In addition to this, the American Chiefs of Staff and at least part of the British government, in the spring and summer of 1950, suggested the 'federal police solution' as the preliminary to military elements.[24] In the late summer of 1950, this method was taken up again by both the British and the Germans as the only feasible official rearmament measure.

Another suggestion made by Chancellor Adenauer, early in June 1950, proved much less problematic. He suggested that, as a temporary measure, German soldiers should be called up into an 'international legion' in France for training[25] because the Chancellor wanted to prove he was prepared to subject a West German defence contribution to Allied supervision. In addition, this plan must probably be seen as an instrument for sounding out the allied attitude and as confirmation of West Germany's willingness to pull her military weight in Western Europe rather than as a concrete suggestion. All the same, the plan was taken up by the French in September 1950, as Paris, under strong US pressure to accept German divisions, tried to find a solution more acceptable to France.[26]

The sounding-out theory is not all that unreasonable in itself, as internal arguments in Great Britain, France and the United States, as well as in some of the smaller Western democracies (The Netherlands, Belgium and Italy) and an inter-allied meeting of the three Western Powers all went to prove that the debate on a German defence contribution had grown out of the official allied attitude by the spring of 1950.

Even though the opinions of Germany's smaller neighbours, The Netherlands and Belgium in particular, were important pointers to the state and change of opinion among the NATO states as a whole, we should concentrate on the attitude of the Occupying Powers, whose word was still decisive in Germany. These had, during a meeting of the parties to discuss the Statute of Occupation, deliberately left open the question of a limited German contribution to defence.[27] In the United States, as early as in the autumn of 1949, plans were drawn up for the creation of a West German armed force. The result was the suggestion that German divisions be included in NATO.[28] The State Department considered these plans somewhat precocious and therefore blocked them. The comprehensive NSC 68 security study, a team effort of April 1950 between the US State Department and the Pentagon, also avoided the issue of German rearmament, but the authors did feel that it might be wise for the free nations 'to conclude separate arrangements with Japan, Western Germany, and Austria which would enlist the energies and resources of these countries in support of the free world'.[29]

The American government (which took French demands for security against Germany very seriously and thus saw the NATO Treaty as a security guarantee against Germany)[30] hesitated for so long because it was convinced that there was no chance at that time of achieving parliamentary majorities in favour of West German rearmament, especially in France, and that US support for this would merely bring more tension into relations with France and Europe. John Foster Dulles, Secretary of State Acheson's Republican adviser, went so far as to allow France a veto on this subject.[31] Indeed, Paris had no wish even to discuss a German military contribution, let alone negotiate.[32] Even so, German soldiers were a feasible concept once again for French politicians. In this regard, Prime Minister Bidault affirmed that he followed the historical principle of never saying 'Never'. In April 1950 he thought it neither wise nor politically feasible to allow the Federal Republic of Germany to join NATO. However, when the Alliance was suitably armed, and the Soviet Union no longer regarded West German rearmament as a threat, he would be happy to consider the matter.[33]

With her plan for a Coal and Steel Community the French government was already drawing conclusions from her conviction that, in the long term, the Federal Republic could be allowed its own sovereignty, including a degree of military power. With the aid of the Schuman Plan, oriented as it was toward the principle of partnership, the most important economic resources of the Federal Republic (coal and steel) were to be open to use by Western Europe as a whole, and West Germany would be permanently anchored in the West, both politically and economically.[34] Using this European solution for Germany, the plan (according to a senior French diplomat) was to prevent her from exploiting her growing freedom and power in order to play East and West off against one another and thus achieve reunification.[35]

The impression given by the files to which the author has had access is that British official bodies were far ahead of public discussion in the spring of 1950 in their private deliberations on the necessity and usefulness of a German military contribution. The Permanent Under Secretary's Committee in the Foreign Office (PUSC), which looked for ways of tying the Federal Republic into

Western organisations, was in favour of West Germany joining NATO and did not rule out the possibility of a military contribution at a later date. As this subject seemed misplaced at that time and was judged to be problematic even for the period after 1952, the committee put forward the step-by-step inclusion of Germany into such alliance political sub-groupings as were still to be formed.[36]

Prime Minister Attlee, at the beginning of May 1950, considered a permanent rejection of the activation of German troops to be unrealistic. Pointing to German tradition, he wrote a note to Bevin saying that Germany would not settle down as a state without some form of armed forces. Attlee argued in favour of German elements being integrated into an allied army in such a way 'that while adding substantially to their strength, the German contingent would not be effective as an independent force. This proposal should be examined.' Attlee saw in integration not only a way of supervising Germany, but indeed a chance of 'diverting' German 'military instincts into a channel which would make for peace instead of war'.[37]

Only one week later, the Cabinet agreed with Bevin that the decision should shortly be taken on how Germany could best contribute to the defence of Western Europe, 'though this raised grave questions which would require most careful consideration'. As a general prerequisite for future West German rearmament, the Foreign Secretary demanded that 'Germany became orientated satisfactorily towards the West and accepted the rules of the Western club'.[38] In any case the British decision-making process was at such an advanced stage that the Cabinet Defence Committee agreed to a recommendation by the Chiefs of Staff on 25 May to the effect that measures be taken to enable Bonn to contribute to joint defence.[39]

On the international level, consultations were taking place between the British and Americans. During the London Foreign Ministers' Conference of the three Western Powers (11–13 May 1950), which mainly concerned itself with the more profound inclusion of the Federal Republic into the Western community, the British and US foreign ministers, Ernest Bevin and Dean Acheson, decided, in the course of talks, to keep Germany's entry into the alliance open for the future.[40] At the end of the conference the three foreign ministers were confronted with the problem by their Dutch colleague, Dirk Stikker, and Bevin declared that West German rearmament was a topic for the future: 'It is our general view that it is premature to rearm Germany, though this may be reconsidered after Germany shows evidence of her cooperative attitude.' He referred to the fact that 'Germany now pays some 300 million pounds per year which represents a share of defence burden'.[41]

By at the same time reinforcing this attitude and accepting the Schuman Plan, they tacitly accepted the fact that France would determine the starting-point for Germany's development towards military partnership. Thus the subject remained off the agenda during the NATO Council meeting which followed the Three-Power Conference.

The plans for West German rearmament put forward prior to the outbreak of the Korean War pointed towards the Federal Republic of Germany making a limited, supervised and integrated military contribution. However, this goal depended upon many factors and developments. The political and economic tying of the Federal Republic to the West, which was regarded as a necessary prerequisite, would, according to British expectations, be accelerated by the Coal and Steel Community, whose structures and presence would surely make it easier for France to agree to German rearmament.[42] For the second important condition, the prior rearmament of Western Europe and France in particular,[43] there seemed to be no quick solution in sight, not least due to the fact that Western European economic reconstruction (as had been planned) had priority over defence,[44] that the necessary US military aid was limited,[45] and that France did not have the required personnel for speedy and realistic rearmament due to heavy losses in Indochina.[46] Finally, there was also no sign of integrated armed forces in which West German elements could have been included on an efficient scale. These few factors and their complexity make it clear how far off a decision in favour of West German forces was, despite the knowledge that a stalemate in atomic terms would occur from 1954 on. The suggestion made by the British High Commissioner, on 22 June 1950, that the basic decision to rearm Germany should be made as soon as possible, but that the question of when and how should be left until later, was wholly unrealistic.[47]

North Korea's attack upon the south on 25 June 1950 led to a decisive political U-turn. There was no doubt among Western governments that the Kremlin was behind the attack. Today it

West German Military Integration

can be said for sure that Moscow did nothing to prevent the attack on the false assumption that South Korea lay outside the USA's sphere of influence and security. Based on long-term political assessments of the Soviet Union as an aggressive power, both for power-policy and ideological reasons (for example US National Security Council study NSC 68 of April 1950)[48] and supported by the latest analyses of the Soviet threat (which could not rule out an attack on Western Europe after a nuclear stalemate had been reached from 1952 on, and in 1955 at the latest)[49], the Atlantic Alliance abandoned its passive stance on defence policy and took dramatic and thorough measures. Possibly the most drastic step was general conventional rearmament within NATO. This was pushed through without much trouble or argument because of the shock effect of the war in Korea, as the importance of doing so had become widely accepted. Correspondingly, the North Atlantic defence organisation was built up until it became a semi-integrated defence community. However, the decision taken by the NATO states in the autumn of 1950 in favour of West German participation in defence was a source of controversy both at home and abroad. The Germans were to fill a gap of ten to twelve divisions in Europe, so that NATO's position would be improved and forward defence made possible.[50]

This decision, made with the greatest reservations by some, was made considerably easier by the speed of general Allied rearmament and the plan to create an integrated armed force for Western Europe, as these factors made it possible for the public to accept a reasonable west German contribution. Suggestions concerning the rearmament of the Federal Republic almost flooded in after the outbreak of the Korean War. Without exception they were based upon international concepts. At the centre of these were quantitative and qualitative limitations and supervisory instruments and bodies.

Now there were two different rival plans competing for attention in Washington. As late as July, the Joint Chiefs of Staff had recommended the creation of West German armed forces at the earliest possible opportunity. Here they followed the prevailing trend of immediate, limited and supervised rearmament under the auspices of NATO, i.e. that there should be no national German army, but rather national German formations.[51]

In mid-August 1950 the US State Department countered the NATO lightning remedy with the concept of a supranational solution to the problem of West German rearmament under the wing of NATO as well as the prior creation of integrative structures in order to make it easier for the French to agree. In a note entitled 'Establishment of a European Defense Force'[52] the State Department put forward the notion of a force comprising reinforced US, British, Canadian, Western European and also West German contingents, which would have an American commander-in-chief with full command authority. He was also to have his own General Staff. The plan for a central organisation for military production and procurement completed the vision of integrated armed forces. The 'European Defense Force' was to operate under the political and strategic command of NATO.

Problems of procedure and security measures concerning the participation of the Federal Republic played a significant role. For example, the German elements were not to exceed division size and were to be included, together with elements of other nationalities, in corps and armies. The plan was to have German land forces only. The State Department considered it a matter of course that the Federal Republic later became a member of NATO – a possible hint towards future equal treatment for Germany.

In August, the British Chiefs of Staff demanded a West German contingent within a NATO army, and that the Federal Republic become a full member. They argued that rearmament be started at once, but also advised that this should occur in stages, to be completed in five years, according to their schedule. The suggested size, twenty active and ten reserve divisions, 2,100 aeroplanes as well as naval coastguard elements, went far beyond anything hitherto mentioned, even if one considers the fact that large naval vessels, submarines, a strategic air force, long-range missiles and NBC weapons were on the list of forbidden topics.[53]

Even before the plans were officially presented there was criticism from the Foreign Office, partly for the simple reason that political implications were not taken into account, and partly because of the size factor.[54] However, British ambassadors in the Western European countries and High Commissioner Sir Ivone Kirkpatrick did much to weaken this plan. They confirmed Foreign Minister Bevin in his opinion 'that the actual re-armament of Germany was not really a practical possibility'.[55] The Cabinet Defence Committee also shared his opinion. They concurred with Bevin's alternative suggestion that the Federal Republic should be allowed to have, as a first step, a federal police force of 100,000 men, on the lines of the Volkspolizei elements in the GDR, and that, in addition, the existing German Labour Service groups serving in the occupying armed forces would, under the direction of the allies, be changed into regular military elements. The border elements would also be strengthened.[56] On 6 September the Cabinet empowered the Foreign Secretary to negotiate on this subject with the French and the Americans,[57] who had already been informed by Bevin both concerning his suggestions and the more extensive demands made by the Chiefs of Staff. He also told Washington that he was prepared to discuss the inclusion of a German contingent if that was what Britain's partners in the Occupying Powers wanted.[58]

France thought it was too early for any kind of West German rearmament. The Paris government did not want to discuss the matter until the NATO states had at least reached the minimum defensive strength.[59] This attitude was mainly due to the fact that the strongest French army elements (in terms of battle-readiness) were committed in Asia and Africa, and there was thus no available equivalent to the envisaged German military potential in Europe.[60] As the French leadership was primarily concerned with preventing the creation of a national German army, Paris was also not prepared to allow the German Federal government to form a federal police force as a counterweight to the Volkspolizei in the GDR. Their reasoning was that, sooner or later, this police force could easily serve as the basis of a national army. According to the French Deputy High Commissioner, Bérard, his government was at the most willing to include West German battalions led by German officers in French, British and US forces.[61]

Since the necessity for and procedure of German participation was the subject of debate among the allies, and because they, for obvious reasons, did not want to be seen to be begging Bonn to join them, the Germans themselves were, at this time, not asked for their views, apart from discreet soundings in July 1950. This changed in mid-August, as West German Chancellor Adenauer confronted the High Commissioners with the urgent nature of the West German security issue, demanding a paramilitary police force of 150,000 men as a concealed way of commencing rearmament. From his point of view, Adenauer, convinced that French public opinion would not tolerate West German rearmament until France herself was armed, and therefore arguing in favour of reinforcing the French armed forces at once and with absolute priority, before starting on his own army,[62] had pointed towards the only feasible course of action with the 'police solution'. Parallel to the increase in French military power, West Germany would prepare for rearmament, something not yet politically feasible, within certain limits and with the tacit approval of the Occupying Powers. Faced with this prospect, High Commissioner John McCloy gave up his former passive stance on the matter. He declared that the diversion via a federal police force was unnecessary, and urged the Chancellor to state his opinion on the European army, brought up during the Consultative Assembly of the Council of Europe. Finally McCloy asked Adenauer to put his ideas in writing and to give them to the US administration.[63]

Thereupon Adenauer had an existing security memorandum (aimed solely at the creation of the police force) rewritten for the three Occupying Powers. In the resulting note of 29 August 1950,[64] he now expressed his willingness to activate a West German contingent within a European Army. So as to guarantee a quick start to rearmament in West Germany and to avoid too much internal wrangling during Parliamentary debate, he suggested, as a first step, the formation of a paramilitary police force as a counterweight to the 'Kasernierte Volkspolizei' in the GDR. The 'police elements', to be trained on military lines, were regarded by Adenauer as the natural preliminary to a German contingent within a European Army.[65] In the 'Memorandum concerning the realignment of the Federal Republic's relations with the Occupying Powers',[66] presented to the allies at the same time, the Chancellor, exploiting US interest, made it clear once again that equality was the condition for West German participation in defence. In a third note to the United States[67] he listed the military prerequisites for his country's inclusion in Western Europe's defence efforts: (a) a protective umbrella of allied armoured divisions for the creation of West German forces and (b) modern and effective rearmament for the Federal Republic.

Regarding a defence contribution under the aegis of Europe, Adenauer agreed 'to bind his government to support his statement, but he does not consider it politically expedient to bind the Bundestag without consulting it. He therefore suggests that the

Foreign Ministers put the issue in the form of a question to the Federal Republic which he can then submit to the Bundestag. This tactic, he feels, would put him in a stronger position in the Bundestag and would assure a favorable reply from it.'[68] The Chancellor could reasonably expect to further strengthen his position when West Germany, as he had demanded, became an equal partner of the Western Powers.[69]

After the German and British positions became clear, President Truman, in agreement with his Chiefs of Staff, decided that West German rearmament was to begin at once within the confines of NATO. In line with this decision, Secretary of State Acheson informed his British and French counterparts that he wanted to bring up the question of Western European defence during the Foreign Ministers' Conference of the three Western Powers, due to begin in New York on 12 September 1950, and that he also wanted the matter to be on the agenda of the NATO Council session which would follow directly afterwards,[70] in which the participants would draw conclusions from the crisis caused by the Korean War.

During the conferences in September 1950, US Secretary of State Acheson demanded that the allies agree to the activation of West German forces for an Atlantic-European NATO army for Western Europe.[71] Based on the conviction that German soldiers were essential, particularly for forward defence, which was seen as vital, and taking full account of Europe's (and especially France's) dependence upon the USA, Washington combined the demand for German troops with the urgent wish for greater Western European rearmament efforts, using as a ribbon attractive offers of American assistance for security, to form a 'single package' which the partners would have to accept or reject as a whole. These offers included a stronger US military presence in Western Europe, American participation in a European NATO defence force, as well as substantial financial aid. Finally, with this guarantee on Western European security,[72] added to increasing French difficulties during the war in her colonies in Indochina, the US administration got the NATO states' approval in September 1950. At the end of that month, they agreed in principle to West German participation in the defence of the West, although France only followed after considerable pressure. There was agreement on the rejection of German elements under national command, a ban on a German General Staff[73] and the demand that the integrated army be created *prior to* the German contingent.[74]

Thus French approval had been achieved with great difficulty. Foreign Minister Schuman, and soon also Defence Minister Jules Moch, facing the fact that both the National Assembly and French public opinion would reject the concept of German troops, and that the result would almost certainly be a crisis within the government, had attempted to bargain their way out of trouble. But this line failed under pressure from Britain and the USA, due to France's isolated position within the alliance, and, most of all, because of fears that the Americans would cancel their urgently needed military aid. Finally, France was forced to agree to a far-reaching compromise, aimed at gaining time in order to achieve internal approval of West German rearmament. Schuman and Moch were pressured into saying they would present the official French document of consent before the next meeting of the NATO Defence Committee at the end of October 1950. Thus Paris also agreed to the recruitment of West German soldiers, albeit in a very hidden way. However, this was not sufficient to persuade Washington to grant the assistance as promised. In a Canadian report on the New York conference, the French negotiators were accused of trying to extract the greatest possible US aid in exchange for their approval of West German forces, although the article does recognise that the internal political situation in France was extremely difficult.[75] It is not possible, however, to find confirmation of the above theory in other sources.

In view of the imminent accord on West German military participation, the Occupying Powers expressly forbade the Bonn government embarking on secret rearmament by means of the federal police force. But the three powers agreed in New York on various 'temporary measures' so as to be able to provide different levels of west German capability. First of all, mobile police forces with a total strength of 30,000 men were to be set up in the West German states (Länder) for internal security purposes (equipped with automatic weapons, mortars and light armoured cars). Then there would be the strengthening of the Labour Service (German Service Organisation), whose German personnel was not, however, to be used as the basis for the drawing up of military units,[76] in order to comply with specific French reservations. It is especially worthy of note that the High Commissioners and Commanders-in-Chief were authorised to employ Germans in anti-sabotage elements, for civil defence, for building fortifications and minelaying, and, above all, for guerilla missions in territory occupied by the Soviets in case of war. Understandably this guerilla project was regarded as so controversial that all reference to it had to be removed from the files, and secrecy was to be observed on the subject when speaking to representatives of the Benelux countries.[77]

The comprehensive suggestions made by US Deputy High Commissioner General George P. Hays to his German negotiating partners were in direct contrast to the agreements made in New York. He said that the mobile police forces would be reformed into two German divisions, and that the Labour Service elements in the British and American Zones could each be formed into another two. These six German divisions would then most likely be placed under the command of an Allied Commander-in-Chief, together with the other thirteen allied divisions. One quarter of the police elements, around 8,000 men, could be trained for a three-month period on special training grounds.[78] Hays was not alone in thinking along these lines. The Commander-in-Chief, US Forces Europe, General Thomas T. Handy, pursued similar plans and was in constant contact with Hays. If the allies rejected a German contingent, or even showed signs of hesitation in their decision, the Labour Service would be increased to 100,000 men and trained with infantry weapons.[79] The ideas of the US Army Chief of Staff, General Lawton J. Collins, concurred with those of his colleagues. He examined the possibility of setting up West German battalions and regiments and training them together with the occupation forces of the United States, Great Britain and France.[80]

While the British saw the Labour Service as necessary for maintaining the combat-readiness of British troops, and thus had no wish to see them used as the potential officer corps of a future German army,[81] the Canadian government supported the formation and arming of West German elements under the command of the occupying forces.[82]

During the month that remained before the meeting of the NATO Defence Committee, Paris was under more pressure than ever to officially approve West German participation, and to find a mode of phrasing this resolution so that it could gain approval in the National Assembly (Assemblée Nationale), thus obtaining the effective US guarantees on security. However, the United

States, Britain and Germany were also taking advantage of the time to define their ideas.

After learning of the results of the New York negotiations from the allies, West German Chancellor Adenauer decided to abandon his plans for secret rearmament and instead to begin official planning for a defence contribution. To this end, Adenauer had his military experts draw up a concept in the form of the 'Himmeroder Denkschrift' at the beginning of October 1950. The Chancellor's foreign-policy advisor, Herbert Blankenhorn, laid down the political limits, so as to prevent the former officers 'marching' along the wrong road. Blankenhorn pointed out that German policy was, above all, aimed at integrating the Federal Republic into Western Europe. The first step towards this goal could be taken via the Schuman Plan. With regard to rearmament, the German government favoured participation in a European army, as this would further European unity. This was already sufficient to prevent the government creating a national army. It was, however, still not clear whether there would be an integrated European army within a European federation or an international army representing NATO.[83]

In the course of the closed meeting at Himmerod, the German military experts planned for a German contingent under Atlantic-European supreme command. This contingent would consist of a land army of twelve divisions, supporting air-force elements and a small coastal defence force with its own air arm. Notwithstanding the clear rejection of a national army, the German contingent was to have a federal command structure and was to be included as a whole in the alliance armed force. The corps was regarded as the highest national command level. These proposals went far beyond any previous American plans. The Himmerod experts aimed at a supranational (European) army. An essential prerequisite for West German participation was complete military equality.[84] Definite ideas on a military reform of future German armed forces, contained in the memorandum together with equally direct statements from Adenauer against the rebirth of 'militarist' traditions, also went to prove that the Germans were serious about entering into the alliance.

At the same time the British government decided to mount an 'attack' in Paris, so as to force the French leadership to formally accept German participation. The main reason for this decision was the fear that a hardening of the French position would place the US go-ahead for her security guarantees in jeopardy. The plan concentrated on demonstrating to the French that it was possible to have safeguards against the risks of German rearmament.[85]

The suggestion made by the British Chiefs of Staff,[86] drawn up soon afterwards, also took account of the French need for security from Germany, and also of the fact that any plan had to be capable of overcoming the hurdle of the National Assembly. Basing their estimate upon a gap in allied forces in Europe of between ten and twelve divisions and 1,700 aircraft (measured against the figures contained in NATO's Medium Term Plan, revised in August) and upon the real planned activation of forces by the Europeans and Americans, the British military leaders proposed a force size of fifteen divisions, together with under 1,000 tactical aircraft and 1,000 interceptors for the joint integrated armed force.

Not only was the entire list of prohibitions from the above-mentioned August plan adopted, but other important limitations were added. The ratio of allied to German land forces was fixed by the draft plan at 2:1, and that of the air forces at 3:1. Any increase in the German proportion was ruled out. A special allied supervisory mechanism was planned for the German rearmament programme. This stated that allied rearmament had permanent priority. In order to allay fears of Germany rearming too quickly, the Chiefs of Staff laid down an approximate time scale. This meant that, even if rearmament was started immediately, as was being demanded, the first German division would be activated within a year at the earliest, and that the first air-force elements would not be at full readiness for two years. 'In general the safeguards would be that West German forces would only be complementary to and integrated with Allied forces, numerically inferior to them and armed as far as possible with weapons of a defensive character'.

The British High Commissioner thought he could accommodate France even more without conflicting with German interests. For example, he limited the number of German divisions to one-fifth, or a maximum of one-quarter of the Atlantic-European armed force. At this time France would hardly tolerate fifteen German divisions. But if only five or six were activated, the technical support elements for the entire army could be recruited from Germany. It was also not yet the right time to confront France with the idea of building up German naval elements for coastguard duties. It was sufficient for the moment secretly to strengthen the German minesweeper flotillas within the British occupation force.[87]

These plans, as well as US proposals on the possible employment of the Labour Service, had nothing to do with the idea of partnership. But Kirkpatrick's main argument, that there was a correlation between West German rearmament and US military commitments in Europe, makes it clear that the plans were formulated in response to military and alliance policy obligations: 'Nobody denies that the gap can only be filled by a German contribution. Unless the gap is filled the battle must be lost. Consequently the Americans cannot reasonably be expected to involve still more troops in an inevitable catastrophe. But if the Americans decide to commit more troops to Europe the gap will be still larger. In fact so large that the Western Powers will have to abandon any idea of effectively defending Europe'.[88]

As a small group led by Prime Minister Attlee, on 20 October, went through the possible decisions the French could take, their hopes rested upon a positive outcome, expecting Paris to make use of the wide-ranging safeguards and to consider them adequate. In any case, Air Marshal Sir W. Elliot was instructed to divert attention towards this point during the preliminary talks of the NATO Defence Committee session.[89]

In Washington, the American model of West German military integration, on the basis of the planned Atlantic-European defensive force for Western Europe, was on paper in the meantime and had been honed down to a definite proposal by the time the session of the NATO Defence Committee began on 28 October 1950.[90] This plan envisaged West Germany making both a military and an economic defence contribution. The first was to consist mainly of 'balanced ground forces'. In addition to this, it was considered necessary to have a small naval force for port-defence purposes. The size of these forces was very different from that demanded by the Germans themselves. The land forces and their support elements would be integrated with non-German elements in corps and other formations. Air support was to be supplied to the German divisions by allied tactical air-force sections assigned to the army corps. There was no mention of a German tactical air force. The proposal included allowing German officers access to the International General Staff of the Allied Commander-in-Chief and to the corresponding staffs in the formations to which the German divisions belonged. The allocation of places at foreign Staff Colleges for initial and further training of senior officers, as well as for special assignments, was also considered.

The entire organisation, training (according to the Commander-in-Chief's general guidelines), armament and administration of the German armed forces was to be the responsibility of a German federal authority, which would if necessary be given a military administrative staff. Because the German sections were to be integrated into the joint armed force from the beginning, there was no need for a 'German General Staff', or for German staffs above division level. It was also envisaged that planning for centralised supply and procurement via a strengthened NATO 'Military Production and Supply Board' would be carried out sufficiently well that full supervision and effective coordination of German arms production with that of the NATO states would be guaranteed.

Alongside the basic safeguards of integration and centralised supply there were other measures such as the following: the numerical limitation of West German forces to a maximum of one-fifth of the total active strength of the Atlantic-European Army; the creation of an 'Allied training mission' within the German federal body, headed by an Inspector-General; the retention of the existing prohibitions and limitations upon industrial production, together with supervision by the allied Military Security Board; arms production restricted to light weapons (which implied a ban on producing aircraft and artillery pieces); and supervision of the choice of officers and restrictions on the reactivation of former Wehrmacht officers.

The American plan kept to the letter of the previous demands, but now the supervisory bodies were strengthened, particularly with a view to well-known French fears of the possible abuse of military might on the part of West German contingents. The recommended safeguards in many ways went against German demands for political and military equality.

After the French position had hardened during the first half of October, and after a further attempt to avoid any kind of German rearmament had foundered under the pressure of continuing massive US demands, Paris used the delay thus caused to work out and agree internally upon an alternative concept, the draft of a supranational solution to the German rearmament question.

This form was seen by the French as a decisive guarantee against the rebirth of a national German army, which might drag France into a reckless policy in order to achieve German reunification.[91] However, internal problems were the main reason for the French choice of the supranational model. Jules Moch frankly explained to the Canadian government that the theme of West German rearmament, which the French Cabinet saw as necessary, had to be handled with the utmost care so as to avoid the break-up of the coalition government, and also so that the French Communists could not gain too much advantage from the agreement on fairly unrestricted West German rearmament.[92]

On 24 October 1950 Paris, in a declaration by Prime Minister René Pleven, announced the plan (later named after him) for the rearmament of the Federal Republic under European auspices, and gained a safe majority for it in the National Assembly.[93]

As the proposal was somewhat hastily drafted, one could not expect it to be a watertight concept. Several additions and amendments during the week after its appearance were the result. Pleven's plan specified that German elements were to be activated within the bounds of a European army which was to 'be linked to the political institutions of a united Europe', 'realise the total fusion of troops and armament' and 'be subject to a joint political and military authority'. A defence minister responsible either to the participating governments or to a council of ministers and a European Assembly was to command this European army. The supranational concept was rounded off by the proposal of a joint budget. A series of (further) safeguards, which at the same time discriminated heavily against the Federal Republic, were added. The national contingents were to be integrated into the European Army on the basis of the 'smallest possible unit', the battalion (which contradicted the widespread opinion that it would only be feasible to have national divisions). Thus each regiment or brigade of the thirty-three allied divisions would have a German battalion.[94] Even one French diplomat admitted that this was both militarily and politically unworkable.[95] After only a few days, Defence Minister Jules Moch was forced to increase the size of the basic national unit to the regiment.[96]

While the individual German soldier would have been under the command of the European defence minister from his first day of service, the French plan not only allowed all other participating countries to continue to have defence ministries, but also permitted them to maintain their own armed forces. At the same time the plan envisaged that these armies would at least partly revert to national command. In addition to this, Pleven made West German military integration subject to the prior signing of the Schuman Plan, the appointment of a European defence minister and the election of the European Parliamentary Assembly.[97]

According to confidential statements made by Defence Minister Moch, the European army would, for a transitional period, be a mere 'training force' of 100,000 men, half of whom would be Frenchmen and one-fifth Germans. Curiously enough, Moch was already considering a final total West German strength of ten divisions, a reasonable and acceptable figure for all concerned.[98] For military reasons, the European army, together with contingents from countries outside this grouping (the USA, Great Britain and Canada) was to be placed under the command of the NATO Commander-in-Chief.[99]

A secret paper [100] concerning the planned military details, presented to NATO on 2 November, contained further unilateral decisions, as one might have guessed considering the emphasis Pleven's declaration placed upon land forces. All present air and naval forces were to remain under national administration. A European air force was envisaged for a later date, but a joint navy was not mentioned in the document. Thus, according to the French, there were to be no West German naval elements, and air formations only at a much later stage. As well as this, Paris wanted to exclude the Germans from NATO membership, thereby preventing them from regaining political sovereignty.[101]

This set-up was obviously designed to pander to French opponents of West German rearmament, but could it also serve the interests of the other partners, particularly the United States? Abroad, the French proposal received a negative response, or at least strong reservations.[102] The reasons for this attitude were, on the one hand, the clear (and intentional) delaying of West German rearmament caused by certain provisos contained in the plan, and, on the other hand, grave doubts about the practicability of its military conception and its political feasibility, but also the fear that a double alliance administration would be ponderous and complex. Nor should the role played by the proposed discrimination against the West Germans and the implied protraction of the build-up of integrated US-led armed forces be dismissed. The British defence minister even suggested the drastic step of tackling the German problem without France.[103] This was never a practical solution, but it does illustrate how difficult the situation had temporarily become.

For the moment the British government played a waiting game. If Paris succeeded in convincing the Continental leaderships, which the British thought highly unlikely, the intention was not to raise objections, but also not to give support to the French proposal. Washington also refused to deliver on its offers of aid, saying that the plan had to be realistic in terms of time, military, psychological and economic factors.[104]

In spite of this, the French government remained steadfast in its opinion that the supranational model was the only feasible way of integrating German forces and refused to discuss the American plan. Even then, the general (and correct) assumption was that behind the French position was her long-term aim of countering the dominant US influence within the alliance and Europe with a group of states of political and military importance.[105] How long would Paris be able to maintain this line in the face of her isolation within NATO, her financial and military dependence on the USA and her desperate situation in Indochina?

Continuing American and British pressure on France and the increasing distress she was suffering in Indochina at the beginning of December, along with the continuing fear of placing the strengthening of the US presence in Europe at risk, or even causing America to pull the troops out if France did not agree: all these factors led to the French acceptance of the plan named after the American chairman of the North Atlantic Deputy Council, Charles M. Spofford. Of course, there was a feeling among the alliance member states that an agreement had to be reached, in view of the fact that the surprise intervention of the People's Republic of China on the side of North Korea had led to Western fears of a Third World War.

Paris, by accepting the Spofford Plan (one of several scenarios under discussion),[106] recognised that immediate West German rearmament was vital. Parallel to and competing with preparations for the creation of a European army on the lines of the Pleven Plan, a start was to be made on 'Provisional Arrangements',[107] the activation of West German elements of combat-group strength, i.e. 5,000 to 6,000 men (a compromise),[108] together with production of military equipment in the Federal

Republic. In addition, a long-term political solution was to be sought without the strictures of lack of time.[109]

During a joint session on 13 December 1950, the NATO Military Committee and the Council of Deputies agreed to this proposal and decided to make appropriate recommendations to the Atlantic Council and the Defence Committee. These recommendations, which concurred with both US and German ideas, contained the following points:

> (a) the activation, at the earliest possible juncture, of German 'regimental combat teams' by the allied occupying forces in Germany, by arrangement with the Atlantic Supreme Commander, under whose command the German elements would then be placed;
> (b) the option of subsequently forming national homogeneous divisions from these teams by the Supreme Commander;
> (c) the activation of tactical German air-force elements and a small naval force for the tasks proposed by the USA;
> (d) a substantial West German industrial contribution to Western European defence.

The French desire to further pursue the European army project under the auspices of NATO was directly accommodated. The recommendations[110] were adopted without amendment by the NATO Council at its joint meeting with the Defence Committee in Brussels on 18 December 1950.[111]

This agreement was important, not only because it was a temporary solution designed to achieve a speedy military effect and 'the highest degree of military effectiveness',[112] but also because, at the same time, it was a successful attempt to commit the alliance to a strong and lasting supervision of German military participation.[113]

In order to guard against independent German military might, the West German government was not to have sole control over the German elements. The permanent allied military presence in West Germany and the superiority of the NATO armed forces were to be seen as direct prerequisites. There were also numerous indirect safeguards in the agreement, such as a ban on central West German institutions for planning, intelligence and operational command, the prohibition of the production of NBC weapons, long-range missiles, heavy weapons, aircraft and larger naval elements – restrictions and bans which were in fact mostly laid down in a treaty after the failure of the EDC in the autumn of

1954. It cannot be over-emphasised that the proposed direct placing of all West German elements and formations under the Supreme Allied Commander in Europe (SACEUR) prevented the Bonn government from creating its own military command structure and thus robbed it of the most important base for the operational command of armed forces.[114]

In general the allies specified that West German forces were to be subject 'at all times to adequate safeguards. These safeguards should be political, military, and possibly economic.'[115] A loosening of military supervision was made dependent upon progress in Western integration and upon the inclusion of the Federal Republic of Germany in the Western community.[116]

The United States now lifted the barrier they had placed on their offers of security. In that same month the three Western Powers and NATO came to a decision on West German rearmament by making official enquiries to the Bonn government. In January 1951 negotiations began between the West Germans and the allies on the definite form of her participation in defence.

The allies, with the Brussels Agreement, achieved a breakthrough on the road to West German military integration. The firm base thus gained not only allowed them to enter into real negotiations with the West German government, but it also allowed France (who had clearly altered her position in the previous months,[117] and had surrendered to the USA and international developments, which were running contrary to Paris' interests) to make the necessary changes to the Pleven Plan so as to have an acceptable military concept.

In spite of this, there were real doubts, at the end of 1950, whether it would be possible to rearm West Germany in the near future. Soviet initiatives following the New York conferences, the presentation of the Pleven Plan, the intensified Korean War, continuing problems within the alliance, and, most of all, uncertainty over the Federal Republic's reaction to the alliance's plans: all these factors made speedy practical steps towards West German rearmament seemingly unlikely.

Internally the alliance was certainly constrained by the fact that it was pursuing both the NATO and European solutions at the same time. Similarly, the French attempt to bring both her own and European interests to the fore in the United States via the Pleven Plan, as well as to coordinate the security policies of the various European states, arguably had the same effect. In any case one could not have foreseen that Washington, in September 1951, would decide to come into line with the French position on solving the German problem, thus going a long way towards realising Paris' long-term goals.

One of the most important conditions for the activation of West German forces was still the strengthening of allied armies on the Continent and the formation of the NATO force for Europe. General Eisenhower's appointment to the post of Supreme Commander and the placing of the first elements under his command was an encouraging start. But on the other hand, at the end of 1950, due to the worsening situation in the Korean War as a result of the Chinese commitment, there were delays not only in sending US troops to Europe[118] but also, very soon, shortages in arms and equipment for the Western European states.[119] For these reasons above all the British government instructed its High Commissioner in Germany to go slow on the military talks with the West German government which were just beginning.[120]

The German reaction to the allied enquiries concerning military cooperation was unclear. Negotiating with the Germans was going to be a lengthy and difficult process for the simple reason that it was no longer possible to give the Germans orders (according to British Foreign Minister Bevin in the Consultative Council of the Brussels Pact), but rather negotiations had to be carried out on the basis of equality,[121] not least because the West German voters had to be shown the advantages of Adenauer's Western course.[122] It was mere speculation that the Federal German government, in an effort at reconciliation with France, would overlook the lack of equal treatment contained in the Pleven Plan and agree to it.[123] In addition to this, the status of West Germany turned out to be a much more important subject for negotiation than the military details. The necessary contractual settlement on the two issues and their passage through the Bundestag would take no less than two years,[124] while the activation of German divisions would take another eighteen to twenty-four months, according to German estimates. This knowledge led the West to take an unhurried view of the situation, which was beneficial to the negotiating climate, and which also removed a lot of the tension from the Eastern problem.

In order to assess the chances of an early West German defence participation, the reception of and the position regarding Soviet initiatives needs to be considered. The well-known proposals made by the Warsaw Pact foreign ministers in the Prague Declaration of 21 October 1950, and written down in the Soviet note to the Western Powers of 3 November 1950, which both suggested the conclusion of a peace treaty with Germany as an alternative to rearming the Federal Republic, had no real effect on the developments leading to the Spofford compromise and the Brussels Agreement. In the West, the majority was inclined to see the Eastern moves as an attempt to disrupt military integration and the final binding of West Germany into the Alliance. Only a few admitted that the Soviets also had security interests. However, the next year saw a tendency to sound out the Soviet proposals. Thus Foreign Minister Bevin recommended that the British Cabinet should not let itself be immovable on the subject of West German rearmament, but that it should keep the option open of reconsidering if there was a chance of achieving a peace treaty for Germany.[125]

Apart from the possibility of a delay in German rearmament due to the planned negotiations with the Soviets, it was clear, even immediately after the Brussels NATO conference of December 1950, that there was little chance of realising a military contribution by the Federal Republic before 1953–4. From the point of view of the acceleration of Western defence efforts, recognised as being vital, this position must have been seen as a disadvantage. But, in view of the size and significance of intra-alliance, domestic policy and military problems which had to be solved, all of which were connected with West German military integration, the timescale envisaged was inadequate. Thus Konrad Adenauer, who for a short time hoped that his country would be made an equal partner in the short term, did not worry overmuch about the delay in rearmament. It was regarded as most positive, and not just by the French, that the Federal Republic would be further woven into the political and economic fabric in the meantime. In this way conditions would be met which had often been demanded in the past, and which had become overshadowed by the outbreak of the Korean War. Apart from this, the above-mentioned timescale meant that there was the chance of a rapprochement between East and West on the questions of Central Europe, even if this chance appeared to be slim at that time.

Notes

1. The author has already dealt with this subject in other works, thereby focusing on different aspects, for example: Überlegungen und Pläne zu einer militärischen Integration Westdeutschlands 1948–1952, in *Kalter Krieg und Deutsche Frage. Deutschland im Widerstreit der Mächte 1945–1952*, mit einem Vorwort von Wolfgang J. Mommsen, Josef Foschepoth (ed.), (*Veröffentlichungen des Deutschen Historischen Instituts London*, vol. 16), Göttingen, 1985, pp. 314–94, and 'Zur Frage einer militärischen Integration Westdeutschlands' (bis Mai 1950) in *Histoire des débuts de la construction européenne (mars 1948–mai 1950)/ Origins of the European Integration (March 1948–May 1950), Actes du Colloque de Strasbourg, 28–30 novembre*, sous la direction de Raymond Poidevin (ed.), Bruxelles, Milano, Paris, Baden-Baden, 1986, pp. 343–66. For this essay it was possible to obtain additional British and Canadian files and documents of the Western European Union (Brussels Pact). This study deals mainly with the half-year following the outbreak of the Korean War.
2. *Foreign Relations of the United States*, Diplomatic Papers, 1945–1950, Washington DC, 1967–1980, (quoted as FRUS), here 1948, III, Washington DC, 1974, p. 5.
3. Quoted in Daniel Yergin, *Shattered Peace: The Origins of the Cold War and the National Security State*, New York, 1977, p. 362f.
4. Bevin and French Prime Minister Ramadier admitted this fact in September 1947. Geoffrey Warner, 'The Labour Governments and the Unity of Western Europe, 1945–1951', in *The Policy of the Labour Governments*, Ritchie Ovendale, (ed.), Leicester, 1984, p. 66.
5. Bevin wrote in his memorandum 'Policy in Germany' of 5 January 1948 that 'the Americans seem determined to make a success of Western Germany since they regard this as one of the pillars of the Marshall Plan'. Public Record Office, London (PRO), Cabinet Office, CAB 129/23 Cabinet Paper (CP) (48) 5, no. 31.
6. For the British government's attitude see David N. Dilks, 'Britain and Europe, 1948–1949: The Prime Minister, the Foreign Secretary and the Cabinet', in *Histoire des débuts* (see Note 1), pp. 391–418; for 1950: PRO, Prime Minister's Office, PREM 8/1203, 1950 Foreign Policy, PUSC (49) 62 FINAL REVISE, The Future of Germany, 19.4.1950; ibid., CAB 129/39, CP (50) 80 Policy towards Germany, 26.4.1950; ibid., CAB 129/40, CP (50) 114, 19.5.1950, Annex B, No. 7 (quotation).
7. PRO, CAB 129/23, CP (48) 5, no. 5. (see Note 4). The possibility of the Germans and Soviets joining forces was a traditional British fear. See John Baylis, 'British wartime thinking about a post-war

European Security Group', in *Review of International Studies*, vol. 9, 1983, pp. 265–81, esp. p. 273ff.
8. Robert McGeehan, *The German Rearmament Question: American Diplomacy and European Defense after World War II*, Urbana, 1971, p. 16 (US Army officers serving in Germany); Laurence W. Martin, 'The American decision to rearm Germany', in *American Civil-Military Decisions: A Book of Case Studies*, Harold Stein (ed.), Birmingham, Alabama, 1963, p. 646 (Operations and Planning Dept. of the G3 Staff of the Army in the Pentagon); for the French military leadership see Pierre Guillen, 'Die französische Generalität, die Aufrüstung der Bundesrepublik und die EVG (1950–1954)' in *Die Europäische Verteidigungsgemeinschaft. Stand und Probleme der Forschung*, Hrsg. im Auftrag des Militärgeschichtlichen Forschungsamtes von Hans-Erich Volkmann und Walter Schwengler. Mit Beiträgen von Alfredo Breccia, Donald Cameron Watt, Anselm Doering-Manteuffel, Alexander Fischer, Pierre Guillen, Peter Jones, Albert E. Kersten, Walter Lipgens, Klaus A. Maier, Wilhelm Meier-Dörnberg, Paul Noack, Raymond Poidevin, Jean-Pierre Rioux, Hans-Erich Volkmann und Werner Weidenfeld, Boppard am Rhein, 1985 (*Militärgeschichte seit 1945*, vol. 7), pp. 125–57.
9. Gerhard Wettig, *Entmilitarisierung und Wiederbewaffnung in Deutschland 1943–1955: Internationale Auseinandersetzungen um die Rolle der Deutschen in Europa*, Munich, 1967 (*Schriften des Forschungsinstitutes der Deutschen Gesellschaft für Auswärtige Politik e.V.*, vol. 25), p. 228f., 273ff.
10. Norbert Wiggershaus, 'Bedrohungsvorstellungen Bundeskanzler Adenauers nach Ausbruch des Korea-Krieges', in *MGM*, vol. 25 1979, pp. 79–122; Wiggershaus, 'Von Potsdam zum Pleven-Plan: Deutschland in der internationalen Konfrontation 1945–1950', in: *Anfänge westdeutscher Sicherheitspolitik 1945–1956*, vol. 1: *Von der Kapitulation bis zum Pleven-Plan*, Von Roland G. Foerster, Christian Greiner, Georg Meyer, Hans-Jürgen Rautenberg, Norbert Wiggershaus, Munich, Vienna, 1982, pp. 1–118, here p. 82 f.; drawings and studies 1947–50 in Nachlaß General Adolf Heusinger, Oppenheim. I would sincerely like to thank Frau Ada Guntrum-Heusinger for allowing me access to this material.
11. On this point and the following cf. Norbert Wiggershaus, 'Zum alliierten Pro und Contra eines westdeutschen Militärbeitrages', in *Militärgeschichte. Probleme – Thesen – Wege. Im Auftrag des Militärgeschichtlichen Forschungsamtes aus Anlaß ihres 25 jährigen Bestehens ausgewählt und zusammengestellt von Manfred Messerschmidt, Klaus A. Maier, Werner Rahn und Bruno Thoß*, Stuttgart, 1982 (*Beiträge zur Militär- und Kriegsgeschichte*, vol. 25), pp. 436–51.

12. On the inadequacy of the defence forces in Western Europe see the files of the Brussels Pact, esp. PRO, DG 1/5/29–35.
13. This is shown by long-term British plans for the creation of a possible 'Third Power Europe' between the United States and the Soviet Union, made in October 1949. PRO, CAB 129/37/1, C.P. (49) 208, 18.10.1949.
14. Bernard L. Montgomery, *The Memoirs of Field-Marshal the Viscount Montgomery of Alamein, K.G.*, London, 1958, p. 510.
15. Guillen, 'Generalität' (see Note 8), p. 126; PRO, DG 1/6/37, Military Committee, 27th session 8.9.1948; 30th session 11.9.1948.
16. PRO, DG 1/4/16, p. 2ff., Doc. no. A/313, 21.6.1949, App.: Memorandum of the Netherlands Government on Policy towards Germany, 16.6.1949.
17. Norbert Wiggershaus, 'Zur Frage der Planung für die verdeckte Aufstellung westdeutscher Verteidigungskräfte in Konrad Adenauers sicherheitspolitischer Konzeption 1950', in *Dienstgruppen und westdeutscher Verteidigungsbeitrag: Vorüberlegungen zur Bewaffnung der Bundesrepublik Deutschland*, Heinz-Ludger Borgert, Walter Stürm, Norbert Wiggershaus, Boppard am Rhein, 1982 (*Militärgeschichte seit 1945*, vol. 6), pp. 11–88, here p. 20ff.
18. Manfred Messerschmidt, Christian Greiner and Norbert Wiggershaus, 'West Germany's strategic position and her role in defence policy as seen by the German military, 1945–1949', in *Power in Europe? Great Britain, France, Italy and Germany in a Post-war World, 1945–1950*, Josef Becker and Franz Knipping (eds), Berlin, New York, 1986, pp. 353–69. See also the drawings and studies made by General Heusinger between 1947–1950 (see Note 10).
19. PRO, Foreign Office (FO) 371/85048, C 3183/27/18G, Germany-Defence Questions: Brief for the Secretary of State at the Foreign Ministers Talks, undated [April 1950], p. 7.
20. On Churchill's proposals cf. Axel Ch. Azzola, *Die Diskussion um die Aufrüstung der Bundesrepublik Deutschland im Unterhaus und in der Presse Großbritanniens, November 1949-Juli 1952*, Meisenheim, 1971 (*Marburger Abhandlungen zur Politikwissenschaft*, vol. 12), p. 33ff.
21. PRO, FO 371/85087, C 2047/57/18, Tel. Wahnerheide No. 118, 18.3.1950.
22. Roland G. Foerster, 'Innenpolitische Aspekte der Sicherheit Westdeutschlands (1947–1950)', in *Anfänge westdeutscher Sicherheitspolitik* (see Note 10), pp. 403–575, here p. 456ff.
23. Reply to questions put to former Ambassador Herbert Blankenhorn by the author on 7.6.1977, Meeting Adenauer-Robertson on 6.6.1950.
24. FRUS, 1950, IV, p. 687 (NSC = National Security Council); ibid., III, p. 934.
25. During talks with the High Commissioners on June 6, 7 and 8 1950.

Reply to questions put to former Ambassador Herbert Blankenhorn by the author on 7.6.1977. On the details see Wiggershaus, 'Zur Frage der Planung' (see Note 17), Chap. III.
26. PRO, PREM 8/1429/1, New York Telegram no. 1009, 14.9.1950.
27. See chapter 12 by Wolfgang Krieger in this book; PRO, CAB 128/13, C.M. (48), 81st Conclusion, 15.12.1948.
28. Martin (see Note 8), pp. 649, 651, 654, 660; FRUS, 1949, III, p. 353.
29. FRUS, 1950, I, p. 275; Steven L. Rearden, *The Formative Years 1947–1950*, Washington DC, 1984 (*History of the Office of the Secretary of Defense*, vol. 1), p. 485.
30. Werner Link, 'Die amerikanische Deutschlandpolitik 1945–1949', in *Die Deutschlandfrage und die Anfänge des Ost-West-Konflikts 1945–1949*, mit Beiträgen von Alexander Fischer u.a. Berlin, 1984 (*Studien zur Deutschlandfrage*. The Göttinger Arbeitkreis (ed.), vol. 7), with reference to FRUS, 1949, IV, p. 109 (Acheson).
31. FRUS, 1950, III, p. 60.
32. Statement by the French Foreign Minister of 24.2.1950, PRO, FO 371/85048, C 3183/27/18G, Germany-Defence Questions, Brief for the Secretary of State (see Note 19), p. 2.
33. Ibid., p. 60f. British Foreign Minister Bevin, however, doubted that Paris would ever accept Germany's inclusion into NATO. PRO, CAB 129/39, CP (50) 92, Memorandum entitled 'Conversations with United States and French Officials', 2.5.1950, no. 7.
34. See Jean Monnet's memorandum of 3.5.1950, the text of which can be found in Gilbert Ziebura, *Die deutsch-französischen Beziehungen seit 1945: Mythen und Realitäten*, Pfullingen, 1950, pp. 195–200 (see esp. p. 199). Cf. also FRUS, 1950, III, p. 699 f., and Edward Fursdon, *The European Defence Community: A History*, London, 1980, p. 57ff.
35. Public Archives Canada, Ottawa, RG 25 External Affairs, A 12, vol. 2088, AR 22/20/1, Telegram from Paris, 24.5.1950 (statement by Parodi).
36. PRO, PREM 8/1203, PUSC (50) 9, Western Organisations, 21.4.1950.
37. Ibid., minute by Attlee for Bevin, 2.5.1950.
38. Ibid., CAB 128/17, C.M. (50), 29th Conclusion, 8.5.1950, minute 3; PREM 8/1202, minute by Bevin, 13.5.1950, quoted from Rolf Steininger, *Deutsche Geschichte 1945–1961: Darstellung und Dokumente*, Frankfurt, 1983, 2 vols., here vol. 2 (Fischer Taschenbuch (paperback) 4316), p. 383.
39. PRO, FO 371/85050, C 4743/27/18G, Mallet's note entitled 'German Federal Police and German Rearmament', 13.7.1950.
40. FRUS, 1950, III, pp. 1021, 1025, 1026, 1062f.
41. Ibid., p. 1056 (Bevin). He had made a similar statement on 13 May. PRO, PREM 8/1202.
42. PRO, CAB 129/41, CP (50) 154, Integration of Western European Coal and Steel Industries. Defence Implications, memorandum by

British Defence Minister Shinwell, 1.7.1950.
43. See e.g. PRO, FO 371/85048, C 2416/27/18G, Chiefs of Staff Committee. Confidential Annex to Chiefs of Staff (COS) (50) 52nd Meeting, 29.3.1950, no. 4: Military Aspects of United Kingdom Policy Towards Germany, contribution by Sir John Slessor; ibid., appendix to COS (50) 108, 3.4.1950, Military Aspects of United Kingdom Policy Towards Germany.
44. PRO, CAB 129/40, CP (50) 118, meeting of the North Atlantic Council, 15–18 May, memorandum by Foreign Minister Bevin, 26.5.1950.
45. PRO, Foreign Office (FO) 371/85048, C 3183/27/18G, Germany-Defence Questions (see Note 19).
46. In any case this was Robert Schuman's opinion. PRO, DG 1/4/19, metric document no. 487 I, record of the Ninth Session of the Consultative Council, 1.8.1950, no. 1.
47. PRO, FO 371/85050, C 3183/27/18G, 13.7.1950, extract from a report by General Robertson of 22.6.1950.
48. See Lawrence Freedman, *The Evolution of Nuclear Strategy*, London, 1982, p. 73. Text of NSC 68: FRUS, 1950, I, p. 234ff., and ibid., III, p. 857ff.
49. Concerning Western conceptions of threat see E. Pikart's essay in this book, chapter 14.
50. On Atlantic military strategy see Christian Greiner's essay in this book, chapter 16.
51. National Archives and Records Service. Modern Military Branch, Washington DC (NA, MMB), Record Group 218, US Joint Chiefs of Staff (RG 218), Geographic File 1948–1950 (GF 1948–1950), CCS 092, Germany (5–4–49), sec. 3, JCS 2124/11 of 27.7.1950. On the American decision-making process, see the essay by Klaus A. Maier, 'Die EVG in der Außen- und Sicherheitspolitik der Truman-Administration', in *Die Europäische Verteidigungs-gemeinschaft* (see Note 8), pp. 31–49.
52. FRUS, 1950, IV, pp. 211–19.
53. PRO, FO 371/85051, C 5371/27/18G, 18.8.1950, COS (59)305, Use of German Resources for the Defence of Western Europe, 18.8.1950; ibid., PREM 8/1429/1, Cabinet-Defence Committee, DO (50)67, Report by the Chiefs of Staff, 30.8.1950.
54. PRO, FO 371/85051, C 5371/27/18G, 18.8.1950, COS (59)130th Meeting, 16.8.1950, minute 4: Use of German Resources for the Defence of Western Europe, Critique by W.I. Mallet of the draft plan formulated by the Joint Planning Staff JP (59)46.
55. PRO, FO 371/85052, C 5425/27/18G, 21.8.1950, Record of Meeting held in the Secretary of State's Office on 21 August 1950 (quotation by Kirkpatrick).
56. PRO, PREM 8/1429/1, Cabinet-Defence Committee, DO (59)66,

German Association with the Defence of the West, Memorandum by Bevin of 29.8.1950; ibid., DO (50) 17th Meeting, 1.9.1950, extract; ibid., CAB 131/8, DO (50) 17th Meeting, 1.9.1950, minute 3.
57. PRO, CAB 128/18, CM (50) 56th Conclusions, minute 6, 6.9.1950.
58. FRUS, 1950, III, p. 246ff., 264ff., ibid., IV, p. 716ff.
59. Foreign Minister Robert Schuman during a press conference. *Stuttgarter Zeitung*, 7.8.1950. Cf. the latest findings in P. Guillen's essay in this book, chapter 7.
60. On 8 June 1950, French High Commissioner François-Poncet gave Adenauer a breakdown of the whereabouts of the French fighting elements as follows: Indochina approx. 120,000, North Africa approx. 150,000, Europe approx. 80,000 men. Questions put to Blankenhorn by the author on 7.6.1977.
61. Reply to questions put to Blankenhorn by the author on 19.6.1979.
62. PRO, FO 371/85049, C 4554/18G, Letter by Kirkpatrick HC/2065, 12.7.1950.
63. See on this point Norbert Wiggershaus, 'Die Entscheidung für einen westdeutschen Verteidigungsbeitrag 1950', in *Anfänge westdeutscher Sicherheitspolitik* (see Note 10), pp. 325–402, chap. IV.
64. *Sicherheitspolitik der Bundesrepublik Deutschland: Dokumentation 1945–1977*, part 1, Klaus von Schubert (ed.), Cologne, 1978, p. 79ff.; PRO, CAB 129/42, CP (50) 210, 18.9.1950, Annex.
65. According to Adenauer in a speech to the Cabinet on August 25. MGFA, Befragungsmaterialien Kapitän z.S. Heinz-Eugen Eberbach. Aktenvermerk über die Fahrt 21.-27.8.1950, Punkt 9. Cf. FRUS, 1950, IV, p. 722.
66. Konrad Adenauer, *Erinnerungen*, vol. 1: *1945–1953*, Stuttgart, 1965, p. 358 f. The west German finance minister had already sent the Chancellor a quickly formulated memorandum on the financing of the German contribution. Bundesarchiv Koblenz (BA), Zwischenarchiv, B 136/2164, Fritz Schäffer to Adenauer, 29.8.1950, annex: memorandum entitled 'Finanzierung des Sicherheitsbeitrages des Bundes'.
67. Princeton University Library, NJ, USA, John Foster Dulles papers, Aide Memoire (translation), undated (beginning of September 1950).
68. NA, Diplomatic Branch (DB), RG 59, Box 15, General Records of the Executive Secretariat, Daily Secret Summary, 18.9.1950.
69. At least the British government was convinced of this. PRO, CAB, 129/44, CP (51) 74, Policy Towards Germany, memorandum by Bevin, 9.3.1951, no. 7, see also ibid., CAB 131/8, Cabinet-Defence Committee, DO (59) 17th Meeting, minute 3, 1.9.1950; ibid., CAB 128/18, Cabinet, CM (50) 56th Conclusions, minute 6, 6.9.1950.
70. FRUS, 1950, III, p. 267.
71. On this point and the following Wiggershaus, 'Entscheidung' (see

Note 63), chap. V.'
72. See for example the reasons for the British government agreeing to this (the chance to pursue a common security policy with the USA and to bind her militarily to Europe; the creation of an integrated armed force for Europe with an American Commander-in-Chief) in PRO, CAB 129/42, CP (50)220, New York Meetings, 6.10.1950; ibid., CAB 128/18, CM (50) 63rd Conclusions, 9.10.1950; ibid., PREM 8/1429/1, Some reflections on the earnest deadlock over the question of German rearmament, memo by Bevin, 19.10.1950. Above all the essay by Geoffrey Warner in this book, chapter 8.
73. PRO, PREM 8/1429/1, DO (50)80, Cabinet-Defence Committee, German Participation in the Defence of the West. Memo by Defence Secretary, 13.10.1950.
74. PRO, FO 371/85054, C 5905/27/18G, 16.9.1950, New York telegram no. 1067, 16.9.1950.
75. Public Archives Canada, RG 2 – Privy Council Office, 18, vol. 243, C-10-9-D (1950), Cabinet Committee. Documents, D 254, memorandum for the Prime Minister, North Atlantic Council, New York.
76. Jules Moch, *Histoire du réarmement allemand depuis 1950, Paris, 1950*, p. 85.
77. Ibid., p. 68 f.; FRUS, 1950, III, p. 340ff.; PRO, FO 371/85055, New York telegram No. 1171 (sketch of the temporary measures including the guerilla project); ibid., New York telegram No. 1216, 26.9.1950 (regarding removal of sentence concerning the guerilla theme).
78. On 27 September 1950 in the presence of Ministerialdirektor Herbert Blankenhorn from the Bundeskanzleramt (Chancellor's Office) and Graf von Schwerin, Bundesarchiv-Militärarchiv, Freiburg (BA-MA), BW 9/3105, Aktennotiz Schwerin, 27.9.1950.
79. NA, MMB, RG 218, GF 1948–1950, CCS 092, Germany (5–4–49), Sec. 4, telegram CINCEUR Heidelberg (Handy), infor. HICOG No. SX 2848, 11.10.1950.
80. Public Archives Canada, RG 2 – Privy Council Office, 18, vol. 139, C-30 Chiefs of Staff, 1950: memorandum of discussions of Lt.-Gen. C. Foulkes, Washington, 16.10.1950, no. 10.
81. PRO, FO 371/85057, C 7720/27/18G, 31.10.1950, Letter from Kirkpatrick to Sir Donald St. John Gainer, 31.10.1950.
82. Public Archives Canada, RG 2, 16, vol. 21, Cabinet Conclusions, meeting 25.10.1950, no. 25.
83. Brief outline of the introductory speech written by Oberst i.G. a.D. (Colonel G.S.(retd.)) Johann Adolf Graf von Kielmansegg, MGFA, Replies to questions put to Kielmannsegg, 5.
84. Hans-Jürgen Rautenberg and Norbert Wiggershaus, *'Die Himmeroder Denkschrift' vom Oktober 1950: Politische und militärische Überlegungen für einen Beitrag der Bundesrepublik Deutschland zur wes-*

teuropäischen Verteidigung, Karlsruhe, ²1985; also in *MGM* vol. 1, 1977, pp. 135–206.

85. PRO, CAB 128/18, CM (50) 63rd Conclusions, minute 3, 9.10.1950, together with ibid., PREM 8/1429/1, draft of telegram to Paris (sent, with minor alterations, as telegram no. 1008 on 9.10.1950).
86. PRO, PREM 8/1429/1, DO (50) 85, Cabinet-Defence Committee: The Military Case for German Participation in the Defence of Western Europe, Report by Chiefs of Staff, 13.10.1950; revised edn. ibid., DO (50) 89, 20.10.1950.
87. PRO, FO 371/85056, C 6582/27/18G, 15.10.1950, telegram Wahnerheide no. 1499, 15.10.1950.
88. Ibid.
89. PRO, PREM 8/1429/1, Note on an informal meeting on 20.10.1950 (participants: Attlee, Bevin, Shinwell, Kirkpatrick, Secretary of State Lord Henderson (FO), Ambassador Sir O. Harvey (Paris) and Elliot).
90. The plan was drafted by October 13 (FRUS, 1950, III, p. 376, See Note 5). It was presented to the 'personal representatives' of the NATO defence ministers on 18 October (however, at that time, Ambassador Bonnet refused to take advice (ibid., p. 396)) and was finally given to the Defence Committee itself in a revised form. The text is in ibid., p. 406ff. The following appraisal is based on this text.
91. The French envoy, de Crouy Chanel, expressed this fear on 26.10.1950. PRO, FO 371/85090, C 6925/57/18, note by Mallet.
92. Public Archives Canada, RG 2, 18, vol. 244, C-10-9-M (1950), Special Meeting, Cabinet Defence Committee with the Minister of National Defence of France, 7.11.1950 (statements by Moch). Further references: PRO, CAB 128/18, CM (50) 69th Conclusions, minute 1, 30.10.1950; ibid., CAB 131/8 Cabinet. Defence Committee, DO (50) 21st Meeting, minute 4, 8.11.1950. See also the critique of the Pleven Plan by Donald Cameron Watt, who describes it as a 'political proposal conceived as a way out of a series of political dilemmas'. D. Cameron Watt, 'Die konservative Regierung und die EVG 1951–1954', in *Die Europäische Verteidigungsgemeinschaft* (see Note 8), p. 83f., quotation p. 84.
93. Text of the governmental statement in *Europa-Archiv* 5 (1950), p. 3518f.
94. This was speculation on the part of Kirkpatrick after the first rumours concerning the French plan while it was in the process of being formulated. PRO, FO 371/85056, C 6263/27/186, 30.9.1950, telegram Wahnerheide no. 1448, 30.9.1950.
95. PRO, FO 371/85059, C 8662/57/18, minute A. G. Gilchrist, 25.10.1950.
96. Cf. the statements in FRUS, 1950, III, p. 411 (in conversation with US

Defense Secretary George C. Marshall: companies; at the most battalions); PRO, PREM 8/1429/1, ZO 384, Report by Defence Minister Shinwell, 28.10.1950 (at the most regiments).
97. Pleven did not specify the last two points of the package until the conclusion. *Keesings Archiv der Gegenwart* 1950, p. 2644. Cf. the explanations by Moch on 27 October, FRUS, 1950, III, p. 410f.
98. PRO, PREM 8/1429/1, ZO 379, 28.10.1950; Public Archives Canada, RG2, 16, vol. 21, Cabinet Conclusions, Meeting 8 November 1950 (50 per cent Germans).
99. Moch on 7.11.1950 in Ottawa (as in Note 92).
100. NATO HQ. Brussels, International Military Staff, Central Registry (IMS) SG 84, Contribution of Germany for the Defence of Western Europe. French Proposal, 2.11.1950.
101. Wettig, *Entmilitarisierung und Wiederbewaffnung* (see Note 9), p. 369 (recognition by Bidault and Alphand).
102. As the source material on the critique of the Pleven Plan is so widely scattered among various archives, see e.g. PRO, CAB 131/9, Cabinet – Defence Committee, DO (50) 95, the Meeting of the NATO Defence Committee in Washington on 28, 30 and 31 October 1950. Memorandum by Shinwell, 7.11.1950.
103. Ibid.
104. PRO, CAB 128/18, CM (50) 69th Conclusions, minute 1, 30.10.1950; FRUS, 1950, II, p. 420.
105. PRO, PREM 8/1429/1, DO (50)100. German Contribution to the Defence of Europe. Memorandum by Bevin, 24.11.1950.
106. See Bevin's plan of an 'Atlantic Alliance Force', which he put before the Cabinet Defence Committee, and which, along with operative integration according to the American proposal, also envisaged an administrative integration. Bevin described this as the least dangerous way of making the Federal Republic into an equal partner. The proposal did not get past the committee, however. The Dutch idea of having a NATO High Commissioner contained the suggestion of administrative control mechanisms for the first time. See for both proposals DO (50)100 (see Note 105).
107. NATO HQ, Brussels, International Military Staff, Central Registry (NISCA), North Atlantic Council Deputies. Documents, D-D/190, Provisional Arrangement for the Participation of Germnay in the Defence of Western Europe. Memorandum by the United States Deputy, 22.11.1950.
108. The Spofford proposal speaks of German elements 'as a small as possible so as to be fully effective, as laid down by the Military Committee'. The Military Committee decided that the sufficiently effective fighting unit (and thus the maximum size of the west German elements) was to be the national 'regimental combat team' or the reinforced brigade (5,000 to 6,000 men). FRUS, 1950, III, p. 518.

109. On Paris' acceptance of the Spofford Plan: NATO, NISCA, North Atlantic Council Deputies, Documents, D-D/174, 14.11.1950, p. 5 (re: the strength of the fighting unit); Wilfried Loth, *Socialismus und Internationalismus: Die französischen Sozialisten und die Nachkriegsordnung Europas 1940–1950*, Stuttgart, 1977 (*Studien zur Zeitgeschichte*, vol. 9), p. 288, and NATO, NISCA, North Atlantic Council Deputies, Summary Records, D-R/41, 11.12.1950, p. 1 (re: Spofford's entire proposal).
110. FRUS, 1950, III, P. 566 ff., together with p. 531 ff. and p. 538 ff.
111. Ibid., p. 585 ff., text of the agreement, ibid., p. 531 ff.; cf. ibid., p. 586, note 2.
112. Ibid., p. 541.
113. The control aspects of the Brussels Agreement is presented in its true light for the first time by Wilhelm Meier-Dörnberg, 'Politische und militUarische Faktoren bei der Planung des deutschen Verteidigungsbeitrages im Rahmen der EVG', in *Entmilitarisierung und AufrUustung in Mitteleuropa 1945–1956*, mit Beiträgen von Alexander Fischer, Christian Greiner, Klaus A. Maier, Ulrich de Maizière, Wilhelm Meier-Dörnberg, Georg Meyer, Manfried Rauchensteiner, Jan Schulten, Hans-Erich Volkmann, Norbert Wiggershaus, Herford, Bonn, 1983 (*Vorträge zur Militärgeschichte*, vol. 4), pp. 184–208.
114. Ibid., p. 195.
115. FRUS, 1950, III, P. 542.
116. Ibid., p. 532 f.
117. General Eisenhower said this at this early stage before members of the Canadian Cabinet. Public Archives Canada, RG 2, series 18, vol. 244, file C-10-9-M, 1951, Special Meeting, Cabinet Defence Committee with General Dwight D. Eisenhower, 25.1.1951.
118. PRO, PREM 8/1429/1. telegram FO no. 5485, 6.12.1950.
119. Ibid., memorandum 'German Rearmament', unsigned, 7.2.1951.
120. PRO, CAB 128/19, C.M. (51) 12th Conclusions, minute 4, 8.2.1951.
121. PRO, DG 1/4/16, Consultative Council, Extract from Record 1, 10th Session, 21.12.1950. The US State Department thought similarly. Steininger, *Deutsche Geschichte*, vol. 2 (see Note 38), p. 402 f., Dok. 67, memorandum of 1.2.1951.
122. PRO, FO 371/85032, C 7533/20/18 22.11.1950 (Kirkpatrick).
123. PRO, PREM 8/1429/1, C.P. (51) 128, The European Army, memorandum by Bevin, 8.5.1951.
124. On the time factor see ibid., on the insecurity over Parliamentary and public reaction in the Federal Republic see ibid., CAB 128/18, CM (50) 85th Conclusions, minute 4, 4.12.1950, and CAB 128/44, C.P. (51) 43, German Rearmament, 7.2.1951.
125. PRO, CAB 128/44, CP (51) 43 (as Note 124).

PART IV
Conclusion

19
Notes Towards a Synthesis

Donald Cameron Watt

Historiography and History: Problems of a Developing Historiography

This conference meets as the historiography of NATO is moving from one stage of development to another. It is essential to recognise the temporary nature of this process of development and not to apply methods and concepts only suitable for a later stage in the historiographical process.

The stages through which the historiography of the immediate present passes as the year studied recedes into the past have still to be properly examined. The example most studied has been the historiography of the period of 'appeasement' (1933–39).[1] From this one can suggest a typology of historiographical developments which divides these developments into six stages.

A Typology of Historiographical Development in Contemporary History

The first stage is that in which current events in a particular year (year X) are analysed in official and public writings contemporaneous with the events analysed. Such analysis ranges from government policy-makers and research personnel, some of which, though by no means all, is made public, to analyses made by public sources such as research institutes like the Royal Institute of International Affairs, the Council for Foreign Relations, Forschungsinstitut der Deutschen Gesellschaft für Auswärtige Politik, etc., political journalists writing in the serious weekly, monthly or quarterly reviews, or writers taking different sides in domestic political controversies or in such within alliances or associations. This stage covers the first five to ten years after the events. One might call this the *political journalism to first narrative stage*.

The second stage, which runs parallel with this but which usually goes on longer (covering the first twenty to thirty years after the event) is occupied by writers concerned to attribute blame or responsibility for errors or disasters in the immediate past and by participants in those events defending themselves against such attributions, by writing memoirs, commissioning sympathetic biographies, etc. This stage is that in which retired politicians, military and civil policy-makers, using whatever personal papers or limited access to government archives they can command, are the main contributors to the historiographical process. The distinguishing mark of the works produced at this stage is that in most cases the writers are viewing the events they are evoking backwards from the present.

The third stage follows on from the second, where it does not coexist with it. In this the first historical version, together with the accompanying myths, simplifications, concepts and misconceptions, take on the status of an authorised, 'received' version, despite the partial and partisan nature of the processes by which it comes to be established. This 'received version' is then drawn upon by academic political scientists and *Politologen*, for case studies, examples of the typologies the evolution of which forms an important part of their discipline. From their work the 'received version' exercises an influence on the new generation of policy-makers, who absorb it through their education, whether formal or informal.[2]

This is the position when, thirty years after the event, the first release of evidence from government archives and private papers takes place. Commercial publishing pressures are so strong at this moment that the time of release generates a wave of writers and historians competing to produce the first publications from the new archives. Critics have with some justice dubbed this the time of the 'Nescafé' school of instant history. The pressure of time impels its members to treat the new evidence, not as the basis of new analysis (which would take time) but as material with which to illustrate, confirm and justify the concepts already established during the previous stages. Paradoxically, the release of new evidence thus strengthens rather than upsets the 'received version', since the evidence is usually wrenched from its context, or selectively mined for statements which could be regarded as confirming the 'guilty men' theses already established. This stage (the fourth in the historiographical process) covers the period from twenty-five to thirty-five years after the event.

The fifth stage sees the re-evaluation and reassessment of *all* the new evidence released by historians working forward in time from study of the preceding events rather than backward from the present. This is the stage at which the main concern of historians is to clear away all the accretions of myths and misrepresentations in the name of historical realism, claiming to be writing history as it really or actually happened. The exigencies of monograph writing still impose on historians the need to cover short periods in time. But, save for the occasional inadequately supervised PhD student of the snotty young know-it-all type, pouring new PhDs into old bottles, historians working at this stage have abandoned the 'history starts now' fallacy.

The fifth stage passes into the sixth when the professional historians begin to reintegrate the myths rejected by their predecessors into the processes of reassessment, recognising that the myths themselves are part of the total historical process, being an essential part of the images and perceptions formed at the time and in the first five stages through which the historiographical process has passed.

The Present Stage in the Development of a Historiography of NATO: Methodological Problems

The current historiography of NATO stands with us somewhere between the fourth and fifth stages. This is a temporary and passing position and should be recognised as such. The temptation to make any assessment that we may now advance too final, too definitive, too elaborate or too rigid to accommodate the plethora of data must be recognised for what it is and rejected. Any individual assessment we make now – and that includes each and every paper presented at this conference – lacks the contexts provided by the other papers and by the political, economic, social and other factors which are part of the whole historical process, in which and against which the individual papers presented at this conference must be assessed.

Donald Cameron Watt

Problems of Imperfect Knowledge

At this moment historical work on the origins and early history of NATO face two kinds of problems. *The first, problems of imperfect knowledge*, can itself be divided into two parts; the first of these arises from the partial nature of the evidence, the second, paradoxically, from the vast amount of evidence that has been released. The wealth of archives, their geographical spread throughout the membership of the North Atlantic Alliance, presents a problem for the individual researcher in time, travel and funding so great that only the most energetic, the most well-funded and the most unscrupulous exploiter of his colleagues' willingness to relieve him of his teaching and administrative duties can possibly cover even a part of the materials available. Among this plethora of materials, it is only too easy for earnest and short-sighted researchers to confine their investigations to those files and papers whose archival classification seems to indicate their relevance.

Of these two problems of imperfect knowledge, the first, that created by the withholding of evidence (which includes, under an agreement of 1978, most if not all materials of NATO provenance) can only be solved, and then only in part, by an improvement in the relations of confidence between the bureaucracies and the historians of all the various NATO members. The second, that which arises from the plethora of research materials, can be persuaded to yield, at least in part, to the kind of research which is represented in the bringing together of the scholars and papers present at this conference and represented in this volume.

Problems of Interpretation, Concepts and Terminology

The second class of problems are those which, in part at least, arise from the imprecision of the concepts and terminology we historians, confronting the shift from stage four to stage five, have inherited from those who have preceded us. This imprecision has already proved a barrier to understanding between those who first developed these concepts, and are proving to be a snare to ourselves. This is particularly true when we consider the wide degree to which the language we use includes *a priorist* concepts ('cold war', 'blocks', 'alliance' are examples of these which are to be discussed later) developed in the heyday of the development of

Notes Towards a Synthesis

international relations theory (1956–1975) largely from American case-examples (themselves often inadequately investigated). These *a priorist* concepts can only be applied to the evidence available by techniques similar to those employed by that well-known Classical inn-keeper, Procrustes, in fitting his beds to his guests.

Another set of problems of interpretation comes from attempting to confine our analysis of the motives and perceptions of the actors to an arbitrarily restricted timeframe. This approach has been christened the 'history begins in 1945' (or 1946, 1947, 1948 or any arbitrarily chosen date) and behaving towards the actors in the events studied as though their existence and political conscience began with the date selected. The existence, experience, acquired knowledge, intellectual and political development of the actors arise, in fact, in an historical past which may extend up to sixty years or more before the date selected. The sources investigated must also be chosen so as to extend back to cover this development.

Yet another set of problems arises as soon as the attempt is made to integrate the work of historians in the Soviet Union in this period into studies based on Western sources. Investigation into the motivation and perceptions underlying Soviet foreign policy requires a completely different methodology, one which employs a far higher element of intelligent speculation and hypothesising than that employed by historians confronted with the detailed documentation of the internal processes of policy-making in Britain and the United States. Current work on Soviet motivation and perceptions is inevitably much more tentative and subject to revision and must be recognised as such in any attempt to incorporate it into any approach based on a synthesis of existing published research.

Terminological and Perceptual Imprecision: the Concept of the 'Cold War'

Let us consider the problems of interpretation which arise from the imprecision of the term 'cold war' as it has developed from its original coinage in 1946 to the general and detailed use made of it today.[3] Consider for a moment the opposite kind of conflict. There is enough disagreement, for example, as to when the Second World War began.[4] But at least each historian, whatever date is chosen, is clear between events which occurred before that date and can therefore be classified as 'origins' and those that occurred after the chosen date, and can therefore be regarded as part of its 'course' or 'development'. Equally it is usually possible to select a date at which the conflict ended (although the peace-settlement process can take several years, and end only with an armistice, as the Korean War did).

By contrast, there is no agreement on when the 'cold war' began, even where the different participants are concerned. There is, therefore, a continual confusion between 'origins' and 'development'. Equally there is no agreement between historians as to the areas covered by the scope of the 'cold war'. Nor is there any agreement over its periodisation. To take the question of origins first: did the 'cold war' begin with Truman's proclamation of February 1947? British policy-makers were inclined to see a major change in Soviet policy from reasonable opposition to covert antagonism by proxy in Stalin's speech of March 1946. Their own determination, that the Soviet Union was bent on the destruction of the British role in Europe and of the economy of Western Europe, dates from the Soviet withdrawal from the Paris meeting in June 1947, the erection of the Cominform and the inciting of the French and Soviet Communist parties against the European Recovery Programme in the autumn of 1947. Soviet historians are inclined to date the beginning of the 'Cold War' much earlier, and some Western revisionists have followed them.

Consider, too, the question of 'scope'. The 'cold war' in the Far East was seen at the time as part of the Moscow-Washington confrontation as though Mao Tse-tung was Stalin's puppet. It is clear now that this was not so. Events in the Far East now seem to be part of a parallel and separate set of events, interlocked and interacting with the events in Europe and the East-West conflict in Europe, but linked mainly through American perceptions and, to a lesser extent, Chinese ideology.

This raises a still further set of problems about the origins of the conflict in the Far East. British policy-makers argued, from the beginning of their conflict in Malaya with the local Chinese Communist party, that their rising followed on directions from Moscow passed on through an Asian Communist Front meeting in Calcutta in 1947. American historians tended to see the 'cold war' in the Far East as following inevitably from the Communist defeat of the Kuomintang in 1949.

These questions are inseparable from any enquiry into the real issues at stake. What was the 'cold war' about? If the issues changed, and they clearly did between the periods 1947–55 and 1958–63, can one talk of a single 'war' or a series of 'cold wars'? And what of the periods of the 'thaw' and the *'détente'*? Should they be seen as armistices or merely lulls in the fighting? It is possible to argue that the main issue in the period 1947–55 was the control of Germany,[5] whereas the period 1958–63, despite such sideshows as the Congo, was concerned with the far narrower issue of the control of Berlin. The 1947–55 period of 'cold war' ended with the Geneva Summit and the Berlin foreign-ministers' conference, at which the perpetuation of the division of Germany and the attachment of its two states respectively to NATO and the Warsaw Pact was assented to by the Soviet Union and the three Western members of the Security Council. That of 1958–63 ended with the failure of Khrushchev's attempt to use the stationing of Soviet missiles in Cuba to force Western withdrawal from Berlin. The hot-line agreement and the partial test-ban treaty of 1963 were positive gains extracted from the Soviet Union in the aftermath of the Cuban crisis. Both blocks were damaged in their cohesion in this period: NATO by the defeat of President Kennedy's 'Grand Design' inherent in President de Gaulle's veto of the British application to join the Common Market; the Soviet Union by the open breach with China consequent on Khrushchev's rebuttal of the Chinese mission to Moscow sent to persuade him not to conclude the partial test-ban treaty.

A further issue is the question of when the 'cold war' began in Europe. It is possible to argue that, before 1947, the conflict lay between Britain and the Soviet Union. If so, it lay below the level of activity to which the term 'war', whether 'hot' or 'cold', can be applied. It was not until the Soviet 'walk-out' of the Paris conference on the Marshall Plan in June 1947, the formation of the Cominform, the incitement of French and Italian trade unionists and politicos against the chance of Marshall Plan aid being accepted by the French and Italian governments that the leading British policy-makers, Attlee and Bevin, were finally convinced that the Soviet Union was Britain's enemy. The failure of the London meeting of the Council of Foreign Ministers in November 1947 launched Bevin on the course of rallying West European resistance as a preliminary to entangling the United States in a permanent alliance. Before the winter of 1947–8 there had been clashes over the future of the Italian colonies, over Trieste, over Soviet actions in Romania, Hungary and Poland, over Soviet support of the Greek anti-government forces in the 1946 outbreak of civil war in Greece and over the Soviet attempt to create a separatist republic in northern Iran. In London these were perceived as deliberate Soviet efforts to embarrass Britain by a policy of assault through proxies. British strategic planners took the Soviet Union as the potential enemy. The Foreign Office created the 'Russia Committee' to coordinate information upon and assess Soviet foreign-policy actions. This could, however, be compared with the manoeuvring or collection of intelligence of rival generals before battle is joined.

With the United States the historian confronts two events: the proclamation of the Truman 'doctrine' and the address of General Marshall, then Secretary of State, on 4 June 1947 at the Harvard graduation ceremonies. The Truman doctrine may be compared with a formal declaration of war; but if this is done their historians are faced with a paradox. In finally acknowledging America's need to take over Britain's role in keeping the Soviets out of the Mediterranean, a decision previous American policy-makers, from early 1944 onwards, had resolutely refused to take, precisely because they feared American involvement in the Anglo-Soviet confrontation they anticipated in the Balkans, the United States administration seems to have involved itself in the 'cold war' *before* Britain did. The point is moot; but it does provide an excellent example of the intellectual and conceptual dilemmas in which the system of categories evoked by the term 'cold war' can involve the unwary historian. Strictly speaking, such dilemmas belong entirely to the category of *'faux problèmes'* rather than the real world, since they stem entirely from the invention of categories based on the use of metaphors, rather than the study of reality; it is hardly surprising, therefore, to discover that the categories invented above prove difficult to apply.

Contemporary Perceptions of the 'Cold War': Problems and Confusions over Priorities

But that is not the end of the problems raised by the concept of 'cold war'. A further group of problems can be found in the different policies and perceptions of the civilian and military policy-makers in France, Britain and the United States. Since historians are stuck with the vocabulary and concepts of the 'cold war', this disagreement can best be described as concerning itself with the stability of the temperature of the 'cold war'. Was the 'cold war' merely a phase before the 'hot war' began, with a Soviet assault on the Western occupying powers in Germany and Austria, and the air bombardment of Paris, London, Brussels and the Hague? Or was it a substitute for 'hot war', something the Soviets would employ at least until 1955 or so, when British intelligence estimates believed the Soviet state would have completed its recovery from the damage done by four years of war to European Russia, and when the Soviet armed forces would once again be ready for a major war? The issues were not purely conceptual. They had very real consequences for the powers of Western Europe.

If the 'cold war' was simply a preliminary phase in the approach of major armed conflict in Central Europe, then it behoved the powers of Western Europe to do all they could to build up their armed forces, to agree on a unified command structure in Central Europe and to prepare for war. Since the economies of the West European states were still barely beginning to recover from the effects of the Second World War, and since available Soviet manpower made possible the assembly in Central Europe of forces considerably greater than any that the signatories of the Brussels Treaty could raise, it was essential that they bring in the United States as their ally, and that the United States be prepared to commit to the defence of Central Europe armies and air power at least on the scale of those General Eisenhower had commanded in 1944–5. Britain, too, should reduce its commitments elsewhere to the minimum, and a way be found to tie the forces thus released firmly into the defence of France. There must be no repetition of the British behaviour of 1940.

If, however, the British view was correct, and the 'cold war' was a Soviet device to obtain the rewards of a victorious war without actually fighting; if the Soviet aims were to disrupt the economic recovery of Western Europe and to destabilise the economies of Britain and France, then the area where Europe's economies were most vulnerable lay in the Middle East, with its enormous resources of energy and the access routes to the raw materials of South-East Asia and Australasia involved in the control of the Suez Canal. The presence of sizeable British forces, backing whatever contingent relations of local political leadership and local military forces were essential to the defence of the area, became an essential weapon for countering Soviet pressure on Europe. It became logical to station Britain's main strategic reserve there, in Palestine, Suez or Kenya, the more so as such a reserve, being poised to intervene anywhere from Turkey's frontiers to South-East Asia, could in turn threaten one of the Soviet Union's more sensitive frontiers. To concentrate all available reserves in Europe would, on this view, be playing the Soviets' game.

Moreover, if 'hot war' should come, it would not be confined purely to Central Europe, the chances of whose successful defence against conventional attack did not fill British strategic planners' minds with optimism. Here British and French perceptions coincided. Both agreed on the necessity of an American commitment. But the British saw such a commitment as a political signal to the Soviet Union. The whole burden of French representations was that it was an indispensable shield for French political stability. It was French opinion that needed reassuring rather than Soviet forces which needed to be deterred. Another occupation and liberation was not a prospect to be viewed with any enthusiasm in France. When and if French opinion could be assured of American protection against invasion, then France's political and military leaders might be prepared to think in terms of winning the 'cold war'. In 1948, however, they were more afraid of losing the 'hot war'.

These disagreements were to be a substantial barrier to the evolution of any agreed strategy within NATO. The question was made much more difficult by the inability of the US Joint Chiefs of Staff to decide on the nature of the situation they faced and by the influence their inability to decide exercised on the debate in the State Department, between the advocates of an alliance policy and those who thought, with Kennan, that Marshall Aid and the Brussels Pact were instruments adequate to 'contain' Soviet expansion in Central Europe without the inflexibility of a military commitment to back them up.

The effect of this confusion of language is to conceal the very similar confusion between the policy-makers, military and political, in Britain, France and the United States, over the nature of the threat against which they believed they were uniting, and the nature of the response that threat required to make a reality of the unity they sought.

Notes Towards a Synthesis

Terminological and Perceptual Confusions: The Concept of Blocs

The elucidation of this confusion by historians is not assisted by the ambiguity involved in a second concept much used by contemporaries and adopted by the numerous political scientists who, anticipating the evidence, have preceded the historians in the elaboration of a whole body of theories on the nature of 'alliances' and 'blocs'. Their attempts, now the evidence is available, to give their theories concrete reality by picking through it in a search for artefacts and structures with which to clothe them are understandable. But, since what they overlook or reject is as valid historically as that which they seize upon, the result is simply to produce a new confusion, if on a higher intellectual plane. These (no doubt intellectually fascinating) logical puzzles are not true history, and historians who get caught up in them are abandoning their role as such. The only questions for historians to answer are: (1) What did the respective signatories of the Brussels Treaty and the North Atlantic Treaty intend by and understand of the obligations into which they entered? and (2) Is the concept of 'blocs' of any use in throwing light on the relations between the signatories – or, for that matter, in throwing light on the relations, military and diplomatic, between the Soviet Union and its East European satellites?

It is clear that alliances play a different role in times of peace than in wartime. In a war they are a means of mustering strength so as to ensure victory. In times of peace they are a means of mustering strength so as to face a potential enemy with the probability of defeat should he proceed to use force against a member of the alliance. Students of the development of NATO or of the debate on the renewal of the Anglo-Japanese Alliance in 1921 (to name but two historical examples) will be aware that an alliance fulfils an extra purpose in time of peace in making it possible for one member of the alliance to control another by making it clear that it reserves to itself the right to decide when and if a *casus belli* has arisen, and that the invocation of the alliance in time of conflict is not automatic.

It is in this light that the historian has to examine both the original coming together of the five signatories of the Brussels Treaty into the Western Union Defence Organisation (WUDO) and the debate on NATO's military committee from the fall of 1949 to the outbreak of the Korean War. To talk of the formation of a bloc is of little help. Once more the British and French perceptions of both WUDO and NATO differed considerably. The matter was further complicated by the evolution of a degree of agreement, in both the Commanders-in-Chief and the Chiefs of Staff Committees of WUDO, on how and where Western Europe was to be defended if war should come, i.e. as far to the east as possible, but in any case on the banks of the Rhine.[6] Even this presented problems: part of northern Holland would thereby be surrendered to enemy occupation, an unhappy prospect for its government's representative. The forces available were, however, so grossly inadequate that the military authorities of WUDO could agree on one issue at least – whether to fight an invasion or to retain sufficient credibility to deter one, they needed American forces. At the first meeting of the WUDO Chiefs of Staff Committee in July 1948, it was the French military representative who pointed out that they would need German manpower too. But the matter was so politically embarrassing that it was not followed up – for the time being.

Did the signatories of WUDO intend it merely to be a response to the American reply to Bevin's original approaches, that is, a demonstration for the benefit of opinion in Congress and in the United States generally of European determination to defend themselves? Was Western Union just 'a sprat to catch a mackerel' and no more? The evidence now available suggests that, in addition to being a means to help French opinion towards acceptance of the movement to create a west German state, it was intended to be much more than mere bait with which to catch or entangle America into an alliance. Rather it was seen as a great improvement in the technology of fishing – that is, as a means of strengthening the European states against America once the alliance between WUDO and the United States was concluded. While WUDO stood alone, the role of the American military delegation to WUDO was to encourage it to approach the Americans for military aid, once investigation had identified WUDO's deficiencies in equipment and *matériel de guerre*, and once it had been shown that these deficiencies were such that self-help between the allies could not cover them.

Whether or not Marshall, Acheson or their advisors understood the purpose behind WUDO cannot be shown. What can be established is that American policy, both within NATO's military-planning structure and in the application of the Military

Assistance Act, had the effect of confining Western Union military planning to one out of five of the command areas into which the North Atlantic area was divided, and of dismantling it as a single agency representing the military needs of the major European parties. There was to be no bloc within a bloc. Nor, in the long run, was there to be any Anglo-American partnership. NATO politics was to become internalised (a new case of *der Primat der Innenpolitik*) in that the main issue was to overcome British and French resistance to the imposition upon them by American planners both of the concept of blocs and, outside the military-aid sphere,[7] the concept of a unified, federal Europe.

The concept of 'blocs', that is of WUDO and NATO forming one bloc, and the Soviet grouping which was eventually to become the Warsaw Pact forming a rival bloc, is thus misleading to political scientists and to any historians unwise enough to accept that analysis. It carries with it the connotations that between members of each bloc there was a unity of purpose and a similar unity of control and leadership – even the temptation to assure, even subconsciously, that the two 'blocs' were organised on similar lines, that their leaders exercised a similar degree of control over their followers and that the group directing each 'bloc' saw their problems as a mirror-image of those faced by their opposite numbers. Now it may be that groupings of this kind can be shown historically to display a tendency to degenerate from an alliance of states equal in sovereignty, if not in comparative strength, towards a relationship more akin to the hegemonial, after the archetype of the confederacy of Delos in the fifth century BC, as described in the writings of the Athenian general turned historian, Thucydides. Such demonstrations, however, have earned a considerable degree of scepticism among British historians who associate them with the monumental but largely discredited work of the late Arnold Toynbee, who, it is now accepted, invented an enormous typology of such cases by a stupendous but indiscriminately wide range of reading which ignored or suppressed all the circumstances which made categorisation of his so-called examples generally illegitimate.

This is not to say that military policy-makers on both the NATO and Soviet sides of the great divide did not themselves use the terminology of 'blocs'. It is, in fact, to argue that in adopting that terminology they misled themselves and their political leaders into assuming a unity of purpose, control and leadership among their opposite numbers which did not initially exist – indeed, it may well be that it was their own assumption that such unity existed, and the courses of action which their assumption dictated, which made that assumed unity a reality. Consider, for example, how often Soviet politics and pressures managed to ingest into the work of WUDO and NATO a sense of threat or danger which rendered the wide differences in aims and perceptions between the NATO powers seem a luxury they could not afford. It is at least arguable (and it was argued at the time) that the drive to create the West German state and then to arm it within NATO played a similar part in unifying the satellite leaderships behind the Soviet Union. The adoption of the concept of 'military blocs' may, in short, be seen to be a self-fulfilling prophecy.

It is useful and rewarding, in this context, to reread the paper contributed by the Canadian member of this symposium. Canadian concepts of an Atlantic bloc, and of Europe, are quite different either from the range of concepts entertained in the United States, or, for that matter, from those entertained in London, Paris, Rome, Brussels, the Hague, Copenhagen or Oslo. Canadian foreign policy and Canadian perceptions are best understood as those which might have been entertained by a United States confined to certain parts of North America, as if the Alleghenies or the Mississippi had never been crossed.

Terminological and Perceptual Confusions: The Concept of Deterrence

A further concept which needs the most careful analysis in the context of the years 1948–52 is that of deterrence as an element in the policies of the individual members of the Atlantic Alliance. At different times one can detect at least four differing conceptions of deterrence, and of who was to be deterred, entering into the deliberations of the policy-makers. There is the straightforward notion that those to be deterred are the political decision-makers in the Soviet Union. This can be divided into deterrence against military attack, deterrence against efforts to subvert the alliance from within, and deterrence against resistance to the processes by which the alliance was becoming a firm and persisting reality. There is the slightly different view that those to be deterred were those responsible for providing the Soviet leadership with military advice and military appreciations of the whole situation. They may be described as measures intended to deter the potential enemy.

But there is also the role that a policy of deterrence must play within the alliance. In seeming to deter the foe, it must counter (or 'deter') those pessimistic, and largely European, currents of opinion within the alliance who believed or argued military resistance to be futile or impossible, and who held that diplomacy should be directed towards reaching an accommodation with the Soviet Union on the best terms possible. Here the targets are the neutralists, the pretenders to a Third Force, those who said 'ohne mich', and the moral defeatists. Equally it had to counter (or deter) the temptation in Washington to react with anger or scorn to such currents, and for these (and other) reasons to write Europe off as indefensible and therefore expendable.

The analysis of this latter aspect of deterrence, that is, how it was perceived by opinion within the alliance is much more complex than that of how it was perceived by Soviet policy-makers. Admittedly we are short of evidence on the Soviet side. But the process of risk analysis which constitutes the acceptance of deterrence on the Soviet side is a fairly simple one. Commenting on a paper given by Henry Kissinger to the International Institute of Strategic Studies in London (the author of this commentary was in the audience), Denis Healey said that the difficulty with deterrence policy was that five times as much power was needed to convince one's own supporters that deterrence was working as was needed to deter one's potential enemies. The context made it clear that he was referring to Western public opinion in general; there is, however, plenty of evidence to show that military advisers, as professional 'worst-case' analysts, are equally difficult to convince, and that domestic opponents can only be prevented from arguing that deterrence policy is a sham by a military expenditure so considerable that they prefer to depict it as grossly in excess of what is required.

The contributions to this book by Professor Kaplan, Professor Guillen and Dr Riste make it clear that differing estimates, of whether those to be deterred were the political or the military policy-makers in the Soviet Union, and of how effective WUDO or NATO was as a deterrent, were the major issues dividing French, British, Benelux and Scandinavian policy-makers and advisers from their American counterparts or WUDO defence-planners from the Pentagon, and the Pentagon from the State Department. Indeed it is often the major issue in intra-NATO politics.

The Dangers of a 'Start Now' Historiography: Political Generations and Perceptions of the Past

Reference was made earlier to the dangers of a historiography which chose any particular date as the basis of its studies, of what is called a 'history starts now' historiography. This conference has selected 1948 as the opening date of our studies. But to write as if events before 1948 were of no relevance is to ignore a range of factors so wide as entirely to distort our understanding. The policy-makers of 1948 and the publics they served entered the year 1948 with an enormous volume of experience, and of conventional hindsight expressed in axiomatic form about that experience, which unfortunately differed enormously from person to person, generation to generation and nation to nation.

European and British policy-makers had already lived through the period of 'cold war' between the democracies and the dictatorships which we now call the age of appeasement, the 1930s. Under the influence of Churchillian historiography and of that group of right-wing historians in Britain (almost entirely those studying Europe) who had opposed appeasement in the 1930s, they arrived at a number of conclusions hostile to any policy of attempting an accommodation with external threats, especially external threats from authoritarian or 'totalitarian' governments. French policy-makers had spent the 1930s obsessed by the threat of military attack across France's eastern frontier; British policy-makers with the threat of sudden catastrophic attack from the air.[8]

To this the policy-makers of Western Europe had to add the experience of defeat, oppressive occupation and violent liberation. British opinion and British policy-makers (this is an often-repeated cliché) had not shared in the experience of occupation and liberation. Britain had, however, undergone both the 'blitz' of 1940–1 and, far more disturbingly, the massive bombardment of 1944–5 by the *Vergeltungswaffen* 1 and 2: the first a primitive cruise missile, the second a crude IRBM. British policy-makers were well aware that only a combination of accurate intelligence,

Notes Towards a Synthesis

preventive bombing and the invasion and reconquest of the French coast had made the V1 comparatively ineffective. They had no defence whatever against the V2. It was assumed that a future enemy would have taken up the development of such strategic missiles where the German scientific effort had ended. Soviet efforts by various measures to recruit German scientific personnel with knowledge of the German programme were well known. Any successful invasion of Western Europe which reached the Atlantic coastline opposite Britain would, it was assumed, be followed in a fairly short period of time by the opening of a new missile bombardment of Britain's southern industrial and administrative triangle, if not of the Midland industrial centres too. It did not seem likely that a new British evacuation of the continent would be followed by time enough to prepare, in comparative invulnerability, a return to mainland Europe on the lines of that mounted in 1944.

To the wartime experience of defeat at Germany's hands there had to be added the first-hand contacts with the Red Army made possible by the meeting of Soviet, American, British and French forces in Central Europe. Opinions of the Soviet air force and the Soviet navy were not greatly enhanced by the experience or observations of the Soviet war effort. Both the Red air force and the Red navy had fought largely in an auxiliary role to that of the Red army. But with the meeting of the victorious armies in Central Europe, their long-term cooperation in the occupation of Berlin and Vienna and the availability for Western intelligence, first of German generals with fighting experience on the Eastern Front, and then of Austrian and German prisoners-of-war returning from captivity in the Soviet Union, much of the wall of secrecy built by Stalin around the Red army before and during the war (to the fury and chagrin of the British and American military missions in Moscow) was irretrievably broken. The Soviet generals, the Soviet private soldiers, the Soviet tank corps and the Soviet military were now known to, observable and encounterable by the most perceptive of British, French and American military observers. There was little room for comfort in what they saw.

The third crucial period of experience was that of the years 1944–5, the years in which the victorious Western armies had landed in France, broken out of the Normandy bridgehead, survived the last German counter-offensive in the Ardennes and driven finally across the Rhine, into the Ruhr and on to the Oder.

Eisenhower, soon to be Chief of Staff to the US Army, Supreme Commander in Europe of NATO forces in 1951–2, and subsequently President, had commanded a host in which five American armies had marched alongside one British army, one Canadian and one French. The idea of overwhelming American strength involved in this experience was increased by the degree to which the non-American forces he commanded were armed with weapons of American provenance. American media coverage of the fighting in France and Germany exaggerated the impression of US might conveyed to Americans at home. American might liberated a Europe without arms or armaments, one largely incapable of contributing to its own liberation. This was the message of the US media.

It is essential to understand this to make sense of the otherwise inexplicable behaviour of American policy-makers towards, first of all, Western Union, and then the European contribution to NATO. To read American criticisms of both, one would not conceive the scale of European mutual aid before the creation of NATO, the paucity and military inadequacies of US military forces in Europe in the years 1947–50, or, even after the commitment of American military forces to NATO in the winter of 1950, the relative scale of US and European military contributions to the defence of Western Europe. The four, later five, American divisions committed to the ground defence of Europe in the Eisenhower era were extremely welcome. But they put the US commitment somewhat above that of Belgium or The Netherlands, and well below the fully mobilised strength of Britain, France or, once the expedient of EDC had been defeated and Western Union revived to provide for control of West Germany, the strength of the Bundeswehr.

The original American contribution to NATO was intended to be purely financial in scope, and was to be subsumed under the military-aid-programme legislation which was funnelling aid to a variety of other (non-European) countries. No American ground forces could be committed to the defence of the Central, Northern or Southern European fronts, for the very simple reason that no such forces were in existence. Indeed, the rapid demobilisation of specialists meant that, by 1947, the forces making up the American occupation of Germany and Austria were simply unable to fight. In the event of an invasion of Western Europe they would have had to run like rabbits for the Channel

Notes Towards a Synthesis

and the Pyrenees.

The actual scale of mutual aid in Europe was reported to the American observer group of WUDO in 1949. Bear in mind that, in 1945, the sole armed forces of Belgium and The Netherlands consisted of those that had escaped the débâcle of 1940 and had taken refuge in Britain where they had been re-equipped with British ships, arms and aircraft. The French had produced one army to fight in France and an army corps or so to fight in Italy. They also had the remains of the Vichy army and of the Maquis. Its arms in 1945 were mainly American. There was no air force and, after the scuttling of the French fleet in Toulon in November 1942, little or no navy. The West European arms industry had been geared to the production of German weapons. It had, in any case, been very largely destroyed by allied air attacks. Design teams had to be built up from scratch.

By the summer of 1948, only three years later, despite French involvement in Indochina and the Dutch troubles in Indonesia, all the European powers had reintroduced conscription, rebuilt their armies, navies and air forces, their command staffs and their military establishments. The major contributor to this process had been Britain. Figures produced by the WU military committee in 1949 for the American observers show that British warships, British military aircraft and a plethora of British military stores had been transferred into continental ownership. The French air force was flying British jets, *Meteors*, built under licence with Rolls-Royce jet engines. In all, British military goods to the value (prior to the 1949 devaluation of sterling) of one and a half billion dollars had passed into European ownership. Dutch and Belgian troops were training in Britain. The major problem was that of how further transfers should be paid for.

By the standards of American aid under Lend-Lease, and by the expectations of Americans who ignored the parlous state of Europe in 1945 to make simple comparisons between the populations of Western Europe and that of the United States, the state of Europe's defence in 1945 left much to be desired. Without the capacity given the United States by the Supreme Air Command and its atomic armament, however, Europe's ground forces, in 1948–9, compared very favourably with those of the United States. European industrial capacity was still, it was true, a mere shadow of that of the United States. If there was scope for valid criticism by American observers of European weakness in

1948–9, it lay in this area. But America, in 1941, had enjoyed an enormous excess of largely unused industrial capacity. Europe in 1945–7 had no such surplus, and Britain's industrial capacity had been under severe strain since 1940.

Enough has been said of the need to take into account the influence on both European and American policy-makers of the experiences of the 1930s, of the years of war, defeat and German occupation, and of the effects of liberation and victory. But historians also need to consider the very different attitudes to these experiences taken by the different political generations now engaged in policy-making. (The term 'political generations' is used to differentiate policy-makers not by their chronological age so much as by the date at which, and the company in which, they began their political experience as policy-makers.) These distinctions are of particular importance in Britain, France and in Western Germany.

In Britain the distinguishing mark of the members of the Labour government of 1945–51 is their survival of the débâcle which overtook the Labour Party in the 1931 General Election, the bitter fight over rearmament against the party's ideological and pacifist wings in the 1930s, their successful resistance (alone among Europe's socialist parties) to the siren-voices of the 'Popular Front', and their entry into government in 1940. The Labour cabinet were opposed to pacifism, suspicious of Communism, adjusted to the role of force in international affairs, and *dirigiste* both by instinct and as a result of the near-total mobilisation of British society for victory in the years 1940–5. They were used, moreover, to working within a system of government where the needs of defence had been increasingly integrated into the policy-making process since before the 1914–18 war. In the first two years after 1945 they were to advance this process still further by establishing a central Ministry of Defence and breaking with a thousand years of British practice by introducing peacetime military conscription.

By contrast, the successive French governments of the Fourth Republic, especially after General de Gaulle's withdrawal in 1946, contained few if any figures with prewar administrative experience and none with any experience of the integration of defence with overall policy-making. The French military leadership were, with a few exceptions, the survivors of the Vichy army, the defeated of 1940. The government of the Fourth Republic was no more integrated than that of the Third, and policy tended, as between the wars, to be made in compartments, whose only links were provided by the informal consensus arising out of the common training and outlook of the products of the *grandes écoles*. In the circumstances of 1945–8, before Jean Monnet put together the remarkable combination of forward–looking talent which was to be engaged by 'planification', these products were both defensive and defeatist in outlook. Military they were not; and their ability properly to assess military threats to the work of reviving, reforming and rejuvenating the French economy was minimal. Panic rather than prudence was the distinguishing mark of much of French alliance policy between 1945 and 1958.

The generational differences in West Germany are even more striking. The new emerging élites of the West German state were a mixture of three separate generations; the old men surviving from the *Kaiserzeit*, the Weimar administrators, and the exiles, internal as well as external, of the Hitler years. All were, by the standards of the interwar years, essentially persons of the second or third rank, some because that was as far as their ability had taken them, some because of their innate inability to fit in with the dominant ethos of Germany before the Hitler period, but most because of the effect that Nazi repression of all rival sources of political leadership in Germany, particularly after the failure of the 1944 attempt on Hitler's life, had in permanently removing the outstanding figures of opposition from German political life. With the fragmentation of Germany into separate zones and the loss of the eastern half of prewar Germany, in part to Poland and the Soviet Union, in part to the Sovietisation of political life in the Soviet-occupied zones, they were, moreover, much more anchored in the interests of their individual *Länder* and their individual regions than in any all-German policy. The need to survive during the Nazi period, reinforced by the experiences of the year 'Null' (1945), had driven them back to their roots. The distinguishing mark of political life in West Germany after 1945 is the unimportant role played by the kind of quasi-ideological, metaphysical debate with which students of the history of German political life and thought are so familiar, and the return of which, in the 1980s, is one of the most worrying phenomena to non-German observers of Germany today. 'Pragmatism' became both the catchword and the watchword.

Under its impulse German self-democratisation proceeded at a pace to which the Germans themselves found it difficult to adjust psychologically, and which lay totally beyond the mental capacity of those who had so recently been both Germany's enemies and victims. The debate in France and Britain over the need and the proposal to rearm West Germany, even the discussion in these countries and in the United States, even the stormy role of Herr Franz-Josef Strauss a decade later, as Germany's Minister of Defence, was conducted in terms of stereotypes to which German politics provided no corresponding reality. But these stereotypes provided the *damnosa hereditas* within which Germany's new political leaders were forced to manoeuvre, and by which their every action was to be judged. The new 'pragmatism' had to realise and accept that too.

One can find the same generational and experiential differences at work in the differing attitudes of French opinion and of French policy-makers, by contrast to those in Britain, towards the extra-European factors with which they had to cope during these years. For France the war years of 1939–45 had involved two campaigns on France's eastern frontiers, one leading to defeat in 1940, one leading to victory in 1945, both fought with the aid of allies who, seen through French eyes, had abandoned them in 1940 and dominated them, or attempted to, in 1944–5. Events in Syria and the Lebanon in 1941, or in Indochina, had been the merest sideshows, arising out of the defeat in Europe in 1940, and inconceivable without it. Much the same is being said by British historians now about the British loss of Malaya, Singapore and Burma in 1942. But, to British opinion in 1945, the great British defeat in South-East Asia was merely one event in a war with a globally distributed hostile coalition which had been blowing up since the early 1930s.

Britain, therefore, had no difficulty, from the beginning, in seeing the 'emergency' in Malaya as part of a worldwide 'cold war' launched against the British Empire by a power whose record in trying to weaken British strength by the back door had begun with Lenin in 1919, and of which ample evidence lay buried in the British archives. Indeed, part of the major difficulty in reconciling British and American attitudes to the breakdown of the British mandate in Palestine and the emergence of Israel lay in the conviction, rooted deep in significant sections of the British policy-making élite, that this was also part of the same process.

Notes Towards a Synthesis

By contrast, the French attitude to the conflict in Indochina began by seeing this purely as a 'colonial war', analogous to many previous such conflicts. It was only at the end of the 1940s, and only when it became necessary to find some means of combating American anti-colonialist sympathies, that French policy-makers began to depict the war in Indochina as part of the global 'cold war'. Even then the real conviction of this was only to take hold of that part of the French military with experience of war and defeat in Indochina. It never really took root in opinion in France. Nor was French opinion ever convinced that Britain's role east of Suez was important in protecting Europe from the loss of vital supplies of energy and raw materials. The British argument that until the Soviet Union was ready to risk war in Europe – which deterrence policy was designed to prevent or at least postpone – Britain's role and presence in the Middle East was essential to protect European (as well as purely British) interests against Soviet 'cold war' tactics (the substitution of subversion and 'informal penetration' for invasion and conquest) therefore found very little echo in France, at least until the rise of Nasser in the mid-1950s. Even then it was Nasser's role in supporting the FLN in Algeria, a French *département*, rather than his presence on the Nile Valley, the Red Sea or the coasts of the Gulf, which brought France to Britain's way of thinking.

To present historians, choosing 1948 as the opening date for a 'Start Now' historiography has one further danger: that is, in the current tendency to see the formation of a Soviet bloc in Europe, economically and militarily integrated, as a Soviet response to the American role in the parallel developments in Western Europe from the original proposals of Mr Secretary Marshall in June 1947 to the signature of the North Atlantic Treaty. The historical evidence now available to us (and the evidence available at the time) shows that the economic integration of the industries and agricultures of the defeated and occupied East European enemies of the Soviet Union was already far advanced when General Marshall mounted the podium at Harvard University's graduation ceremonies. This was particularly true of the economies of Romania and the Soviet zone of eastern Germany. The process of integration, however, was also well under way in Poland and Hungary. Only in Czechoslovakia did it need the coup of 1948 to reverse the Czech attempt to rebuild the trade pattern of the pre-war years: an attempt which was greatly handicapped by the absence of any German market comparable with that which had obtained in the 1930s, and the physical weaknesses of trans-German road and rail links. The establishment of the Cominform in the autumn of 1947 provided a more overt institutionalisation of a process already well under way.

In much the same way, it did not need the final signature of the Warsaw Pact, in 1955, to provide the integration of east European armed forces with the Soviet command structure. Even as early as 1946, British military planners assumed – no doubt on more than adequate military evidence – that Polish, Hungarian, Romanian, Bulgarian and indeed Yugoslav military forces were at the disposal of the Soviet military planners (save for the 20–30 per cent of the satellite armies which would be needed to maintain internal security) in the event of war. As for the SBZ, the development of German paramilitary *Kasernierte Volkspolizei* units by the Soviet occupation authorities was well known to the British authorities through the evidence of defectors or deserters. The military planners of Western Union declared, in 1949, that an intrusion by East German forces of this kind into Western Germany would be treated as 'aggression' on the same basis as an attack by Soviet forces themselves. It did not need the outbreak of the war in Korea in June 1950 to awaken the military staffs of the WUDO powers to the possibility of what was later called 'aggression by proxy'.

Terminological and Perceptual Confusions: The Concept of Alliance

The concept of alliance is one that, both in the public mind and in historical usage, carries with it a number of ambiguities stemming from the double purpose to which the conclusion of an alliance has been put in the past. In using the term 'alliance' here, we are, of course, employing it as the term is used in diplomatic and military usage, that is, involving a written undertaking to support any signatory in the event of that party being involved in war, given on behalf of the other signatories. An alliance is thus a precisely defined term, the reality of which may be judged by the attachment to the political side of the alliance of a series of military conventions detailing the aid which each signatory will give to the other signatories in the event of the alliance being activated. The term should not be used by serious historians as synonymous with merely amicable relations, understandings or deals over the political support one state might give to another generally, or other such agreements. An *entente* is not an alliance (witness the sad story of the Anglo-French entente between 1906 and 1914), though it may lead to one. Contrariwise, two co-belligerents may be merely 'associated' in war, as the United States was with Britain and France in 1917–18. An unwritten alliance is, in the words of the legendary US film magnate, Joseph P. Mayer, stigmatising a 'gentleman's agreement', 'not worth the paper it's not written on'.

Having said this, one can distinguish at least five different conceptions of a North Atlantic Alliance, current in the years 1945–52, in such a way as to cause confusion if not outright conflict between its advocates before April 1949, and its signatories thereafter. It was, in the first place, conceived as a warning to potential aggressors and therefore as *political reassurance* against aggression for the more nervous or more vulnerable of its signatories. The initial US reaction to Mr Bevin's approach in January 1948 was to unleash a bitter debate within the State Department between those who could not see why Britain, France and the west European powers should need, or be given, any more American reassurances than those America had already given (a point of view taken, for example, by George Kennan, whose expression of it betrayed a considerable degree of ignorance of the little (in military terms) America was capable of doing after the potentially crippling level of American military demobilisation in 1946). Incidentally, the degree to which the North Atlantic Alliance, once concluded, was effective as a reassurance to different elements in the differing national groups of policy-makers provides a crucial, quasi-barometric guide to the atmosphere of confidence engendered by its signature within the alliance.

In the second place, the North Atlantic Alliance functioned as a *double military guarantee*, against aggression by the Soviet bloc, and against an American strategic withdrawal or panic evacuation of the European continent in the event of a crisis in East-West relations. British thought on this subject was not widely understood by her European co-signatories, for whom Dunkirk was still taken as indicating the lack of any real British intellectual conviction in the necessity of defending mainland Europe. Certainly there were moments when Britain's military planners, in some desperation at the disparity of forces between East and West, envisaged an evacuation of British forces from mainland Europe. But this counsel of despair gave way, from 1948 onwards, to an ever-increasing involvement in and commitment to a defence in Europe. The experience of the bombardment of Britain by the primitive cruise missiles and intermediate-range ballistic missiles, which Hitler called *Vergeltungswaffen 1 and 2*, had convinced the Chiefs of Staff that a Britain driven from the Atlantic coastline of mainland Europe was a country left defenceless and on the verge of defeat. French opinion had survived occupation and liberation. Despite Allied bomb attacks in 1944, it had no real concept of either the 1940–1 or the 1944–5 *Blitzes*. Soviet tanks and Soviet paratroopers dropping out of an autumn or winter mist around Paris were the nightmares which haunted the beds of France's political leaders, not an attack from the air of a form to which there was no reply.

However, if the North Atlantic Treaty was to be effective as a political reassurance and a military guarantee, it also had to appear plausible as a means of *winning a war* against the Soviet bloc. Here French tunnel-vision and American and British preoccupations with Soviet power elsewhere were at cross-purposes. To British and American military planners, it seemed obvious that a war with the Soviet bloc would be fought as much on the Soviets' borders with Turkey or Iran, on the Soviet maritime frontier with Japan, the United States and Canada as on the Norwegian and Central European fronts. To British eyes a demand to make the defence of Central Europe the main priority made the defence of the Middle East difficult if not impossible. To Britain's strategic air-offensive planners, British air bases in Cyprus and Iraq offered the only means of striking at the new Soviet industrial complexes and oil fields from the Caucasus to trans-Caspia. This argument was found more and more convincing – it need hardly be said – by allies and successors to Marshal of the Royal Air Force 'Bomber' Harris than by the policy-makers, political and military, who congregated in Paris, Brussels and the Hague. It reinforced the already-noted British tendency to lay more stress on the political defence of the Middle East, while the French political scene trembled before the threat to the military defensibility of Central Europe. French military thought seemed to many simply to have moved the *horizon bleu* some 250 miles eastward.

Notes Towards a Synthesis

Modern mid-twentieth-century alliances had, however, come a long way from the eighteenth or nineteenth-century notions of mere military coalitions. Since the German offensives of March 1918 had summoned a unified allied command structure under Marshal Foch into existence on the Western Front, alliances, in military terms, had moved towards permanently integrated command structures on the model of Eisenhower's SHAEF. But with a global war, an integrated command for NATO, which would be a purely European front-command structure, would simply become one of a number of regional commands. Britain and the United States, with their global commitments, could not be integrated into NATO in the same way as France, Italy, the Benelux powers, Denmark or Norway. NATO became, or threatened to become, an instrument by which *Kleineuropa* could be established at the military level; as was to be dramatically demonstrated once West German rearmament within a consciously European framework was mooted. NATO, Bevin's brainchild, became an instrument which threatened Britain's status continuously, both diplomatically and in terms of military commitment. NATO became an instrument for *European integration*.

Indeed, to an increasingly influential, if never completely dominant, group of American policy-makers, NATO became such an instrument consciously and deliberately, a way of 'getting Europe off our backs and on its feet'. In the beginning such opinion welcomed Western Union as completely adequate to fill such a role. There was no need for anything more. The more politically conscious (and militarily ignorant) of State Department figures recognised, however, that, in political terms, WUDO's forces represented the addition of a set of military zeroes. To give Western Europe, especially the French, the sense of political security for which they clamoured against an increasingly hostile Soviet Union and an increasingly resurgent West Germany, it would be necessary to go further than the provision of aid to remedy WUDO's arms deficiencies.

America's Chiefs of Staff, facing America's own military weaknesses, were by no means enthusiastic even about letting American-manufactured arms go to European armies. They were, however, adamant that there could be no US military commitment to the defence of Central and Western Europe. This resulted in the paradox that the senior US military observers present at all WUDO military committee meetings, in 1948–9, could not attend any meetings for the Northern and Central Commands of NATO once the treaty had been signed. US aid to NATO would be just that – military aid – and not troops. Britain, France and the Benelux countries found that, when they pressed for the participation by American military personnel in military discussions and staff planning for the central front, they ran into procrastination designed to conceal the awkward fact that the US Chiefs of Staff had no troops available for commitment to the immediate defence of Europe, and did not plan to make any available. In current American military thinking, Europe was not capable of being defended against any initial Soviet attack; it was somewhere to be liberated, not defended.

To the British and French, especially to the British military and French political leaderships, this was unthinkable. British military planning, given British commitments in the Middle East and in Malaysia, was not prepared to commit troops to the defence of the European continent without similar American commitment. Such an attitude seems, at first sight, to confirm all that has been written about the isolationist element in British 'Atlanticism'. It is, however, so difficult to reconcile with the dire prophecies that the Chiefs of Staff were currently making to the Cabinet about the almost-total defencelessness of Britain against Soviet air and missile power, should the latter become established on the Atlantic coasts of France and the Low Countries, that this facile interpretation is obviously incorrect. The Chiefs of Staff position has therefore to be seen essentially as a political manoeuvre designed to thwart any American pressure to confine Britain to a purely European role, and to ensure that American policy-makers would be forced to commit American forces to the defence of a free Europe rather than the liberation of a continent overrun by and subject to the Soviet armed forces. Only the presence of adequate American forces in Europe would, in their view, have any chance of deterring or restraining a Soviet attack.

To the French political leadership, the doubt over American military commitment was alarming in the extreme. To their way of thinking the only form in which deterrence could work would be by confronting Soviet decision-makers not with the chance but with the certainty of defeat, and that in the initial battles of encounter. France, in their view, had only one chance of survival. In the 1914–18 war, invasions had been stemmed short of Paris; but recovery of that part of France which the invaders had over-

Notes Towards a Synthesis

run necessitated French subordination to an Anglo-American link-up, and had cost France the blood of a generation. In 1940 France had not survived the initial battles of encounter. If there was to be a third European war, France would have to be able to count on victory at the beginning. They regarded the lack of an American commitment as disastrous and as a betrayal of France itself. In 1947–8 they had rejected an accommodation with the Soviets and the siren voices of Third Forceism, of European neutralism in a Soviet-American conflict. Whatever might happen to France, their political existence – and, if a Soviet invasion did come, their physical existence – was at stake. Defeat and liberation was not an option, and a North Atlantic Alliance whose major partner formulated its military policy in such terms was not an alliance but a sham.

It was to take some time for the Truman administration and the Joint Chiefs of Staff to realize that the alliance could not survive if it were simply to be regarded as a substitute for military commitment to the defence of Europe. Even when the commitment was made, after the outbreak of the Korean War, the political view of the alliance, that is, that its purpose was to create a predominantly European shield for the United States, persisted. The American commitment of four US divisions was intended as a temporary one, designed to reassure the French and to bridge the period until a major German commitment to the defence of Europe had been made and had become acceptable to French and Benelux opinion. It was a commitment for five years at most, so General Eisenhower told a group of American senators in the winter of 1951. Thereafter, presumably, a Europe unified and integrated, revived and revivified by US aid would be capable of undertaking her own defence.

The main concern of United States policy-makers lay, as so often, not with the proper consideration of how her potential allies and co-signatories conceived and construed the notion of an alliance, but with how Congress would take it. The Truman administration laboured under two convictions; firstly that bipartisanship in policy-making was essential to avoid the issue of isolationism as against Atlantic commitment becoming an issue of inter-party politics, especially in a Presidential election year; and secondly, that, without very careful handling, budgetary conditions which argued for a drastic limitation of governmental expenditure on aid and defence would dominate Congress rather

443

than the necessity of an 'entangling' alliance with Europe as an essential element in the defence of America.

They decided, therefore, in putting the issue of American participation in a European defence system to Congress, that they would have to make it an issue of ideals rather than interests. In so doing they introduced two distortions into the American image of NATO which still persist. The first is that an American commitment to NATO was, like the earlier American commitment to the United Nations, a *peace-keeping commitment*, and thus *an act of expiation for American guilt*, in not ratifying Versailles, not joining the League of Nations and thus paving the way for the outbreak of World War II. The second distortion followed from this. If American support for and participation in the North Atlantic defence organisation was an *act of grace* rather than one of overriding self-interest, then America's co-signatories in Europe should be duly and continually grateful for it. The expurgation of American guilt for the breakdown of the inter-war security system does not, after all, presuppose any European expurgation of their own role in bringing about the Second World War. If America's co-signatories rejected American leadership and the act of grace this constituted, then the obvious corollary was that the American commitment to the defence of Europe, being a mere act of generosity, of grace, could and should be withdrawn.

The importance of Congress, the source both of money and of legitimation for American participation in NATO, carried with it a whole series of consequential implications. The first was that aid to NATO's European members would have to be made part of America's mutual aid legislation, making America's European allies merely the leaders in a process of aid which covered Latin American countries, Saudi Arabia, the Philippines etc. As related above, this had the effect of destroying Western Union as an instrument for the military integration of Western Europe, since the Mutual Aid legislation provided for aid to be given only on a one-to-one relationship, that is, of the United States as donor and the individual European state as recipient. Not only did this undo all that America's would-be integrationists of Europe had so far achieved, especially in relation to British integration. It also destroyed any but the most tenuous of developments towards inter-European cooperation in arms development and procurement. Moreover, it led to the direct lobbying of Congress by the

Notes Towards a Synthesis

American arms industry to secure a preference for American arms sales to Europe (to be paid for by US aid) over the development of European cooperation in arms development. The Congressional budgetary cycle became of overriding importance to the recipients of aid, who found themselves forced to abandon their own constitutional and parliamentary budgetary cycles in order to provide information at the appropriate time to Congressional enquiries. Pressure to standardise equipment (but not American, unless the model of standardisation was American), to integrate forces (but not American ones) in the European Defence Community, the concentration of European forces (but again not American) on the defence of Europe, all followed as a matter of course.

The last role the American conception of alliance played in distorting American attitudes to the new alliance lay in the only model with which American military opinion had any recent experience, that is in the model of the 1944–45 integrated alliance as it functioned in North-West Europe. Here we hark back to the point made earlier about the importance of the American experience of 1944–45. When he became president, General Eisenhower's conceptions of the Alliance were inevitably governed by his memories of 1944–45, as were those of his entourage. This distortion operated in both a positive and a negative fashion. Positively it reinforced all the tendencies already operating towards the dominance by American commanders of the command structure in Europe. In the Mediterranean, in Europe, and in the Atlantic, American commanders predominated. It was desirable to win Congressional approval, to counter any argument that American forces and lives were being put at the disposal of European military commanders. But it also fitted Eisenhower's own memories of the period in 1944–45 when he commanded five US armies to the two European armies, and laboured under the necessity of having to listen to the interventions and consider the susceptibilities of a British prime minister, British commanders and British opinion.

During his period as Supreme Commander Allied Forces Europe in 1951–52, the forces at his command would after mobilisation have comprised some twenty-one divisions, of which the United States would have contributed only four. This is hardly an overwhelming contribution. Yet both Eisenhower and his senior military advisers from 1952 onwards, most of them veterans of

445

wartime experience, shared the same conviction that the predominant role played by American forces to the defence of Western Europe by land, sea and in the air was such that American command and dominance over the alliance was the natural way of things. In the years after 1950, save for the role of the US Strategic Command (which was not part of NATO) in the deterrence of Soviet attack, this conviction, insofar as it related to the relationship of American forces in Europe to European forces, was misplaced. The rationale for American command – in the Central European front, in the Mediterranean and in the Atlantic, was political. It was the price of American commitment, the price paid by the European members of NATO for the commitment which, in their view and in that of the electorates they represented, was a necessary guarantee for peace.

Conclusions ad interim

Any historical conclusions at the moment have to be *ad interim*. The time has not yet come for any definitive typological or conceptual analysis of the evidence, which is, in important respects, both overwhelmingly rich and riddled with *lacunae*. To attempt, at present, to force a definitive analysis, especially one couched in terms adopted *a priori*, is to apply the principle of Procrustes' bed, either in the distortion or the elimination of such evidence as cannot be accommodated.

We historians need to be much more precise, both in our use of the concepts in which our discussion is cast, and in recognising the degree to which the policy-makers whose perceptions, decisions and actions we are studying were entrapped and misled by the ambiguities and imprecisions of these concepts, and failed to communicate to each other or to comprehend the different and individual fears, anxieties and calculations which motivated them.

Equally, any historical account of the origins, establishment and early history of NATO needs, whatever the date selected for its starting point, to comprehend how those we are studying viewed the past through which they had already come, the lessons they believed the past to embody for them and the consequences this past, as they conceived it, carried for the future they anticipated.

Notes Towards a Synthesis

It is important for the future health of the North Atlantic Alliance that historians understand and be allowed to explain how the views of NATO's origins current among the opinions of its various members fail to correspond with or be justified by the evidence, now available to historians, of the true motives, perceptions and misperceptions of those who brought NATO into existence. Insofar as current views are not in line with or confirmed by historical research, it is desirable that the work of demythologisation and public enlightenment be carried out by professional historians rather than by those who wish to readjust the past to benefit a particular political position in the present.

In the light of all these considerations, it is essential that a solution be found to reconcile the needs of the historians with the security and other considerations at present governing the withholding of NATO documentation from historical research.

Notes

1. See, for example, D. Cameron Watt, 'The Historiography of Appeasement' in Alan J. Sked and Chris Cook, *Crisis and Controversy. Essays in Honour of A.J.P. Taylor*, London, 1976.
2. This concept is developed in D. Cameron Watt, *Succeeding John Bull: America in Britain's Place, 1900–1975*, Cambridge, 1984, pp. 13–16, and the works cited therein.
3. For this argument see also D. Cameron Watt, 'Rethinking the Cold War, a Letter to a British Historian', in: *Political Quarterly* XLIX (1978).
4. Chinese historiography places the opening of the Second World War in 1937; the catalogues of the Library of Congress date it firmly to December 7, 1941. British and French historians, ignoring the date of the German attack on Poland, choose September 3, 1939.
5. Cameron Watt, 'Rethinking the cold war', op. cit.
6. The process may be followed in the files of the Military Committee of WUDO, first released on microfilm in the British Public Record Office and in other public repositories.
7. See Alan Milward, *The Reconstruction of Western Europe 1945–1951*, London, 1984.
8. See especially U. Bialer, *The Shadow of the Bomber*, London 1975.

Abbreviations

ACUE	American Committee on a United Europe
ADF	Archives Diplomatiques françaises, Vincennes
AdG	Archiv der Gegenwart
AE	Affaires étrangères
A.M.A.E.	Archivio storico del Ministerio degli Affari Esteri (Italian Ministry of Foreign Affairs Historical Archive)
ATAF	Allied Tactical Air Force
AUC	Atlantic Union Committee
BA	Bundesarchiv, Koblenz
BALTAP	(Allied Command) Baltic Approaches
BA-MA	Bundesarchiv-Militärarchiv, Freiburg
BLEU	Belgisch-Luxemburgse Economische Unie
CAD	Centraal Archieven Depot, Den Haag
CCS	Combined Chiefs of Staff (USA/Great Britain)
CD	Classified Document
CDN	Comité de Défense Nationale
CED	Communauté européenne de la défense
CINCEUR	Commander-in-Chief, Europe (USA)
Cominform	Communist Information Bureau (1947-56)
Comintern	Communist International (1919-43)
COS	Chief of Staff
CUSRPG	Canadian-United States Regional Planning Group
C.V.P.	Christelijke Volkspartij (Christian People's Party) (Holland)
DC	Defence Committee (NATO)
DELWU	Delegation to the Western Union (USA)
DNA	Det norske arbeiderparti (Norwegian Labour Party)
EA	Europa-Archiv
ECA	1. Economic Cooperation Administration 2. Economic Cooperation Agency
EMDN	Etat-Major de la Défense Nationale
ERP	European Recovery Program
EUCOM	European Command

449

Abbreviations

EDC	European Defence Community
EEC	European Economic Community
FHFS	Forsvarshistorisk Forskningssenter (Research Centre for Military History), Oslo
FLN	Front de la libération nationale
FRUS	Foreign Relations of the United States
GATT	General Agreement on Tariffs and Trade
GDR	German Democratic Republic (DDR)
GF	Geographic File
GOP	Grand Old Party (= Republican Party)
GPO	Government Printing Office
HICOG	(Office of the) High Commissioner for Germany (USA)
HKGS	Hoofdkwartier Generale Staff (see CAD) (HQ General Staff), Den Haag
IHEDN	Institut des Hautes Etudes de la Défense Nationale
IMS	(NATO HQ, Brussels) International Military Staff, Central Registry
INSOC	Institut Universitaire d'Information Sociale et Economique
JCS	Joint Chiefs of Staff (USA)
JO	Journal Officiel de la République Française
LTP	Long Term Plan
MDAP	Mutual Defence Assistance Programme
MGFA	Militärgeschichtliches Forschungsamt, Freiburg
MGM	Militärgeschichtliche Mitteilungen
MMB	Modern Military Branch
MOD	Ministry of Defence
MTDP	Medium Term Defence Plan
MTP	Medium Term Plan
NA	National Archives, Washington DC
NATO	North Atlantic Treaty Organisation
NERPG	North European Regional Planning Group
NISCA	(NATO HQ, Brussels) International Staff, Central Registry
NSC	National Security Council (USA)
OECD	Organisation for Economic Cooperation and Development
OEEC	Organisation for European Economic Cooperation
OSD	Office of the Secretary of Defence

Abbreviations

P&O	Plans and Operations Division, US Army
PCI	Partito Communista Italiano
PPS	Policy Planning Staff
PRO	Public Record Office, London
- CAB	Cabinets
- CP	Cabinet Papers
- DC	Defence Committee
- FO	Foreign Office
- PUSC	Permanent Under-Secretary's Committee
- TS	Top Secret
RAF	Royal Air Force
RG	Record Group
SAC	Strategic Air Command (USA)
SACEUR	Supreme Allied Commander Europe (NATO)
SACLANT	Supreme Allied Commander Atlantic (NATO)
SBZ	Sowjetisch Besetzte Zone (Soviet Occupied Zone)
SCFR	Senate Committee on Foreign Relations
SG	Archives Sécrétariat général du ministère des Affaires étrangères
SGCI	Sécrétariat Général de Coordination interministérielle
SGDN	Sécrétariat Général de la Défense nationale
SHAEF	Supreme Headquarters Allied Expeditionary Forces
SHAFR	Society for Historians of American Foreign Relations
SHAPE	Supreme Headquarters Allied Powers Europe (NATO)
SMG	Sectie Militaire Geschiedenis (Military History Division) (Holland)
STP	Short Term Plan
USSR	Union of Soviet Socialist Republics
UN	United Nations
UNO	United Nations Organisation
USA	United States of America
VfZG	Vierteljahrshefte für Zeitgeschichte
WEU	Western European Union; WEU Archives, London
WP	Warsaw Pact
WUDO	Western Union Defence Organisation

Contributors

Donald Cameron Watt
MA (Oxon), FBA, FRSA, FR Hist. S. (born 1928), Stevenson Professor of International History at the University of London, Department of International History, London School of Economics and Political Science, Houghton St., London WC2A 2AE. Official historian for the organisation of British defence policy in the period 1945–64.

Publications include: *Britain Looks to Germany: British Opinion and Policy towards Germany since 1945*, 1965; *Too Serious A Business: European Armed Forces and the Approach of the Second World War*, 1975; *Succeeding John Bull. America in Britain's Place 1900–1975, A Study of the Anglo-American Relationship and World Politics in the Context of British and American Foreign-Policy-Making in the Twentieth Century*, 1984; *How War Came: The Immediate Origins of the Second World War, 1938–1939*, 1989.

Luc De Vos
Professor, Dr phil. (born 1946). After a long period of active service as an officer in the Belgian Army, Prof. de Vos now lectures in History at the Royal Military Academy, Renaissancelaan 30, B-1040 Brussels, at the War College and the Catholic University of Leuven.

Publications include ten books and a number of essays on Belgian military history in the nineteenth and twentieth centuries.

Roland G. Foerster
Oberst i.G. (Colonel G.S.), Dr. phil. (born 1937), Director of Abteilung Historische Bildung (AHB) at the Militärgeschichtliches Forschungsamt, D-7800 Freiburg.

Publications include: *Herrschaftsverständnis und Regierungsstruktur in Brandenburg-Ansbach 1648–1703: Ein Beitrag zur Geschichte des Territorialstaates im Zeitalter des Absolutismus*, 1975; 'Innenpolitische Aspekte der Sicherheit Westdeutschlands 1947–1950', in *Anfänge westdeutscher Sicherheitspolitik 1945–1956*, vol. 1: *Von der Kapitulation bis zum Pleven-Plan*, 1982; *Military History in the Federal Republic of Germany and the Bundeswehr*, 1991.

Contributors

Christian Greiner
Dr phil., MA (born 1937), Oberstleutnant (Lieut.-Col.) and historian at the Militärgeschichtliches Forschungsamt, D-7800 Freiburg, and also Lecturer for International Politics and Political Theory at the University of Freiburg.

Publications include: 'Die alliierten militärstrategischen Planungen zur Verteidigung Westeuropas 1947–1950', in *Anfänge westdeutscher Sicherheitspolitik 1945–1956*, vol. 1: *Von der Kapitulation bis zum Pleven-Plan*, 1982. In addition to this Dr Greiner has published essays on seventeenth century military history.

Pierre Guillen
Professor for Modern History, Dr (born 1929); has held the Chair for Modern History since 1970, and is Director of the Centre de Recherche d'Histoire de l'Italie et des pays alpins at the Université des Sciences sociales de Grenoble II, F-38040 Grenoble, and since 1974 Director of the review *Relations internationales*.

His latest publication in a long series is entitled *L'expansion. 1881–1898 (Collection Politique étrangère de la France)*.

Lawrence S. Kaplan
University Professor for History and Director of the Lyman L. Lemnitzer Center for NATO Studies at Kent State University, Kent, Ohio 44242–0001, USA. Formerly on the staff of the Historical Office at the Office of the Secretary of Defence.

Publications include: *A Community of Interests: NATO and the Military Assistance Program, 1948–1951*, 1980, *The United States and NATO: The Formative Years* (1984), and *NATO and the United States: The Enduring Alliance*, 1988. He is co-editor of the following: *NATO after Thirty Years*, 1981, *NATO and the Mediterranean*, 1985, and *NATO After Forty Years*, 1990.

Manfred Knapp
Professor Dr (born 1939), Professor for Political Science, esp. International Relations at the Universität der Bundeswehr, Postfach 70 08 22, D-2000 Hamburg 70.

Publications include: *Die Stimme Amerikas – Auslandpropaganda der USA unter der Regierung John F. Kennedys*, 1972; *Sorgen unter Partnern. Zum Verhältnis zwischen den USA und der Bundesrepublik Deutschland*, 1984 and, together with other authors, *Die USA und*

Deutschland 1918–1975, 1978. In addition he has edited the following: *Die deutsch-amerikanischen Beziehungen nach 1945*, 1975, *Von der Bizonengründung zur ökonomisch-politischen Westintegration*, 1984, and (together with G. Krell) *Einführung in die Internationale Politik*, 2nd edn 1991.

Wolfgang Krieger

Professor Dr (born 1947), senior research fellow at the Stiftung Wissenschaft und Politik, D-8026 Ebenhausen; Privatdozent for Modern History at the University of Munich.

Publications include: *Labour Party und Weimarer Republik 1918–1924*, Bonn, 1978, and *General Lucius D. Clay und die amerikanische Deutschlandpolitik 1945–1949*, Stuttgart, 2nd edn 1988.

Paul Létourneau

(born 1949), Professor of Modern and Contemporary German History at the Université de Montréal, Département d'histoire, C.P. 6128, succursale A, Montréal, Québec H3C 3J7, Canada. He lectures in Modern History at the Université de Montréal, Département d'histoire, C.P. 6128, succursale A, Montréal, Québec H3C 3J7, Canada.

He has published essays on German, Canadian and European security policy as well as in the more general field of International Relations. He published his book on *Walther Rathenau (1867–1922)* in 1987. In 1990 he co-edited *Défense et sécurité: onze approches nationales*, which was also published in English in that year. Then, in 1991 he edited *Le Canada et l'OTAN après quarante ans* as well as *L'Allemagne dans une Europe nouvelle*.

Wilfried Loth

Professor Dr (born 1948), was Professor for Political Science at the Freie Universität Berlin and at the University of Münster. Since 1986 he has lectured in Modern History at the University of Essen, Postfach 10 37 64, D-4300 Essen 1.

Publications include: *Die Teilung der Welt. Geschichte des Kalten Krieges 1941–1955*, 1980; 8th edn 1990, in English 1988; *Geschichte Frankreichs im 20. Jahrhundert*, 1987; *Documents on the History of European Integration*, ed., 1988–91; and *Der Weg nach Europa. Geschichte der europäischen Integration 1939–57*, 1990, 2nd edn 1991.

Contributors

Pierre Melandri

Professor (born 1946), graduate of the Ecole Normale Supérieure, Professor at the Université de Paris X, 200, ave. de la République, F-92001 Nanterre Cedex. (Private address: 16, blvd. Soult, F-75012 Paris). In particular Professor Melandri has researched in the field of American history and International Relations from 1945.

Publications include: *L'alliance atlantique*, 1979; *Les Etats-Unis face à l'unification de l'Europe 1945–1954*, 1980 and *La politique extérieure des Etats-Unis de 1945 à nos jours*, 1982. His latest work is entitled *Une incertaine alliance: les Etats-Unis et l'Europe de 1973 à 1983*, 1988.

Nikolaj Petersen

Professor (born 1938), lecturer in Public Policy at the Institute of Political Science at the University of Aarhus, Universitetsparken, DK-8000 Aarhus C from 1970–85, and then Professor of International Relations. Since 1986 he has been Co-chairman of the Danish Commission for Security and Disarmament Affairs.

Co-editor of *The European Missiles Crisis: Nuclear Weapons and Security Policy*, 1983 and *Dansk Udenrigspolitik Arbog*, 1983 f., and has also published numerous essays in international scientific periodicals. Recent monographs on Germany's unification and political union in the EC.

Eberhard Pikart

Professor Dr (born 1923), Professor for Modern History at the Universität der Bundeswehr Munich, Werner-Heisenberg-Weg 39, D-8014 Neubiberg, with the emphasis of his research on military elements of the cold war from 1945 to Eisenhower's Presidency.

He has published (among others) a book entitled *Theodor Heuss und Konrad Adenauer*, 1975 and is helping to compile the *Staatslexikon der Görres-Gesellschaft*, vol. 3, 1987 under 'Militär'.

Romain H. Rainero

Professor (born 1929), is Professor for Contemporary History at the Faculty of Political Science at the University of Milan, Via Conservatorio 7, I-20122 Milano, and a member of the Historical Committee in the Italian Defence Ministry.

He is the author of several publications on the history of Italian colonialism, anti-colonialism and the reclamation of Tunisia in the age of Fascism.

Olav Riste
Professor, Director of the Norwegian Institute for Defence Studies at the National Defence College, Tollbugt. 10, N-0152 Oslo 1, Adjunct Professor for History at the University of Bergen (Norway) and President of the Norwegian Commission for Military History.

Among his many other publications, Professor Riste is the author of a two-volume work on the history of Norway in the wartime alliance 1940–1945, 1973–79 and the study 'Isolationism and Great Power Protection: The Historical Determinants of Norwegian Foreign Policy', in J. Holst (ed.), *Norwegian Foreign Policy in the 1980s*, 1985. He is also co-author and editor of the following: *Norway and the Second World War*, 1966 and other editions; *Norway 1940–1945: The Resistance Movement*, 1970 and other editions; and *Western Security: The Formative Years: European and Atlantic Defence 1947–1953*, 1985.

Jan Schulten
Lieut.-Col., Dr (born 1933). After lengthy service as a line officer in the Dutch armed forces, he has lectured in Military History since 1976 at the Royal Military Academy, Postbus 9 01 54, NL-4800 RG Breda.

Publications include: *Nederland neutraal?*, 1980; 'Die Aufstellung des königlich-niederländischen Heeres nach 1945', in *Entmilitarisierung und Aufrüstung in Mitteleuropa 1945–1946*, 1983; *Met toestemming van de opperbevelhebber*, 1984 and *Het Amerikaanse leger en de bevrijding van Nederland*, 1986.

Klaus Schwabe
Professor Dr (born 1932), Professor for Modern History at the Rheinisch-Westfälische Technische Hochschule Aachen, Kopernikusstr. 16, D-5100 Aachen.

Publications include: *Wissenschaft und Kriegsmoral: Die deutschen Hochschullehrer und die politischen Grundfragen des 1. Weltkrieges*, 1969; *Deutsche Revolution und Wilson-Frieden*, 1971, English edn 1985; *Gerhard Ritter: Ein politischer Historiker in seinen Briefen*, 1984. Editor and co-author of *The Beginnings of the Schuman-Plan*, 1988.

Contributors

Goeffrey Warner
Professor, MA, FR Hist. S. (born 1937), taught at the Universities of Reading, Hull and Leicester (Great Britain), at the Australian National University in Canberra, and was Visiting Professor at the Johns Hopkins School of Advanced International Studies in Bologna. He took early retirement from the Open University in Milton Keynes (GB) at the end of 1989 and is now a Visiting Fellow in the Department of Politics and International Studies at the University of Birmingham (GB).

Publications include: 'Britain and Europe in 1948: The View from the Cabinet', in Josef Becker and Franz Knipping (eds), *Power in Europe? Great Britain, France and Germany in a Post-War World – 1945–1950*, 1986, and also numerous other works on British foreign policy after the Second World War and on the origins of the cold war.

Norbert Wiggershaus
Oberst (Colonel), Dr phil (born 1939), Head of Research Dept. IV 'Internationale Militärgeschichte und Konflikte seit 1945' at the Militärgeschichtliches Forschungsamt, D-7800 Freiburg.

Publications include: 'Von Potsdam zum Pleven-Plan: Deutschland in der internationalen Konfrontation 1945–1950' and 'Die Entscheidung für einen westdeutschen Verteidigungsbeitrag 1950', in *Anfänge westdeutscher Sicherheitspolitik 1945–1956*, vol. 1: *Von Potsdam zum Pleven-Plan*, 1982; he is author of a series of publications and articles on West German foreign and security policy, on German military history and on problems connected with German military tradition and co-editors of *Das Nordatlantinche Büuduis 1945–1956*, 1993.

Wichard Woyke
Professor Dr (born 1943), Westfälische Wilhelms-Universität Münster, Bispinghof 3, D-4400 Münster.

Publications include: *Oppositionsparteien und Verteidigungspolitik im gaullistischen Frankreich 1958–1973*, 1975; *Die NATO in den siebziger Jahren*, 1977; *Erfolg durch Integration – Die Europapolitik der Benelux-Staaten 1947–1969*, 1985. *Handwörterbuch Internationaler Organisationen*, 1985.

Index of Persons

Acheson, Dean G. 18f., 21, 51, 140f., 144, 155, 164, 191,193,199f., 211f., 264, 296, 307, 354, 358, 362, 383, 389, 426
Achilles, Theodore C. 47, 64, 212, 255
Adenauer, Konrad 37, 320, 329, 378–381, 387f., 392, 401f.
Alexander, Harold R.L.G. Earl of Tunis 52
Alexander, A.V. 152, 236–238, 241, 243, 355
Alphand, Hervé 135–138, 275f.
Amendola, Giorgio 22, 174
Anderson, Eugénie 209, 216, 219f.
Aspremont Lynden, C. d' 99
Attlee, Clement 91, 154, 156–158, 163f., 166, 234, 299, 307, 383, 394, 421
Auriol, Vincent 127, 134, 141, 143, 145, 148, 235, 275, 297, 300

Baele, Etienne 62
Baldwin, Hanson 117
Benes, Edvard 11
Bérard, Armand 275, 387
Bevan, Aneurin 161f., 165f.
Bevin, Ernest 32f., 47f., 71f., 91, 95, 97, 127, 150–152, 154–157, 161–164, 168, 185, 232–235, 242f., 252f., 258, 261f., 291, 293, 301f., 305, 336, 347, 355, 375, 383, 386f., 401f., 421, 426, 439, 441
Bidault, Georges 11, 33, 47, 95f., 140f., 234f., 254, 291, 295, 301f., 305, 307, 382
Billotte, Pierre 252, 380
Blankenhorn, Herbert 392
Bohlen, Charles 233, 255, 300, 308
Bonnet, Henri 138, 140, 307
Bradley, Omar 50f.
Brentano, Heinrich von 380
Bruynincx, Leon 98
Burgess, Guy 153
Buset, Max 98
Butler, Richard Austen 168
Byrnes, James F. 231

Caffery, Jefferson 298, 308
Cauwelaert, van 92
Chauvel, Jean 295, 300

Cherrières, Jean 135, 137, 140
Chevillon, 63
Chiang Kai-shek 17, 280
Churchill, Winston S. 22, 30, 36, 90, 93, 174, 191, 276, 380
Claxton, Brooke 77
Clay, Lucius D. 15, 54, 236, 240, 256, 275f., 278, 305, 380
Collins, J. Lawton 59, 391
Connally, Thomas T. 100, 254, 260–262, 296, 345
Cossée de Maulde, Vincent 92
Coste-Floret, Paul 127
Courten, Raffaele de 180
Couve de Murville, Maurice 295
Cripps, Stafford 160–162

Dalton, Hugh 158f.
De Gasperi, Alcide 174f., 180, 182f.
Defraiteur, Raoul 99
Diepenrijkx, Pierre J. 119
Douglas, Lewis W. 51
Drees, Willem 299
Droste, Jan H. 119
Dulles, John Foster 289, 302, 307, 382

Eden, Anthony 91
Eisenhower, Dwight D. 54, 73, 109, 112, 119f., 157, 168, 195, 282, 290, 317, 333, 401, 423, 432, 441, 443, 445
Elliot, Sir William 394
Ely, Paul 131f., 137, 236
Eyskens, Gaston 97, 103

Fayat, Henri 98
Foch, Ferdinand 441
Forrestal, James V. 59
Franks, Sir Oliver 253

Gaitskell, Hugh 162f., 165–167
Gaulle, Charles de 174, 261, 421, 434
Gerhardsen, Einar 186, 194
Griffiths, James 159
Gronchi, Giovanni 181
Gruenther, Alfred M. 256
Guderian, Heinz 109
Gutt, Camille 94
Guzenko, Igor 79, 81

459

Index

Handy, Thomas T. 391
Hansen, Poul 217
Hansen, Rasmus 207, 210, 214, 217
Harriman, W. Averell 50, 163, 298, 301, 356, 358f., 362
Harris, Sir Arthur T. 440
Harvey, Oliver C. 51, 56
Hasselman, B.R.P.F. 118
Hauge, Jens-Christian 160, 187f., 190
Hays, George P. 391
Healey, Dennis 429
Hedtoft, Hans-Christian 199, 203f., 206, 209f., 214, 216, 218
Heusinger, Adolf 320f., 329, 334f., 376
Hickerson, John D. 47, 64, 234, 255, 302
Hitler, Adolf 279, 435, 440
Hoover, Herbert C. 109
Howard, Michael 245
Huebner, Clarence R. 46, 57, 60, 240
Humbert, Jean 125

Inverchapel, Archibald J., Lord 354

Jaujard, Robert 100, 239
Johnson, Louis A. 19, 50, 317
Joll, James 244

Kaspi, André 53f.
Kauffmann, Henrik 210–212
Kennan, George F. 13f., 233, 255, 275, 278, 295, 305f., 345, 355, 424, 439
Kennedy, John Fitzgerald 421
Khrushev, Nikita S. 421
Kibler, A. Franklin 46, 57, 60–63
Kim Il-sung, 20
King, W. L. Mackenzie 70–72, 76–79, 81
Kirkpatrick, Sir Ivone 386, 394
Kissinger, Henry 429
Kleffens, Eelco N. van 101
Kraft, Ole B. 214
Kruls, Hendrik J. 113, 116–119, 237

Lange, Halvard M. 187, 190, 193, 194, 195, 199, 209, 211f.
Lattre de Tassigny, Jean-M. G. de 51, 54, 100, 115, 118, 127, 237, 239f.
Lechères, Charles 50, 61
Lefèvre, Théodore 99
Lemnitzer, Lyman L. 46, 57–60, 256, 293
Lenin, Wladímir Iljítsch 436
Leopold III., 88f., 103f.
Letourneau, Jean 142
Lie, Haakon 186
Lieftink, Piet 118

Lipgens, Walter 29, 46
Longo, Luigi 22
Lovett, Robert A. 254, 257f., 292, 296, 302, 354, 356
Lundestad, Geier 244
MacArthur, Douglas 20
Maclean, Donald 101, 153
Malenkow, Georgij M. 10
Mallaby, George 233, 240
Mao Tse-Tung, 17, 280, 420
Marshall, George C. 11, 14f., 17f., 30f., 33, 47, 49, 51, 71, 75, 94, 96, 100f., 128f., 176, 187, 217, 253f., 291, 302, 347, 356, 422, 426, 437
Massigli, René 305
Mayer, Joseph P. 439
McCarthy, Joseph R. 79, 80
McCloy, John Jay 51, 388
McNeil, Hector 159
Meyer, René 289
Milward, Alan 229
Moch, Jules 127, 194, 390, 396f.
Moe, Finn 192
Møller, Andreas 219
Monnet, Jean 34, 36, 159, 435
Montgomery, Bernard L. 46, 51, 54, 62, 100, 115, 117f., 127, 231, 237, 239f., 257, 293, 305f., 333, 378
Morrison, Herbert S. 157, 159, 167
Mussolini, Benito 173f.

Nasser (Abd an-Násir, Gamal) 437
Nenni, Pietro 179, 182f.
Nitze, Paul H. 162f., 361

Opsomer, Adrianus T.C. 117
Oster, Hans 119

Pacciardi, Randolfo 174
Pearson, Lester B. 70, 75f., 80
Petersen, Harald 217
Petsche, Maurice 139–141
Pierlot, Hubert 119
Pineau, Christian 127
Piron, 91
Pleven, René 37–39, 137, 140, 142–144, 155, 159, 194, 214, 396f.

Quaroni, Pietro 177f.
Queuille, Henri 127, 132f., 259

Ramadier, Paul 53, 60, 125, 131f., 126, 239, 236, 303
Rasmussen, Gustav 199, 205, 210, 213f., 216–218

460

Index

Reid, Escott 70f.
Révers, Georges 126, 252
Rey, Jean 98
Reynaud, Paul 380
Rhee, Syngman 20
Ridgway, Matthew B. 112, 120
Robb, James 100, 239
Robens, Alfred 159
Robertson, Brian H. 14, 380
Roey, van 102
Rollin, 92
Roosevelt, Franklin D. 94

St. Laurent, Louis Stephen 70, 72, 76, 78, 80, 255
Sas, Gijsbertus Jacobus 119
Scala, Edoardo 179
Schryver, August de 92, 98
Schuman, Robert 29, 36–39, 128f., 137, 141, 144, 152, 155, 159, 242f., 261, 307, 354, 390
Schwerin, Gerhard, Graf v. 380
Scotti, Gallarati 177
Secchia, Pietro 22
Sforza, Carlo 174f., 178, 182f.
Shinwell, Emmanuel 160, 163, 165, 167, 238
Slim, William Joseph 164
Smith, Walter Bedell 14
Spaak, Paul-Henri 89–98, 101–104, 231, 238, 241, 251, 302
Speidel, Hans 320, 322, 328f.
Spofford, Charles M. 38, 138, 194f., 353, 398
Spoor, Simon H. 113
Stalin, Josef W. 10, 13, 20, 22, 80, 90f., 93, 231, 251, 420
Stehlin, Paul 52, 53
Stikker, Dirk Uipko 111, 236, 298, 300, 383

Strachey, E. John 158f.
Strauß, Franz-Josef 436
Sturzo, Don S. 174
Sutherland, R.J. 73

Taggart, Joseph H. 60
Tedder, Arthur William 50, 62
Teitgen, Pierre-Henri 125f., 131
Tito, Josip Broz 23
Togliatti, Palmiro 22, 179
Toynbee, Arnold 427
Tromme, Albert 100
Truman, Harry S. 14f., 18f., 21, 23, 50, 71, 100, 191, 193, 212, 254, 257, 266f., 275, 282, 293, 301f., 317, 360, 362, 389, 420

Vandenberg, Arthur 12, 71, 92, 100, 253f., 257, 279, 296, 345, 355
Vanlangenhove, Fernand 93, 97
VanLoo, 238
Varga, Eugen 10
Vleeshauwer, Albert de 89
Vos, Hermann H. 99
Vychinsky, Andrei J. 101, 251

Washington, George 47
Wedemeyer, Albert C. 59
Wilgress, L. Dana 79
Wilhelmina, 110
Wilson, Harold 166
Wrong, H. Hume 70

Younger, Kenneth 152, 154, 156f., 161, 166

Zeeland, Paul van 89, 104, 335
Zemaco, Demezio 179
Zhdanov, Andrei 10, 23